Collins

BTEC NATIONAL

Business

Level 3

Charlotte Bagley, Andrew Dean
Louise Stubbs and Mark Gardiner

Published by Collins Education
An imprint of HarperCollins Publishers
77-85 Fulham Palace Rd
Hammersmith
London
W68JB

Browse the complete Collins Education catalogue at
www.collinseducation.com

©HarperCollins Publishers Limited 2011
10 9 8 7 6 5 4 3 2 1

ISBN 978 0 00 741847 3

Charlotte Bagley, Andrew Dean, Louise Stubbs and Mark Gardiner assert their
moral rights to be identified as the authors of this work

British Library Cataloguing in Publication Data.
A Catalogue record for this publication is available from the British Library.

Commissioned by Charlie Evans
Project Managed by Jo Kemp
Design and typesetting by Joerg Hartsmannsgruber and Thomson Digital
Cover design by Angela English
Printed and bound by L.E.G.O.S.p.a

Contents

Photo Acknowledgements

Advertising Archives: 154
Alamy: 4, 5, 8, 10, 11, 15, 19a, 19b, 21, 23, 25, 26, 27, 30, 31, 32, 37, 38, 41, 45a, 45b, 46, 49, 51, 53, 55, 65, 66, 70, 71, 73, 82, 83, 87, 95, 100, 104, 107a, 107b, 108, 111a, 111b, 113, 115a, 115b, 116, 117, 119, 123, 125, 129, 136, 139a, 139b, 143a, 143b, 144a, 144b, 147, 148, 149, 153, 155, 156, 157, 162, 166, 167, 173, 175, 180, 181, 184, 189, 191, 197, 200, 203a, 203b, 203c, 205, 213, 218, 225, 231, 237, 241, 259, 262, 267, 269, 270, 273, 275, 276, 277, 278, 281, 284, 285, 287, 290, 291, 292, 296, 300, 311, 324, 325, 326, 327, 339, 341, 349, 361, 363, 369, 371, 377, 385, 390, 393, 395, 396, 399, 401, 403, 407, 409, 413, 421a, 421b, 423
Antonia Krieger: 351
Business Link: 381
Companies House: 229
Corbis: 235
Doritos: 195
Elle au naturel: 340
Getty Images: 9, 323, 327, 330, 423
Grumbletext: 275
www.pepsico.co.uk: 198
Istockphoto: 6, 12, 29, 33, 39, 47, 50, 56, 68, 81, 86, 101, 121, 156, 177, 187, 211, 222, 227, 231, 239, 243, 244, 252, 253, 258, 293, 295, 302, 305, 307, 309, 313, 319, 321, 328, 329, 332, 336, 344, 348, 358, 374, 391
Online Kitchen Design: 266
Privacy Policy: 343
Rex Features: 196, 209, 214
Screenshot: 171
Shelter: 339
Shutterstock: 5a, 5b, 5c, 7, 13, 16, 20, 22, 23, 34, 35, 36, 41, 43, 51, 54, 59, 62, 64, 66, 72, 74, 75a, 75b, 76, 77, 78, 79, 80, 84, 85, 88, 94, 95, 121, 123, 137, 164, 175, 176, 177, 179, 194, 207, 215, 245, 250, 251, 265, 283, 299, 303, 309, 310, 312, 316, 331, 333, 338, 352, 353, 354, 372, 375, 382, 408, 411, 415, 417, 419a, 419b
Simon Seeks: 209
Trading Standards Institute: 378
Yahoo: 280

Introduction

Welcome to BTEC Level 3 Business.

This course book is written for students aiming to achieve one of the following BTEC Level 3 Business awards:

BTEC Level 3 National Certificate in Business	(30 credits)
BTEC Level 3 National Subsidiary Diploma in Business	(60 credits)
BTEC Level 3 National Diploma Business	(120 credits)
BTEC Level 3 National Extended Diploma Business	(180 credits)

The material in this book covers twelve units of the BTEC Level 3 Business award. All of the units that you need to complete to obtain a certificate or subsidiary diploma award are contained in this book. All of the mandatory units required for the diploma and extended diploma awards in Business are also covered in this book.

Each chapter of the book covers a specific BTEC Level 3 National Business unit. You will see that the chapters are divided into topics. Each topic provides you with a focused and manageable chunk of learning and covers all of the content areas that you need to know about in a particular unit. You should also notice that the material in each topic is clearly linked to the unit's pass, merit and distinction grading criteria. This mapping of the content against the grading criteria should help you to prepare for your assignments. The assignments that you are given by your tutor will require you to demonstrate that you have the knowledge and are able to do the things which the pass, merit or distinction criteria refer to.

Overall this course book provides a comprehensive resource for the units of the BTEC Level 3 National Business programme that it covers. You can be sure that the content is closely matched to the BTEC specification and is designed and presented to help you achieve the grades you are aiming for and which you are capable of. The book provides case studies, activities and realistic examples to develop your interest in and understanding of business.

Students often begin a BTEC National Business course with the aim of undertaking further professional training or to get a job in business. We hope that the material in the book is accessible, interesting and inspires you to pursue and achieve this goal. Good luck with your course!

The authors

1 | The business environment

LO1 Know the range of different businesses and their ownership

- ▶ How do businesses differ?

- What are the different purposes of businesses?

- ▶ What are the different ownership structures of businesses?

- ▶ Who is influenced by a business?

LO2 Understand how businesses are organised to achieve their purposes

- ▶ How are businesses organised?

- ▶ How are businesses divided up?

- ▶ Why is strategic planning so important?

- ▶ What influences a business?

- ▶ What do businesses aim for?

LO3 Know the impact of the economic environment on businesses

- ▶ How does the economic environment affect businesses?

- ▶ What makes demand change?

- ▶ What makes supply change?

- ▶ How does the global economy interact?

LO4 Know how political, legal and social factors impact on businesses

- ▶ How do political changes affect businesses?

- ▶ Do laws help or hinder a business?

- ▶ Does society impact on business decisions?

The range of different businesses

Business scale

Businesses operate on many different scales. For example, you don't find an IKEA on every street, nor are smaller shops from the UK spoken about in the USA. The **business scale** varies from local through to global.

Local

If you needed a plumber, taxi or just a pint of milk, you would probably go to a local business. This means businesses that operate in just one area, serving the local community. Businesses on this scale will often be small, privately owned sole traders who employ very few people.

National

In the UK, there are many businesses that operate all over the country, on a national scale. Innocent smoothies are now available on a national scale — what used to be a small local business is now selling to millions of people all over the UK. National-scale businesses are usually much larger in size than local-scale businesses and employ a large number of people, often in different regions.

International

If you go to Spain, you may be surprised to see many of the same brands and products that you see in the UK. You may see the Seat Ibiza being driven around, or a Subway being opened on the high street. Some companies operate on this international scale, selling to many different countries. This allows them to sell to a larger market, increasing their customer base and, hopefully, increasing their revenue.

Global

Go to anywhere in the world and you will be able to find a bottle of Coca-Cola. This is because Coca-Cola has become a global firm. Firms on this scale are public limited companies, which use the capital generated through selling shares to help fund their expansion.

Your assessment criteria:

P1	Describe the type of business, purpose and ownership of two contrasting businesses

🔑 Key terms

Business scale: the size of the area or region within which a business operates

🔍 Research

For each of the different business scales, find examples which are all in the same industry or market.

💬 **Discuss**

Discuss whether you think all businesses want to grow to a global scale.

Public, private or voluntary?

Around 40 per cent of the business activity in the UK is through the public sector. This is the sector that provides goods and services through the government or local authorities; for example, the NHS. This sector focuses on providing services for everyone, without charging large amounts.

The private sector is made up of businesses privately owned, with no direct interaction with the government. The private sector is often regarded as profit driven, although many firms now follow a corporate social responsibility plan, which aims to give something back to the community.

The voluntary sector is made up of over 170,000 organisations in the UK. This sector aims to help people around the world in all situations. Charities such as Save the Children, Love in a Box and Cancer Research UK all work towards a social aim of helping the community. The sector itself is made up of both volunteers and paid staff who are funded through donations.

Sectors of business activity

It is possible to classify businesses into sectors based on the processes they perform. In the primary sector, raw materials are extracted and food is grown; for example, farms and mines. The secondary sector uses the raw materials, transforming them into goods ready to be sold. This can be seen in factories and car plants. The tertiary sector provides services such as transport, leisure and education and goods that are sold through retail outlets such as Next, IKEA and Boots.

Primary   Secondary   Tertiary

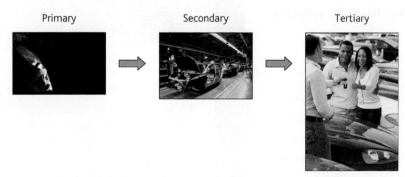

Figure 1.1 Primary, secondary and tertiary sectors

Business aims and ownership

Businesses have different aims or purposes. Not all businesses set out to make huge **profits**, or to spread their name all over the world. Some have a more social aim, or supply a service that will help people directly.

P1 Profit or not?

Goods and services

Not all businesses sell a product, some may sell both **goods** and **services**, whereas some just offer a service. Retailers on the high street stock the latest fashion accessories, gadgets, cosmetics, etc all of which are products. However, businesses such as doctors, solicitors and lawyers make their money through offering a service. Some businesses offer a product with a service attached; for example, Dyson may sell their new vacuum cleaners with a 3-year warranty service and after-sales service.

Profit and not-for-profit organisations

When asked to think of a successful business, many would mention Coke, Nike, Tesco or Microsoft. However, there are plenty of firms that have generated huge successes from operating as **not-for-profit organisations**. Angelbear sends hand-knitted teddy bears to disadvantaged children around the world and reinvests a percentage of its **profit** back into the business. Not all businesses are driven by shareholders; many focus on making a difference locally, nationally or globally.

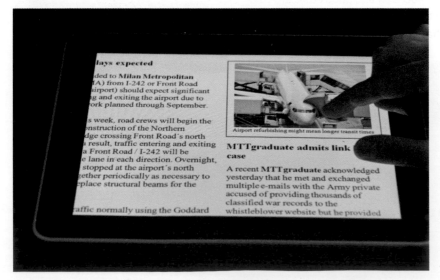

High-street retailers sell products such as the latest electronic gadgets.

Sole trader

A **sole trader** is the most common form of business ownership in the UK and is the quickest and simplest form of business ownership to set up. Although sole traders can employ more than one person, they are often run as single seller businesses such as taxi drivers, carpenters or small business servicing the local area.

Figure 1.2 The advantages and disadvantages of being a sole trader

Advantages	Disadvantages
• All profits are kept by the owner of the business. • The owner has total control of the business decisions and operations. • Setting up as a sole trader is quick and easy, and relies on only basic paperwork.	• Sole traders have unlimited liability. This means the business is not separate from the owner. If the business goes into debt, the individual will have to pay the creditors with their own money. • Operating as a sole trader can often lead to a difficulty in accessing finance. Banks are often unwilling to lend to sole traders due to their risk. • Smaller businesses cannot easily achieve economies of scale (achieving a lower cost per item through increased production). This means their products are likely to be more expensive than those of larger businesses, e.g. a convenience store is more expensive than Tesco.

Operating as a sole trader can mean that other businesses avoid dealing with them as they can be a riskier supplier or customer than other ownerships.

Key terms

Sole trader: a business owned by one person who makes the key decisions and absorbs all the risk

Discuss

In pairs, discuss the following: 'All businesses should start up as a sole trader.'

Sole traders often work on their own.

P1 Partnership

Ben and Jerry's is an example of a high-profile, successful **partnership**. However, not all partnerships operate on this scale. Partnerships are businesses with between 2 and 20 owners and are set up by issuing a deed of partnership, which outlines the following:

- the amount of capital invested by each partner

- how profits are to be divided between the partners

- how a partner can leave or a new partner be chosen.

Figure 1.3 The advantages and disadvantages of setting up a partnership

Advantages	Disadvantages
• Additional partners bring experience and skills to the business.	• Partnerships mean sharing the profit with other partners.
• The risk of the business failing is spread among more owners.	• There are often disputes over the spread of the workload with some partners not working as hard as others.
• New partners bring with them credibility and resources which help the business to reach new customers.	• Making decisions can often be difficult in a partnership with differing views and ideas.

Many sole traders decide to move into a partnership to help expand their businesses. For example, painters may wish to bring in a partner who can offer other skills such as plastering or plumbing.

 Case study

When setting up The Wise Revise, Gareth seemed happy with the structure of his business. He had brought on board Stephen, his brother in law, as an equal partner in the business. Having identified the skills he lacked, Gareth seemed certain that Stephen would complete the business.

However, after just a few months' trading, Gareth noticed that he was putting in most of the work despite investing half the start-up money. Stephen had become involved in some other ventures which were taking up his time. Gareth discussed the issue with friends, but in the end, he decided it was difficult to tackle the problem with Stephen as they had not signed a deed of partnership.

1. What is a deed of partnership?

2. Why is a deed of partnership so important when setting up a partnership?

3. How would you advise Gareth in the situation outlined above?

Your assessment criteria:

 P1 Describe the type of business, purpose and ownership of two contrasting businesses

 Key terms

Partnership: *a business made up of 2–20 people who share the ownership and workload*

 Research

Using your research skills, find other famous examples of businesses that either operate or operated as a partnership.

Discuss

Should all business operate as a partnership?

P1 Private or public?

Limited companies are owned by shareholders, run by directors and have limited liability. This means the business is a separate entity to the shareholders. If the business runs into debt, the creditors cannot take the money or possessions of the shareholders themselves. All limited companies have to register with Companies House, and are issued with a certificate of incorporation. The business also has a memorandum of association, which outlines the business's purpose and industry, as well as articles of association which are internal rules for the shareholders and directors.

Microsoft is a public limited company.

Private limited companies do not make their shares available to the general public. They are often sold to families and friends. This can reduce the amount of capital available to these businesses.

Public limited companies sell their shares on the stock exchange. They can be bought by the general public.
Share capital is raised by selling shares (£50,000 minimum)

Advantages
- Limited liability protects the shareholders.
- The business has control over who owns the shares.

Advantages
- Large amounts of capital can be raised by selling shares to the public.
- Becoming a plc can lead to quick growth and enhanced reputation.

Disadvantages
- There is a loss of control, with shareholders often voting on major decisions.
- Profits are spread among all shareholders.

Disadvantages
- Some information has to be made available each year, which competitors can see; e.g. sales and profit.
- Plcs are costly and difficult to set up – a large amount of paperwork and legal proceedings.

Figure 1.4 The differences between private and public limited companies

🔍 Research

Use the London Stock Exchange website, www.londonstockexchange.com, to find the share prices of Tesco, British Airways and BP.

🔑 Key terms

Private limited company: a privately owned business, the shares of which are not sold to the general public

Public limited company (plc): a larger business, the shares of which are available on the stock exchange

P1 Other business ownerships

Government agencies and departments

Government departments operate on behalf of the government. For example, the Ministry of Defence operates as a department of the government, representing the entire population. Other departments such as the Department for Education focus on more specific matters aimed at part of the population.

Government agencies are separately run organisations which are funded by the government. The Driver and Vehicle Licensing Agency (DVLA) is one example of an agency that undertakes a role within the government's responsibilities. Although agencies run as a separate entities, they operate to very strict guidelines.

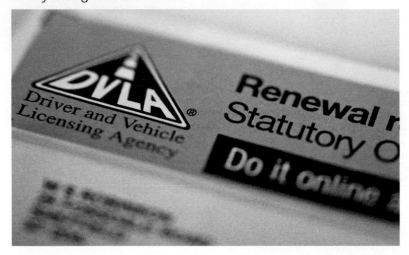

Worker co-operatives

A worker co-operative is an organisation that is owned by the workers who produce the products or services. Divine Chocolate is a good example of this. The farmers who grow the cocoa that is used to produce the chocolate, own 45 per cent of the company. They therefore help make decisions that influence the business's aims and objectives. This open form of business encourages all workers to produce more, as they receive part of the profit.

Charitable organisations

A charity can be organised in many different ways. It can be an unincorporated association, a trust or a limited company. Each of these differs in its structure but all exist with the same aim: to raise funds to help the specific cause they represent. A charity that is formed as a registered company needs to have a board of directors, whereas a charitable trust needs to have a board of trustees in place.

Your assessment criteria:

P1 Describe the type of business, purpose and ownership of two contrasting businesses

Key terms

Charity: an organisation founded to promote public good

Government agencies: separately run, government-funded organisations that hold responsibilities given by the government

Government departments: specific organisations that represent the nation on specific issues, such as defence or schools

Worker co-operative: a business that is part owned by the workers

Charities are run as businesses, with paid staff and overhead costs. They are governed by legal documents which outline their duties. They are also expected to produce financial accounts and a transparent operating system. Examples of charities in the UK are Cancer Research and Oxfam.

Once registered, charities have to follow certain rules. These cover the accounts, management and ethos of the charity. Charities that register as a company also have to follow the laws set out for any normal registered company.

Charities must make sure they use any surplus cash to enhance the achievement of their aims. They also remain independent of any government intervention or agenda. This allows them to remain focused solely on their overall aims.

 Did you know?

In the UK, there are over 500,000 voluntary organisations, with less than 200,000 registered as charities.

 Discuss

Do you agree with charities saving money in their bank accounts for 'rainy days'?

Research

Research a charity of your choice and find out the total amount of donations made to it in 2010.

 ## Case study

On 1 January 2011, many iPhone users woke up late thanks to a glitch with the iPhone alarm system. The change of year caused mayhem for thousands who were late for work or other engagements. However, with the huge success of the iPhone, Apple will not be worried. By June 2010, over 1.7 million phones had been sold, with Apple's share price rising daily.

1. Describe the type of business and ownership of Apple.

2. Apple has seen recent products such as the iPhone and iPad sell well all over the world. Describe the purpose of Apple.

Key stakeholders

Who are stakeholders?

A **stakeholder** is any organisation, individual or business that is affected or influenced, in any way, by a particular business. Stakeholders can have a large influence on the business and can have a variety of roles in the decision-making of the business. Some stakeholders have a bigger influence than others. As an example, trade unions and employees are both stakeholders in British Airways. When the company proposed pay and job cuts, the influence of the employees and trade unions eventually meant fewer job cuts and an increase in pay.

Your assessment criteria:

P2 Describe the different stakeholders who influence the purpose of two contrasting businesses

M1 Explain the points of view of different stakeholders seeking to influence the aims and objectives of two contrasting organisations

Key terms

Stakeholder: *an individual, organisation or business that is affected or influenced by a particular business*

Research

Using your research skills, note down as many stakeholders as you can for Manchester United Football Club.

Figure 1.5 **Different stakeholders**

 ### Discuss

Which stakeholder do you think is the most important to a business?

M1 Stakeholder points of view

Customers
Customers are those who purchase goods or services from a business. They are often driven by price and quality, and value for money is a key aim.

Local community
Businesses can directly impact local and national communities through their operations. People in the local community often want jobs with the businesses, as well as minimal pollution and damage to the area.

Owners/shareholders
The owner of a business may be an individual, partners or shareholders. Owners and shareholders are often seen as key stakeholders as they have put the most time and money into the business. They often want large profits.

Trade unions
Trade unions represent the interests of the employees. They try to secure higher pay and better working conditions for their members.

Employees
Employees seek job security as well as promotional opportunities and good pay.

Suppliers
Suppliers often strive to gain large and steady contracts with other businesses with which they can work closely in a respectful relationship.

Employer associations
These represent the employers themselves and help to settle disputes with the company's employees.

Governments
Governments want businesses to provide jobs and tax revenue, and to help the economy grow.

Figure 1.6 The different aims of various stakeholders

Describe

Make a list of your school's/college's stakeholders. Can you put them in order according to their importance?

? Did you know?

British Airways lost £150 million due to the employee strikes in 2010. A powerful stakeholder!

The influence of stakeholders

D1 Nike's stakeholders

Stakeholders have a variety of influences on how a business is run. As reputation plays such an important role in the success of a business, firms try to avoid negative publicity. This can increase the influence of some stakeholders. Nike attracted negative publicity when it was exposed for using low-paid staff in factories abroad to produce its products.

Figure 1.7 The influence of various stakeholders on Nike

Customers	Customers can stop buying products displaying the Nike logo. Word of mouth means that Nike can be seriously damaged by customer shifts. They have a huge influence on the aims and objectives of Nike. However, Nike may feel that it has sufficiently strong brand loyalty to ignore customer input.
Employees	Employees can make firms alter their aims and objectives to include staff needs and wants. Nike altered their company objectives to include the working conditions of its staff. However, at a time when unemployment is high, employers are in a position of greater power as employment is harder to find.
Suppliers	Suppliers are very important to Nike's aims of quality and innovation. Therefore the company needs to have secure and reliable suppliers in place. If Nike doesn't treat its suppliers well, they may let the company down, damaging its name.
Owners	The shareholders have a direct influence on the aims and objectives of Nike. They often influence the business to increase profits through expansion or growth, although some shareholders may prefer sustainable growth.
Trade unions	Unions mainly focus on the treatment and pay of their members. Nike has employees who are members of unions. Therefore the unions may be able to influence the aims and objectives of Nike to some extent.
Employer associations	Although they give advice to Nike, employer associations have little direct influence on the company's aims and objectives.

Your assessment criteria:

D1 Evaluate the influence different stakeholders exert in one organisation

Key terms

Trade union: *an organisation that represents employees in business negotiations and day-to-day issues*

Figure 1.7 (continued)

Local and national communities	Local and national communities can bring significant media coverage to a company like Nike if it damages them in any way. For example, pollution created by Nike would cause negative media coverage. Therefore the local and national communities have to be considered when planning future aims and objectives.
Governments	Governments should have very little direct influence on private companies such as Nike. However, through taxation, support and employment laws, they have a strong influence on how the business behaves. Therefore, their influence is hard to measure.

 ## Case study

On 20 April 2010 an oil rig off the Gulf of Mexico exploded, starting a chain of events which caused 40,000 barrels of oil a day to spill into the sea, killing millions of birds, fish and other wildlife. The explosion brought worldwide media coverage of BP and its clean-up operation. The US government decided to take legal action against BP for the leak. Many of BP's stakeholders demanded that the company change its aims and objectives. BP announced that its shareholders would not be receiving a dividend for up to 2 years.

1. Describe the different stakeholders that influence BP.

2. Explain the points of view of BP's different stakeholders after the spill.

3. Evaluate the influence the different stakeholders exert over BP after the spill.

 Did you know?

Nike has factories in 45 different countries. It therefore has global stakeholders.

 Discuss

BP was forced to spend billions of dollars to clear up the oil spilled in the Gulf of Mexico crisis of 2010. Do you think this was fair?

Discuss

Should external stakeholders, such as local communities, be able to influence a business's aims and objectives?

The purpose of an organisational structure

A business must make sure it chooses the correct organisational structure so that its stakeholders can clearly see:

• the communication channels and lines of control

• how the workload is broken up between staff and departments.

An organisation divides up its work in this way so that:

• staff are clear what their roles and duties are

• there is no time-wasting overlap in decision-making

• staff at all levels can see who they should be reporting to.

The **chain of command** allows all staff to see how decisions from the top are to be cascaded down to lower levels. For example, if Mark Zuckerberg, owner of Facebook, wanted all staff in the organisation to know about the release of the film *The Social Network*, he would pass this on to the managers below him, who would then pass it on to their teams, until it filtered down to the lowest level of staff.

Your assessment criteria:

P3	Describe how two businesses are organised

🔑 **Key terms**

Chain of command: *the order in which decisions and orders are passed down the organisational structure*

Organisational structure: *the hierarchy and layout of a business*

🔍 **Research**

For each of the following organisations, find or create an organisational chart that shows the structure of the company:

• *Google*

• *your school /college*

• *Boots.*

Types of organisational structure

As businesses grow, it is very important that they build the organisation using the most appropriate structure. Choosing the correct type of structure could mean the difference between success and failure. There are a number of ways in which an organisation can structure itself.

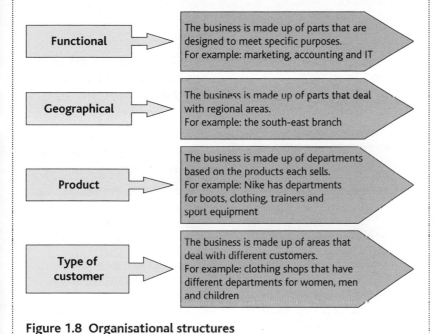

Functional	The business is made up of parts that are designed to meet specific purposes. For example: marketing, accounting and IT
Geographical	The business is made up of parts that deal with regional areas. For example: the south-east branch
Product	The business is made up of departments based on the products each sells. For example: Nike has departments for boots, clothing, trainers and sport equipment
Type of customer	The business is made up of areas that deal with different customers. For example: clothing shops that have different departments for women, men and children

Figure 1.8 Organisational structures

 Discuss

In pairs, discuss the following questions, ready to feed back to the class:

1. *As companies grow, why can decision-making become slower?*

2. *Why is it important to break a company such as Apple into product departments?*

 # Case study

Having merged with its main competitor, Rainbow Gym had grown into a national franchise. It now operated 18 gyms across the breadth of the UK. Each gym had its own manager, assistant manager and staff, which included gym instructors, cleaners, chefs and, in some cases, lifeguards.

Throughout 2010, the company grew again, taking over more smaller firms until there were 28 franchises. However, all was not well. The managing director, Wayne, started to see a delay on the monthly reports, as well as a drop in customer satisfaction.

1. Why are problems starting to arise for Rainbow Gym?

2. How could Wayne improve customer satisfaction?

P3 Organisational charts

Organisational charts are used to show the structure and key areas of an organisation. The chart should be simple and clear so that all stakeholders can understand how the business is divided up.

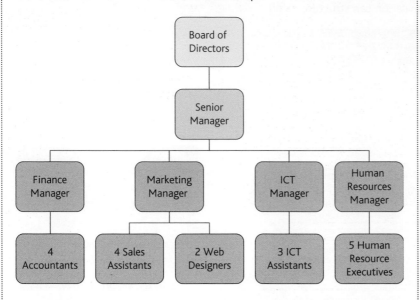

Figure 1.9 The organisational chart of a simple, well structured organisation

Figure 1.9 clearly shows how each department fits into the organisation and the line of control of each department. Each manager reports to the senior manager who then reports to the board of directors. The **span of control** of each manager is fairly small. For example, the marketing manager has a span of control of six people. As the organisation gets larger, the spans of control tend to increase. However, organisations need to be careful as an increase in span of control means an increase in the time needed to manage the individuals within the span of the control. This can cause managers to be overworked.

Tall or flat?

Organisational structures can differ depending on the organisation's ethos or industry. In the past, most organisations had many layers in their organisation (a **tall structure**). Companies such as Dyson, Google and Vodafone have reduced numbers of layers (a **flat structure**). This speeds up communication as there are fewer levels for the decisions to pass through. This also helps to boost motivation as staff feel they can talk directly to the senior managers. The more layers an organisation has,

 Key terms

Flat structure: an organisational structure with few layers and small chains of command

Span of control: the number of people directly responsible to an individual

Tall structure: an organisational structure with many levels or layers of staff and departments

 Reflect

Why is it important that companies such as Google minimise their spans of control?

 Discuss

Why do some larger businesses choose to keep their structure as flat as possible?

the harder it can be to adapt and make quick decisions, which is often crucial in an ever-changing business environment.

 ## Case study

In 2009 Carol Bartz took over from the founder of Yahoo, Jerry Yang. She is seeking to improve the firm's fortunes by cutting costs and jobs and changing the organisational structure. Yahoo is moving towards functional departments, with fewer layers. At present, Yahoo holds only 17 per cent of the search engine market in the US, although it claims that the search market is only 50 per cent of its overall business. Yahoo is now working hard to improve its range of products and expanding on its 200 million customers.

1. Describe how Yahoo is organised using an organisational chart.

2. How will this new organisational structure help Yahoo fulfil its purpose?

Functional areas

P3 The functional areas of a business

Within an organisation, duties are often broken up into **functional areas** or departments such as:

- finance
- production
- sales
- marketing
- human resources
- customer service.

Finance

The finance department's duties include:

- keeping financial records for all transactions in the business
- designing and updating budgets for each department
- helping managers with costing and financial forecasting.

The finance manager must constantly monitor the department to ensure that it can always give an up-to-date and accurate report on the company's finances. Staff in this department may therefore be split into two teams:

- financial accounting – keeps records of all business transactions such as sales, pay and tax
- management accounting – works with the other functional areas to help with budgeting and project costing.

Your assessment criteria:

P3 Describe how two businesses are organised

Key terms

Functional areas: *the grouping of individual staff based upon their skills and knowledge*

Discuss

How important is the role played by finance in a large organisation such as Microsoft and Vodafone?

Marketing

The marketing department's main role is to identify the customer's needs and wants and then make the customers aware that there is a product that matches these. For example, Apple used various marketing tools to make customers aware that the new iPhone 4G was about to be released.

The marketing department is judged on how well the products sell, so it must make sure it chooses the correct *product* for the market. For example, a car manufacturer must make sure it produces cars that customers actually want. It then decides on an appropriate *price* to attract customers and give value for money. The product must then be *promoted* in the most appropriate way; for example, TV, magazines or leaflets. Finally, the product must be sold in the appropriate *place* so customers can access it. These 4Ps make up the marketing mix.

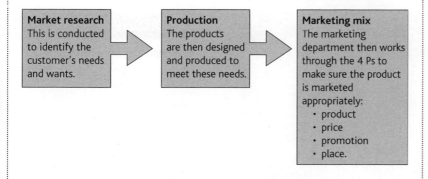

Market research
This is conducted to identify the customer's needs and wants.

→

Production
The products are then designed and produced to meet these needs.

→

Marketing mix
The marketing department then works through the 4 Ps to make sure the product is marketed appropriately:
- product
- price
- promotion
- place.

Figure 1.10 The role of the marketing department

P3 The functional areas of a business
continued

Human resources

Human resources is the department responsible for the employees of the company. Its work includes:

- recruitment – recruiting staff based upon department managers' specifications

- employee welfare – making sure the firm provides all the necessary facilities and implements safety measures

- support – supporting all departments to improve their work

- administration – completing all paperwork such as contracts, discipline letters and payroll

- training – helping to keep staff up to date with the skills needed.

Production

The production department is in charge of taking the raw materials, designs and other resources, and making the product. The production manager must make sure the work is carried out to the highest standards with all staff following company procedure to maintain quality and safety. This is very important as reputations can be seriously damaged if standards are not maintained. For example, in December 2010 Honda had to recall over 143,000 of its 2007/2008 plate Honda Fit hatchbacks for safety reasons. The production manager is responsible for making sure that his or her supervisors are allocating production staff in the most appropriate way.

 Your assessment criteria:

P3 Describe how two businesses are organised

 Discuss

Discuss the following statement: 'The human resources department is the most important department for a successful business.

 Research

Using your research skills, describe the production process of a large multinational company such as Nike.

? **Did you know?**

Saudi Arabia produces over 8 million barrels of oil per day!

Customer services

This department aims to maintain a positive relationship with all the firm's customers. Word of mouth is the most powerful marketing tool available, and firms are very aware that they must be seen to support and understand their customers. Most firms operate their own customer service area. Department stores and supermarkets have customer service departments and most company websites have a customer service area that offers customers various ways to contact the company. Many firms now have customer service call centres in the UK.

Sales

This department works closely with the marketing department to ensure that customers can purchase the product. The marketing department focuses on making the customers aware, while the sales team must try to close deals. This can be done in various ways. Some firms identify potential customers, and then use personal visits or phone calls to try to sell; for example, window salesmen. Other firms have regional sales team that focus on a specific area through email and phone sales. The manager of this department must make sure his or her team is suitably qualified and trained as the firm will struggle to exist without any sales.

 Discuss

Which department do you think is the most important in developing a successful company?

Strategic planning

P4 Directing a business

Every business is different in terms of its ethos, aims and objectives. A charity such as Save the Children will have a totally different set of ambitions to Apple or BP. However, all firms need a long-term plan or strategy. **Strategic planning** is at the heart of all successful businesses and charities. The plan is formulated using the key values and principles of the organisation as outlined by the board of directors and managers.

Mission and value statements

Nearly all organisations set out their mission and values in these two documents:

- **Mission statement** – This document is usually very short, and sets out the overall vision of the organisation. It has to be clear and concise so all stakeholders can understand it.

- **Value statement** – This statement sets out, usually as a list, the key values of the organisation, which it tries to build into all of its day-to-day business.

Developing strategic aims and objectives

While the mission statement sets out the values and ethos of a business, strategic **aims** set out broad targets for the business to achieve through its strategic plan. The aims will reflect the same message as the mission and value statements, but offer more of a sense of direction. These aims are then broken down into more specific **objectives** which help achieve the aim. Objectives should be like building blocks that help a business work towards its overall aim.

Your assessment criteria:

P4 Explain how their style of organisation helps them to fulfil their purposes

Key terms

Aims: *the overall goals of a business*

Mission statement: *a short statement setting out the overall vision of a business*

Objectives: *the smaller steps that help a business to achieve its aims*

Strategic planning: *the setting out of a business's long-term aims and how to achieve them*

Value statement: *a statement outlining the key values of a business*

Research

Using your research skills, find the mission statement for your three favourite organisations. Were they difficult to find? Are they easy to understand?

Figure 1.11 Working towards the overall aim of a business

Cascading objectives

Within an organisation, objectives are set at different levels. However, the organisation must set objectives for the entire business to work towards. These are then cascaded down to individual departments that set their own functional objectives. Within each functional area, each team may then set its own objectives. Finally, individuals in the organisation may set personal objectives.

Corporate objective
Increase revenue of the company by 15 per cent by 29 June 2011

Functional objective
Each department, from ticket sales to the club shop, is set the objective to increase its revenue by 15 per cent

Team objective
Each team within the departments is set the objective to increase its revenue by 15 per cent

Individual objective
Each individual working for Manchester United FC is then set the objective of increasing revenue by 15 per cent

Figure 1.12 How the cascading of objectives could work within Manchester United FC

Design

Design your own short-term objectives and long-term aims. Remember, the objectives should help you achieve your broader overall aims.

The strategic planning process

This process brings together the organisation's major decision-makers who create the major future plans for the business. They meet to compose broad corporate aims and more specific objectives. They even design the functional plans which will help them meet their objectives. The key to this process is putting in place performance management procedures to measure the success of the plan.

Using SMART objectives

SMART objectives are used to make sure objectives are set out correctly.

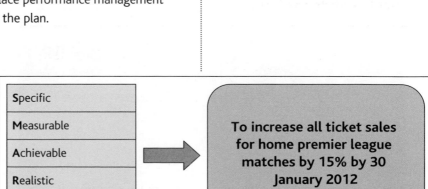

Specific
Measurable
Achievable
Realistic
Time related

To increase all ticket sales for home premier league matches by 15% by 30 January 2012

Figure 1.13 Using SMART objectives

Influencing factors

P4 ▶ The three influencing factors

Stakeholders

Each business has different stakeholders depending on its industry and location. A stakeholder can have a varied degree of influence on a business. For each of the stakeholders below, the values, mission and aims of the business are reflected in the stakeholder's beliefs:

- Dyson employees may have chosen to work for Dyson because of its innovative and laid-back approach to business.

- Volunteers at charity shops give up their time to help others.

- Divine Chocolate stockists choose Divine Chocolate to attract ethical customers.

Business environment

Every business has to respond to the **business environment** as it sets out its strategic plans. The better a firm can respond and understand the environment, the better it will do. External factors such as government law, the economy, customer tastes and availability of resources will have a big impact on a business. For example, in 2009 Cadbury started to produce its Dairy Milk bar using Fair Trade cocoa in response to changing customer expectations. At the present time, businesses are being significantly affected by the drop in spending as the economy struggles to gain momentum. This means expansion strategies may be halted to be replaced by cost-cutting in the labour force and marketing.

Your assessment criteria:

P4 Explain how their style of organisation helps them to fulfil their purposes

🔍 Research

Using your research skills, look into a company of your choice. Who influences the values, aims and objectives that it sets out? How much influence do the stakeholders have over this business?

🔑 Key terms

__Business environment:__ the climate within which a business operates

Business type and ownership

The strategic planning of Cadbury and Divine Chocolate differ significantly because of the companies' differing ownership types. Profit-driven organisations such as Cadbury will be driven by returns on their investment. However, as Divine Chocolate is a co-operative, partly owned by the cocoa farmers themselves, it may choose to continue to provide Fair Trade chocolate that supports the communities of Ghana. Private businesses run as a sole trader, partnership or limited company normally have few owners who can contribute to the strategic plan, whereas in a public limited company, these decisions are agreed by the board of directors.

 ## Case study

In the autumn of 2009, Cadbury announced its Cocoa partnership, which led to the award of the Fair Trade logo, which is now displayed on the packaging of Cadbury Dairy Milk bars. However, the amount of Fair Trade cocoa beans actually used by Cadbury is very low.

1. Why did Cadbury move over to Fair Trade in 2009?

2. Which stakeholders have influenced the company's decision to move towards Fair Trade?

 Research

Focusing on a large company of your choice:

- Research its aims, values and mission statements. Which stakeholders can you see have influenced these?

- Look at the firm's business environment. How has this changed in the past year? How has this affected the business?

 Discuss

Fair Trade is becoming a common feature in supermarkets. Do you agree with the label being used by firms such as Cadbury?

 Describe

Describe the business ownership of Divine Chocolate. Visit its website, www.divinechocolate.com, for help.

 Did you know?

Of the UK population, 72% recognise the Fair Trade mark on products. Do you?

The aims of private sector businesses

Private sector aims

The private sector is made up of privately owned businesses, with their own shareholders and directors. These shareholders have a significant influence on the eventual aims of the business.

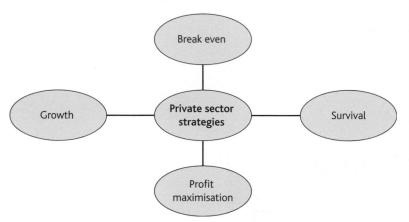

Figure 1.14 The four main aims of private sector businesses

Break even

Break even is the most important aim for start-up businesses and those looking for survival in the short term. Break even is the point at which sales revenue covers all of the businesses costs. At this point, the business has not made a profit or a loss, but simply broken even.

To work out the costs of a business, it is necessary to separate the costs into two types.

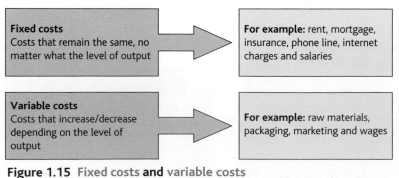

Figure 1.15 Fixed costs and variable costs

Key terms

Break even: costs are exactly the same as revenue

Fixed costs: costs that do not change with a change in output

Variable costs: costs that change with a change in output

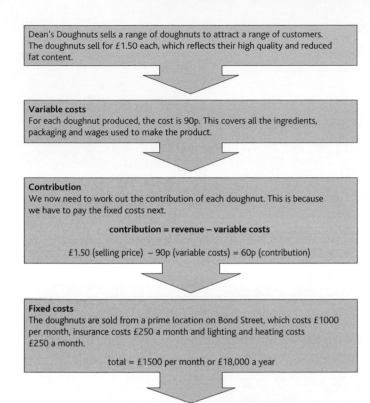

Dean's Doughnuts sells a range of doughnuts to attract a range of customers. The doughnuts sell for £1.50 each, which reflects their high quality and reduced fat content.

Variable costs
For each doughnut produced, the cost is 90p. This covers all the ingredients, packaging and wages used to make the product.

Contribution
We now need to work out the contribution of each doughnut. This is because we have to pay the fixed costs next.

contribution = revenue − variable costs

£1.50 (selling price) − 90p (variable costs) = 60p (contribution)

Fixed costs
The doughnuts are sold from a prime location on Bond Street, which costs £1000 per month, insurance costs £250 a month and lighting and heating costs £250 a month.

total = £1500 per month or £18,000 a year

Break even
To work out the number of doughnuts that Dean's Doughnuts has to sell to break even, we use this formula:

$$\text{break even} = \frac{\text{fixed costs}}{\text{contribution}}$$

$$\frac{£18,000 \text{ (fixed costs)}}{60p \text{ (contribution)}} = 30,000 \text{ doughnuts}$$

With each doughnut contributing 60p, Dean's Doughnuts has to sell 30,000 doughnuts each year to break even.

Figure 1.16 Calculating the break-even point

In most cases, rent or mortgages are the biggest fixed cost for a business.

P4 Private sector aims *continued*

Survival

Survival may seem like a strategy that only sole traders and start-up businesses would use, but with the economy struggling, larger companies can also see its importance. In any high street or shopping centre, you will see a range of shops that seem to have been around for years. However, even larger companies can fall foul of changing tastes and poor quality. In late December 2009, Woolworths closed its stores. This was a huge shock to the shopping world, as Woolworths had been in business since 1909. Other stores such as River Island and Marks and Spencer have dramatically changed their image and product range in an attempt to keep up to date in a hugely competitive market, and in order to avoid a similar fate.

Profit maximisation

The emergence of social enterprises such as Divine Chocolate and Livity has altered the perception that all businesses aim for **profit maximisation**. Although all businesses aim to make a profit, some have slightly different approaches to this. Profit maximisation can be difficult to achieve in the short term as large initial investments in advertising or production processes may be required before long-term benefits can be realised. Remember that profit does not occur until all the business's costs are taken away from the revenue.

Your assessment criteria:

 P4 Explain how their style of organisation helps them to fulfil their purposes

 Key terms

Profit maximisation: setting achieving maximum profits as the key aim

Survival: a business continuing to trade

 Describe

Identify five changes that Marks and Spencer have made in the last 5 years to make the store more attractive to younger shoppers. You may find www.marksandspencer.com helpful.

Growth

Growth is a natural aim for most successful businesses. It can occur internally through reinvestment of profits, perhaps into new technology or increased staff. A business can also expand externally, through a **merger** or **takeover**. For example, Orange and T-Mobile merged in September 2010.

Figure 1.17 Ways in which businesses can grow

Increased sales	By taking a larger share of the market sales, a business can increase its sales overall. Online firms such as Amazon and Play have increased their sales and reduced those of HMV.
New markets	Firms can produce products in new markets to help increase their customer base and overall sales. For example, Apple now produces products in the phone and music industry rather than just computers.
Increased retail outlets	By increasing their presence on the high street, firms can increase sales automatically. Businesses can attract more customers if they operate out of a large number of outlets. Jack Wills Ltd, the clothing retailer, has opened 37 stores across the country in just under 8 years to increase its sales.
Overseas expansion	Businesses can find large pools of new customers by taking their brand overseas. For example, Jack Wills Ltd opened its first store in the US in 2010.

Tesco has tried to enter the US market with their new store.

The aims of public sector organisations

P4 > Expectations of the public sector

Service provision

Businesses in the public sector are significantly influenced by different stakeholders, including the government and taxpayers, who expect the businesses to put profit behind quality of service. This is certainly the case for the BBC, which is funded through annual television licences sold to those who watch television. The BBC aims to produce high-quality viewing by investing this money into new programmes.

There are many other organisations funded by the government to provide a service to the public. The National Health Service, state schools, the police and Her Majesty's Revenue and Customs are all funded by the government.

Cost limitation

Despite taxation increases, the government has to borrow money from the World Bank and other countries in order to maintain services for the public. As the government reduces its spending, it has to limit its outgoings in some areas and be sure to use its money wisely. The public is a key stakeholder in the government's activities, and expects the government to be transparent in its spending.

? **Did you know?**

Switzerland's television licence is nearly twice as much as the UK licence: a mammoth £277.32 a year.

💬 **Discuss**

Between 1 April 2009 and 31 March 2010 the cost of the UK TV licence was £142.50 – the equivalent of £11.88 per month or just under 40p per day. Do you think this represents good value for money?

Q **Research**

Using the website www.hm-treasury. gov.uk, research the government's budget which outlines the funding given to public sector services. Find the 2010 budget for government spending on:

• education

• health.

Value for money

A key aim for the government is to maintain value for money. This means that the public should receive a full and high-quality service for the tax that it pays. Government-funded organisations should produce goods and services efficiently and at the lowest cost possible. In the past, the government has come under fire for going over the budgets set for its departments and not giving value for money.

Meeting government standards

Public services are set standards or targets by the government. For example, the National Health Service is set targets for the time taken to see patients. These organisations are given funding to help achieve the standards that are set. However, many would argue that government standards are often inflated and are aspirational rather than achievable.

Growth of range of provision

Public sector organisations must ensure they provide the services that are needed by the public. The government must continually adapt to changes in demand. This could be in the form of new roads or hospitals, or through extra funding for the NHS in a state of crisis. The government is heavily influenced by the general public, and must constantly look for changes and improvements to its provision of services.

Discuss

Which of the following public sector organisations do you think should receive the most money:

- *education*
- *the NHS*
- *security (the police and MI5)*
- *the armed services?*

? Did you know?

In November 2010, the UK government had overspent by £23.3 billion!

The impact of the economic environment

There is a range of factors outside a business that can have a direct impact on it. These could stem from political, social, legal and economic changes. The recession of 2008/9 caused many businesses to have concerns about the future economic climate and gave rise to uncertainty about how the global economy could impact on business aims and objectives..

P5 The economic environment

The **economic environment** is made up of chains of decision-makers who turn raw materials into products and services that are bought by consumers. To enable this chain to continue, banks and governments alter their behaviour according to what is needed to maintain a healthy economy. For example, the recession of 2008/9 caused a dip in consumer confidence, a fear of high unemployment and a tendency for families to save rather than spend. This caused businesses to receive less revenue.

The importance of stability

Economic stability has become key to a successful economy. Businesses prefer stability as it removes additional pressure on the finances of a business. Credit can be given in the knowledge that customers should be able to pay it back. Also, stability means that businesses can make longer term forecasts with more certainty.

The impact of changes in the economic environment

Growth

Prior to the recession of 2008/9 the UK experienced an extended period of **economic growth**. This occurs when the goods and services being produced are being consumed at an increasing rate. As consumption of goods increases, businesses are encouraged to produce more and therefore start to employ more staff. With more and more people in work, household spending increases, leading to more goods and services being consumed.

Recession

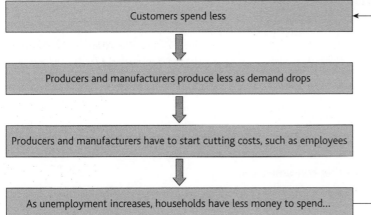

Figure 1.18 The ripple effect

The ripple effect shown in Figure 1.18. shows how a reduction in consumer spending leads to businesses becoming more cautious and therefore cutting back on staff, and a slowdown in the economy. If this drop in the value of the goods and services sold decreases for two quarters (3 months per quarter) then the economy is said to be in a **recession**.

The ripple effect has been seen in the UK economy since 2008/9 when there were considerable job losses in construction, retail and finances. Without government intervention, the ripple effect can continue, and get worse, for a long time.

P5 Inflation

Inflation is the general rise in the price of goods and services. Inflation means that money becomes worth less than it was previously. For example, in 2001, a bar of chocolate cost on average 35p; today it costs around 60p. You therefore use more money to buy this product than you previously did. In the UK, inflation is measured using the Consumer Price Index (CPI).

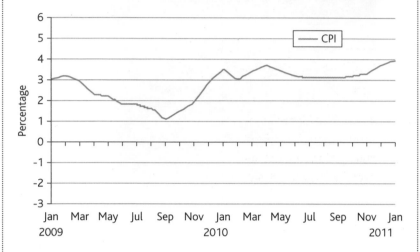

Figure 1.19 The Consumer Price Index (CPI) in the UK Jan 2009–Jan 2011

For businesses, high inflation can signal uncertainty and a change in consumer spending. If prices are rising, this may mean that the costs of materials, wages and fuel are also increasing in price. Businesses may also see demand drop if they produce luxury items that consumers can no longer afford. Businesses have to think carefully about whether or not to increase their prices.

Credit

The **interest rate** in the UK is set monthly by the Monetary Policy Commitee (MPC). It is set as a percentage. This is then used to calculate the cost of credit. For example, if Vodafone borrows £100,000 from its bank at an interest rate of 6 per cent, it will pay back £106,000 (£6000 being the interest accumulated).

Your assessment criteria:

P5 Describe the influence of two contrasting economic environments on business activities within a selected organisation

 Key terms

Inflation: the general rise of prices for goods and services

Interest rate: the cost of borrowing or the money received on savings

Discuss

You work for Caterham Cars, Surrey, that produces bespoke sports cars to the consumers' requirements. Rising inflation has meant demand has dropped. What should you do? Should you increase wages, reduce prices or accept a drop in profits?

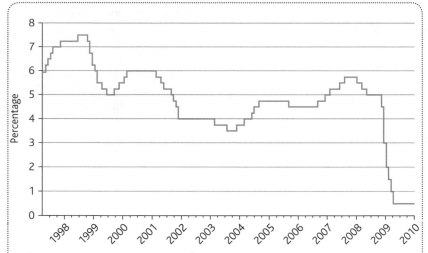

Figure 1.20 Interest rates in the UK 1997–2010

As you can see in Figure 1.20 above, interest rates have remained low for an extended period of time as the MPC tries to encourage businesses and consumers to borrow money to increase spending. However, despite interest rates being so low, consumer spending over the 2010 Christmas period was still well below the historic average.

Labour

For many businesses, labour costs are the highest costs they incur. Recruiting the best labour force can help businesses grow and succeed, even at difficult times. However, this can prove difficult when there is a lack of staff with the desired skills. The labour market cannot always supply the necessary staff and shortages occur. For example, the NHS employs doctors and nurses from around the world as a result of the shortage of staff in this industry.

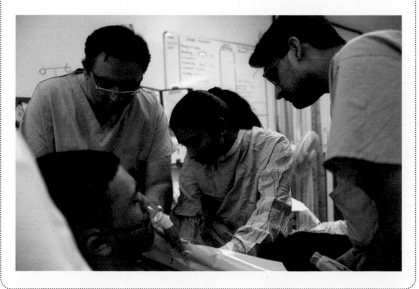

P5 Changes in government policy

The government is elected to manage and support the UK economy.

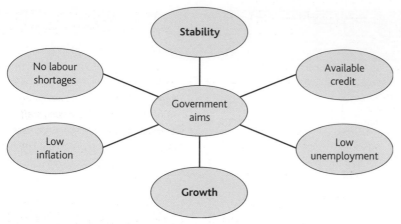

Figure 1.21 The government's aims

Interest rates are used to help stimulate spending so that the government can achieve many of its aims. However, in 2009, the UK government agreed to a phase of **quantitative easing**. As part of **monetary policy**, the government allowed the Bank of England to print more money, therefore making more money available to lend. This is one tool the government can use to halt the ripple effect (see page 35).

One of the government's aims is low unemployment.

Your assessment criteria:

P5 Describe the influence of two contrasting economic environments on business activities within a selected organisation

Describe

Outline two ways that would help to encourage businesses and consumers to increase their spending.

Key terms

Monetary policy: regulation of money supply and interest rates by the Bank of England

Quantitative easing: increasing money supply through the printing of money

The government also uses its **fiscal policy**. Within this, the government can alter its spending and the rates of taxation. Through these policies, the government can encourage businesses to spend and employ.

The government can also influence businesses by passing certain laws. These can, for example, encourage businesses to improve their efficiency by setting quotas for wastage and pollution.

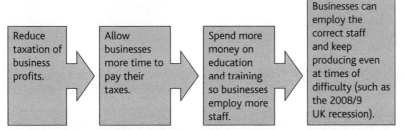

| Reduce taxation of business profits. | Allow businesses more time to pay their taxes. | Spend more money on education and training so businesses employ more staff. | Businesses can employ the correct staff and keep producing even at times of difficulty (such as the 2008/9 UK recession). |

Figure 1.22 The government's attempts to encourage businesses to spend and employ

Key terms

Fiscal policy: government decisions on taxation and spending in the UK

Describe

You have been asked to write a letter to local businesses to encourage them to start employing more staff. You will need to include the advantages of new staff, how increasing staff numbers could help the businesses develop and any government support they may receive.

? Did you know?

In 2010, the Bank of England injected £200 million into the economy through quantitative easing.

Discuss

At a point when the UK economy is only just coming out of a recession, spending is still down and unemployment is rising, do you think the Bank of England should agree to another phase of quantitative easing?

The demand for goods and services

P5 Demand

Demand is the quantity of goods and services that consumers buy at a given price. Imagine Sony priced its PlayStations at £1200 or the new Nike football boots cost £900 – demand would be heavily affected. The more expensive a good is, the fewer people can afford it. However, there are other factors that influence demand:

- affordability
- availability of substitutes
- level of Gross Domestic Product (national income)
- needs and aspirations of consumers.

The relationship between the demand for a product and its price can been shown in a demand line graph.

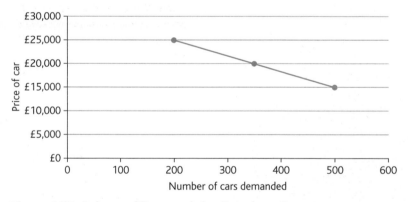

Figure 1.23 A demand line graph for Caterham Cars

Affordability

As the price of a product drops, consumers see the product as more affordable. This means they feel they have the spare money to be able to buy the product without causing themselves financial difficulty in the long run. Individual consumers have a maximum price they think they can afford for each product. For example, it may be that as the price for Caterham sports cars decreases, consumers start to feel they can afford them. Therefore, finding the correct pricing is crucial for businesses.

Your assessment criteria:

P5 Describe the influence of two contrasting economic environments on business activities within a selected organisation

Key terms

Demand: quantity of products and services bought by consumers at a given price

Gross Domestic Product (GDP): value of goods and services produced in a country

Design

Create your own cash flow statement showing any money you receive each week, as well as the items you spend money on. Do you have any extra to spend? Do you save?

? Did you know?

In 2010, the most sought after children's Christmas presents were dancing rubbish trucks and mini video cameras.

Competition and availability of substitutes

All businesses have to attract customers with quality, low prices and good customer care. The level of competition will affect demand as customers go elsewhere for their products. If alternatives, or **substitute goods**, are available then businesses will have to offer something special to keep their customers.

Level of Gross Domestic Product

Income has a big impact on demand. The more money we have, the more we feel we can buy. This is true for individuals and countries. Gross Domestic Product (GDP) measures the goods and services produced and sold in a country. The higher the GDP, the more that country can spend. Countries such as the USA and India can spend more as they have more money.

Needs and aspirations of consumers

Do we need a TV or PlayStation? No. We buy them because we want them. However, products such as food, drink and fuel are necessities. Therefore, products that are necessities are often less responsive to price increases as demand remains relatively stable.

 Key terms

Substitute goods: *goods that satisfy the same need as another good*

 Discuss

As petrol prices increase, oil companies continue to see record profits. Do you think these companies should be able to raise their prices despite the fact that drivers have no alternative but to buy the petrol?

The supply of goods and services

How much to produce

Supply is the quantity of a good or service that a business is willing to supply at a given price. Suppliers will provide more as the price increases. For example, a tailor makes five bespoke suits each week at a cost of £200 per suit. However, if customers are willing to pay £400, the tailor may make more suits and sell eight suits each week. If customers then decided they would pay £500 per suit, the tailor may employ additional staff and produce ten each week.

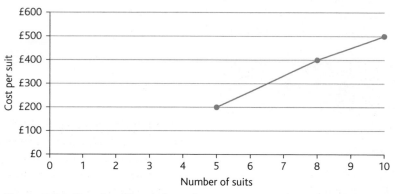

Figure 1.24 Supply of bespoke suits

Although suppliers may wish to increase production, there are factors which will influence the extent to which they can adapt. The most important factor for the supplier is the profitability of increased production. If the business feels that the increase could lead to a major profit boost, it will be more likely to make this change. The other factors are:

• availability of raw materials and labour

• competition for raw materials

• logistics

• government support.

Availability of raw materials and labour

The supply of oil can only be increased once oil fields have been discovered. Supply can only be increased if the materials and labour required are available. During a recession, supply can increase quickly as there is a vast labour pool from which to choose. However, during a boom, businesses can struggle to find the labour they need.

Key terms

Supply: *the quantity of a product available for purchase at a given price*

Discuss

In pairs, discuss factors which:

• *encourage suppliers to produce more*

• *discourage producers from increasing their supply.*

Discuss

Discuss in pairs how the four factors listed to the left might affect the increased supply of Apple's iPads. Which factor would have the biggest influence on the increase in production?

Logistics

The movement of the raw materials to the business, and of the products to the retailer is called the supply chain. If this system is not managed properly, the producers will be more reluctant to increase supply as they will not make sufficient increases in profit.

Competition for raw materials

In November 2010, countries including Russia, UK, the USA and Argentina claimed they had found oil off the Falkland Islands. The scarcity of oil means that competition for this raw material is strong.

As countries such as India and China grow, their economies use more resources. Therefore countries compete to gain access to stable and long-term supply chains.

Government support

In May 2010, the UK government started the car scrappage scheme, which offered £2000 to those who scrapped an old car and bought a new one. This scheme saved over 4000 jobs in the UK car industry. This government support helped to subsidise the production of cars and kept supply high. Governments can also use subsidies to encourage the production of goods that are needed but are yet to be produced on a sufficiently large scale.

 Discuss

As countries disagree over oil reserves, many have called for a focus on using new sources of power. Do you think this is the way to go?

? Did you know?

Under the car scrappage scheme introduced by the government in 2010, 330,000 new cars were sold.

Changes in supply and demand

The relationship between supply and demand

In the **marketplace**, the price of goods is determined by the relationship between supply and demand.

Figure 1.25 Supply and demand for Nike trainers

Price of trainers	Quantity demanded	Quantity supplied
£30	1000	400
£35	850	550
£40	700	700
£45	550	850
£50	400	1000

As shown in Figure 1.25, Nike will want to produce more trainers at the higher price in order to maximise returns. However, customers will demand more at lower prices. Therefore, they will meet at the equilibrium point.

It is clear from Figure 1.25 that the market will, if untouched by other influences, find a way to set the price in line with customer demands.

Your assessment criteria:

P5 Describe the influence of two contrasting economic environments on business activities within a selected organisation

Key terms

Marketplace: where suppliers and customers meet and price levels are determined

Discuss

Why may firms like Nike price their products above the equilibrium price, despite the knowledge that some will go unsold?

Design

Using Figures 1.25 and 1.26 as templates, produce your own supply and demand question for a member of the class.

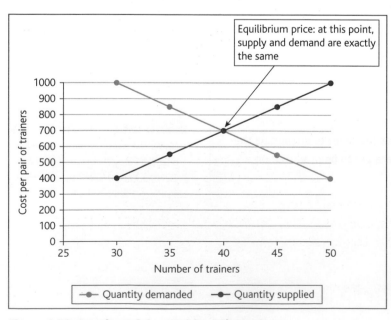

Equilibrium price: at this point, supply and demand are exactly the same

Figure 1.26 Supply and demand for Nike trainers

Despite a clear equilibrium point, markets do not always work at this point. In the example above, it may be that Nike continues to sell its trainers at a higher price, with many pairs going unsold.

However, the market can be influenced by other factors including the government, which may interject to help boost supply or demand.

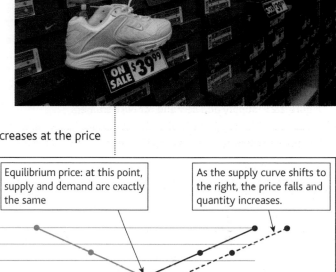

Supply

On a supply and demand graph both demand and supply curves can shift both left and right. If supply increases at the price given, then the line will shift to the right, whereas if the amount supplied at the given price is reduced then the line will shift to the left.

An increase in supply (a shift right) could be caused by:

• Technology – Advances in technology can lead to higher production in the time given and waste can be reduced as computers make a business more efficient.

• Weather – Changes in the weather can allow producers of food to grow more.

• Labour – An increase in the labour force or an improvement in skills can allow a business to produce more.

Equilibrium price: at this point, supply and demand are exactly the same

As the supply curve shifts to the right, the price falls and quantity increases.

Cost per pair of trainers

Number of trainers

—•— Quantity demanded   —•— Quantity supplied

Figure 1.27 Supply and demand graph showing increased supply

Demand

Demand can also shift to the left (indicating that demand has dropped at a set price) and right (indicating that demand has increased at a set price) depending on the marketplace. Demand may shift to the right if:

• tastes and fashions change. For example, when in July 2010 David Beckham announced his love for Lego on *Friday Night with Jonathan Ross*, sales for some of Lego's products rose by 663 per cent.

• the income of consumers increases, allowing them to purchase more products.

Elasticity and price sensitivity

The **elasticity of demand** measures how responsive the demand for a product is with a change of price. Products can be classified as:

- **Elastic** – The quantity demanded changes dramatically with a small change in price. For example, if Cadbury increases the price of its chocolate by 2p, there would be a big shift of customers over to alternatives such as Nestlé or Galaxy.

- **Inelastic** – The quantity demanded changes very little when price is changed. For example, petrol prices have been rising constantly, but demand has remained very high. Goods that are inelastic are usually necessities that have very few, if any, substitutes. They may also be products that have such a good brand image that customers don't shift to another product despite price increases.

Elasticity of demand can be calculated using the following formula:

$$\text{elasticity of demand} = \frac{\%\text{ change in quantity demanded}}{\%\text{ change in price}}$$

- If the elasticity of demand is a figure greater than 1 the demand is *elastic* – the percentage change in quantity demanded is greater than the percentage change in price.

- If the elasticity of demand is a figure less than 1 the demand is *inelastic* – the percentage change in quantity demanded is less than the percentage change in price.

If you are struggling to remember this, imagine holding an elastic band. If the product is inelastic (e.g. petrol) the elastic band will not stretch – this is because the demand won't be affected by a change in price. However, the elastic band will stretch for an elastic good (e.g. chocolate) as a change in price will cause the demand to change.

Your assessment criteria:

P5 Describe the influence of two contrasting economic environments on business activities within a selected organisation

 Key terms

Elasticity of demand: the responsiveness of the demand for a product to a change in the price

Discuss

In pairs, note down five items that you think would be

- *elastic*

- *inelastic.*

? **Did you know?**

Due to the huge increase in petrol prices, 5 per cent of drivers in the UK have stopped driving altogether.

Petrol: an inelastic good

Price sensitivity

If a product is price sensitive, it will be very responsive to a change in price. For example, demand for new cars can be heavily influenced by the wrong price. Therefore it is crucial not to under- or over-charge for a product. For more on pricing, see page 148 in Unit 3.

Price sensitivity differs for each product depending on:

- the number of substitutes it has – the more it has, the more sensitive customers will be as they know they can find an alternative

- whether it is a luxury – if the product is a luxury item, customers may feel they do not need it if the price is too high

- whether the product is a must have – if it is, a rise in price will have little effect on the demand.

Influence of branding on price sensitivity

If a firm can create brand loyalty, then its products will be price inelastic. This means customers will continue to buy the product despite its price because they feel the product has features that no other product has. For example, McDonald's has created a global customer base through its branding. Its television adverts, packaging and unique products have made it a global success.

Key terms

Price sensitivity: the extent to which demand changes with a change in price

Chocolate: an elastic good

Describe

Make a list of three products or services which have no alternatives.

Discuss

Why has the Snickers bar become a global brand?

Global interaction

P5 The features of globalisation

The development of global communication has allowed businesses to operate all over the world, selling products in markets around the globe. This is called **globalisation**. The key features of globalisation are:

- global brands – Nike, Coca-Cola and Microsoft are known all over the world

- global communication – businesses have offices all over the world which communicate with suppliers and retailers 24 hours a day

- global products – Coca-Cola sells the same product all over the globe, using the same advertising and packaging.

Levels and types of interdependence

Interdependence is the link between different parts of the supply chain, with each part relying on and working with the others. It is not only businesses that depend on each other, but individuals, countries and worldwide organisations such as Oxfam.

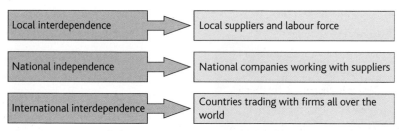

Figure 1.28 The different levels of interdependence

Supply chains

Businesses of all sizes rely on their supply chain to make sure they can produce their products on time and to the standard required. For example, Tropicana buys the fruit it needs for its juices from countries such as Brazil. It then send the fruit to its plants in Florida and, after producing the juice, transports the products all over the world. Without the supply chain in place, Tropicana would not be able to produce its products.

Key terms

Globalisation: *the growth of a business to a global scale*

Discuss

What negative impacts do countries face as a result of globalisation?

? Did you know?

In 1955 global trade of merchandise accounted for $95 billion. In 2005, this had risen to $10,431 billion.

Ownership of businesses

Multinational businesses own companies all over the world. They often purchase shares (normally over 50 per cent of the shares) in firms abroad so they can control production. By operating abroad, firms like Honda, Google and Tesco can increase their revenue. Many firms produce products in a range of countries to make use of the skilled labour force or reduced costs. For example, many car manufacturers operate in the UK to make use of the labour force.

In March 2008, the Indian firm Tata bought Jaguar from Ford for £1.15 billion. Tata decided that this was a good way to get into the UK market and expand its operations. The acquisition of other firms or joint ownership is appealing to multinational firms as it allows a quick expansion into new markets, sharing risk and making use of local skills and knowledge.

Movement of capital and business operations

All businesses need a supply of capital to make sure production continues. In the modern business world, businesses trade all over the world, with money moving between economies. Investors from all over the world can now invest in firms in a range of countries. The UK has encouraged this investment, called Foreign Direct Investment (FDI), to help sustain the economy and maintain employment. In 2009, FDI in the UK fell to £97 billion (around half the previous year's level), and was mainly in ICT and communication and financial services such as banking. A good example of FDI into the UK was the takeover of Manchester City FC by Sheikh Mansour.

The ability of governments to regulate global business

Although governments receive many benefits from FDI, it can cause major long-term problems as it becomes more difficult to regulate. Despite offering employment and taxation revenue for the government, the investors can leave very quickly. Governments therefore often reduce the tax rate to attract and keep the investment in place.

🔍 Research

Go to Divine Chocolate's website, www.divinechocolate.com, and find out about the supply chain that enables Divine to offer its bars for sale all over the UK.

? Did you know?

Japanese firms employ over 95,000 staff in the UK. Fujitsu alone employs 17,700 people.

M2   Challenges to business activities

Having looked at the factors that make up the economic environment, you will need to decide whether those factors will benefit or hinder a specific business. The ever-changing environment means businesses must be adaptable, with staff that are multi-skilled and able to adapt to new procedures and conditions.

Interest rates

At the beginning of 2011 interest rates in the UK were at an all-time low. As such they could only fall slightly and an increase in interest rates was highly likely. This increase would affect businesses in various ways. Start-up firms that have borrowed money could be dealt a devastating blow if they took out loans at a variable interest rate. The increase in rates would increase their payments, perhaps pushing the business towards bankruptcy. However, cash-rich firms with only small loans would feel little effect.

All firms, however, could face reduced revenue. An increase in interest rates would mean that customers would be less likely to borrow (due to a higher interest rate on the credit) and would be encouraged to save (earn more interest on their savings).

Your assessment criteria:

 M2   Compare the challenges to selected business activities within a selected organisation, in two different economic environments

 Discuss

Various companies advertise short-term loans that can be deposited into your account within an hour. However, they often charge interest rates as high as 2000 per cent. Do you think that firms should be able to give credit to customers at such high interest rates?

 Discuss

What could be the possible effects on the present economy if people started to save more money?

Research

What is meant by 'Gross Domestic Product per capita'? Why is this a better indicator of a country's wealth than Gross Domestic Product?

Gross Domestic Product

If Gross Domestic Product (GDP) is increasing, this suggests that the economy is doing well, with consumers consuming what is produced. It also suggests that exporters are doing well. A positive by-product of this is increased consumer spending. This benefits businesses as they increase their revenue. However, it also reduces unemployment, and boosts taxation revenue for the government. This frees up capital for the government to invest in education and healthcare, to improve the standard of living, and to support businesses though grants and loans.

Inflation and deflation

A high inflation rate can cause major issues for businesses. Consumer spending drops as money buys less than it did previously. This means producers of luxury items suffer the most. Companies that own cheaper brands often do well at this time. High inflation leads to employees asking for pay rises as they look to maintain their standard of living. If a business agrees to these rises, its costs increase. Deflation can also cause problems for businesses. Consumers save rather than spend so firms are forced to lower prices, thus reducing revenues and profit margins.

 ## Case study

In 2011 the future for John Lewis looked positive, with the retail giant posting a 30 per cent rise in pre-Christmas sales in 2010. However, 2011 looked less rosy as VAT rose to 20 per cent, and employment was expected to be reduced. With over 24 per cent of the retail industry claiming they expected to make staff redundant in 2011, consumer confidence and spending looked set to drop. The UK economy was also suffering from rising inflation, at around 3.3 per cent. The UK's interest rates were also set to rise at the start of 2011, meaning customers were likely to reduce their spending even further.

1. Describe the influence of the UK's economic environment on John Lewis's business activities.

2. What do you think were the major immediate challenges for John Lewis in 2011?

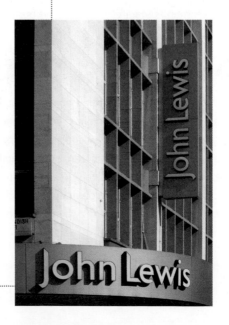

The impact of political factors on businesses

Levels of government

Political decisions affect businesses of all sizes, as the laws and regulations set will have a direct impact on their day-to-day practice. A change in government can, overnight, change the environment for businesses. A new government will often change the taxation on businesses, as well as other factors such as grants and spending. There are different levels of government that influence businesses:

- The European Union – The UK is a member of the EU and is affected by the decisions made on subjects such as international trade.

- National government – The UK is governed by an elected government, which has a direct impact on the running of businesses. The UK elects a party into government through a general election. The elected party's leader becomes the Prime Minister, and elects a Cabinet (a group of ministers) which is in charge of education, foreign policy, transport, etc.

- Local government – Local councils make decisions on local issues such as recycling, council tax and education.

Political factors affecting a business

Political stability

In the UK, once a government has been elected, businesses can look forward to years of stability in terms of the policies and targets as outlined in the government's manifesto. This allows businesses to plan for the future and, if necessary, change their product line.

Government support

Governments try to provide a fair marketplace in which all firms can compete. They may do this by investigating mergers and takeovers or removing barriers to entry, for example by helping with start-up costs. They may also offer grants. Voluntary organisations can receive grants; for example, from the National Lottery. They are often also given relief on assets such as property. In the voluntary sector, the government will often part-fund projects, especially if they benefit society.

Your assessment criteria:

P6 Describe how political, legal and social factors are impacting upon the business activities of the selected organisations and their stakeholders

Research

What are the benefits and drawbacks of the UK being a member of the EU?

Discuss

In February 2011, Egypt experienced the start of government instability. What is the impact of such instability on a country's businesses?

Taxation

Taxes are a substantial cost for businesses. The government sets taxes at a national level and taxes profits and wages. From January 2011, Value Added Tax (VAT) increased from 17.5 to 20 per cent. The associated record-keeping and payment of tax is often a burden, especially for smaller firms.

Direct support and supporting organisations

Governments give grants and loans to support businesses. These can help to keep unemployment low and taxation revenue high. Government loan schemes support industry, enabling the purchase of up-to-date technology. Organisations such as Business Link, Companies House and the Inland Revenue are funded by the government to support businesses.

Infrastructure

Governments also play a major role in providing the infrastructure of an area. Internet access, roads and other transport links allow businesses to grow. Without government pressure to expand the internet in the UK, many businesses would be without an internet connection. Access to motorways allows businesses to visit customers all over the UK and to trade abroad – all over the EU and further afield.

Education and training

The government's policies on education can have a direct impact on businesses in the long term. The introduction and funding of new courses, such as the Diploma and BTEC courses, is usually aimed at solving a labour shortage and opening education up to all. Firms rely on the government to identify, through research, shortages in the labour force and to educate the labour force so that it can meet the market needs of the future. The government may also invest in training schemes that focus on a certain industry or regional area to help improve the labour force.

? Did you know?

Gas and electricity are only charged at 6 per cent for VAT.

Discuss

Should the government reduce VAT on products such as bikes, health equipment and healthy food?

Discuss

Discuss how the political factors covered on these pages (52–53) influence the day-to-day running of a business of your choice.

P6 ▶ Legal factors

Businesses all over the world must operate within the **legislation** set out by the country within which they operate or face large fines, imprisonment and loss of customers. The three main areas of law that affect firms in the UK are:

• company law   • contract law   • competition law.

Providing a framework for business

Company laws exist to regulate who sets up a business, as well as setting out the procedures required each year to maintain the business. One of the main parts of company law is the 2006 Company Act, which outlines the following:

• Company names – The law stops new firms using existing business names. Firms must register their business, filing in information such as shareholder names and address. (The names registered are on the Companies House website.)

• Separate identity – The act sets out laws which protect the shareholders of the business, giving them a separate identity to the business.

• Shareholders – The law sets out the rights of shareholders as regards gaining information about the business and the process of buying and selling shares.

• Accounts – The business's accounts need to be published and audited each year, before being sent to Companies House. The board of directors must agree the accounts, placing responsibility for any mistakes with them. Failure to do this can result in hefty fines and suspension of trade for the firm.

Protecting consumers

Businesses form contracts with a range of stakeholders, but the key relationships covered by contract law are those between employees and customers.

The main law in place to protect customers is the Sale of Goods Act 1979. This law entitles the consumer to products that:

• are of satisfactory quality – products cannot have faults that have not been disclosed upon sale.

Your assessment criteria:

P6 ▶ Describe how political, legal and social factors are impacting upon the business activities of the selected organisations and their stakeholders

🔑 Key terms

Legislation: a law or set of laws, or the act or process of making new laws

❓ Did you know?

The Companies Act is one of the longest Acts in the UK, made up of over 1000 pages.

- fulfil their purpose – products must do what they should do, e.g. a waterproof jacket should not let in water.

- are as described – products must be as described on the packaging or labels, e.g. a Red Nintendo DS can't be white.

Customers can also expect a service of good quality, delivered within an expected time frame and price.

Consumers can also expect protection from the:

- Consumer Credit Act 2006

- Weights and Measures Act 1963

- Trade Descriptions Act 1968.

Protecting employees

Many would argue that employees are the most important aspect of a business. Once a contract is signed, employees can expect:

- a set amount of paid holiday each year

- a clear pay structure

- a disciplinary procedure to be in place

- a clear complaints procedure to be in place.

Employees are also protected by laws across the European Union:

- Equal Pay Act 1970

- Minimum Wage Act 2010

- Equality Act 2010

These pieces of legislation ensure that businesses treat staff in an equal and fair manner, with working conditions and pay above the minimum standard.

Discuss

'The minimum wage doesn't really benefit employees or employers.' Do you agree with this statement?

Ensuring fair and honest trading

Businesses are regulated by competition law to ensure they participate in the market environment in an honest and transparent way. The Competition Commission works to ensure that any mergers or takeovers are for the good of the industry, with consumer welfare their top priority. The recent merger of Orange and T-Mobile was allowed as it was felt that this would improve the market, increasing competition with larger networks such as O_2 and Vodafone.

P6 ▷ Social factors

There are many social factors that can influence a business over an extended period of time.

Demographic issues

Demographic changes are always taking place and can have considerable impact on businesses. An increase in population increases the pressure on businesses to produce using limited resources. However, it also increases the pool of labour, which can help economies to grow. For example, India has seen a large increase in population, which is helping to sustain the economy.

There is a global shift in population structure, with more people living to an older age. As people retire, the demand for certain products and services increases, such as retirement homes, NHS support and pharmaceutical products. However, in Japan, the population is ageing so much that younger people are worried about the government being able to afford their pensions. They are therefore saving, causing firms to lower prices and suffer reduced revenues.

Education

Education standards in the UK are well above those around the world, and help businesses recruit staff with the appropriate qualifications and skills. The importance of maths and English has now been joined by ICT skills, as businesses require staff with appropriate computer skills.

Your assessment criteria:

P6 Describe how political, legal and social factors are impacting upon the business activities of the selected organisations and their stakeholders

 Key terms

Demographic: *relating to the size and characteristics of a human population*

💬 **Discuss**

How important is education to achieving success in life?

 Discuss

How will an increase in the number of over-60s in the UK impact businesses of all sizes?

The government must make sure that education caters for all of the population (vocational courses and apprenticeships alongside degrees) to help keep the labour market up to date.

Attitudes to work

The attitudes of employers and employees are important, as firms seek staff who show commitment and are reliable. Some employees actively seek employment with firms who mirror their own beliefs and culture. For example, Divine Chocolate and The Body Shop tend to attract staff with beliefs and lifestyles that match the aims of those companies.

Religion

Businesses have become more sensitive to religious beliefs and how they can impact business activities. Within the UK, there are workers from a large variety of religions. Employers must be ready to act appropriately, in accordance with anti-discrimination legislation, allowing staff the flexibility to enjoy their religious beliefs.

Attitudes to male and female roles

The acceptance of equal rights and the ban on sexual discrimination has meant females now hold roles that used to be male dominated. Businesswomen such as Sophi Tranchell MBE, Karen Brady and Jacqueline Gold are now seen as role models.

Ethics

Business ethics dictate the behaviour, aims and values of a business. For example, a business may focus on:

- Fair Trade

- improving the industry

- reducing waste and pollution

- fair treatment of all stakeholders.

These policies are often written into a firm's corporate social responsibility plan, which outlines how the firm plans to achieve it aims. For example, In November 2010, NatWest issued a customer charter to outline its aims for customer care during the year.

Describe

Describe your perfect job. You will need to outline the daily duties, wages and outcomes. Remember, enjoyment of your job is the most important thing.

Design

Design a corporate social responsibility statement (aims, objectives and key areas) for a firm of your choice.

The impact of political, legal and social factors on businesses

M3 The impact of political factors

Governments can have a major impact on firms through changes to taxation, which can reduce cash flow, increase costs and reduce dividends to shareholders. Businesses need to plan for changes in the political field as stability can be lost overnight. Firms can compensate for this by operating in more than one country or selling a range of products. Businesses often judge their success at a time of political transition according to market share and revenue streams.

The impact of legal factors

Changes to the minimum wage and working conditions bring about increased costs for businesses. These changes are often decided in advance, so firms can prepare for them. The increased costs are usually passed on to the consumer, so despite a general increase in wages, employees often lose out as a result of a general spending increase. Improvements to employees' rights and working environments can mean that businesses struggle to keep up with the changes and their costs.

The impact of social factors

In the UK, changes to educational qualifications and standards are a regular occurrence. The changes to university fees and to school-based qualifications will mean changes to the labour market in the future. Businesses may struggle to find employees with the skills they desire, and many people are likely to face unemployment. Businesses may need to change their training and recruitment policies as a result. Firms in the UK are also adapting to customers' demands for the use of Fair Trade suppliers. The costs of altering suppliers and minimising pollution can damage businesses' cash flow and destroy relationships with existing suppliers. As the expectations of customers change, however, firms can lose customers very quickly.

D2 The impact of political factors in the future

A change of government can be foreseen but planning for it is very difficult. One of the major issues facing firms in the UK in 2011 was the increase in VAT to 20 per cent. Firms used this change to start new advertising campaigns. Rises in interest rates and high inflation rates are also important factors for businesses. Once interest rates rise, costs increase as loans and mortgages become more expensive. These burdens also reduce customers' disposable income, reducing spending in the economy.

Your assessment criteria:

M3 Analyse how political, legal and social factors have impacted on the two contrasting organisations

D2 Evaluate how future changes in economic, political, legal and social factors may impact on the strategy of a specified organisation

  Discuss

Which factor, political, legal or social, has the biggest impact on larger companies based in the UK?

The impact of legal factors in the future

The future of legal change can be difficult to predict. New laws that can have a direct impact on businesses are discussed in parliament every year. If the government brought in new laws that enforced firms to employ a set number of over-60s or employees with certain qualifications, some would struggle to adjust. The consequence of failing to adjust to new laws is so significant that businesses have to adhere, even if they feel the change is short term.

The impact of social factors in the future

Society is always changing, which makes the future difficult to predict. Trends suggest that the ageing of the UK population is likely to continue, with businesses having to adapt to the a changing pensions environment. Many also believe that society is moving towards ethical trading, with consumers demanding Fair Trade products as the norm. Whatever changes occur, society will continue to dictate to businesses, as consumers form the basis of the supply and demand relationship.

 Discuss

Why do increased interest rates reduce spending by consumers?

 Design

Create your own law. This could focus on protecting the customer, promoting trade or allowing the government to make more tax revenue.

 Case study

In 2011, the Labour leader Edward Miliband said that the VAT increase would hit poor families the hardest, with the additional cost per week estimated at around £10. This change was also set to have a direct impact upon business costs. Start-up businesses were likely to be hardest hit, struggling to pay additional employment costs, and losing out to larger firms with established customer bases.

There were also other changes in 2011. The rise in university fees looked likely to bring a drop in the availability of skilled labour, with many starting to look aboard for further education and employment. The growth in the number of older people is also likely to affect the labour pool.

1. Describe how changes in the political, legal and social factors were likely to impact Nisa Local in 2011.

2. Which of the factors listed in question 1 do you think were likely to have the biggest impact?

3. Evaluate how future changes in these factors could influence Nisa Local.

Assessment checklist

To achieve a pass grade, my portfolio of evidence must show that I can:

Assessment criteria	Description	✓
P1	Describe the type of business, purpose and ownership of two contrasting businesses	☐
P2	Describe the different stakeholders who influence the purpose of two contrasting businesses	☐
P3	Describe how two businesses are organised	☐
P4	Explain how their style of organisation helps them to fulfil their purposes	☐
P5	Describe the influence of two contrasting economic environments on business activities within a selected organisation	☐
P6	Describe how political, legal and social factors are impacting upon the business activities of the selected organisations and their stakeholders	☐

To achieve a merit grade, my portfolio of evidence must show that I can:

Assessment criteria	Description	✓
M1	Explain the points of view of different stakeholders seeking to influence the aims and objectives of two contrasting organisations	☐
M2	Compare the challenges to selected business activities within a selected organisation, in two different economic environments	☐
M3	Analyse how political, legal and social factors have impacted on the two contrasting organisations	☐

To achieve a distinction grade, my portfolio of evidence must show that I can:

Assessment criteria	Description	✓
D1	Evaluate the influence different stakeholders exert in one organisation	☐
D2	Evaluate how future changes in economic, political, legal and social factors may impact on the strategy of a specified organisation	☐

2 | Business resources

LO1 Know how human resources are managed

▶ What are human resources?

▶ How can businesses maintain their operations?

▶ How is the recruitment process used?

▶ What are employability skills?

▶ What are personal skills?

LO2 Know the purpose of managing physical and technological resources

▶ What are physical resources?

▶ How are physical resources used within a business?

▶ What are technological resources?

LO4 Be able to interpret financial statements

▸ Why should a business understand its costs?

▸ How are budgets used?

▸ Which financial statements are used in business?

▸ How are basic ratios used?

LO3 Know how to access sources of finance

▸ What internal sources of finance are available to a business?

▸ What external sources of finance are available to a business?

Working as a team

Human resources

Employees are often regarded as the most important part of a business because without them the firm would be unable to produce its goods or offer its service — it would cease to exist. Employees are the human resource and need to be treated and managed in a certain way.

The changing environment

With the workplace ever changing, both employers and employees need to adapt quickly to keep up. This starts at the **recruitment** stage, with employers choosing staff with the desired skills. They can then give the staff **training** to enhance their skills, helping both the business and employee to improve.

However, they must always try to plan ahead. The main problem facing businesses is adapting to changes in demand. If the number of customers shopping in a Tesco store at any given time increases, there must be enough staff on duty with the required skills, for example, to operate the checkouts. Training has grown in importance as staff are asked to carry out a variety of tasks.

In some larger organisations such as Nike, Boots and Nestlé, members of staff often liaise with those in other departments on a daily basis. New projects such as the launch of a new football boot or new chocolate bar will need an input from all departments. This can be in the form of meetings, emails or video conferencing — all of which require employees to be able to work together as a team.

Managing employees

An organised and well managed team can bring success to any organisation. Finding the correct structure is therefore vital. The use of team leaders can reduce the workload of managers, allowing them to focus on wider issues and projects. If the team is well lead and given a clear direction it will often achieve its targets.

Your assessment criteria:

P1 Describe the recruitment documentation used in an organisation

Key terms

Recruitment: *finding new employees for a specific role or business*

Training: *courses or activities that lead to an expansion of skills or knowledge*

Discuss

In pairs, discuss and note down the different things that employees will want and need from their employers. Then put these in order of importance to the employee.

No matter how good a team is, employers still use monitoring systems to make sure teams are making sufficient progress. This monitoring can be formal or informal. Formal monitoring often leads to feedback to the employees, with consequences clearly explained. Informal monitoring may be in the form of routine drop-ins or checks as well as informal conversations with customers and other employees. Monitoring can include:

- Target setting – This can monitor the team's overall results, such as whether the sales team met its sales target for the day.

- Team meetings – Regular team meetings are often used to give updates to managers or team leaders.

- Feedback – This can be from clients, individuals or team leaders and can indicate how the team is performing.

Key terms

Monitoring: observing employees

Discuss

Discuss a team or group situation of which you were a part or that you observed and that worked well. Why was this? Did the team have a clear leader?

 Case study

Some firms, like Google, are well known for their human resource management techniques. At Google, staff are given 10 per cent of their time to use for their own projects and ideas. They are trusted to use this time in a positive way. This is in contrast to many other businesses, both large and small, that monitor staff with extensive systems and procedures, which some argue limit employee creativity.

1. Explain the possible benefits that Google may experience as a result of giving staff this extra time.

2. Describe the negative impacts that businesses may face if they overuse monitoring of staff.

The working environment

P1 Business culture

The image of any firm is crucial to its success. You wouldn't buy a house from a dodgy estate agent or a takeaway from a restaurant with a poor reputation for cleanliness. This image relies on the firm creating a professional **business culture** which clearly sets out how employees are expected to behave. In some businesses, it is expected that all staff wear suits and address each other as Mr and Mrs, or Sir and Miss, whereas some firms prefer a more relaxed approach. Whatever the firm chooses to do, it must make sure employees are aware of the expectations. This is often done through the contract of employment. Key issues that employees must be aware of include:

- Uniform – Are they expected to wear a suit, a uniform or specific colours?

- Relationships – Are they allowed to have a relationship with someone within the same team or organisation?

- Second job – Are they allowed to have a second job?

Your assessment criteria:

P1 Describe the recruitment documentation used in an organisation

Key terms

Business culture: code of behaviour that outlines social expectations

Discuss

In pairs, discuss the business environment that you would find most comfortable. Think about what you would wish to wear to work.

Creativity

In firms such as Google, Dyson and Vodafone, the business culture is very relaxed, and creativity and enterprise are encouraged. Employees are often given 'down time' to work on new ideas and projects, or to bond with fellow colleagues. By allowing staff the time to be creative, firms of all sizes can adapt and expand into new products which they would have struggled to come up with in a stricter environment.

Incentives

Organisations need to have a clear **incentive** structure in place in order to optimise the performance of their employees. Various different schemes are used as shown in Figure 2.1.

Discuss

Which incentive shown in Figure 2.1 would you prefer?

What incentive could your school or teachers use to make you work harder?

Key terms

Incentive: a positive reinforcement through a reward or praise

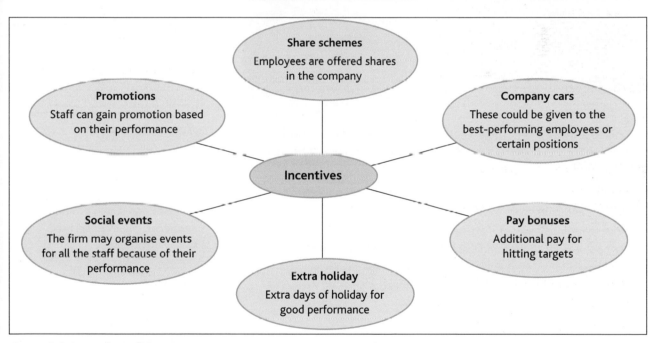

Figure 2.1 Incentive schemes

Outsourcing

Despite businesses often recruiting the best staff available, they may still choose to outsource part of the business's operations. **Outsourcing** is employing other firms to carry out tasks on your behalf, rather than doing them in house (internally). For example, many small businesses outsource their accounts to individual accounting firms. This means they do not have to worry about carrying out this task or finding someone with the necessary skills. Some firms even outsource production, only taking on the product once it has been made. Outsourcing can free up time for employees to concentrate on the tasks that they have the skills to perform.

Key terms

Outsourcing: sub-contracting out duties or responsibilities to a third party

P1 Maintaining business operations

In 2006, Nintendo launched the Wii console. Within weeks it was sold out and customers were waiting weeks for new deliveries to arrive. Nintendo had not managed its **resources** properly, meaning it disappointed customers and lost out on increased revenue. No matter how large a business, it must make sure it manages its resources well enough to continue on a day-to-day basis. A business needs the following in order to maintain its operations:

- staffing
- equipment
- working capital
- administration
- facilities
- monitoring.

Staffing

Businesses need to ensure that they have enough staff on shift with the appropriate skills. However, they must be careful not to have too many on shift when it is quiet as this increases costs. These needs may change at different times of the week, month and year. For example, supermarkets need more cashiers on a weekend at 12–4pm. Flexibility of staff is often crucial for a business to succeed. Some prefer to hire staff who live close to the premises so they can come and go more easily.

 Discuss

Should businesses aim to employ people who only live in the local area?

? Did you know?

In March 2009, sales of the Nintendo Wii reached 50 million, overtaking the PS2 as the fastest-selling games console ever. Nintendo achieved this even with its initial poor management of business operations.

 Key terms

Resources: physical, human or technological entities

Equipment

Without the correct equipment, staff cannot carry out their duties. Equipment may be in the form of the correct uniform, safety equipment or machinery.

Working capital

working capital = current assets − current liabilities

This is the money used on a day-to-day basis by the firm. It is crucial in keeping the business functioning. The business does not want to have too much working capital in its accounts as this would mean it is not being utilised (e.g. gaining interest from the bank). However, if there is not enough, the firm may struggle to pay its bills.

Administration

To make sure the business runs smoothly, administration staff and procedures are vital. Some firms have specific staff dedicated to the admin tasks that have to be carried out daily. These can range from deliveries to answering telephones. Without administration a business simply stops functioning.

Facilities

Staff need the appropriate facilities to produce the products demanded. It would be very difficult for fire fighter to operate without fire engines, and chefs couldn't produce food without a kitchen and the necessary equipment. In some situations, certain equipment is required by law. For example, construction workers are required to have a toilet, access to a recreational area where they can sit down and consume food and drink. These requirements can be costly and some employers try to avoid them.

Monitoring

In all businesses, employees are monitored in some way. This can be in the form of production levels, time management or computer usage. Some companies try to limit their monitoring as it can demotivate staff. Monitoring can involve programmes and procedures that enable a business to troubleshoot and solve problems, reducing the negative impact on the business of any problems that occur. This can then help deal with customers and ensure consistent practice across the business.

Research

Using your research skills, find out the equipment that must be in place for the employees of a car manufacturer such as Nissan, Ford or Renault. Think about the equipment that individuals use, and that which is needed by the entire workforce.

Key terms

Current assets: *cash or stocks that can be easily converted to cash*

Current liabilities: *money owed within 12 months*

Working capital: *money used in the day-to-day operations of a business*

Did you know?

It is legal for a business to monitor its employees' phone calls and internet usage.

Human resources

P1 Recruitment and retention

The recruitment of staff with the appropriate skills is a key factor in the success of a business. A firm cannot run with the incorrect staff. Once they have been found, the **retention** of these employees is also vital for continued success. Recruitment now takes place via many different media, with online advertising allowing firms to attract applications from all over the globe.

Online recruitment has now taken over as the preferred avenue in many industries. The speed of access and simple format means many businesses prefer online applicants.

Recruitment is, however, only the first step. Once employers have found the correct staff, they must make sure they retain them. Recruitment is an expensive and time-consuming process that businesses do not want to repeat on a regular basis.

Key terms

Retention: keeping staff at an organisation

Research

Find examples of job adverts and other recruitment material using the different techniques in Figure 2.2. Try to find adverts and application forms for different industries.

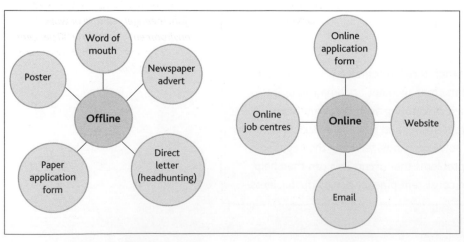

Figure 2.2 Methods of recruitment

70

Retention can be difficult for businesses for a number of reasons.

Businesses measure the **staff turnover** by using the calculation below:

$$\frac{\text{number of staff leaving per year}}{\text{number of staff employed}} \times 100$$

The higher the staff turnover is, the more concerned a firm will be. A high staff turnover could mean there are problems with the business ethos or culture which may need addressing.

🔍 Research

Using your research skills, find job adverts for the following positions:

- *business studies teacher*

- *marketing executive.*

- *retail manager.*

🔑 Key terms

Staff turnover: the percentage of the workforce that leaves each year

❓ Did you know?

Around 90 per cent of employees leave because of issues with their 'job, manager, culture or work environment', yet nearly 90 per cent of managers believe that 'employees leave for the money'.

```
                    ┌─────────────────┐
                    │   Poached by    │
                    │ other firms because of │
                    │   their skills  │
                    └─────────────────┘
  ┌──────────┐                          ┌──────────┐
  │  Having  │      ┌──────────────┐    │ Change of│
  │ children │──────│  Reasons     │────│  career  │
  └──────────┘      │ for staff    │    └──────────┘
                    │  leaving     │
  ┌──────────┐      └──────────────┘    ┌──────────┐
  │  Moving  │           │              │ Dislike  │
  │  abroad  │           │              │ of the firm or their │
  └──────────┘     ┌──────────┐         │ co-workers│
                   │  Lack    │         └──────────┘
                   │ of promotional │
                   │ opportunities  │
                   └──────────┘
```

Figure 2.3 Reasons for staff leaving

Documents for employees

Finding new employees is difficult and businesses have to work hard to attract the correct applicants. Once new employees have been chosen, they must be issued with correct and up-to-date contracts of employment and job descriptions.

Your assessment criteria:

P1 Describe the recruitment documentation used in an organisation

P1 Contracts of employment

Once a job offer has been made, the employee will be sent a **contract of employment**. This sets out the details of the employment offer, including:

- the length of contract
- the pay and additional bonuses available
- the rights of the employee
- the discipline procedure
- any extra information on the expectations of the employee.

Once this is signed, the employee enters into a binding relationship with the employer and is expected to follow the rules and regulations outlined in the contract.

Job descriptions

The employee should also be given a **job description**. This outlines the day-to-day duties of the role they have been offered. A job description also gives details of the pay, hours and holiday attached to the role.

 Key terms

Contract of employment: *agreement between the employer and employee over the details of a job*

Job description: *outline of the responsibilities of a given role*

Discuss

Is the contract of employment more important to the employee or the employer?

Case study

Every year, retailers such as Topman, HMV and Sony recruit additional staff to cover the increase in customer numbers over the Christmas period. This adds to recruitment costs but the companies often balance this with large revenues through sales. This increase in staff can cause difficulties in monitoring and leading bigger teams. At such a busy time of the year, retailers need to be able to cope with additional customers, but at the same time continue to liaise with and maintain their employees.

1. Describe the process retailers such as HMV go through to recruit temporary workers over Christmas.

2. Suggest ways in which HMV can reduce recruitment costs at Christmas.

3. Suggest ways in which HMV could manage its human resources.

Required skills

P2 Employability skills

Employability skills are the specialist skills that can be transferred from one career to another. They include:

- suitable **qualifications**

- experience of the role and industry

- knowledge of the product or service

- the ability to meet different levels of targets

- the ability to improve and raise professional standards.

Different industries require different qualifications. Some require GCSEs, whereas others require a degree. Employers set out the expected qualifications depending on the post. Skills such as problem solving and team work are also important to employers.

In the modern world, experience is often required. This can be difficult, especially for those who are applying for jobs at a young age. Work experience and part-time jobs are therefore vital in demonstrating to employers that an applicant has the necessary skills they are looking for.

Those with experience, especially in the same industry, can bring new ideas and skills to a business. Knowledge of the products or services that the business offers makes an applicant particularly appealing to an employer. For example, you would expect a car salesman to be able to tell you in detail about the cars they sell. Businesses also look for employees who can meet personal and team targets on a regular basis. Being able to meet your BTEC deadlines is a good example of time management and effective target-setting, which employers will value. The ability to help improve the standards of a company is a very important employability skill. Employers now look for staff who will continue to work despite reaching their target and who offer suggestions on procedures to help improve efficiency.

Key terms

Qualifications: *achievement of a recognised skill or test*

Discuss

For the roles below, discuss the experience you would expect a new employee to have:

- *manager of Manchester United FC*

- *head physiotherapist for the women's England rugby team*

- *marketing executive for Sony.*

M2 ▸ The importance of employability skills

Employability skills have become more and more important as businesses look beyond qualifications. Employers want staff who will add something extra to the business through experience, creativity or knowledge of an industry. At times of economic hardship when businesses are struggling, they look for new staff to bring with them hunger and drive to meet targets which may be particularly optimistic.

Although suitable qualifications are essential for many posts, they are becoming the minimum requirement as firms seek out more employability skills. In the modern world, you must be able to show proven success in a similar role, or one that you can link to the new post.

📋 Case study

Audi prides itself on its products (cars) but also the service customers receive when they visit showrooms and garages. The staff at Audi are often highly experienced, having worked in the industry for some of Audi's competitors. When new cars are released, the staff have to learn all the details about the new product.

Audi only employ the most highly skilled staff. They expect applicants to have the necessary qualifications, but also to demonstrate a variety of personal and employability skills.

1. Why is expertise and experience so important to Audi?

2. Describe and explain two personal skills that Audi would look for.

3. Why would the ability to raise professional standards be a skill that Audi looks for in new employees?

4. Discuss the importance of employability and personal skills in the recruitment and retention process at Audi.

💬 Discuss

Which of the employability skills do you think is the most important for the following roles:

- *headteacher of a school*

- *new research and development officer for Dyson*

- *managing director for a new sports brand?*

P2 ▶ Personal skills

Personal skills are those that are transferable from any industry or job. They are highly regarded by employers. Employers are looking for:

- patience
- willingness to work hard
- team-work skills
- interpersonal skills
- cooperation skills
- negotiation skills
- interviewing skills.

Patience is a key skill, especially in a job that requires a large amount of customer interaction. Employees who can demonstrate patience, no matter what the situation, are highly prized as they can help a business to gain a good reputation. Every business wants its employees to be hard-working. Employees who maintain focus on the tasks set help businesses become more productive. This can often mean staying late, for no extra pay, just to finish a report or order. This is very highly thought of but can go unnoticed by employers, leading to employees reducing their effort levels.

Working in a team of strangers is often used within the interview process at large firms as a way of identifying the best applicants. The ability to work with people of different ages, ethnic backgrounds and gender is a valuable skill that can help businesses to improve their customer image. Being able to work well with managers and colleagues is crucial for the business, as it creates a productive environment.

Your assessment criteria:

P2 Describe the main employability, personal and communication skills required when applying for a specific job role

M2 Assess the importance of employability, and personal skills in the recruitment and retention of staff in a selected organisation

💬 Discuss

For each of the following jobs, discuss which skills are the most important:

- *headteacher of a school*
- *chef*
- *pilot*
- *policeman.*

Negotiation skills are very useful in the workplace as they may help when **negotiating**:

- with customers over problems and issues

- with suppliers over prices

- with the employer over promotions, pay rises and holiday

- individual and team targets with a manager.

Interview skills allow you to show off your employability and personal skills. Practising interview situations gives you the opportunity to outshine other candidates.

M2 ⟩ The importance of personal skills

Personal skills are vitally important for any applicant. Many high-profile business leaders have said that they believe these are the skills that will determine whether a new employee is a success. Neither Lord Sugar nor Richard Branson attended university, but their personal skills have compensated for a lack of qualifications and have lead to them being hugely successful.

The ability to work well in a team and leadership skills are both very important. Businesses often seek new managers and team leaders who can demonstrate these skills at a young age, for example through experience as a sport captain or by leading a small team in the workplace.

Many would argue that personal skills are very important in the recruitment process, with interview skills perhaps the most important. Many applicants have a great Curriculum Vitae (CV), demonstrating relevant qualifications and experience, but lack the ability to sell these skills during an interview.

Physical resources

Physical resources are the **tangible** resources that are needed to maintain the day-to-day running of a business.

P3 Buildings and facilities

A business needs space and **facilities** to work from. These will vary from business to business, with some working from small office rooms, and others from large buildings such as Canary Wharf. Buildings are no longer just the place of production. They have become part of a company's image, representing the firm's ethos and culture. In London, the banks all operate from very large buildings within close proximity to each other. This helps to create an image of prestige as well as easy access for its customers. The location of a building is important because if customers cannot access the business, it will struggle to exist.

The inside of a building is also very important. The outside of a building may attract customers in, but if there are inadequate facilities, they may not stay. These facilities may be as simple as toilets, chairs and warmth, but also include meeting rooms and private rooms. Some firms keep equipment to a minimum in order to reduce costs.

The growth of online businesses means that many firms now operate through a website rather than an actual building. Customers do not go to the business to receive their products or services. This has meant businesses can reduce overhead costs such as buildings, and thus increase their profits.

Key terms

Facilities: a building or place that helps provide a service or product

Tangible: can be seen or touched

? Did you know?

Number 1 Canada Square, Canary Wharf, has 50 floors, 3960 windows and 32 lifts. You can ride from the top to the bottom in 40 seconds!

Discuss

Are buildings and location as important to businesses as they used to be?

Materials and waste

All businesses use materials in their day-to-day running, though the amount and type vary. For example, a painter and decorator needs paint, brushes and transport. The materials used in a business can range from large sheets of metal to plastic used for packaging.

The resources used by businesses, such as paper, are now produced using more efficient processes, therefore reducing pollution. The UK government also puts pressure on British firms to use recycled material. Businesses must also be very cautious about the amount of waste they produce. Material such as oil, plastic and metal can be very harmful to the environment, and costs large sums to take away and destroy.

Equipment

Equipment is vital if a firm is to operate effectively. For example, the police would struggle to catch and hold on to criminals if they didn't have handcuffs. It is critical that a business identifies and then purchases the equipment it needs to succeed. Computers have become increasingly important as firms move much of their day-to-day running onto ICT systems. Computers now form the core of offices around the world, as we use them to complete nearly all our daily tasks. The use of ICT has enabled businesses to increase their customer base and improve efficiency.

It is also important for a business to manage its machinery and the plant in which it is used. These are expensive to buy and to maintain but allow a business to guarantee orders and maintain efficiency.

Discuss

Inner London is one of the most expensive places for a business to have a building. Why do you think this is?

Research

Find out about recycling initiatives within the UK and your local area. Try to find out about specific businesses that have been involved in these schemes and initiatives. How does your school reduce waste?

Did you know?

We fill about 300 million square metres of land with rubbish every year. That is the same as covering the pitch at Manchester United Football Club's ground 28,450 times.

Did you know?

Globally, an estimated 1 million birds and 100,000 marine mammals and sea turtles die every year from entanglement in, or ingestion of, plastics.

P3 Planned maintenance and refurbishment

In order to keep running smoothly, businesses need to maintain and **refurbish** their machinery. Marmite is produced on one of the most efficient production lines in the world, which stops for only for 1 hour per day so that the machinery can be checked. **Maintenance** and refurbishment is essential because:

- it allows time to make adjustments and corrections

- if it doesn't take place the machines may break down

- it keeps the working environment clean and safe

- it can save the business money by making the machine more efficient and eco-friendly.

Emergency provision

Your school or college should run regular fire drills to make sure everyone is aware of what the procedure is in the event of a fire. This became law as part of the Health and Safety Act 1974 which states that organisations must have provisions in place in case of an emergency. This also covers equipment such as fire extinguishers and fire alarms. These must be updated and checked regularly. The last thing a business wants is for an employee or customer to be injured.

🔧 Key terms

Maintenance: *caring for and cleaning a product or machine*

Refurbish: *renovate or improve in some way*

💬 Discuss

Why are some businesses reluctant to stop production for maintenance?

❓ Did you know?

Marmite has fitted self-cleaning pipes at its factory in Burton on Trent to help minimise its water wastage each year.

Insurance

Just as individuals insure their car and home, businesses insure their buildings, machinery and equipment. For a monthly or yearly fee, the businesses buy protection for their assets in case of an expected event, such as a fire or leak.

Businesses can choose the level at which they want to be covered. They can even cover the loss of income that would be caused if their building burnt down. However, many firms see **insurance** as an unnecessary expenditure as many do not make claims for years on end.

Businesses also have other forms of insurance:

- Employers' liability insurance – This is compulsory and covers employees against death or serious injury at work.

- Public liability insurance – This covers the general public in case of injury caused by a business.

Security

Security guards, safes and alarm systems are just some of the ways businesses protect themselves. Business buildings can become vulnerable after hours and must be protected. Security systems, using cameras, are now available to monitor buildings from other locations and help firms to minimise losses through theft or fire.

 Discuss

To what extent do you think security and insurance are necessary for a successful business?

 Did you know?

The value of retail goods stolen in the UK rose by 20 per cent to £4.8 billion, in the year to June 2009. Globally, the only countries in the world with a higher value of shoplifted goods are the US and Japan.

 Key terms

Insurance: *financial protection from damage, theft or loss of earnings*

DANGER MEN WORKING OVERHEAD

Technological resources

P3 Invisible resources

Technological resources are not just computers; they include **intellectual property**, accumulated experience and skills, software licences and **patents** and **copyright**. These are often invisible and hard to place a value on.

Intellectual property

People and companies own the rights to videos, designs, drawings, text and music that they have created. They decide when it can be used and charge for this. For example, musicians and music companies own the intellectual rights for their songs. If a company wishes to use a song in its adverts, for example, it must pay.

Accumulated experience and skills

Once someone has worked in an industry or job for an extended period of time, they are said to be experienced. This comes from years of work gaining skills and knowledge that others do not have. Employees with these skills and knowledge can help a business achieve goals that other businesses cannot achieve. However, in some situations, when these employees retire, a void is left in the business which cannot be filled. This can cause businesses to decline. Through training and apprenticeships, these skills can be passed on to the next generation.

Software licences

Software such as Windows Live is often purchased by individuals, schools and businesses to help with the day-to-day running of their activities. The fee paid for the software is called a licence. The software is protected by licensing laws – if people use it without paying, they are breaking the law.

Key terms

Copyright: exclusive rights to publish words, diagrams or designs

Intellectual property: intangible property that is the result of creativity

Patents: sole rights to an invention

Patents and copyright

Patents and copyright give businesses some protection against other firms using their ideas and inventions. On the TV programme *Dragons' Den*, Peter Jones and James Caan often ask those who are presenting their ideas if they have had their product patented. A patent stops competitors using the invention. Dyson has patents protecting its products and stopping other firms using its cyclone technology.

 Discuss

The cost of patents, trademarks and copyrights can be very high. Is this expense worth it?

? **Debate**

When buying a new laptop, you often have to pay extra to have Microsoft Office installed. Do you agree that with having to pay extra for this?

? **Did you know?**

Patent number 5,255,252 was issued to Michael Jackson for the 'Smooth Criminal' leaning shoes. The special shoes have hinges attached that allow the dancers to lean forward with their feet firmly stuck to the floor.

 ## Case study

In 1902 Marmite received a patent for the recipe for its spread. The main factory in the UK is in Burton-on-Trent, which is now regarded as the home of Marmite. In 2006, Marmite embarked on a campaign to improve its water usage. As a result of upgrading equipment, improving its systems and training staff, Marmite managed to improve its efficiency by 40 per cent. The management of physical and technological resources are both very important to Marmite.

1. Explain why investment in new machinery can help businesses improve efficiency and increase production.

2. In 1902, Marmite received a patent for its recipe. Explain why managing technological resources is important to a firm like Marmite.

3. The new equipment Marmite purchased helped it become more efficient and productive. Evaluate how managing its resources in this way will help Marmite continue to improve in the future.

Improving performance

M1 Management of human resources

Businesses that truly value their employees, and show this through their **management**, will often achieve greater growth and success than those that do not. Recruitment is an expensive process. The advertisement of the job, and the time taken to sort through applicants and interview them costs large amounts of money. Therefore, businesses that can retain their staff will save money. This can then be used to help the business grow, provide financial incentives for the employees and maintain a good working environment.

Maintaining happy and productive human resources means that training and support must be at the forefront of the company's workforce strategy. Through training, a business is able to develop its staff, helping the business increase in efficiency and **productivity**, but also enhancing its reputation within the business environment. This can lead to long-term benefits such as:

- more applicants for vacancies
- increased production leading to increasing profits
- lower staff turnover.

With the right staff, a business can grow and grow. Staff allocated to the right jobs will be able to perform them quicker and with less waste. The business must make sure that job descriptions and contracts of employment are written in a fair and motivating manor, allowing staff the time they need to complete tasks.

Your assessment criteria:

M1 Explain how the management of human, physical and technological resources can improve the performance of a selected organisation

Key terms

Management: *pulling together people and resources to achieve a common goal*

Productivity: *the amount produced per hour*

Design

You have been asked by the government to design a slogan that it will use to convince employers to manage their employees better. The slogan must put across the idea that employees are important and the management of them will have serious repercussions on the business.

Management of physical resources

Managing the buildings and facilities of a business can help to improve the performance of the business. Online businesses, such as Amazon and eBay, do not need to spend large amounts on customer-facing buildings. This can save millions of pounds, which can then be used elsewhere in the business. Buying in cheaper equipment and machinery reduces costs and, at the same time, helps improve efficiency. Maintaining the machinery reduces pollution and repair costs, and improves quality.

As the business world continues to change, one thing is clear: reducing wastage and pollution has become a necessity. The power of the media and the strength of consumers mean that businesses must show they are working hard to reduce their impact on the environment. By managing the amount of waste produced, businesses can become more efficient and cut their costs. This will enable them to invest in other areas such as research and development and design, which can improve the performance of the business in the short term and even more so in the long term

Security can also have a big impact on performance if well managed. The safety of the buildings, stock and produce is essential to the business doing well. Therefore, small increases in security can have a dramatic impact on profits.

Management of technological resources

Would Nike be so successful if everyone could use its historic Nike tick logo? How would Dyson compete if other firms were allowed to copy its cyclone technology? The management of technological resources such as patents and copyright can maintain a firm's dominance in a market and keep profits high. It is therefore vital to employ staff who have responsibility for maintaining these rights and monitoring other firms to make sure they are not using the company's intellectual property, trademarks or patents. If these rights are managed well, companies like Dyson, Nintendo and Apple can expand their market share.

> **Discuss**
>
> *Which of the three areas – human, physical or technological resources – do you think has the biggest impact on a company if it is well managed?*

D1 The benefits of good management

If a firm can manage all its resources in an efficient and appropriate way, it will reap the benefits in the long term. On a day-to-day basis, a business has to manage a range of resources, all of which require a different technique.

Management of human resources

Staff who are given the right resources to complete the tasks they are set will be able to do their job quicker and to a higher standard. Therefore, businesses should operate an open communication ethos, allowing employees the chance to speak their mind. However, some firms dislike this, as it can lead to any discontent being communicated around the entire workforce.

Businesses need to ensure that their staff are working to their full capacity. Monitoring staff, however, can lead to a 'big brother' feel, with managers putting pressure on their employees. Staff may then feel they are constantly being scrutinised, which can lead to a drop in performance and productivity. Staff may also look to leave, increasing recruitment costs. An appropriate and staff-led incentive programme can remove the need for constant monitoring.

The effective management of human resources is vital for improving performance and can keep recruitment costs down, allowing a business to increase pay, invest in training and reward those staff who stay at the firm. Extra money may have to be spent, however, on training, incentives and the time taken to speak to staff.

Your assessment criteria:

D1 Evaluate how managing resources and controlling budget costs can improve the performance of a business

Key terms

Communication: *the conveying or passing on of information in verbal or non-verbal forms*

Discuss

To what extent do you think giving staff extra time to be creative will help improve the performance of a business?

Management of physical resources

Maintaining buildings can be a huge expense for a business. Therefore, an efficient maintenance programme can help save large amounts of money. Reducing the turnover of equipment and furniture helps a business to reduce its costs. However, a firm must make sure it does not allow machinery to break down for long periods of time. If equipment is not managed properly, it can cause a reduction in revenue as efficiency and productivity drops. It may also pose a health risk to staff.

Managing wastage and stock levels also help to improve the performance of a business. A reduction in wastage costs saves money, but can also help to improve a business's reputation and possibly attract staff and customers. Choosing the correct insurance and security cover can also reduce costs. Any reduction in costs can help a business to improve its longer term performance as it frees up capital for other uses.

Management of technological resources

Technological resources are difficult to manage but can help a business achieve much higher revenues. Businesses that manage their intellectual property can keep ahead of their competitors, achieving increased sales in the long term. If firms do not protect their logos, designs or text with patents, trademarks and copyright, they could lose large amounts of revenue. It is also important to find and retain staff with the relevant technological skills and experience as they can train other staff and help the business perform better in the future.

Management of budget costs

A budget is used to help set targets and give structure to a business's spending. If budgets are managed correctly, businesses can become more efficient and productive. It is important to dedicate time to collecting data so that the budgets are realistic and accurate. If budgets are not monitored or set correctly, a business risks wasting large amounts of money, leading to poor performance.

Those who hit their targets or stay within their budgets help the business to improve its performance and continue with other projects. Incentives can encourage staff to hit targets and stay within budgets.

 Key terms

Budget: sum of money allocated to a project

 Discuss

Using a business of your choice, explain how managing a budget can help improve performance.

Internal and external sources of finance

Internal sources

A business can access funds in two ways: internally or externally. **Internal** sources of finance can be the owner's own savings or the capital made from profits.

Figure 2.4 Internal sources of finance

Owner's savings	Capital from profits
This is often the source chosen by sole traders who are setting up a small enterprise, such as painting and decorating. Sole traders' requests for finance are often rejected by banks, so savings are a good option. There is no interest payment, and the owner understands the risks.	Once a business starts to make a **profit**, it has to decide what to do with the money. It may choose to pay the money to shareholders or give bonuses to staff. However, the profit is often put back into the business to help it grow.

External sources

External sources of finance are perhaps the most obvious sources of money for a business – we automatically assume a bank will lend money to a business. However, in times of **recession**, banks tighten up their lending. Businesses may then ask friends and family for the funding before going to one of the other sources of finance.

Key terms

External: *outside the business*

Internal: *within the business*

Profit: *revenue minus all costs*

Recession: *reduction in the economy for at least two quarters of a year in succession*

Discuss

Glenn is reluctant to reinvest the profit he is making from his plastering business. Discuss the ways in which you could convince him that it is the best option.

Figure 2.5 External sources of finance

Source	Information
Banks – overdraft	A popular short-term facility allowing a business to access money. Banks can recall an overdraft at any time. The business has to pay interest on the amount used.
Bank – loan	Loans are usually given to businesses that have assets against which the loan can be secured, such as properties or vehicles. The amount available varies depending on the age and success of the business.
Mortgage	A loan specifically for purchasing property and buildings. Interest is paid on the amount lent.
Venture capital	People or organisations invest money for shares in the business; e.g. the dragons on *Dragons' Den*.
Hire purchase	Equipment is used by the business in return for a monthly fee. Once the balance of the agreement is paid off, the business owns the equipment. If payments are missed, the business may lose the equipment.
Leasing	The business pays a monthly fee to use the equipment or vehicles.
Factoring	Used when a business is owed money. The business sells the debt to another company (for less than the original amount) and receives money straight away.
Share issue	Private and public limited companies sell shares in order to raise capital for new projects.
Other	There are also other organisations that help fund businesses. The government often runs funding schemes aimed at small start-up businesses. The Prince's Trust has helped many people start their own business.

 Case study

In January 2010, LuxLimo Ltd was opened by Mike and his partner, Becky. With his passion for cars and redundancy from British Gas, Mike decided this would be an exciting and profitable new career.

However, the start-up costs for the company were large. Mike could only input a small amount of his own savings and, even after selling his beloved Lotus Elise, they were still £35,000 short.

Figure 2.6 Internal sources of finance for LuxLimo Ltd

Cars x 3	£42,000
Property	£800 per month
Advertising	£2,000 initial cost
Insurance	£4,000
Total	**£46,000**

1. Suggest two sources of finance that Mike and Becky may wish to consider.

2. Mike has decided to bring in an investor. He will receive the £35,000 he needs but will lose 40 per cent of the company. Discuss whether or not you think this was a good decision.

 Discuss

Mike, of LuxLimo Ltd, doesn't want any input from others in his business but needs around £4000 for new equipment. What type of finance would you suggest he chooses? Why?

Financial statements

Businesses must monitor their financial performance on a regular basis. Once a business becomes incorporated (private and public limited companies) it will need to publish its accounts for shareholders to see. The two key financial reports you must understand are: the **profit and loss account** and the **balance sheet**.

Your assessment criteria:

P5 Interpret the contents of a trading and profit and loss account and balance sheet for a selected company

P5 ▷ Profit and loss account

A profit and loss account (P and L) is used to show a business's performance at the end of the financial year. It is used in many different ways. It can be used by investors to compare public limited companies and to decide which is worth investing in. Other firms may use a profit and loss account to see how well they are doing, before making decisions on future expenditure and budget setting.

A profit and loss account can be very complicated and larger organisations, such as Tesco, Microsoft and BP, may include more detail than smaller businesses need to include.

Key terms

Balance sheet: snapshot of a business's financial situation

Profit and loss account: statement showing a business's turnover and expenses

Research

Using your research skills, find the most recent profit or loss account for the following:

• Tesco

• HMV

• a business of your choice.

Figure 2.7 Profit and Loss account for Dean's Doughnuts Ltd

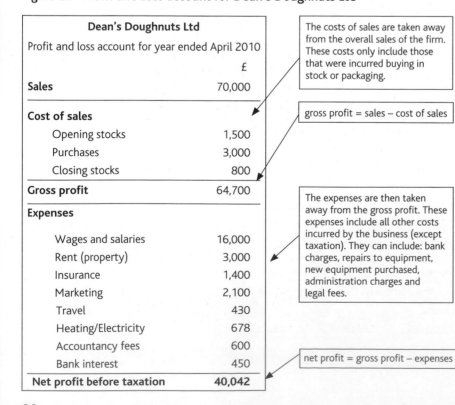

Dean's Doughnuts Ltd	
Profit and loss account for year ended April 2010	
	£
Sales	70,000
Cost of sales	
Opening stocks	1,500
Purchases	3,000
Closing stocks	800
Gross profit	64,700
Expenses	
Wages and salaries	16,000
Rent (property)	3,000
Insurance	1,400
Marketing	2,100
Travel	430
Heating/Electricity	678
Accountancy fees	600
Bank interest	450
Net profit before taxation	**40,042**

The costs of sales are taken away from the overall sales of the firm. These costs only include those that were incurred buying in stock or packaging.

gross profit = sales − cost of sales

The expenses are then taken away from the gross profit. These expenses include all other costs incurred by the business (except taxation). They can include: bank charges, repairs to equipment, new equipment purchased, administration charges and legal fees.

net profit = gross profit − expenses

Balance sheet

The balance sheet is used as a snapshot to show how healthy the business is at a particular point in time. It shows the value of the business at a given time. Public limited companies have to publish balance sheets, which show how much they are worth and the amount of assets they own.

Figure 2.8 Balance sheet for Mecky Mechanics Ltd

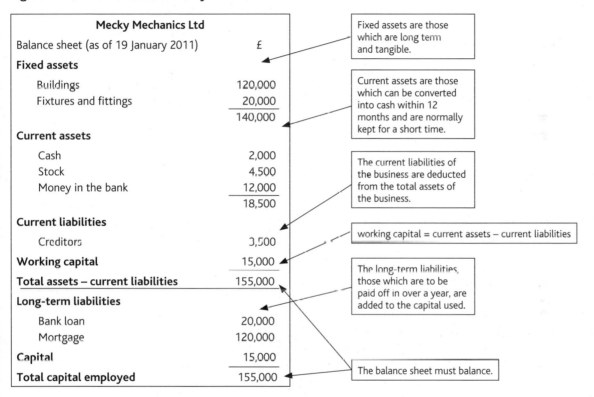

Mecky Mechanics Ltd	
Balance sheet (as of 19 January 2011)	£
Fixed assets	
Buildings	120,000
Fixtures and fittings	20,000
	140,000
Current assets	
Cash	2,000
Stock	4,500
Money in the bank	12,000
	18,500
Current liabilities	
Creditors	3,500
Working capital	15,000
Total assets – current liabilities	155,000
Long-term liabilities	
Bank loan	20,000
Mortgage	120,000
Capital	15,000
Total capital employed	155,000

Fixed assets are those which are long term and tangible.

Current assets are those which can be converted into cash within 12 months and are normally kept for a short time.

The current liabilities of the business are deducted from the total assets of the business.

working capital = current assets – current liabilities

The long-term liabilities, those which are to be paid off in over a year, are added to the capital used.

The balance sheet must balance.

 ## Case study

Every year, Apple publishes its accounts, including a profit and loss account and a balance sheet. These accounts are eagerly anticipated by shareholders who hope to see the business making large profits, which will mean that they receive large dividends. The balance sheet is an important reflection of the business's health. The launch of the iPhone and iPad brought an increase in Apple's profits. In 2010 the company was valued at $222 billion.

1. Which other stakeholders would be interested in Apple's profit and loss account?

2. Why does Apple need a large amount of working capital?

Budgets and costs

Costs

Managing **costs** is crucial for a business. Identifying the costs that a business will incur allows the business to **budget** for them. However, the business needs to ensure that it keeps to the budget. There are two key costs that must be identified and then monitored in order to make a realistic budget. These are:

- Fixed costs – These are costs that do not increase with a change in output; for example, rent, salaries, marketing and insurance.

- Variable costs – These are costs that change with a change in output; for example, electricity, wages and stock.

Budgets

Monitoring budgets is a difficult process for businesses. Trying to judge what each department or staff member will need can prove tricky. The previous year's data is very useful. Firms can choose many different ways to issue budgets. The two extremes are:

- Zero budgeting – no budget is issued. Each time a department or employee wants to buy something, they must justify it to their manager/ team leader.

- Allocated budgeting – each department is given an allocated budget that they must stick to. They may not need the entire amount but they can use it for whatever they choose.

A firm may also use:

- Incremental budgeting – taking last year's budget and adding on a certain amount.

Variance analysis

Businesses set their budgets based upon their predicted sales forecasts. Measuring the difference between the predicted and the budgeted value is called variance analysis. For example, Dean's Doughnuts had budgeted on sales figures of £120,000; however, the actual figure was £140,000. This is a *favourable* variance for the business. However, if the sales had been lower, or the costs higher, the variance would have been *adverse*.

 Key terms

Break even: *the point at which sales revenue is exactly the same as fixed costs (no profit or loss is made)*

Budget: *to plan the expenses for a project*

Costs: *total spent on goods and services*

 Discuss

Why is it important for businesses to use budgets?

Break-even point

Break even is the point at which sales revenue is matched by the costs the business is accruing. At this point, the company is not making a profit or a loss, but is breaking even. As shown in Unit 1 on page 29, we must first work out the contribution each product makes to paying off the fixed costs. We can then work out the break-even point.

contribution per unit = unit price − variable costs per unit

$$\text{break even} = \frac{\text{fixed costs}}{\text{contribution per unit}}$$

This formula shows how many products the business needs to sell to break even.

The break-even point can be demonstrated in a graph format. This helps to show the:

- break-even point

- margin of safety – the amount a business can afford to see its sales reduce by before it makes a loss

- revenue/cost figures for other sales figures.

💬 Discuss

Start-up businesses often aim to break even in their first year. Why is this?

Figure 2.9 Graph to show the break-even point

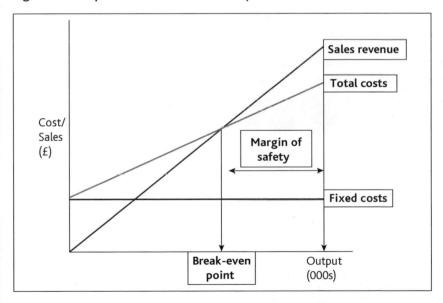

Figure 2.10 The advantages and disadvantages of a break-even graph

Advantages	Disadvantages
• It is easy to see the sales needed to break even.	• The graph doesn't take into account any change in prices, discounts or promotions.
• The graph is easy to create.	• The graph is based on one product being sold, which is unrealistic for many firms.
• It can be used to plan for the future.	• Predictions made on the basis of the graph can change overnight.

P6 Financing the future

Many businesses experience **cash flow** problems and, at times, need additional investment or a short-term loan from the bank. Budgeting can help to reduce the regularity of this event. Businesses can look for investment from other organisations or individuals (see pages 88–89), but this can lead to a loss of control in the business. Some businesses are also eligible for grants. These are aimed at firms that produce products that have a positive impact on society. For example, firms that produce wind turbines are supported by government grants.

Liquidity

Businesses often try to maintain high levels of **liquidity**. This allows them to maintain their cash flow, keep up to date with supplier invoices and pay their staff. Businesses also purchase liquid assets which can be quickly converted into working capital.

Working capital is the money used on a day-to-day basis to pay the bills. It is very important to the continued running of a business. The working capital of a business can be worked out by using the following calculation:

working capital = current assets – current liabilities

Businesses often offer a payment period of around 30 days but it can be up to 60. Until this is paid, the business which is owed the money will have to finance the costs. The larger the contract on offer, the longer the payment period will be.

Your assessment criteria:

 P6 Illustrate the use of budgets as a means of exercising financial control of a selected company

Key terms

Cash flow: movement of money through a business

Liquidity: ability to pay off debt with cash or turn stock into cash

 Discuss

Businesses should not give credit to customers or suppliers. Discuss.

Sometimes debts are not paid. The business may then have to take legal action to see the money repaid. **Factoring** may also be used to recover some of the debt.

Businesses can plan for events like this by building up a reserve fund. This can help them in a crisis or emergency, such as a major piece of machinery breaking down, or a customer not paying on time.

 Key terms

Factoring: selling off debt for a reduced amount

Discuss

Would you advise businesses that are owed large amounts of money to use factoring?

 Case study

Nike is to launch its new range of running clothing but has had to rethink its marketing campaign. The initial research and development cost over £2 million, and identified new technology that would help runners endure longer distances. However, the production and design went over budget in terms of both time and money. The variable costs increased as the development stage dragged on, meaning the finance department has changed the budgeting to zero budgeting from now on.

1. Identify three variable costs Nike would have encountered in the production of this product.

2. Why is it important for projects like this to have strict budgets?

3. The project must at least break even in the first 6 months. Explain why working out the break-even point can help Nike choose its price.

Ratios

Ratios are used to help analyse the financial information shown in profit and loss accounts and balance sheets. However, to be most effective, they need to be compared to previous years' figures or competitors' figures.

Your assessment criteria:

P7   Illustrate the financial state of a given business

P7   Determining solvency

These ratios allow a business to determine its **solvency** – to see if it has enough capital to meet its liabilities.

🔑   **Key terms**

Solvency: ability to meet financial commitments on a regular basis

Current ratio

This shows how easily a business can pay off its debts. A ratio of 1:1 could mean the business would struggle to pay all of the liabilities. A figure of 2:1 means the business has twice as much asset as liability.

$$\text{current ratio} = \frac{\text{current assets}}{\text{current liabilities}}$$
$$= x\text{: 1 (shown as a ratio)}$$

Acid test ratio

This is very similar to the current ratio. However, it takes away the option for a business to sell its stock to meet its liabilities. This makes it more accurate.

The same rules apply as for the current ratio: above 1 is crucial, above 2 is very good.

$$\text{acid test ratio} = \frac{\text{current assets} - \text{stock}}{\text{current liabilities}}$$
$$= x\text{: 1 (shown as a ratio)}$$

Determining profitability

These ratios show how profitable a business is at a certain point in time or in the longer term.

Gross profit percentage/margin (GP%)

The higher the percentage, the better. A higher percentage shows that the business is controlling its stock levels and the costs of production.

$$GP\% = \frac{\text{gross profit}}{\text{turnover of business}} \times 100$$

Net profit percentage/margin (NP%)

This figure is more focused on the actual profit of the business as a percentage of the turnover. If the NP% is higher than the GP% it means that the business is not managing its day-to-day costs.

$$NP\% = \frac{\text{net profit}}{\text{turnover of business}} \times 100$$

Return on Capital Employed (ROCE)

This ratio shows the return a business or investor is receiving on its investment. It enables them to decide whether they have made a worthwhile investment. It can be directly compared to the interest rate of a bank.

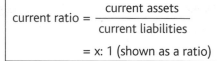

$$\frac{\text{net profit before interest and tax}}{\text{capital employed}} \times 100$$

Determining performance

Stock turnover

In some industries, a short turnover period is essential, as perishable items will become worthless if not used. This means an efficient stock control and ordering system are essential.

$$\text{stock turnover} = \frac{\text{average stock}}{\text{cost of sales}} \times 365$$

= the number of days it takes to turn over the stock

Debtor collection period (debtor days)

This shows how good a business is at choosing who to issue credit to, as well as how well it collects its debt. The higher the number of days, the longer a business has to wait for its payment.

$$\text{debtor collection period} = \frac{\text{debtors}}{\text{credit sales}} \times 365$$

= the number of days **debtors** take to pay (debtor days)

Asset turnover

This ratio shows how much the business earns for the investment in assets it makes. The higher the number, the more the business is making on its investments.

$$\text{asset turnover} = \frac{\text{sales}}{\text{total assets}}$$

Key terms

Debtors: those who owe money

Stock turnover: regularity of the selling of stock

Case study

Figure 2.11 Financial data for Penfold Stationers

Sales	£230,000
Gross profit	£150,000
Net profit	£89,000
Total assets	£60,000
Capital employed	£50,000

1. Using the information above, calculate the:
   a. gross profit margin
   b. net profit margin
   c. asset turnover.

2. Explain how using ratios can help Penfold Stationers monitor its performance.

3. To what extent are the ratios you have calculated a true reflection of the business?

Discuss

How useful do you think the different ratios are? Do you think this differs for businesses of different sizes?

Using ratios

M3 Interpreting financial statements

By interpreting the statements below, it is possible to see how the business is doing.

Figure 2.12 Balance sheet for Mecky Mechanics Ltd

Mecky Mechanics Ltd	
Balance sheet (as of 19 January 2011)	£
Fixed assets	
Buildings	120,000
Fixtures and fittings	20,000
	140,000
Current assets	
Cash	2,000
Stock	4,500
Money in the bank	12,000
	18,500
Current liabilities	
Creditors	3,500
Working capital	15,000
Total assets – current liabilities	155,000
Long-term liabilities	
Bank loan	20,000
Mortgage	120,000
Capital	15,000
Total capital employed	155,000

Your assessment criteria:

M3 Interpret the contents of a trading and profit and loss account and balance sheet for a selected company explaining how accounting ratios can be used to monitor the financial performance of the organisation

D2 Evaluate the adequacy of accounting ratios as a means of monitoring the state of the business in a selected organisation, using examples

$$\text{current ratio} = \frac{18,500}{3,500} = 5.3 : 1$$

This shows that Mecky Mechanics is doing well. It has plenty of assets in place to pay off liabilities. However, it may be missing out on earning interest or investing in new projects. As with all ratios, this should be compared to those from previous years and competitors' ratios.

$$\text{acid test ratio} = \frac{118,500 - 4,500}{3,500} = 4 : 1$$

This shows that the business would not need to sell stock to meet its liabilities. This is very healthy and shows the business has plenty of assets available.

Return on Capital Employed (ROCE) is also a very useful figure if you want to see whether a business is working well. If the ROCE rate is lower than the interest rate set by the bank, the business may have been better off investing its money there.

You can also look at the debtor days and stock turnover of a firm. These figures are partly dependent on the industry in which the business operates. Supermarkets enjoy a large stock turnover and need it to keep their cash flow fluid. However, antiques shops operate on a low turnover of stock. Generally, the shorter the length of time that debtors take to pay, the better. A shorter debtor collection period allows the business to utilise its capital. It would also show a lack of management and decision-making if the debtor collection period increased. If it increased each year, or was more than that of competitors, it would highlight an issue that the business needs to resolve.

Figure 2.13 Profit and Loss account for Dean's Doughnuts Ltd

Dean's Doughnuts Ltd	
Profit and loss account for year ended April 2010	
	£
Sales	70,000
Cost of sales	
Opening stocks	1,500
Purchases	3,000
Closing stocks	800
Gross profit	**64,700**
Expenses	
Wages and salaries	16,000
Rent (property)	3,000
Insurance	1,400
Marketing	2,100
Travel	430
Heating/Electricity	678
Accountancy fees	600
Bank interest	450
Net profit before taxation	**40,042**

$$\text{gross profit \%} = \frac{64,700}{70,000} \times 100$$
$$= 92\%$$

This shows the business is doing well and maintaining its stock levels.

$$\text{net profit \%} = \frac{40,042}{70,000} \times 100$$
$$= 57\%$$

This shows the business loses a fair amount of profit through its expenses. In this case, the business may look to reduce its expenses to help raise this ratio.

D2 ▶ The adequacy of accounting ratios

Accounting ratios need to be compared to previous years' ratios to see whether or not a business has improved. If these figures are unavailable, it becomes difficult to make a judgement. It is also useful for firms to compare their ratios to those of their competition.

Ratios can be used to help a business identify areas in which it needs to improve. For example, the ratios above for Dean's Doughnuts show that the company needs to address its expenses as the net profit margin drops significantly from its gross profit margin. However, the use of ratios does not show the full story. There are aspects of a business, such as morale, which are hard to measure and do not show up in ratios. Ratios also fail to show how the business could be doing if it was managed better, if staff received more training or if incentives were improved.

 Discuss

How could Tesco improve its stock turnover rate?

Controlling costs

M4 Why control costs?

Controlling costs becomes even more crucial in times of recession. Keeping costs as low as possible gives a business a better chance of making a profit, as well as freeing up working capital for investment or research.

If costs are not controlled it can lead to:

- underachievement of the business. The business may have the potential to generate much larger profits but is unable to due to poor management of costs. This reduces the prospect of investors wanting to buy shares.

- the business not being able to pay its debtors, and therefore accruing large amounts of interest and increasing the possibility of legal action or bankruptcy.

- the business missing out on new opportunities with its existing or a new market (because it does not have the capital to invest in machinery, staff or marketing).

If budgets are not monitored it can lead to:

- staff spending more than they need to on expenses or equipment which doesn't benefit the business

- some departments spending their entire budget when they don't need to, just so they can justify asking for the same amount the following year

- the hard work of departments or individuals (to hit their targets or finish a project under budget) not being noticed. Staff may therefore not be promoted or rewarded.

Your assessment criteria:

M4 Analyse the reasons why costs need to be controlled to budget

D3 Evaluate the problems they have identified from unmonitored costs and budgets

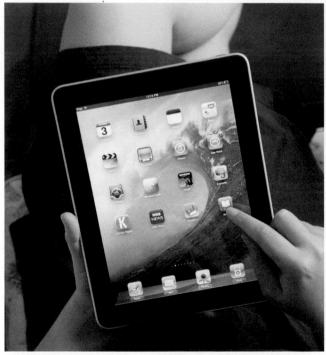

Controlling costs allows businesses to research and develop new products, like the iPad.

 Design

Write an email to the new managing director of Samsung explaining why it is important that Samsung manages its costs and monitors its budgets.

D3 Unmonitored costs and budgets

A failure to monitor costs and budgets can cause long-term problems for a business. If budgets are continually not monitored, staff may feel they can be wasteful and work below their maximum ability. This can lead to the business developing a reputation that could attract the wrong sort of applicants, which in turn could lead to reduced profits and a slow down of production. Uncontrolled budgets and costs can also lead to short-term problems. Working capital is vital to the day-to-day running of a business. If it is wasted on rising costs or overspending, then this can cause cash flow problems, which can affect suppliers and customers who may not receive their products.

The development of new products, such as new vacuum cleaners by Dyson or the new Kindle by Amazon, requires large amounts of capital. If a business is running above its estimated costs, as well as not hitting sales targets, it won't be able to compete with its competitors. This can cause a reduction in market share.

Discuss

Why are unmonitored costs so dangerous for a business?

Case study

The final cost of building the Channel Tunnel was £10 billion. This was almost £5.2 billion over budget. The spiralling costs of materials, as well as increased wastage led to large demands being put on the UK government to help fund the project. These costs have had a considerable long-term impact on the project and government.

1. Analyse why costs need to be controlled.

2. Evaluate the problems that have been caused by the Channel Tunnel project being over budget.

Assessment checklist

To achieve a pass grade, my portfolio of evidence must show that I can:

Assessment criteria	Description	✓
P1	Describe the recruitment documentation used in an organisation	☐
P2	Describe the main employability, personal and communication skills required when applying for a specific job role	☐
P3	Describe the main physical and technological resources required in the operation of a selected organisation	☐
P4	Describe sources of internal and external finance for a selected business	☐
P5	Interpret the contents of a trading and profit and loss account and balance sheet for a selected company	☐
P6	Illustrate the use of budgets as a means of exercising financial control of a selected company	☐
P7	Illustrate the financial state of a given business	☐

To achieve a merit grade, my portfolio of evidence must show that I can:

Assessment criteria	Description	✓
M1	Explain how the management of human, physical and technological resources can improve the performance of a selected organisation	☐
M2	Assess the importance of employability, and personal skills in the recruitment and retention of staff in a selected organisation	☐
M3	Interpret the contents of a trading and profit and loss account and balance sheet for a selected company explaining how accounting ratios can be used to monitor the financial performance of the organisation	☐
M4	Analyse the reasons why costs need to be controlled to budget	☐

To achieve a distinction grade, my portfolio of evidence must show that I can:

Assessment criteria	Description	✓
D1	Evaluate how managing resources and controlling budget costs can improve the performance of a business	☐
D2	Evaluate the adequacy of accounting ratios as a means of monitoring the state of the business in a selected organisation, using examples	☐
D3	Evaluate the problems they have identified from unmonitored costs and budgets	☐

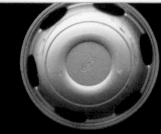

3 | An introduction to marketing

LO1 Know the role of marketing in organisations

▸ What is marketing and how are clear marketing objectives set?

▸ What marketing techniques can businesses use?

▸ Are there any limitations and constraints on how marketing departments operate?

LO2 Be able to use marketing research and marketing planning

▸ What is primary research and how is it carried out?

▸ How can secondary research help inform marketing strategies?

▸ What are SWOT and PESTLE and how do we carry them out?

LO3 Understand how and why customer groups are targeted

- ▶ What do we mean by customers?
- ▶ How do businesses identify who their customers are?
- ▶ Do customers behave differently in business to business markets?

LO2 Be able to develop a coherent marketing mix

- ▶ What is a marketing mix and why does it need to be coherent?
- ▶ How do different product ranges suit different customers?
- ▶ What different methods are used for setting prices?
- ▶ What different methods are used for promoting products?

The overall concept of marketing

P1 What is marketing?

Marketing is the process of understanding the market within which a business operates and satisfying customers' needs in order to meet the business's objectives. The role of marketing within a particular organisation will depend on the organisation's overall objective. The objective of many businesses is to make a profit, but this is not the purpose of many voluntary and public (government owned) organisations. Marketing is, however, equally important for them.

In order successfully to identify, anticipate and satisfy customers' needs, a business needs to carry out **market research** to assess its competitive position and its customers' needs. Once a business knows more about its customers and competitors it can set clear and **SMART** marketing **objectives**. The marketing department's objective should fit in with the overall **strategic objective** of the organisation.

When the marketing department has a SMART objective it can then implement its marketing strategy – commonly referred to as the marketing mix or the 4Ps. The **marketing mix** consists of the following:

- Price – businesses must set a price for their products (goods or services) that meets both the customers' and the organisation's expectations. Setting a price too low may well attract a lot of customers but might not be profitable for the business. Its objective would therefore not be met.

- Product – a marketing department also needs to consider a successful mix of suitable products or services. Researching competitors and customers will help a business to develop a successful mix of products – a **product portfolio**.

- Promotion – this is the process of informing customers about products and persuading them to buy them. There is little point having a successful product that is priced to meet customers' expectations and provide the business with the required level of income to meet its objectives if the customers doesn't know about it.

- Place – the final part of a traditional marketing mix is to consider how customers can buy the products. There is a wide range of ways to reach customers. Some businesses sell direct to the customer; some sell to someone else (an intermediary) who then sell on to the end consumer.

Some organisations need to consider an additional three aspects, making their marketing mix the 7Ps.

 Key terms

Marketing mix: *an integrated strategy for marketing a product, which normally includes price, product, promotion and place*

Market research: *the process of collecting and collating information on a business's market, customers and competitors*

Product portfolio: *the range of products offered by a business*

SMART objectives: *objectives that are Specific, Measurable, Achievable, Realistic and Time related*

Strategic objective: *a broad target for the whole of an organisation*

Promotion – promotional offers inform customers about different products and try to persuade them to buy.

- People – a company that provides a service needs well trained and knowledgeable staff in order to offer good customer service. Businesses that offer exceptional customer service can often charge more for their product.

- Process – businesses that offer a service need to consider how this service is consumed and how the business can improve the service that it offers.

- Physical environment – for retail businesses the environment in which they sell their product or service is important for customer satisfaction.

Physical environment – a well organised retail outlet helps improve customer satisfaction so is therefore an important aspect of the marketing mix.

P1 Corporate objectives

Every organisation has an aim that it wishes to achieve. As this aim is something that that whole organisation wants to achieve, it is often referred to as a corporate aim. This corporate aim can then be split into objectives. Each year, businesses set themselves different objectives that they want to achieve in order to reach their aim.

Marketing objectives

A business's corporate objectives (or strategic objectives) give direction to individual departments, such as the marketing department. The marketing department sets objectives in accordance with what the whole organisation wants to achieve over the year.

Marketing objectives often relate to:

- increasing **brand awareness**

- improving customer perceptions

- improving market share and achieving market leadership.

Your assessment criteria:

P1 Describe how marketing techniques are used to market products in two organisations

Key terms

Brand awareness: *how aware customers are of a particular brand in the market*

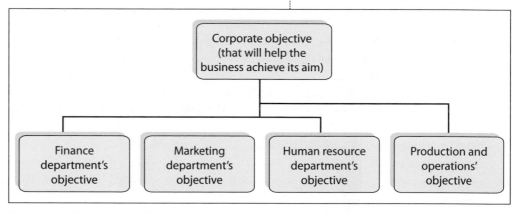

Figure 3.1 The relationship between marketing and corporate objectives

Brand awareness

A brand can be described as what the customer associates with a particular product, service or business. It can be a symbol, a logo, a particular design of packaging or a name. Over time, customers build up an understanding of what they think of this brand. The more good experiences they associate with the brand, the better their opinion of the brand will be. Once customers associate quality with a particular brand it makes it easier to charge higher prices for those products. By increasing brand awareness a business makes that particular brand better known to the public.

Marks and Spencers has worked hard on developing a brand that represents quality for its food range.

Customer perceptions

Customer perception of a business or a product is very important as it affects the strength of the brand. It is not imperative that customers perceive a particular product to be of the highest quality, as long as the price reflects the quality of the product. Value ranges and supermarket own brands are rarely perceived to be the best quality but they still sell. This is because customers perceive the products to offer value for money. Businesses try to improve customers' perceptions of their products in order to build a successful brand and to gain loyalty from the customers.

Market share and market leadership

The market is the place where buyers and sellers meet to exchange goods for money. From the point of view of the seller, the market is all of the potential customers for its goods. Businesses also refer to their competitors as being in the market, as they are trying to sell to the same customers. A common objective of a business is to increase its market share. The more customers a business has, the larger its share of the market. Businesses with dominant market shares are often called market leaders. Market leaders tend to have more power over their competitors and can often set a benchmark for pricing that competitors follow.

Key terms

Customer perception: *how different customers view a particular business or brand*

Market share: *the number of customers that a particular business sells to – a percentage of the total market*

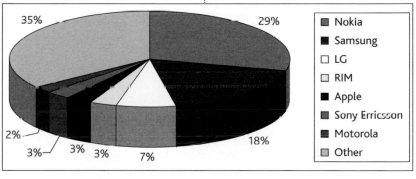

■	Nokia
■	Samsung
□	LG
□	RIM
■	Apple
■	Sony Ericsson
■	Motorola
■	Other

35%   29%   2%   3%   3%   3%   7%   18%

Figure 3.2 Nokia currently holds a 29 per cent share of the global mobile device market.

SMART objectives

It is important that the objectives of a marketing department are SMART. The success of the objectives can then be measured over a period of time. Changes can then be implemented to a particular strategy to make the objective more achievable.

S	Specific – a SMART objective is not too vague and is easily measured, e.g. to increase the market share of our men's footwear range.
M	Measurable – a SMART objective needs to include something that can be measured against a set criteria, e.g. to increase the market share of our men's footwear range by 10%.
A	Agreed/Achievable – a SMART objective should be agreed by everyone in the marketing department as it will need an integrated effort from the product, price, promotion and place teams in order for it to be achieved.
R	Realistic – a SMART objective should be realistic in terms of what the business is capable of and the resources that are available.
T	Time related – a SMART objective should include a time limit within which the objective should be achieved, e.g. to increase the market share of our footwear range by 10% in the next year

Figure 3.3 SMART objectives

Design

In pairs, create a brief outline of a marketing mix (4Ps or 7Ps) for a business of your choice that wishes to increase its brand awareness.

Discuss

Who would you consider to be the market leader in the MP3 market? How does that market leader impact on the rest of the business?

Growth strategies

P1 Helping a business to grow

Part of the overall aim or objective of an organisation might be to grow. Growth can have many benefits, including:

- increased brand awareness

- increased sales

- higher levels of profit

- more valuable shares if the business is a plc

- cheaper production costs through economies of scale.

A marketing department can help a business grow by looking at four possible strategies, which were originally classified by Igor Ansoff.

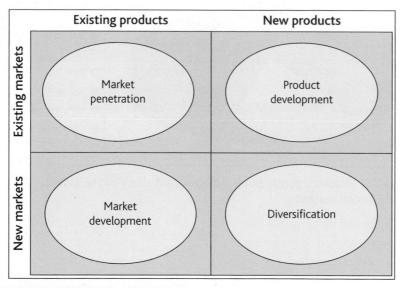

Figure 3.4 Ansoff's matrix

Market penetration

Of the four strategies in Ansoff's matrix, **market penetration** is the least risky. The business is simply taking an existing product and trying to sell more of it in its current market. This type of strategy requires a marketing mix that is planned around increasing market share. Pricing and promotion decisions are made to sell more of the existing product and penetrate the market. Promotional deals and an emphasis on promotion help businesses to attract customers of other brands. Brand loyalty, although important, is often not as important to customers as price, so lowering the price for a short period could help market penetration.

Your assessment criteria:

P1 Describe how marketing techniques are used to market products in two organisations

 Key terms

Market penetration: improving the sales of an existing product line in its current market

Product development

This strategy means bringing out a new product or service in a business's existing market. **Product development** is, of course, riskier than market penetration as although the business has knowledge of the market, it may have only limited knowledge of the product that it is developing or it may need to build the brand in order for customers to continue to buy the product. Businesses with well established brands find market development far easier as they can bring out product lines under the same brand so the market already has an association with them. The iPhone and the iPad, for example, have been introduced to the market as part of the same brand as the iPod.

Product development – the iPad is a new product that is targeted at an existing market.

Market development

Moving an existing product into a new market carries a similar level of risk to product development. The type of market will determine the level of risk some highly competitive markets are difficult to enter. **Market development** can also mean venturing into an overseas market which requires much more planning and careful consideration of not only the external factors in the UK but also those affecting the host country.

Diversification

Taking a new product into a new market is the riskiest of the four main strategies highlighted by Ansoff. The level of risk is far higher as the business has to carefully research the market and plan the product launch. Due to the risk involved, it is normally bigger businesses that opt for **diversification** as they can afford to take the associated risk.

Market development – Lucozade used to be marketed as a medicinal drink.

Key terms

Product development: *the introduction of a new product or line of products in a market where the business already operates*

Key terms

Diversification: *the introduction of a new product or line of products in a market where previously the business did not operate*

Market development: *moving an existing product into a new market*

Research

Using your research skills, research the history of Lucozade. Use Ansoff's matrix to analyse how Lucozade changed what it was doing in the early 1980s.

Design

In pairs, create a copy of Ansoff's matrix and annotate it with how Tesco has grown from a small grocers in 1929 to where it is now.

Branding

P1 What is branding?

A brand can be the name, logo, packaging or reputation of goods or services. A good brand stands out against similar products and by reinforcing the core values of the product (quality or value for money, etc.) encourages a repeat purchase. A poor brand image can be difficult to change.

The benefits of branding

As a brand becomes established, a relationship forms between the customer and the brand. This can influence consumer buying behaviour as psychologically customers identify with a brand and continue to choose that particular brand in preference to another. This is particularly important for businesses that are operating in very competitive markets where it becomes harder to retain customers as they become more price conscious. Once brands are established, their buyers perceive there to be less risk involved with a purchase as they are used to the brand and what it represents. Premium pricing strategies can therefore be easier to apply to established brands.

Your assessment criteria:

P1 Describe how marketing techniques are used to market products in two organisations

Figure 3. 5 The benefits of developing a good brand

Benefits to the customer	Benefits to the business
• Less risk involved with the purchase • Less time spent on shopping as good brands are easily identifiable • Can provide assurance when purchasing another product under the same brand name	• Can develop a good relationship with the customer which encourages repeat purchases • Helps the product to stand out in a competitive market • Makes it easier to apply premium pricing • Makes it easier to promote new products under existing brands

Brand positioning

Before a brand can be developed, an organisation needs to consider where it wants to position the brand and how it wants customers to view the brand. This will directly influence and be influenced by:

• the price charged for the product
• how the product is promoted
• the quality of the product
• the place from which the product is available.

Positioning a brand depends on the quality that the organisation wishes to portray. Not all products need to be perceived as high quality. Value ranges in supermarkets are branded to give the impression of 'no frills' quality but this is reflected in the price, so consumers are happy to continue to purchase. Other businesses are intent on customers perceiving their products to be of the highest quality (for example, Gucci and Versace) and their prices reflect this.

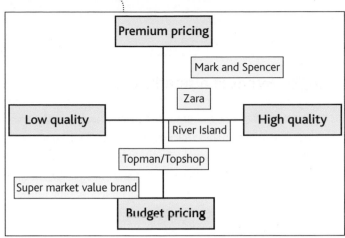

Figure 3.6 **Brand positioning in the high street clothing market**

Brand building

Building a brand requires a cohesive approach to marketing. A brand can be built through developing a unique selling point (USP) – something that this brand alone offers and others do not – but this is often not possible. When building a brand, advertising is very important at the outset to gain exposure and build brand awareness. However, once the brand is established, advertising becomes less important.

For organisations that have limited financial resources, public relations and public image are important. In the public sector, consumers want to see a brand that represents value for money and reliability, so negative media coverage can be very damaging. The price of a brand needs to be consistent and in line with the brand's core values. Brands associated with quality usually warrant a high selling price either to cover the additional costs of manufacture or to maintain the perception of high quality. The place from which products are available will also influence **brand building** as some outlets are deemed more exclusive than others and are therefore chosen by certain manufacturers to sell their brands.

Brand extension

The stretching of a brand name to cover a range of products is called **brand extension**. The products take on the name of the brand rather than the name of the manufacturer. For example, the Dettol brand is no longer just associated with antiseptic, but also includes kitchen and bathroom cleaner, soap and pain relief spray.

Brand extension – the Dettol brand now covers a range of different products.

Relationship marketing

P1 Building a relationship

The process of building a relationship between the buyer and the seller is known as **relationship marketing**. Most organisations no longer see a customer purchasing a product as a one-off discrete transaction. Instead, the purchase provides them with a chance to strengthen the customer's loyalty to the brand and the business's understanding of the customer, helping to establish a relationship.

Lifetime customers

In order to encourage customers to continue buying a particular product or service, organisations try to make the process of buying the product as convenient as possible. More importantly, however, once the transaction is finished, the organisation wants the relationship with the customer to continue. (This contrasts with **transactional marketing** where, once a transaction is made, the relationship is over.) If an organisation can gain information about the customer, it can then start to personalise its marketing mix to meet the needs of that customer. A marketing mix that can be personalised to suit a particular customer is likely to satisfy that customer's needs more than a generic marketing mix that might be offered by a business with little knowledge of its individual customers.

Lifetime customers or customers who continue to use one brand, creating a stronger relationship, are normally cheaper for a business in the long run as attracting new customers normally involves a larger marketing investment.

Gaining information

Most organisations keep a detailed record of who has bought their products. Retail businesses use methods such as store cards and loyalty cards to build up a database of customers' buying behaviour. This information can be used to help develop a marketing mix around that customer in order to build a relationship.

Tesco Clubcard holders provide Tesco with a wealth of information: their name, email address, postal address and details of every purchase they have made at a Tesco store (providing the card was used) since they took out the Clubcard. If a customer buys a lot of a particular product then Tesco can send an email to that person every time offers are made on that product. Points gained on the card also give discounts to the customer to encourage repeat purchases.

Your assessment criteria:

 P1 Describe how marketing techniques are used to market products in two organisations

Key terms

Lifetime customer: a customer who remains loyal to a brand

Relationship marketing: a form of marketing that puts emphasis on building a long-term relationship between the buyer and the seller

Transactional marketing: a form of marketing that considers individual transactions to be more important than a long-term relationship

E-marketing

E-marketing or electronic marketing is a relatively new aspect of marketing that enables businesses to build and manage customer relationships using online facilities.

Figure 3.7 The e-marketing mix

Product	Place
• Buying products through the internet can give customers access to more information about the purchase. • Customers can easily adapt their product and select the relevant product specification.	• Products can be easily purchased via secure Paypal services and often delivered at a time and date that suits the customer. • Customers can track their product to find out where it is so they know when it will be delivered. • Secure customer accounts mean that purchasing is far easier and available 24 hours a day.
Promotion	**Price**
• Emails and pop-ups can be personalised to meet an individual customer's needs. This is a cheaper and often more effective method of promotion. • The more customers buy, the more offers and suggestions can be refined to meet their needs.	• Due to the low costs associated with e-marketing, the prices of products can be lowered. • Customers who show repeat purchases can often collect points that can be exchanged for money off future purchases.

E-marketing – customer account pages can be personalised with suggested products and promotions.

> ### 💬 Discuss
>
> *In pairs, consider one particular loyalty card for a retail outlet that you are aware of. What information do you think that business has on customers who use the card? How will this help the business with its marketing?*

M1 ▸ Types of business

An organisation's objectives and marketing techniques depend upon the nature of the organisation.

Product or service

The process of marketing and the main concepts involved are different depending on whether the business offers a product or a service. For instance, a restaurant business gives careful consideration to the physical environment, the people (waiters and chefs) and the process of serving food, as well as the price, products on offer, promotion and place. However, a business selling products, for example an online retailer such as Amazon, spends more time developing a marketing mix that consists of price, product, promotion and place, as the other three are not really applicable to what it does. Many public and voluntary sector organisations provide a service rather than a product.

Customers or businesses

The marketing techniques used also vary depending on who the business's customers are – whether they sell to individuals or to businesses. Nokia, for example, sells communication devices (phones) to millions of individual people all over the world; other technological companies sell their technology to businesses such as Nokia, so their customer is in fact another business.

Private, public or voluntary sector

The type of business also affects the objectives and marketing techniques. A private sector organisation normally has a strategic objective based around making a profit. This means that the marketing department has to develop a marketing mix that is geared around making as much profit as possible. A public sector organisation is more likely to have an objective that is to do with providing the public with a good service that makes the most of taxpayers' money. Its marketing needs to be geared around providing the best value for money and offering a range of services that meet the requirements of the public. A public sector organisation is likely to have far less finance available for marketing.

A voluntary sector organisation does not usually have as much money as a private or public organisation so its marketing will be very different. A charity, for example, might depend largely on individuals making donations so it has to be clear about how it spends its money (ensuring that it is

🔑 Key terms

Private sector organisation: *a business owned by private individuals, not by the government*

Public sector organisation: *an organisation owned by the government and paid for through taxes*

Voluntary sector organisation: *an organisation normally run and owned by a group of volunteers (it normally exists to provide help for people or the environment rather than make a profit)*

Private sector organisations have more scope to advertise as they are profit driven and accountable to their shareholders not the general public.

being used to get 'results'). It is usually harder to measure the success of public and voluntary sector objectives than private sector objectives.

Government-owned organisations have less scope to advertise as their budget is put towards providing a service.

D1　Evaluating the marketing techniques of an organisation

In order to evaluate how marketing is used within an organisation, you need to consider how important marketing is to that particular business. Marketing departments are allocated funds through a marketing budget. The funds available to a marketing department largely depend on how much money the organisation has and how important it deems marketing to be. Some organisations might not see marketing as a particularly important aspect of the business. If a business is product orientated it might allocate far more funds to the operations department and the development of new products than to devising a strategy to satisfy customers. Market-orientated organisations tend to see more value in marketing as time and resources are required to research the customers' needs in order to satisfy a gap in the market.

It is also important to consider the market in which a business operates. You should look at how many competitors the business has, how the customers currently perceive the business and whether the business is a market leader or trying to generate a larger market share and compete with more established competitors. Whether the business operates in a b2b market or a b2c market may also influence its marketing.

Key terms

Business to business (b2b): *a business that sells to other businesses*

Business to customer (b2c): *a business that sells to individuals*

Marketing budget: *the amount of money that is allocated to spend on marketing activities*

Market-orientated organisations: *businesses that use their resources to research what the market needs and then develop a product to satisfy that need*

Product orientated: *a business that puts its resources into developing products and then tries to persuade customers to buy*

Research

In groups, choose a business you are familiar with. Discuss the type of business and the market that it operates in and choose a suitable marketing objective that can be measured and would benefit the whole organisation. Recommend a marketing strategy that best suits the objective and discuss how the process might be evaluated.

Limitations and constraints on marketing

P2 Legal constraints

Organisations are faced with a number of legal constraints that impact on how they market their products. Organisations that do not abide by the legal framework that affects how they operate will run the risk of heavy fines and negative media that can lead to a poor public image. There are a number of Acts that relate to the marketing of products:

- Sale of Goods Act 1979 – This law states that goods that are sold should be fit for the purpose that they are intended; as described and of satisfactory quality with no minor faults or defects unless they are pointed out at the time of purchase (for example, reduced in price because of damaged packaging). This law impacts on the product and promotion aspect of the marketing mix.

- Sale of Goods and Services Act 1994 – This law states that services and contracts must be carried out with due care and skill and within a reasonable time. This impacts on the product aspect of the marketing mix where the business offers a service.

- Trade Descriptions Act 1968 – This law makes it an offence to apply a false description of goods or services that are being sold, including things such as accommodation. In 1974 Thomson Holidays Ltd published false information about a hotel in Greece. Customers bought the holiday on the basis of the description; Thomson Holidays were found guilty of misleading customers and were subsequently convicted. Products should also disclose where the product was manufactured. This law impacts on the product (including the packaging of products) and promotion aspects of the marketing mix.

- Consumer Credit Act 1974 – This law forces anyone who lends money or offers credit deals (paying for a goods or services over a period of time) to have a licence to do so from the Office of Fair Trading. They also have to clearly communicate any charges and interest rates and allow time for the consumer to change their mind and cancel the agreement. This law impacts on the product and pricing aspects of the marketing mix.

- Data Protection Act 1998 – This law requires that any data collected be fairly processed and used for the purpose it was collected. Personal data on individuals must be accurate, up to date, not kept for any longer than is necessary and not passed on to anyone else without the subject's permission. This law impacts on the way that market research is conducted and the promotion aspect of the marketing mix.

Your assessment criteria:

P2 Describe the limitations and constraints of marketing

Controlling advertising

The Advertising Standards Authority (ASA) is the UK's independent watchdog committed to ensuring that adverts, wherever they appear, are legal, decent, honest and truthful. The rules, written by the Committee of Advertising Practice (CAP) and Broadcast Committee of Advertising Practice (BCAP) ensure that advertising does not mislead, harm or offend. There are additional protections for children and vulnerable people and specific rules for certain sectors such as alcohol, health and beauty, environmental claims, gambling and direct marketing.

Ethical constraints and pressure groups

Businesses should follow a moral code of practice when marketing their products or services to consumers. Business activity is coming under increasing scrutiny and consumers want transparency and openness in the advertising, labelling and description of what they are buying. For example, environmental concerns mean that customers may want to know that the product they are buying is ethically sourced and is not having a detrimental impact on the environment. Using Fairtrade suppliers is also important to certain customers.

Businesses that act ethically often make this a key part of their promotion in order to appeal to customers who consider ethics important. Businesses that do not act ethically are often subject to interest from pressure groups that can use the media to damage a business's reputation and affect customers' perceptions of the business.

Key terms

Advertising Standards Authority (ASA): *an independent regulator of advertising across all types of media*

Broadcast Committee of Advertising Practice (BCAP): *writes and reviews the advertising code for advertising on television and radio*

Committee of Advertising Practice (CAP): *writes and reviews the advertising code for non-broadcast advertising*

Pressure groups: *organisations that lobby for a particular cause*

Research

Using your research skills, find out how the advertising code of practice affects the promotion of products in two different industries.

P3 What is market research?

In order for a business to launch a successful marketing campaign and develop a marketing mix that best suits its customers, it needs to research those customers. This is what businesses refer to as market research – the process of collecting and collating information about their customers. It is important that businesses see this as a continual process and not just a one-off activity. Customers' views and expectations change, so if a business is going to continue to satisfy its market it needs to change and adapt its marketing strategy.

Before deciding on what methods are most suitable to obtain the information required, businesses should look at the type of information they need. If they need to know *what* is happening, then closed questions are more suitable. If they want to know *why* something is happening, then open questions are more suitable.

Quantitative data

Closed questions that have pre-determined responses will generate quantitative data. This is information in the form of numbers and can therefore be easily collated, analysed and displayed. For example, the question 'How often do you visit the supermarket?' can have set responses so the researcher might be able to draw the conclusion that 61 per cent of people visit the supermarket at least once a week.

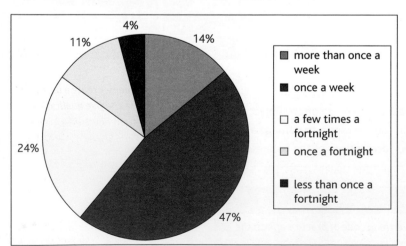

Figure 3.8 A pie chart can be used to display the quantitative data collected in response to the question 'How often do you visit the supermarket?'

Your assessment criteria:

P3 Describe how a selected organisation uses marketing research to contribute to the development of its marketing plans

 Key terms

Quantitative data: *information collected in the form of numerical data*

Qualitative data

This information is in the form of in-depth opinions and views. Qualitative data is far harder to analyse – a question to 100 people might come back with 100 different answers – but can provide a business with information on *why* something is happening.

Primary research

Primary research is research that a business carries out itself, or pays another organisation to carry out on its behalf. As the business carefully selects who and what to ask, the information gathered (primary data) is often specific to a particular need, for example pricing strategies. The information collected is first hand and up to date, but the research is often time consuming and expensive.

Primary research – data is collected first hand, for a specific purpose.

Secondary research

Secondary research makes use of information that already exists. It is often quicker, easier and therefore cheaper to carry out than primary research. However, as the information is collected for another purpose, secondary data can be slightly misleading, irrelevant and out of date.

Secondary research – newspapers and magazines can provide a valuable source of secondary research.

P3 The purpose of primary research

When devising a strategy to collect primary data, an organisation must consider its objectives and how it will use the information to make marketing decisions. The purpose of primary research may be to:

- find out about a new product or service
- find out about changes to an existing product or service
- find out customers' opinions on existing products or services
- find out about a suitable price or whether a change in price is possible
- find out how a product might be promoted
- gauge the success of a particular promotion campaign
- understand the best possible means to sell a product or service
- gauge the success of a particular method of selling a product.

Methods of collecting primary data

There are a number of methods of collecting primary data, each with its own advantages and disadvantages.

Surveys

This is a good method for collecting quantitative data. As the market researcher can ask any questions that are deemed relevant, the results are very relevant. Surveys can be carried out via the phone, face to face or through the internet.

Your assessment criteria:

P3 Describe how a selected organisation uses marketing research to contribute to the development of its marketing plans

Key terms

Surveys: *data collected through the use of a questionnaire*

Figure 3.9 The advantages and disadvantages of face-to-face surveys

Advantages	Disadvantages
• Interviewer can elaborate or explain a question if the interviewee is unsure. This helps remove ambiguity from the questions, making the results more accurate. • Normally a series of closed questions that are quick to ask and easy to answer.	• If the survey is time consuming, interviewees may not give an honest response. • May not give all the possible outcomes. • Not much scope to view the interviewee's opinions. • Can be time consuming and expensive. • Difficult to find people who are willing to answer the questions. An incentive is often needed, adding costs.

Figure 3.10 The advantages and disadvantages of telephone surveys

Advantages	Disadvantages
• Interviewer can elaborate or explain a question if the interviewee is unsure. This helps remove ambiguity from the questions, making the results more accurate. • Normally a series of closed questions that are quick to ask and easy to answer, • Can ask a far broader range of people than face to face.	• If the survey is time consuming, interviewee may not give an honest response. • May not give all the possible outcomes. • Not much scope to view the interviewee's opinions. • Can be time consuming and expensive. • Can be difficult to find a willing respondent.

Figure 3.11 The advantages and disadvantages of online surveys

Advantages	Disadvantages
• Cheap to carry out. • Can be done via pop-ups or emails which enables access a wide range of people. • Requires little to no human involvement, which reduces costs. • Responses can be fed into a database automatically, making collation and analysis of results easier.	• Often discarded as junk mail. Pop-ups are often considered a nuisance and can easily be removed.

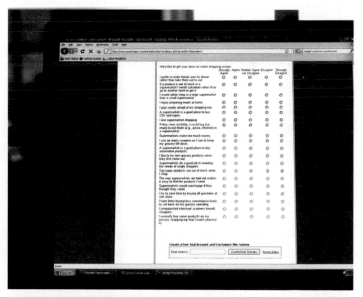

Telephone surveys – interviewers can elaborate on the questions, removing any ambiguity.

Online surveys – these are very cheap and easy to carry out but can be discarded as junk mail.

Methods of collecting primary data *continued*

Your assessment criteria:

 Describe how a selected organisation uses marketing research to contribute to the development of its marketing plans

Interviews

Interviews enable an organisation to gain in-depth views on particular products or services from a small number of respondents. There is scope for open questions and the collection of qualitative data. Interviews are either structured: the interviewer sticks to a series of pre-determined questions and doesn't stray too far from them, or semi-structured: there are a few pre-determined questions but the interviewer has scope to change the questions to fit the interviewee. Interviews are often carried out face to face or on the telephone.

Key terms

Interviews: pre-set questions are asked of an individual or number of individuals

Figure 3.12 The advantages and disadvantages of interviews

Advantages	Disadvantages
• Open questions can lead to more in-depth answers.	• Open questions often give a large range of different responses that are difficult and time consuming to collate and analyse.
• Requires little to no human involvement, which reduces the cost.	• More difficult to ask personal questions.
• Responses can be fed into a database automatically, making collation and analysis of results easier.	• Time consuming for the interviewer and interviewee. This limits the number of people who can be interviewed.
• Can read the interviewee's facial expressions.	
• The interviewer can elaborate and adapt questions so the interviewee fully understands.	• Quite expensive to set up and carry out. Respondents often need an incentive to take part.

Deciding whether to carry out face-to-face or telephone interviews depends on:

• Resources – Some businesses can allocate far more of their budget to market research and can therefore spend more on interviewing respondents

• Time – Telephone interviews are easier and quicker to set up and carry out.

Some businesses use a combination of both.

Interviews can allow for both quantitative and qualitative responses but can be very time consuming.

Observation

Watching customers in action and observing their behaviour and attitudes towards certain products can give specific information about how different sets of customers behave. This is time consuming and the information gathered is often qualitative. It is particularly useful for retail organisations.

Focus groups

In a focus group, a small number of consumers are asked to discuss their opinions on a series of points. Focus groups are popular within retail, and existing customers of a particular product or service are often asked to take part. This technique gathers qualitative data that can often be used to explain why something is happening or why customers perceive one brand to be better than another. The reliability of focus groups often depends on the group dynamics as one dominant person can influence others within the group.

Key terms

Focus group: a small group of people, thought to represent the population, who discuss questions in a relaxed environment

Discuss

In small groups, discuss the most suitable way a car manufacturer might be able to collect market research in order to gather the right balance of qualitative and quantitative data. You may wish to discuss what questions might be required for each.

Secondary market research

P3 The purpose of secondary research

Secondary data is less specific than primary data. Instead of addressing individual needs to do with particular decisions on the marketing mix, secondary research can be used to provide supporting data and help an organisation see the bigger picture and what is happening in its market. Secondary data, such as that collected from the government, can canvas a far wider range of respondents than primary research. It can therefore provide a view as to what is happening in the whole market.

The purpose of secondary data may be to find out:

- about trends across the whole market

- if a market is growing or reducing in size

- who the major competition is and what their strengths and weaknesses are

- about the ranges of products and services that already exist and how successful they are

- about trends in the market, such as changes in levels of spending, social trends and levels of inflation.

Methods of collecting secondary data

The method of collecting secondary data depends upon its source.

Internal data

Internal secondary data is data that already exists within an organisation that can be used for an additional purpose another time.

External data

External data is information that already exists, but has to be obtained from another source. This sometimes incurs a small cost.

Your assessment criteria:

P3 Describe how a selected organisation uses marketing research to contribute to the development of its marketing plans

---

 Key terms

External data: *data gathered from outside the organisation in order to inform decision-making*

Internal data: *data gathered from inside the organisation in order to inform decision-making*

Figure 3.13 Sources of internal data

Sales figures and accounts	Results from prior research	Management information systems
Looking back over past sales figures and accounts can help businesses establish trends in levels of sales of profits that can be used to help forecast in the future.	Results from past surveys or focus groups might still be useful and have some relevance for future research campaigns.	Information held on customers, collected through things such as loyalty cards can help organisations gain vast information about customers' buying patterns.

Sources of external data include:

- The government – Information available from the government can be used to help make decisions. It includes data on changes in the population, for example changes in ages, ethnicity and social trends in different regions.

- Publications – Many publications can be used for secondary data.

- Trade journals – These are publications targeted to people in a specific industry. They often contain research that is relevant to the particular market.

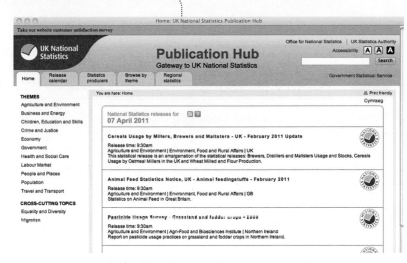

Government data – the UK National Statistics Publication Hub provides valuable data for businesses.

- Newspapers – Many of the broadsheet papers release reports on financial markets and often contain business supplements that have information on specific industries including information on leading businesses' market shares and the size of the market.

- Online sources – The internet is a very useful resource for businesses and entrepreneurs and can be used to carry out research into competitors' prices and product ranges. A number of specialist agencies also offer data in various different forms (see Figure 3.14).

Research

Using www.statistics.gov.uk, try to find a pattern in consumer spending over the last year. How could this be used to help you make marketing decisions?

Figure 3.14 Specialist agencies offering market research

MINTEL	DUN & Bradstreet	Datastream
MINTEL specialises in researching different markets and creating reports that can help businesses gain an insight into what is happening in the market in which they operate (for example, market size and relative market shares). Many reports contain both quantitative and qualitative data.	D&B is one of the world's leading market intelligence companies. They have over 151 business records that can be used to make more informed decisions. Much of the data included is quantitative.	Datastream is a database consisting of quantitative data on company accounts, market trends, the stock market and macro-economic indicators such as national income, unemployment and inflation.

Although these databases are primarily available online, hard copies of the reports are available through some libraries.

Discuss

In pairs, discuss what information an organisation like Tesco might have on a customer who uses its Clubcard for every shop. How might this affect Tesco's marketing decisions?

Sampling

M2 › What is sampling?

Primary research is very time consuming and the data collected is used to inform important decision-making. The research should therefore be carefully planned to ensure that the responses given are accurate and will provide the best information. Organisations do not have the time or the financial resources to research the **total population**, so they use sampling.

Sampling is the process that enables an organisation to question a small, but representative, number of people that it thinks best matches the total population. The total population is not necessarily everyone in the country, but rather anyone who might be interested in buying the product or service.

Sampling should, if carried out correctly, give the same results as if the organisation had researched everyone. Therefore, sampling cuts the amount of time required for the research and the amount of money spent on the research. However, if the **sample** is too small or not representative of the total population then the subsequent decisions made are likely to be riskier and more likely to fail, costing the organisation far more in the long run.

There are various methods of sampling:

- Random sampling – Everyone who you might select has an equal chance of being selected. This may require a database of potential customers – the total population. A number of respondents are then randomly selected for research purposes. In order to be completely random, by mathematical standards, the nth person criterion is often used.

- Quota sampling – Quotas of individuals are filled, depending on the characteristics of the total population. For example, if a school wished to make a decision that impacts every pupil, then all the pupils in the school would be the total population. Random sampling could select a far higher number of Year 11s than Year 7s as everyone has an equal chance of being selected. Quota sampling would ensure that a certain number of respondents were chosen from each year group. This should give a more accurate representation of the total population.

Your assessment criteria:

 M3 Explain the limitations of marketing research used to contribute to the development of a selected organisation's marketing plans

 Key terms

Sample: *a small number of the total population that is supposed to represent the views of everyone*

Total population: *the total number of people that are customers or are considered to be potential customers*

• Stratified sampling – Similar to quota sampling, stratified sampling requires knowledge of the characteristics of the total population. It is used when only a specific group that shares similar characteristics is needed for research – this is called the strata. For example, if a decision made by a school only really required research from sixth-form boys, then researching the total school would be misleading. Therefore, only sixth-form boys would be selected for research. This would be the strata. Within this strata, quota or random sampling principles could be applied in order to determine the actual respondents chosen.

• Systematic sampling – A formulaic approach to selecting who is chosen for research is applied; for example, every seventh person. The method of displaying the list of possible respondents will determine how biased the selection is. Systematic sampling can be used as part of a quota sample and a stratified sample.

• Cluster sampling – A group or cluster of people is chosen that are thought to best share the views of the total population. This is often used by businesses that wish to launch a new product. They can rarely seek the views of the whole country so instead they research one area that they consider best represents the whole country. Once a cluster is chosen, an additional sampling method can be applied.

• Convenience sampling – Although many businesses aim to select their sample of respondents as accurately and scientifically as possible, this often adds to the time and financial resources needed to complete the research. Convenience sampling saves time and money by simply asking anyone who might answer. This can give biased results that affect the reliability of the data collected and ultimately add risk to the decisions that subsequently might be made.

Cluster sampling – the views of shoppers in this retail centre may well be representative of the city's shopping population.

Discuss

In small groups discuss what the most suitable method of sampling might be for the following:

• *a mass market coffee manufacturer wishing to bring out a new instant coffee range*

• *a publishing company launching a new BTEC National in Business textbook*

• *a local sandwich shop wishing to change its opening hours.*

Improving the validity of data

D2 Evaluating market research techniques

When evaluating market research techniques you need to consider the suitability of an organisation's current techniques, the reliability of the results and how the information can be used to inform decision-making.

In order to determine whether the method is suitable, it is important to consider the type of organisation and what the research is needed for – what the organisation's objective is. To do this, it is useful to look at the model of the marketing planning process in Figure 3.15. This reinforces the fact that everything to do with marketing is part of an integrated process.

Organisations rarely find all the information they need simply from one piece of primary or secondary research. It is important that they have the right mix of both. This may include internal and external sources of secondary research so that they can make accurate assumptions about what is happening in their market and be able to give a more accurate forecast of what might happen in the future.

It is also important to consider what primary research is needed. One survey will rarely be adequate. Surveys often give valuable quantitative data, which can then be added to by organising interviews or focus groups. Specific questions can then be used to find out qualitative data. It is important that the interviewer does not ask any leading questions.

The reliability of results

When looking at primary research you will need to consider the method of sampling used. You should consider whether the sample size was big enough. There is no definitive sample size – the larger the sample size, the more accurate the results. However, a sample of 1000 may be more than large enough for one type of business, but inadequate for another. It depends on the purpose of the research and the nature of the product or service. A mass market product such as instant coffee will require a far larger sample than a more specialist product such as fencing equipment.

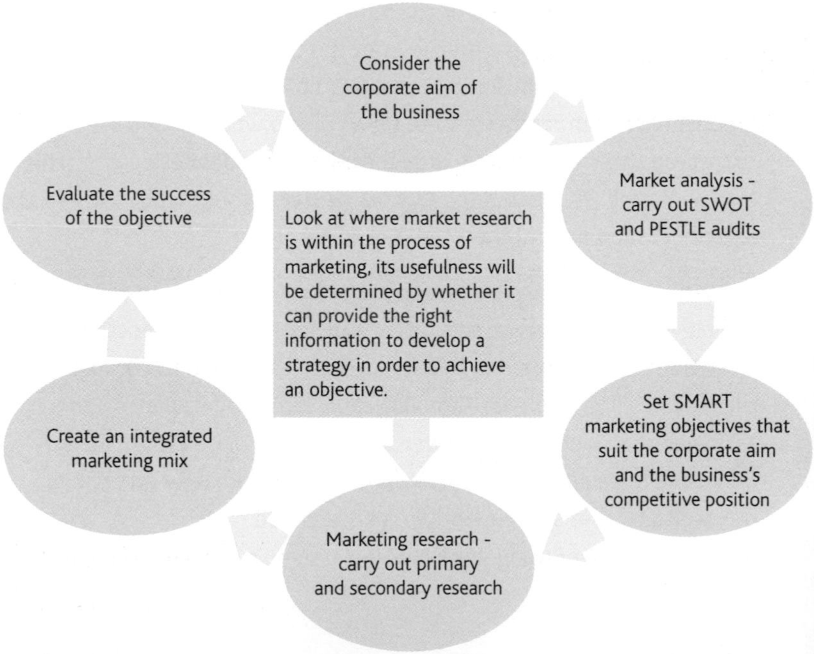

Figure 3.15 A model of the marketing planning process

It is important to consider how the sample was selected and whether there was any **bias** in who was selected for research. Convenience sampling, although cheap, is often very biased and can lead to misleading results.

You should also consider whether the secondary data used was suitable. For example, data collected in 2006 is likely to be out of date and would therefore not provide particularly useful information on which to base a decision. Secondary data can also be misinterpreted and used out of the context for which it was intended.

Using the information to inform decision-making

The Data Protection Act 1998 inhibits organisations from collecting and using data for anything other than its intended purpose. It is important to consider why market research is carried out. Its purpose is to help make more informed decisions. This does not mean that it will guarantee the success of a particular product launch or marketing mix decision. Researching the market can only ever make the decisions slightly more informed and reduce the risk of failure and wasting valuable resources.

Recommendations for improvement

To recommend improvements to an organisation's market research technique, you could start by asking a number of questions:

- Have they considered both primary and secondary research?

- Does the primary research use a range of different methods that provide both qualitative and quantitative data?

- Does the primary research contain any leading questions or ambiguous questions that can be misinterpreted?

- How is the information displayed? Are there easier and quicker ways to analyse the data?

- Is there evidence of using sampling? Is the sample size large enough?

- Does the method of selecting the sample sufficiently reduce the threat of bias in the results?

- Has the secondary data used come from internal and external sources?

- Has the data been misinterpreted or is it out of date?

- Does the data fit the purpose of the research?

Key terms

Bias: *a tendency to make a decision based on personal opinion rather than fairness*

Discuss

In pairs, discuss what the impact is on a marketing mix if the data used to inform the strategy is out of date.

P4 ▸ The marketing plan

In order for marketing to be successful everything the marketing department does needs to be carefully planned to suit the business's objectives and resources. A **marketing plan** is a detailed outline of what a marketing department will do over a period of time. Some businesses have far larger marketing departments so their marketing plans may be broader and more detailed than those of smaller organisations where less emphasis might be put on marketing.

The marketing planning process is made up of six steps.

Corporate aim

The first part of the marketing plan is to know what the organisation wants to achieve. An organisation will consider its current position before setting or agreeing on its corporate aim. It will have to take into account its internal capabilities, such as the finance available to it, the level of expertise within the workforce and its production capabilities.

Market analysis

When the marketing department knows what the organisation wants to achieve, it can begin to formulate its own objectives to help achieve the corporate objective. Before it does this, it will need to do an audit of the department's internal capabilities and the external environment that it operates within. This is done by carrying out techniques such as a SWOT analysis and a PESTLE review (see page s 134–7). Once the marketing department knows its position it can then set realistic and achievable marketing objectives.

Marketing objectives

SMART marketing objectives should fit in with the capabilities of the department and the existing product range. Market analysis will help highlight the current level of brand awareness and customer perception so the objectives set can be realistic and achievable.

Market research

Once the objectives have been set, the marketing department can start carrying out specific research to help it achieve its objective. The research carried should be both primary and secondary and should

Key terms

Marketing plan: a detailed statement that outlines marketing objectives and how they will be achieved in a given time frame

contain information that will help the marketing department put together an integrated marketing mix in order to achieve its objective.

An integrated marketing mix

Once research has been carried out, the marketing department can then go about developing an integrated and cohesive marketing mix that will achieve the objective set.

The success of the objective

The success or otherwise of the organisation's objective will help determine whether the marketing plan was successful or not. However, most businesses value the success of the smaller or tactical objectives as well. Achieving its objectives will help to ensure that the marketing department is allocated more funds in future in order to further develop its product range or increase the amount of promotion that takes place. Evaluating the success of the objective should be an ongoing process so that changes can be implemented if necessary to ensure the objective is met.

The importance of planning

Planning is important as it enables businesses and individual departments and teams to have a clear direction. Achieving objectives is far easier once there is a clear plan of what needs to be carried out. Planning the process carefully can also help a marketing department and a business make the best use of their resources so they can allocate tasks and projects to specific teams within the department. Setting deadlines for projects to be finished helps the overall process; for example, a successful marketing mix may not be possible unless market research information has been collated and made available. Careful planning also allows for alterations as constant evaluation can take place. At any stage, if a particular strategy is not working then alterations and amendments can be made.

Consider the corporate aim of the business

Market analysis – carry out SWOT and PESTLE audits

Set SMART marketing objectives that suit the corporate aim and the business's competitive position

Marketing research – carry out primary and secondary research

Create an integrated marketing mix

Evaluate the success of the objective

Figure 3.16 A model of the marketing planning process

Discuss

In pairs, discuss how easy you think it would be to complete a BTEC National if there was not a clear plan of how this could be achieved.

133

SWOT analysis

Understanding its position in the market helps a business to decide on the most suitable marketing strategy to help it achieve its objective. Carrying out a review of its internal strengths and weaknesses and then identifying the key issues with the external business environment enables a business to understand its competitive position and move towards making more informed decisions in terms of marketing strategies.

Your assessment criteria:

P4 Use marketing research for marketing planning

Key terms

SWOT analysis: *a tool used to identify a business's Strengths, Weaknesses, Opportunities and Threats*

P4 Using a SWOT analysis to aid marketing planning

A SWOT analysis is a marketing tool that can be used as part of a marketing audit to classify a business's key strengths, weaknesses, opportunities and threats.

Figure 3.17 A SWOT analysis

Internal	Strengths	Weaknesses
External	Opportunities	Threats

Internal factors

The internal factors make up the top half of a SWOT analysis and consist of strengths and weaknesses.

Strengths

A business's strengths are the strong points about a business. As the strengths are internal to the organisation they are easily controllable and marketing decisions can be based around them. The strengths themselves do not have to be marketing based and a business could draw upon a number of different strengths in order to aid their marketing of products.

A business's strengths could include:

- years of manufacturing expertise
- a strong brand name
- a large range of products
- a large marketing budget.

Weaknesses

A business's weaknesses are the areas that it considers to be a weakness and that it has control over. These are normally areas that the business has highlighted as working on in order to improve.

A business's weaknesses could include:

- high levels of returns
- poor customer service
- high staff turnover
- limited expertise in a particular market.

External factors

The external factors make up the bottom half of a SWOT analysis and consist of opportunities and threats.

Opportunities

Opportunities are the developments to a particular market that might be of use to a particular business. However, it is important to remember that opportunities are external and therefore not controllable. They are also the same for all of a particular business's competitors and it is often organisations that can successfully exploit these opportunities that gain an edge in the market.

Opportunities for a business could include:

- advancements in technology
- growth in the market
- increases in consumers' spending.

Threats

Threats are uncontrollable events that might limit a business's future growth plans or chances of success. These are normally threats that are conceivable. Although businesses make contingency plans for most eventualities, some threats would not normally arise from an audit of the external environment. For example, in April 2010 a volcanic ash cloud brought most air traffic to a standstill. This was not something that could have been foreseen so it would not have appeared on a business's external audit.

Threats to a business could include:

- economic decline or recession
- drop in the value of the market
- government legislation
- influence from pressure groups
- changes in social opinions.

? Did you know?

The UK's beauty industry was worth £9.6bn in 2009 and is expected to grow by 3–4 per cent for the next few years. This provides a number of opportunities for businesses operating within this market.

Design

In pairs, choose a business of your choice and carry out a SWOT analysis on it.

PESTLE analysis

P4 Analysing the external market

In order to gain a better understanding of the **external environment**, a business can carry out a **PESTLE analysis**. This breaks the external environment down into six categories, each of which has an impact on how a business operates. Sometimes abbreviated to SLEPT analysis or simply PEST, this tool analyses a business's political, economic, social, technological, legal and environmental issues.

Political issues

These are similar to legal issues but are to do with government policy rather than necessarily the law. Political issues may include government policy on education or health. For example, the cutbacks made by the Conservative government in public sector spending from 2010 onwards had an impact on the public sector and any private sector business dealing directly or indirectly with the public sector.

Economic issues

Closely linked to political issues, economic issues have a huge effect on a business's marketing decision-making. Changes in government spending affect the economy of the country. For example, if the government decided to increase spending on the transport infrastructure, this would have an impact on the country's bus and train manufacturers, energy providers and petrol suppliers, to name but a few. It would also affect the levels of employment, which could increase demand for various products. The government's decisions about taxation also affect the economy. **Indirect taxes**, such as VAT, impact on the cost of a particular product, while **direct taxes** such as income tax impact on the amount of money people have to spend on products. Changes to these taxes impact both the range of products offered by businesses and how they price their products. The Central Bank of England (which is separate from the government) dictates the rate at which people borrow money,

Economic issues – changes in levels of taxation, such as VAT increases, impact on how businesses operate.

🔑 Key terms

Direct taxes: *taxes that are imposed directly on to an individual or business. e.g. income tax or corporation tax*

External environment: *factors that are a beyond a business's control that impact on how the business operates*

Indirect taxes: *taxes that are imposed on producers of goods that are then normally passed on to the customer, e.g. VAT*

PESTLE analysis: *a tool used to analyse a business's Political, Economic, Social, Technological, Legal and Environmental issues*

💬 Discuss

In pairs, discuss how government pressure on healthy eating has influenced marketing decisions for businesses in the food industry.

🔍 Research

Research the base rate of interest over the last few years. How might changes in this affect a business's marketing strategy: their price, place, product and promotion?

which impacts on how much people receive for their savings. A high rate encourages customers to save and not to spend too much as bank loans and buying on credit become more expensive.

Social issues

The characteristics of human populations are called demographics. Knowledge of the country's demographics can help a business shape its product portfolio. The increase in the Eastern European population in the UK, for example, has impacted on the way in which many businesses operate, and the products that they offer. The fact that the UK has an ageing population is also important as people of different ages have different levels of disposable income and different buying habits.

Technological issues

Changes in technology present both opportunities and possible threats to a business. They can impact on the manufacturing of products, enabling economies of scale or higher quality products. Technological advancements can also affect the ways in which a product is sold and promoted.

Technological issues – the growth in social networking sites such as Facebook has provided new opportunities for businesses.

Legal issues

Legislation can be an opportunity or a threat to a business. Legal issues often place considerable constraints on how a business markets its products. Legislation such as the Trade Descriptions Act 1968 and Sale of Goods Act 1979 have an impact on how a business promotes its products. The Data Protection Act 1998 impacts on how market research information is collected and used.

Environmental issues

Environmental issues can impact on all the other parts of the external audit. They can lead to changes in social trends and opinions, and to new legislation being passed and political pressure, for example to reduce carbon footprints and help the environment. Environmental issues have a direct impact on how businesses package their products. Businesses that can turn environmental issues into a selling point often gain a competitive advantage in the market. Those that do not are likely to experience bad public relations and a lowered public perception of their brand.

Q | Research

When was the smoking ban in public places introduced in the UK? Discuss how you think this has impacted on both the tobacco industry and the restaurant industry.

Q | Research

Using your research skills, research One Water. Discuss how the company used an environmental issue to its advantage and managed to find a gap in the market.

137

Identifying customers in consumer markets

Not all **customers** are the same. Most products and services that a business offers are targeted at specific customers who normally share some similar characteristics. Therefore designing a marketing mix to suit those customers helps to increase demand among that particular segment of the market and reduces the risk of wasting resources on trying to target customers who are not really interested.

Your assessment criteria:

P5 Explain how and why groups of customers are targeted for selected products

P5 What is a target market?

An organisation's **target market** is anyone who might be interested in buying or using its product or service. For a very few products this includes everybody. However, it is important to consider that most businesses offer a wide range of products, and it is possible that each product has a slightly different target market. The more customers a business appeals to, the less risk there is of failure and the more chance it has of improving brand awareness, sales and ultimately profit.

Mass market and niche market products

In order for a business to gain a better understanding of who its customers are and what characteristics they share, it is important to consider the nature of the product and service it offers. Some products appeal to most people – these are called **mass market products**. Other products are very specialist and have a clearly defined type of customer – these are called **niche market products**.

Figure 3.18 Mass market and niche market products

Mass market products	Niche market products
• Generally appeal to most people, for example tea bags. • Appeal to the masses so are produced in large quantities. This can often reduce manufacturing costs, making the product cheaper for the customer.	• Appeal to a particular type of customer, a more specialist product, for example Earl Grey tea bags. • Often produced on a smaller scale so can have larger costs, which can make the products more expensive for the customer.

Key terms

Customer: the person who exchanges money for a particular product or service

Mass market products: products that appeal to the total market

Niche market products: products that suit a small, specialist section of the market

Target market: a section of the market at which an organisation targets its products and services

Mass markets – traditional tea is regarded as a mass-market product.

Niche markets – specialist products such as Earl Grey tea would be classified as a niche market.

Key terms

Consumer: the person who is the end user of a particular product or service

Customer decision-making

As well as understanding that all customers are different, it is also important to understand the decision-making process that the customer goes through before purchasing a particular product or service. Some products that are cheap and have short life spans can be bought with very little thought from the customer. With other products, customers can take a long time to research and plan the purchase. Businesses should be aware of the customers' needs and reflect this in their marketing mix as they persuade customers to buy.

Consumers and customers

The decision to buy a product is not always made by the end consumer. It is important for businesses to appreciate this if they are to develop a successful marketing mix. For example, when developing a marketing mix for a children's clothing range it is important to consider that the end consumer might be a child but the purchasing decision is normally made by the parent or carer. The marketing mix should be structured around developing a price that suits the parent or carer but also gaining the child's interest in the product as the child will influence the decision to buy.

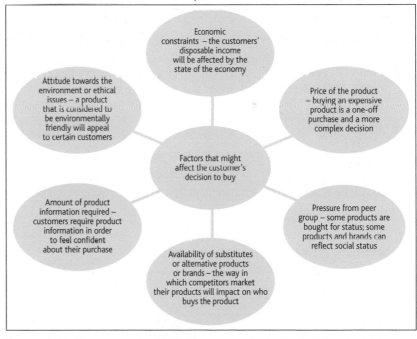

Economic constraints – the customers' disposable income will be affected by the state of the economy

Price of the product – buying an expensive product is a one-off purchase and a more complex decision

Attitude towards the environment or ethical issues – a product that is considered to be environmentally friendly will appeal to certain customers

Factors that might affect the customer's decision to buy

Pressure from peer group – some products are bought for status; some products and brands can reflect social status

Amount of product information required – customers require product information in order to feel confident about their purchase

Availability of substitutes or alternative products or brands – the way in which competitors market their products will impact on who buys the product

Figure 3.19 Factors that might affect a customer's decision to buy

Discuss

In pairs, discuss the influences that might affect a consumer's decision to buy a:

* car   * holiday   * laptop.

P5 ▶ Why segment the market?

Businesses that sell mass market products do not segment the market; instead they sell their products to everyone as one person is no more inclined to buy than another. This is called market aggregation.

The products and services of most businesses, however, appeal to a certain 'type' of customer – a segment of the market. Market segmentation allows a business to target these particular customers and develop a marketing mix around their needs. The marketing mix can ensure that the:

- price of the product meets the customers' expectations and matches their level of income.

- product is targeted at the customers through an appropriate type of media. Different people buy different magazines and listen to different radio stations, so advertising can be directed to reach certain types of people.

- availability of the product, such as where it is sold and how it is sold, is tailored towards the customers.

- product itself is designed, customised and adapted to satisfy those customers.

Targeting smaller groups of people helps an organisation to use both financial resources and time effectively by not trying to sell its product to an audience that is not interested. If a business that should segment the market fails to do so, it is likely to fall behind competitors that treat the market as lots of smaller segments of individuals.

Methods of segmenting the market

Geographically

Markets can be split according to where people live. Different parts of the country have different tastes so businesses can target a marketing mix to suit the needs of a particular area. The most obvious type of geographical segmentation is that practised by smaller organisations with limited resources that are likely to only target their local area.

Demographically

Demographic segmentation is splitting the market according to a descriptive feature such as age, sex or occupation.

Your assessment criteria:

P5 Explain how and why groups of customers are targeted for selected products

Key terms

Market aggregation: *choosing to treat the market as a whole and not targeting particular segments of the market*

Market segmentation: *the process of splitting the market into segments within which customers have similar characteristics*

Segment: *a smaller group of individuals in a market that share similar characteristics*

Figure 3.20 Demographic segmentation

Demographic characteristic	Explanation
Age	This is a fairly obvious method of splitting the total market into smaller segments. The buying decisions of younger people are very different to those of older generations (sometimes referred to as the grey market).
Sex	Men and women have very different buying habits and respond differently to particular marketing tactics. Segmenting the market by sex is obviously very important in the fashion and cosmetics industry.
Occupation and income	People's occupations dictate their income, which has a large impact on the choice of product and brand. By understanding the level of income that might suit their product, businesses can decide on a suitable pricing strategy.

Geodemographically

People's lifestyles and aspirations are believed to reflect the place where they live (their neighbourhood). Geodemographical segmentation identifies groups of people with the same demographic characteristics who are living in the same geographic area.

Two common systems used for geodemographical segmentation are:

- ACORN – this stands for A Classification of Residential Neighbourhoods and roughly splits neighbourhoods in to: wealthy, urban prosperity, comfortably off, moderate means and hard up.

- MOSAIC – created for Experian, a credit information agency, this database breaks families down into 11 different groups with an additional 61 sub-groups.

Understanding a particular neighbourhood's lifestyles and aspirations is vitally important, especially when setting up retail outlets, choosing how and where to sell a product and deciding on areas for direct mail campaigns. It is also important to consider the nature of the product that is being targeted at certain groups. Some products and brands carry a social status and therefore might be considered more important to own by one of the lifestyle segments.

Psychographically

Psychographic segmentation refers to splitting the market according to consumers' lifestyles. This is sometimes called behavioural segmentation. Marketing departments could use socio-economic groupings as an indicator to consumer behaviour or could classify consumers according to their stage in the personal life cycles, for example, individuals who are dependent on parental income, couples who are yet to start a family (often referred to as DINKY – double income no kids yet), families and older generations (sometimes referred to as empty-nesters).

Q | Research

Using your research skills, find out the different classifications of lifestyle that are highlighted using ACORN and MOSAIC.

P5 What is different in a b2b market?

The process of segmenting the market is different for businesses that supply products (suppliers) in b2b markets. The customers' decision-making is likely to be different as the customers are often not the end consumers, but rather another business that will sell the product on to the end customer or consumer. The decision-making is also likely to be carried out by a group of people that may have a formalised process and set criteria for what it looks for in its suppliers.

A number of factors influence market segmentation in b2b markets:

- size
- region
- value
- sector
- product or industry.

Size

The size of an organisation affects the way it goes about selecting its purchases. It is important that businesses that sell to large organisations take this into consideration when creating their marketing strategy. Larger organisations are likely to want a specific type of product with a certain specification and are able to negotiate cheaper prices per unit because of the volume that they order. Smaller businesses have simpler buying procedures and decisions might be made by one or two individuals who are likely to order a smaller quantity of the product.

Region

Some organisations might choose to segment the market by location if a particular area in which they operate has strong links with a particular type of industry. Although manufacturing in the UK has declined over the past 40 years some areas still specialise in manufacturing certain products or offering certain services. London is still one of the world's leading financial markets so software manufacturers in the South East might adapt their product range to meet the needs of the financial sector.

Value

Some markets have shown considerable growth over recent years. Markets that show growing value are likely to attract large numbers of organisations willing to supply them. This is particularly applicable within technological markets as innovation requires suppliers to continually change and adapt their product ranges to suit changing market needs.

Sector

Some businesses might segment the market by sector and target businesses in either the private or the public sector. Education suppliers may well decide to target the public sector over the private sector as there are far more education institutions under government control. Pricing decisions are affected by this because public sector organisations often work on tighter budgets. The same applies to the voluntary sector as donations often provide much of their income.

Product or industry

This type of segmentation acknowledges that the same product can have many different uses depending on the product that the buying business offers and the industry that it operates within. For example, a glass manufacturer might segment the market according to the type of industry in order to develop a product that best suits that industry's needs. The motor industry, for example, has different requirements of a glass supplier compared to the food industry that might use the glass for packaging.

Segmentation by industry or product – glass manufacturers can develop their products to suit a particular industry, such as the food industry (above) or the car industry (below).

Decision-making units (DMU) in b2b markets

It is not just customers who make decisions about what and when to buy. Businesses also have to these make decisions, and make them in decision-making units (DMU) or buying centres. For example, a business such as Debenhams has a DMU for each of its clothing ranges. Each DMU is responsible for buying in products to suit the customers' preferences.

In b2b markets it is important to create buyer–seller relationships as, depending on usage, continual orders can be made, often to the benefit of both the buyer and seller.

Benefits for the seller:

• Sales can become easier to forecast with repeat customers.

• Payments are more likely to be prompt.

• The marketing mix can be developed to meet the need of that customer; a more specific marketing mix can increase profitability.

Benefits for the buyer.

• Price negotiation becomes easier with an existing supplier.

• If a supplier understands an organisation's needs it can reduce the risk involved with purchasing.

• Stock handling costs can be reduced by developing Just-In-Time (JIT) stock ordering.

Developing a suitable product mix

P6 Coherent marketing mix

The marketing mix is a combination of finding the right product, charging the right price, promoting the product and being able to sell it to the customer. The purpose of developing a marketing mix is to help the business achieve its objective by satisfying the needs of a particular target group of customers. In the long term, however, it can also help to build a brand. A successful brand enables the business to bring out new products within that brand, with which customers already have an association, whether for good quality or value for money.

Each individual element of the marketing mix needs to be carefully planned to fit in with the marketing strategy and objectives. In order to be successful, the marketing mix must also be integrated – the different elements must all work together. Consider, for example, a brand that is recognised for quality, such the Gucci clothing label. Gucci's marketing mix includes a carefully devised pricing strategy to meet its customers' perception of its products. The products are advertised and promoted specifically at their target market through exclusive magazines and carefully selected slots on television. Gucci also considers carefully where it sells its products, only using high street retailers that stock similar brands and specialist online retailers.

Your assessment criteria:

P6 Develop a coherent marketing mix for a new product or service

Key terms

Product portfolio: the range of products that a particular organisation offers

Developing a coherent marketing mix – Gucci's marketing mix is carefully planned around customers' perceptions.

Product range and the Boston matrix

The term 'product' applies to both a physical product that can be touched by the consumer and a service. Most businesses offer more than one product. These products normally have specific features or benefits that make them appeal to a particular type of customer or segment of the market.

A product portfolio is the term given to the range of products that a business offers. A wider range of products not only spreads the risk of failure, but also means it is possible to reach a greater range of customers. This gains wider exposure for the brand and reaches more customers, which should increase a business's sales and profit levels.

Product portfolio – most businesses offer a range of different products.

The **Boston matrix** (see Figure 3.21) is a useful tool for analysing a business's product portfolio in order to make informed marketing mix decisions. Each product in a business's product portfolio can be positioned on the matrix according to its market share relative to its competition and its potential for market growth. The product can then be identified as one of four types.

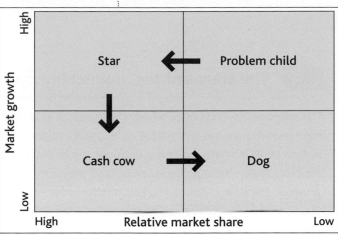

Figure 3.21 The Boston matrix

Cash cow

This type of product is named the cash cow because the business will milk it for cash. If a product has a high market share, yet there is little potential for growth in the market then that product will be milked for as long as it is successful and the money it makes will be used to fund other products in the portfolio.

Problem child

Sometimes referred to as a wild card, this product is currently experiencing problems as it has a low market share. However, the product has potential and, with the right marketing mix behind it, sales could increase significantly as the market in which it operates is still growing.

Star

This is the leading product within the portfolio. This type of product can be considered a market leader as it has a high market share in a growing market. It is important that this product is protected and supported by the right marketing mix in order to remain competitive. As the market in which it operates is growing, many new products may enter the market – money from the cash cow can be used to maintain the star's market share.

Dog

These products have little value within their market. The market itself has stopped growing and could be declining and the product has a low market share. Sometimes these products can be revived (for example clothing items can become popular again as fashions tend to repeat themselves). However, technological products in this sector are generally obsolete and continuing to produce and market these products is a strain on the business's resources.

Key terms

Boston matrix: *a tool to analyse a business's product range in accordance with its potential in the market*

Reflect

Reflect on how you think Gucci's brand image would be affected if it lowered its prices and started using outlets such as Argos and Tesco to sell its products?

P6 The stages of the product life cycle

The **product life cycle** maps where a product is in relation to its expected lifespan. The product life cycle is split into four stages and at each stage different marketing decisions can be made to maximise the profitability of the product. The product life cycle is often used alongside the Boston matrix in order to make more informed marketing decisions and to identify more established and successful products that can be used to help fund the marketing of products that are less well established and need more backing to reach their potential.

Your assessment criteria:

 P6 Develop a coherent marketing mix for a new product or service

Key terms

Penetration pricing: an introduction pricing strategy that involves pricing a product at a lower price to gain a market share

Product life cycle: a marketing tool that helps a business map a product's sales against its lifespan

Skimming pricing: pricing a product at a high introductory price

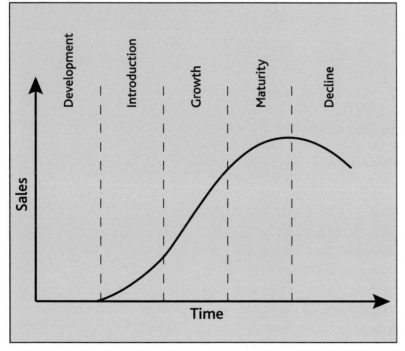

Figure 3.22 The product life cycle

Introduction

Products at this stage are new to the market. Depending on their brand, they might not be that well known. Therefore marketing efforts could be used to increase the brand awareness and gain exposure for the product. The pricing is likely to depend on the product. If the product offers something new to the market then a high price (**skimming pricing**) could be used. Otherwise a lower price to gain a market share (**penetration pricing**) might be more suitable.

Growth

After the initial launch stage, providing the product is successful, it will enter its growth stage where sales see a sharp increase. As sales begin to grow, the profit that the business makes on the product may also increase. Marketing decisions are then made accordingly.

Maturity

The maturity stage is when a product has been out for a certain amount of time. This is the stage at which there is little more growth available. Similar to a cash cow in the Boston matrix, this type of product is likely to achieve high sales so the marketing mix behind it will be devised to prolong its lifespan for as long as possible. This is called an **extension strategy** – changing aspects of the marketing mix in order to prolong the product's lifespan.

 Key terms

Extension strategy: a measure taken to extend the life cycle of a particular product

Extension strategy – the Wii Fit has brought out new additions to the original product to extend its life cycle.

Decline

The decline stage is when a product's sales start to decline. This is similar to a dog in the Boston matrix. At this point a business is normally faced with two options. If the sales are falling because the product isn't successful then it might be worth trying to revive the product. However, if the sales are falling because the market is falling then there would be little point continuing to market.

 Discuss

In pairs, discuss how the product life cycle of an item of food is different from that of a technological product.

 Design

Draw a product life cycle and then place the individual products of a business of your choice where you think they are on the graph.

Pricing strategies

Pricing strategies are an important part of the marketing mix as the right price helps to determine how much profit a business makes and most customers see price as the most important part of a making new purchase. If the pricing is wrong, the product is unlikely to be a success.

Your assessment criteria:

P6 Develop a coherent marketing mix for a new product or service

P6 Introductory pricing strategies

Some pricing strategies are particular suitable for products that are entering the market.

Penetration pricing vs market skimming

Penetration pricing is the strategy of setting a low introductory price in order to undercut the competition. Once the product is established, the price can be raised. This 'normal', long-term price is related to customers' perception of the product and in line with the competition. This pricing strategy is normally taken when there is a highly competitive market or the brand name has little recognition.

Skimming pricing is the strategy of setting a high introductory price. This normally happens when the product offers something new or unique to the market. Once the product has been out for a while, new competition is likely to enter the market so the price is then lowered to remain competitive.

Competitive pricing

Some new products are already part of an existing brand. Therefore their prices are likely to reflect the rest of the brand's image and where the products are perceived to be in relation to the competition. Some businesses launch a new product with a price that best suits their existing brand, then change it over time as and when competitors' prices change.

Long-term pricing strategies

Once a product is established in the market, a long-term pricing strategy should be used.

Psychological pricing

Once a product has become established, a business may wish to pursue a psychological pricing strategy. This means that products are priced at a figure just below a round number; for example, £1.99 instead of £2, or £4.99 instead of £5. Contrary to popular belief, this is not to fool customers

🔑 **Key terms**

Pricing strategies: a series of different methods for pricing a product as it goes through its lifespan

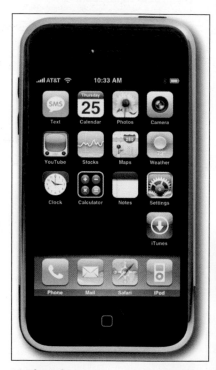

Market skimming – products that are technologically advanced often start with a high selling price.

148

directly as few people are fooled by having a product just 1p cheaper. Instead, this strategy means that the product can be legally advertised at less than £5.

Cost plus pricing

Cost plus pricing means that a business calculates the average cost of making a particular product and then adds a mark-up on top. For example, if a product costs £10 to make and the business adds a 50 per cent profit margin then the selling price will be £15. Although this method allows the business to make a clear profit on each product sold, it is not very flexible, especially if the business is not prepared to lower the profit margin.

Economy pricing

Economy pricing is used for products that are offered in order to provide customers with a cheaper alternative. Supermarkets often offer these products. A very low cost of manufacture and no frills packaging allows for a cheap selling price.

Premium pricing

This is the opposite of economy pricing. A product or service is marketed to offer the customer quality goods for a high selling price.

Short-term pricing tactics

Sometimes a short-term tactic will be used to sell a product.

Promotional pricing

Promotional pricing is when a product is put on offer for a short period of time. Offers such as '25% extra free' and 'buy 3 for the price of 2' are common promotional pricing offers that allow a business to increase sales for a short period of time. If this was done over too long a period then the product line may become unprofitable.

Captive product pricing

This is when a business sells a product at a loss, at a price far lower than that offered by the competition and even lower than the cost of production. This tactic is short term and is designed to draw customers in with the cheap product and make a profit on the other products that are available. This technique is commonly used in cafes and sandwich shops where some products might be exceptionally cheap but profit is made on the additional products.

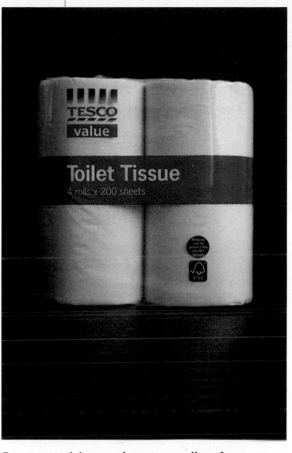

Economy pricing – value ranges allow for a cheaper selling price.

🗩 Discuss

In pairs, discuss what Apple would have considered before devising a pricing strategy for the iPad.

🔍 Research

Using your research skills, find examples of different pricing strategies being used by various online retailers.

Place in the marketing mix

Place does not just mean location – it is the term that refers to the physical process of getting a product or service from a business to a customer. Place is primarily about making sure that the product or service is available to the customer when and where they want it. As with the other aspects of the marketing mix, the place or the **distribution** of the product is largely dependent on the actual product. The distribution of some products is purposefully exclusive in order to create the perception of a high quality exclusive brand. Other products are far more widely available in order to increase the appeal of the product.

Your assessment criteria:

P6 Develop a coherent marketing mix for a new product or service

Key terms

Distribution: the physical process of getting a product from a business to a customer

Retailer: a business that exists to sell manufacturers' products

P6 Methods of distribution

Manufacturers commonly use two main methods or channels of distribution, either going direct to the customer or involving a **retailer**.

Using a retailer

Using a retailer within the method of distribution makes things simpler for most manufacturers as the retailer acts as their customer. The end consumer then purchases the goods from the retailer at a slightly higher price than the retailer paid.

Manufacturer	The manufacturer of a product makes the product and then sells it to a retailer, or a number of retailers, depending on the type of product. Mass market products are sold to many different retailers in order to widen their appeal.
Retailer	Retailers add on a mark-up to the product and then sell to the customers in a situation with which they are familiar. Some larger retailers can store large quantities of goods before they're sold; however, most use regional distribution centres.
Customers	Customers then go to the retailer at their convenience in order to buy the product. Retailers can normally hold enough stock to satisfy demand.

Figure 3.23 Using a retailer

Figure 3.24 The advantages and disadvantages of face-to-face surveys

Advantages	Disadvantages
• Just as customers have a perception of the quality of products, they also have a perception of the quality of shops/retailers, which makes it easier for manufacturers to place their product with a suitable retailer. • The manufacturer has to deal with a smaller number of customers as the retailers are effectively their customers. • Retailers can often store products until they are sold which can free up space and keep costs low for the manufacturer.	• Retailers will treat certain brands differently depending on how established they are. This may mean that new brands struggle for shelf space. • Once the retailer has bought the product from the manufacturer, the manufacturer has limited control over the final price of the product which may affect customers' perception of the quality of the product. • If a retailer offers its own brand it may try to push that brand ahead of the others that it stocks.

 Case study

A large UK-based crisp manufacturer, Runners Crisps, that has an 11 per cent market share of the UK crisp market is thinking of bringing out a new product range. After carrying out a PESTLE analysis, the company has discovered that the market for healthy snacks has grown significantly and is expected to continue to grow by 4 per cent over the next few years.

The product line that the company is considering launching is baked oat biscuits that have far less fat and salt content than Runners Crisps' current non-crisp snacks. The marketing department is considering bringing out the product line as a brand extension of it current 'light crisps' range, as these have been considered star products by the sales and marketing team. This range of products is premium priced as past sales data suggests that customers are happy to pay more for a healthy alternative to traditional snacks.

In the past, healthy snacks have been considered a niche market, but the market is growing fast and can be considered a mass market. Runners Crisps' marketing department thinks that if the product is launched, the marketing mix should reflect this.

1. Explain the following key terms from the case:

    a. star product b. market share   c. niche market.

2. Explain the importance of gaining both primary and secondary research before launching a new product.

3. Explain how sampling can be used to aid primary research.

4. Using Ansoff's Matrix, explain the strategy that Runners Crisps is using.

5. Recommend a pricing strategy for the new product line.

P6 More methods of distribution

Some products are sold directly to the customer.

Selling straight to the customer

Selling straight to the customer removes the need for a retailer. For some businesses that sell large quantities of relatively cheap products, this is not possible. However, this method is becoming increasingly popular as the customer can often find cheaper deals as the manufacturer does not need to add the profit margin that the retailer would have added.

Your assessment criteria:

P6 Develop a coherent marketing mix for a new product or service

Manufacturer	The manufacturer of a product makes the product and then sells directly to the customer. Traditionally, this has been very difficult for manufacturers; however, the internet has enabled customers to remove the middle man and buy direct from the manufacturer.
Customers	By using the internet, customers can choose from a wide variety of manufacturers with relative ease. For many products there is no need to use a retailer. For example, the demand for package holidays booked through travel agents has dropped in demand.

Figure 3.25 Selling straight to the customer

Figure 3.26 The advantages and disadvantage of selling straight to the customer

Advantages	Disadvantages
• Products and services are cheaper for the customer and the manufacturer can increase their profit margin as the retailer's mark up is removed from the process.	• For the manufacturer, this can add to stock-holding costs as retailers that can hold large amounts of stock are placing smaller orders.
• The internet has given customers far more power when buying products and services as there is a wider choice and more product information available.	• Many products require transportation to the customer. For customers, this makes returns harder and incurs an additional cost for postage and packaging.
• Manufacturers can access more data on the end consumer as they are dealing directly with them rather than a retailer. This can help future marketing decisions.	• It is very difficult for customers to try before they buy if they are using the internet to buy a product.

Selling online or through a physical outlet

As the internet has revolutionised the customer's buying process, it has also provided a choice for businesses. They can opt to sell online or through a physical outlet or through a combination of both. Most high street retailers, for example, also have an online retailer.

Figure 3.27 The features of selling online and through a physical outlet

Selling online	Selling through a physical outlet
• Products can be bought 24 hours a day from the comfort of the customer's home.	• It is easier for consumers to return products.
• It is easier for customers to search for products as more information is available.	• Products can be easily tried on, which can aid the decision-making process when thinking of buying.
• More intense competition and more information for customers reduce prices and profit margins.	• Shopping itself is an experience that is enjoyed by many people.
• Businesses can reach a far wider market, which can help them to grow.	
• Online fraud can make customers reluctant to purchase online.	
• It can be difficult to return items.	

Q Research

Using www.expedia.co.uk research the different holidays that you can create by selecting the services directly from the service provider. Compare these with holidays on offer through a travel agent.

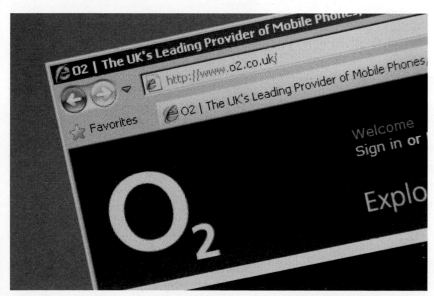

O₂ sells its products and services through retail outlets and online.

Above-the-line promotion

The purpose of promotion is to inform and persuade customers about a particular product or service. The type of promotion differs depending on the type of product and who the customers are. It also depends on the type of organisation selling the product and the resources that it has available to spend on promotion.

Your assessment criteria:
P6 Develop a coherent marketing mix for a new product or service

Key terms

Above-the-line promotion: promotion that reaches a mass audience

P6 Types of above-the-line promotion

Above-the-line promotion concerns promotional methods that are geared around a mass-market audience; it is therefore difficult to control who actually sees the promotion. Some methods do, however, make it easier to control who sees the promotion.

Television advertising

Mass-media advertising is normally for mass-market products and businesses with large advertising budgets. Businesses can choose the time slots when their advertising is shown so that the advertising is more specific; for example the adverts at half-time in a football match are likely to be more male orientated.

Television advertising – Lynx can reach a mass audience through its television advertising campaigns.

Radio advertising

Radio advertising is another mass media method, but is considerably cheaper than television. Local radio stations can be chosen to promote businesses that have segmented the market geographically.

Newspaper/magazine advertising

This form of advertising can be fairly specific as businesses can select the type of newspaper or magazine depending on who the 'typical' reader might be. More information can be given on these adverts as they are not time constrained in the way that radio or television advertising is.

Newspaper/magazine advertising – adverts can be more detailed and placed in specific magazines.

Billboards and posters

These can be targeted at specific customers, depending on where they are put. On a large scale, billboards can be seen by motorist; on a far smaller scale, posters advertising a product or service can be placed in order to best reach the target market. Businesses that segment the market geographically can select different areas in which to place billboards. Buses and bus stops are popular ways of displaying promotional posters.

Billboards – large-scale billboards can be seen regularly by many motorists.

E-advertising

Advertising through electronic means is becoming increasingly popular due to its low cost. It is therefore available to businesses regardless of their size and resources. The internet provides businesses with a medium through which to promote their goods. Businesses can choose a suitable website on which to advertise their products, depending on which customers they want to reach. Pop ups can also be an effective way of promoting products; although they can cause irritation, they are comparatively cheap and can be seen by a huge range of people in different international markets. Text messaging is also a popular means of communicating with customers – many restaurants and nightclubs send information promoting offers via text messages. Social networking sites, such as Facebook, where groups can be created provide organisations with a quick and cheap method of communicating with their customers.

Cinema advertising

Cinemas offer a number of methods of advertising. There are the adverts that precede the films, posters in the foyer and adverts that can be shown in between film releases and trailers on the smaller screens.

 Design

In pairs, design a mind map of ideas for above-the-line promotion methods for the following scenarios:

- *an international plc that is bringing out a new chocolate bar*

- *a highly specialist camera manufacturer that is bringing out a new state-of-the art camera for professional photographers*

- *a local restaurant that has recently been refurbished.*

Below-the-line promotion

P6 — Types of below-the-line promotion

Your assessment criteria:

P6 — Develop a coherent marketing mix for a new product or service

Below-the-line promotion concerns promotional methods that can be aimed at specific types of customers and segments of the market. Although some methods of above-the-line advertising can be placed to reach specific customers, below-the-line methods allow for more control over who will be exposed to the promotion.

Key terms

Below-the-line promotion: promotional methods that can be aimed at specific types of customers and segments of the market

Personal selling

This is when trained individuals take the time to personally promote a product or service to the customer. This normally occurs for very expensive purchases such as a new car, where a salesman would take the time to cover the features of the vehicle, inform on any special offers and allow the customer the opportunity of a test drive.

Personal selling – trained individuals can persuade and inform customers about products.

Sales promotions

There are a number of sales promotions that businesses can use to promote their products:

- Coupons and vouchers – This is a method of increasing short-term sales. Offering customers vouchers and coupons through point of sale, newspapers and circulars and direct mail can improve brand loyalty as customers are encouraged to make repeat purchases.

- Buy one get one free (BOGOF) – These deals can be used to sell large amounts of products in the short term. Although the profit per unit falls this is likely to be compensated by the increase in the amount of the products sold and off set by the increased brand awareness and repeat purchases in the future.

- Special offers – Businesses offer a wide range of special offers. The type of offer depends on the nature of the product or service. Many consumable products have offers such as '25% extra free' or 'buy 3 and get the cheapest free'. These add value for the customers and improve brand loyalty. Service businesses can offer introductory rates, such as, 'sign up for a year and get the first month free', or many credit cards offer interest-free periods on purchases.

Sales promotions – short-term offers are useful in promoting particular product lines.

Sponsorship

This happens when an organisation pays to be associated with a particular event or individual. Normally organisations will pick a suitable event or individual that represents their target market. This can lead to customers associating a particular brand with an event, subsequently increasing brand awareness.

Public relations

Public relations or PR is the process of improving the image of a particular business in the eyes of the public. Rather than improving the public's perception of a particular product, PR is about improving a business's public image. Many businesses do this by ensuring that the public is aware of their ethical stance and their commitment to giving something back to society. For example, Sky are now committed to helping preserve and restore the Amazon Rainforest, and supermarkets such as Tesco and Morrisons run schemes that reward their customers' local schools.

Trade fairs and exhibitions

This is a useful method for businesses that sell niche-market products as it provides an opportunity for an organisation to display their products or services to potentially interested customers. Trade fairs and exhibitions are particularly useful for small firms as they can help build presence in the market and are cheaper than a mass-market advertising campaign.

Sponsorship – Vodafone's sponsorship of Manchester United has helped promote the brand.

🔍 Research

Research the Clothes Show Live. *How many different types of business and industry are involved with the show? Do these include any brands that you have not heard of?*

Developing a coherent mix to suit a target market

M3 How to segment the market

Your assessment criteria:

M3 Develop a coherent marketing mix that is targeted at a defined group of potential customers

When developing a marketing mix to suit a particular type of customer it is important to consider how the customer group is chosen. Different customers behave differently and therefore a marketing mix needs to be developed to meet the particular customers' needs.

Customer groups that share a special interest

Some product ranges are specifically designed to meet a particular niche in the market. For example, horse-riding equipment is sold in specific outlets, such as specialist sport shops and horse-riding schools, in order to reach its customers. Making the products available anywhere else would probably be a waste of the business's resources. Promotion is also chosen to meet the needs of the particular customer group and may be placed in specialist horse-riding magazines.

Figure 3.28 The 4Ps for customer groups that share a special interest

Product	The product is made specifically to meet the particular needs of that specialist group.
Price	The price reflects the quality of the product. Depending on how small the market is, a business might be able to charge more as there is less competition.
Place	Where the product is available to be purchased is specifically chosen to reach the customer. Specialist retailers and websites are likely to be used.
Promotion	Targeted advertising is used to ensure that the advert reaches the right type of audience.

Customer groups with a similar income

Groups of customers who share similar levels of income are likely to share similar tastes when it comes to buying products. Individuals within the group will still be different, however, as the level of disposable income is only a small factor for customers when deciding on purchasing a product.

Figure 3.29 The 4Ps for customer groups with a similar income

Product	The quality of the product and the brand are changed to meet different levels of income. High-income groups may buy products with higher quality raw materials and more elaborate packaging to portray the quality of the product.
Price	The pricing strategy chosen reflects the product and the group of customers. Economy pricing might be more suitable for a product that is targeted at low-income groups whereas premium pricing might be more suitable for higher income groups.
Place	The price and quality of the product have a direct impact on the choice of where to sell the product. 'Exclusive' retailers are more suitable for products aimed at the higher earning part of the market, whereas using as many retailers as possible is more suitable for lower income groups as larger volumes need to be sold in order to make a profit.
Promotion	The choice of advertising and the information that the advert gives differ depending on the target customer. A product that is geared around 'value for money' is likely to give the impression of longevity and reliability while adverts for a 'quality' product might try to reflect a particular image or lifestyle.

Customer groups of the same sex

Male and female buying habits are clearly very different and certain products are targeted specifically at women and some at men. This is particularly true in the fashion and cosmetics industries.

Figure 3.30 The 4Ps for customer groups of the same sex

Product	Products and packaging are designed to appeal to a particular sex. Female packaging tends to use lighter colours such as cream and pink, while men's products and their packaging tend to be darker.
Price	The price depends partly on the product, but male clothing is traditionally more expensive than female clothing as the demand is not as high. Women are also prepared to pay more for certain items such as products in the cosmetics and beauty industry.
Place	Retailers differ depending on the sex of the target market. There are a number of single-sex orientated retailers and a growing number of online retailers that appeal to either males or females.
Promotion	The choice of promotion depends on the sex of the individual. Adverts are placed in particular magazines to reach either males or females. Television adverts are positioned during particular programmes or on certain channels in order to gain more exposure to one sex or the other.

Q | Research

Using the internet, research how the marketing mix for Stella Artois and John Smith's is different. What type of customer is each company targeting?

Assessment checklist

To achieve a pass grade, my portfolio of evidence must show that I can:

Assessment criteria	Description	✓
P1	Describe how marketing techniques are used to market products in two organisations	☐
P2	Describe the limitations and constraints of marketing	☐
P3	Describe how a selected organisation uses marketing research to contribute to the development of its marketing plans	☐
P4	Use marketing research for marketing planning	☐
P5	Explain how and why groups of customers are targeted for selected products	☐
P6	Develop a coherent marketing mix for a new product or service	☐

To achieve a merit grade, my portfolio of evidence must show that I can:

Assessment criteria	Description	✓
M1	Compare marketing techniques used in marketing products in two organisations	☐
M2	Explain the limitations of marketing research used to contribute to the development of a selected organisation's marketing plans	☐
M3	Develop a coherent marketing mix that is targeted at a defined group of potential customers	☐

To achieve a distinction grade, my portfolio of evidence must show that I can:

Assessment criteria	Description	✓
D1	Evaluate the effectiveness of the use of techniques in marketing products in one organisation	☐
D2	Make justified recommendations for improving the validity of the marketing research used to contribute to the development of a selected organisation's marketing plans	☐

4 | Business communication

LO1 Understand different types of business information

- How many methods of business communication are there?
- What is the purpose of this communication?
- Where does information come from? Is it internal or external?

LO2 Be able to present business information effectively

- Meeting the needs of the receiver
- Output requirements
- How to communicate an appropriate image

LO3 Understand the issues and constraints in relation to the use of business information in organisations

- What are the legal issues to consider?
- The importance of behaving ethically
- What are the operational issues a business should consider?

LO4 Know how to communicate business information using appropriate methods

- What does the audience want and need?
- Should a business use electronic methods of communication?
- Are non-electronic methods sometimes more suitable?
- What skills are needed to be an effective communicator?

Different types of business information

A business communicates with its customers on a daily basis through face-to-face interaction on the shop floor, via its website and through its advertising. Even the layout of its store and colour of its staff uniform is communicating a message about who and what a business is. It has to communicate with its suppliers about orders, quality requirements, health and safety expectations and with its staff about codes of conduct, targets and rewards. In order to do this effectively, it has to employ different types of information.

P1 Types of information

Figure 4.1 Types of information used by businesses

Type	Explanation
Verbal	Usually face to face or via the telephone
Written	A letter, memo, email or any information that is written down
On-screen	The staff intranet, the internet or through touch-screen information points
Multimedia	DVDs, TV, training films, adverts, etc.
Web-based	The company website or through related sites (e.g. a restaurant taking bookings through a website such as www.sugarvine.com)

Purpose of information

A business must first identify the purpose of its communication before selecting the type of communication. Getting this wrong can be damaging for its relationships with its staff, customers and the public. Perhaps the most famous case of failing to match the type of information to the purpose took place in 2003 when The Accident Group, a personal injury claims firm, went into liquidation and chose to sack its staff by text.

Dream2be Coaching is a company that offers life coaching. It uses many different types of communication. It has an e-newsletter and a blog and it uses Twitter to keep its customers updated about future developments and sales promotions and to ask for support with charitable events. Its website is used to update customers about theories of coaching. The company has to keep stakeholders such as its creditors informed about its strategic direction and its SWOT analysis and it does this through reports. It uses social media to follow competitors and to keep abreast of their activities. It also uses social media to call on its business network for support when taking part in charitable events.

Sources of information

The information a business communicates originates either internally or externally.

The business needs to consider how reliable the information is. Business decisions are based on the information a firm has, be it internal or external, so getting it wrong can be very damaging.

Figure 4.2 Sources of information

Internal sources	External sources
Financial data (e.g. cash flow statements, profit and loss accounts)	Government statistics (e.g. unemployment figures, GDP)
Human resources (e.g. labour turnover rate)	Commercial reports (e.g. those carried out by a market research company into a particular product or into marketing trends)
Marketing reports	Customer databases (purchased from other companies, e.g. mobile phone companies whose customers have agreed to their data being used in this way)
Sales figures	Competitors' annual reports
Manufacturing outputs	Trade associations (e.g. Chamber of Commerce)

Key terms

Social media: *online tools that enable people to communicate and share resources via the internet, e.g. Facebook, Bebo and Twitter*

SWOT analysis: *a strategic planning method used to evauate the Strengths, Weaknesses, Opportunities and Threats involved in a project or a businesses*

Research

How many different types of information does your college/school use on a daily basis? Record a day's diary of all the different types of information you receive from your school/college, the purpose of the communication and its source. For example, it could be an email advising you about changes to student loans issued by the government or a magazine published by students publicising the week's social events.

Using business information

M1 Get the information right

If a business is to get its message heard and acted upon, it needs to be confident in the reliability of its information sources and then to match the purpose of its communication to the type of information it uses.

Back in 2006 Starbucks produced an e-voucher offering customers a free iced coffee. This was sent to employees who were told to email it to family and friends. The company anticipated use of the voucher in one state. As you can imagine, it was circulated far more widely than this. The company then became anxious about the potential costs of the offer and refused to honour the coupons. This led to a lawsuit against the company.

Starbucks was widely criticised for failing to understand how the internet works and in this instance clearly got the information type wrong.

Your assessment criteria:

M1 Analyse different types of business information and their sources

D1 Evaluate the appropriateness of business information used to make strategic decisions

Q Research

Select a business with which you are familiar – it could be the company where you have a part-time job or where you have done a work placement. Select three different types of information the company has used, analyse the choice of type of information, the purpose of the information and the source.

Case study

In 2011 the British Government was criticised for making drastic cuts to the funding of public services in an attempt to balance the books. The Armed Forces was one of the services affected. Thirty-eight soldiers, one who was in Afghanistan at the time, were informed by email that they were to lose their jobs and that they should begin planning their re-settlement. The Army was criticised for its use of this medium to deliver the news, and the Chief of Staff for the Armed Forces admitted it was a mistake and that the emails should have gone to their commanding officers who would have delivered the news personally face to face.

1. Why was the Army criticised for conveying this message via email?

2. Why would face-to-face delivery of this message be more appropriate?

D1 Strategic direction

Businesses make strategic decisions about their future direction based on the information they have to hand.

Tesco is the UK's biggest supermarket chain. Back in 2004 the company recognised that it had only 5 per cent of the UK non-food market, 6 per cent of the convenience market and 2–3 per cent of the banking market.

This information was used to inform the company's strategic direction.

• The company now includes Tesco Direct. Customers can order non-food items such as electrical goods, toys and furniture from a catalogue in-store or online. Despite the recession, which saw people cut back on non-food purchases, in 2009 Tesco Direct had sales of £12.5 billion and clothing sales were up 11 per cent.

• Tesco has expanded the number of Tesco Express stores and bought the One Stop store chain (these continue to trade as One Stop).

• In 2008 Tesco Personal Finance (bought from Royal Bank of Scotland that year) made approximately £400 million profit. The company plans to have personal financial advisers in its stores and has set a target of £1 billion profit in the next few years.

Q Research

Select a business with which you are familiar – it could be the company where you have a part-time job or where you have done a work placement. Investigate how the company has used information to plan its strategic direction.

? Did you know?

When film director Kevin Smith (Jay and Silent Bob Strike Back) was deemed by Southwest Airlines to be too fat to fly he used Twitter (he has 1.6 million followers) to vent his frustrations about the airline. Southwest airlines used Twitter to apologise and make clear its 'customer size' policy. The airline also issued an apology via its website.

P2 ▶ Presentation methods

Businesses can use a number of presentation methods to meet the needs of their users:

- written documents (e.g. instruction manuals, leaflets) in either a formal or informal style

- verbal presentations (e.g. holiday reps holding a welcome meeting)

- role plays (e.g. in a staff training session)

- on-screen multimedia presentations (e.g. in a tourist information centre)

- images (e.g. to promote a product or in a training manual)

- web-based presentations (e.g a film of a city on a travel website)

- multilingual support (e.g. a presenter may need a translator, a hotel website may need to be in a number of different languages).

Output requirements

Businesses have to consider the output requirements of their communications:

- Users' access to software and hardware – For example, a travel website that uses a range of multimedia presentations will not be successful if the user does not have the hardware or software to access them.

- The resolution of images (in print or online) – Is the quality good enough? Will the images slow the website down?

- Page layout (in print or online) – This needs to be matched to the user. Too much white space can make a document look boring; too little and the text can be difficult to read.

- Choice of font – This has an impact on users. For example, Comic Sans is used by primary schools because it is one of the easiest fonts to read but it is not suitable for a business document.

- Tables – These are used to make information easier to understand, particularly when making comparisons.

- Combining information from a range of applications – For example, a financial report often combines text with data and graphs from a spreadsheet.

Presenting corporate communication

Everything a business does communicates a message to its customers. Its staff uniforms, its buildings, livery and packaging all tell the customers something about that business. For example, IKEA uses blue and yellow, the colours of the Swedish flag, for its buildings, logo and staff uniforms. Many businesses also endorse events, sports and TV programmes in order to communicate a message to customers. The furniture retailer Harveys sponsors *Coronation Street*. As most people watch the programme while sitting on their sofas, this puts the company firmly in viewers' minds as the place to go to for home comforts.

An example of presenting information

Mini Movers is a company providing dance classes for children. It is very successful and therefore there are plans to franchise the business model. Business information has to be prepared for potential franchisees, including:

- a spreadsheet of costs and revenues that a franchisee can expect to pay and receive

- graphs and charts showing profitability

- promotional material on the website including images and a mission statement.

This information has to be tailored to the needs of the audience (potential franchisees) and must promote the business and be a true reflection of the franchises' earning potential.

Three methods of presentation

To achieve a pass you need to present information using three different methods. This could be: a verbal presentation (1), accompanied by a PowerPoint (2) containing graphs of financial data (3) or: a webpage (1) that has a link to a pdf of a leaflet (2) that contains images (3).

You also need to include a statement about the purpose of the information and its likely audience.

Key terms

franchise: *sale of the right to use a firm's name and sell its products in a particular area*

livery: *the colours/designs on transport, buildings, staff uniforms to signify they are part of a larger organisation*

logo: *a graphical representation of a company*

strapline: *a secondary sentence or logo attached to a brand or company name*

Research

Research the presentation methods your school/college uses to present information to you.

- *Does it use written/ verbal/ electronic methods?*

- *Do the messages have the intended effect on you?*

- *How do the methods used in your school/college compare to those in your local university?*

- *Look at the mission statements, logos*

straplines *and images of both organisations. How do they compare?*

External corporate communication

P3 Producing corporate communications

To achieve P3 you need to produce a corporate communication for a business of your choice. This could be a poster advertising a new product or service or a leaflet communicating information about an event or a new business launch.

When Mini Movers first launched Street Fleet they used the leaflet shown here.

street fleet
arrives in Chorley

re you the next Street Dance star? Step up to the challenge of Street Fleet and show us what you've got! We offer classes on Thursday evenings for all ages and abilities and promote self confidence, teamwork and most importantly fun!

Tel: 07510 104228
www.minimoversdance.co.uk

 Join us on Thursday 23rd of December for our Christmas Party Workshop of at aves Green Community Centre, 10am-3pm. Please book early as places are limited.

Your assessment criteria:

P3 Produce corporate communications

P4 Evaluate the external corporate communications of an existing product or service

Discuss

How would you improve the Street Fleet leaflet? Does it, in your opinion, project the right message?

P4 Evaluating external corporate communications

A business uses a variety of communication methods to communicate with its customers. The success of the business depends to some extent on how effective these communications are. Gabe and Grace is an **e-tailer** and wholesaler supplying baby products. The company does not have a retail outlet and sells to the public through its website. The website is the company's main communication method with its customers so it is vital that its content is correct and represents the company accurately.

Gabe and Grace believes in natural products and its main product is Australian lambskins used in baby car seats and strollers.

Key terms

e-tailer: a web-based retailer that has no physical shop or retail premises and conducts all its sales electronically

The 'About us' section of the website states:

*At Gabe and Grace we supply exclusive natural, organic and innovative baby products. Our mission is to bring you high quality, yet practical products to promote the **wellbeing, comfort** and **safety** of our tiny customers because we know how mums feel about their precious babies...*

We have developed one of the largest ranges of first grade luxury lambskins for babies including pram liners, rugs, booties, footmuffs and underlays. We truly believe in the natural benefits lambskins offer babies and have experienced them ourselves when used by our own children, in aiding sleep and comforting them when ill.

This opening section clearly states the company's beliefs, puts the emphasis on wellbeing and safety, and makes the company appealing to mums.

In order to evaluate a business's external communications it is important to look at how successful they are and to identify their failings. Gabe and Grace only communicates to its customers through its website and via email. Not having physical premises, such as a shop in a town centre, does reduce its overheads, but we should evaluate whether limiting sales to the website means the company is missing out a proportion of its potential market.

Discuss

Gabe and Grace sponsors a little boy in Bangladesh through World Vision.

- What message about the business does this communicate to customers?

The company founder, Mari Williams, has a photograph of herself on the 'About us' page.

- Why do you think she has included this?

The owner's daughter is also featured using some of the products.

- Why has the business done this rather than using a professional child model? What message does it give to customers?

Legal and ethical issues related to the use of business information

P5 Legal issues

Your assessment criteria:

P5 Explain the legal and ethical issues in relation to the use of business information

There are a number of **legal** issues related to the way that a business uses information.

Data Protection Act

The Data Protection Act 1998 was introduced to protect the information stored about individuals. All businesses that store information must register with the Data Protection Registrar and adhere to the eight principles of the Act. Data must:

- be fairly and lawfully processed
- be accurate
- be relevant to the purpose it is stored for and not excessive
- be processed for limited purposes
- be kept only for as long as is necessary
- be processed in line with individual's rights
- be secure
- not be transferred to countries without adequate protection.

In 2007 TK Maxx, the retail chain, had to admit that 45.7 million payment card records had been stolen from the company's computers. It was heavily criticised for keeping debit card information for 3 years, as under the Data Protection Act data should only be kept for as long as it is necessary.

Computer Misuse Act

Businesses are also vulnerable to attacks on their computer systems from viruses, hackers, copyright infringements and fraud. The Computer Misuse Act 1990 was introduced in an attempt to prevent this. The Act makes it illegal to:

- gain unauthorised access to a computer's data (hacking) – this includes the illegal copying of programs
- gain unauthorised access to a computer's data for blackmail purposes
- gain unauthorised access to a computer's data with the intention of altering or deleting it – this includes the planting of viruses
- copy programs illegally (software piracy).

Key terms

Legal: *doing something that has its basis in law, e.g. driving at the speed limit*

Ethical: *doing something that is perceived to be right, e.g. giving up your seat for an old lady on the bus*

Ethical issues

A business also has **ethical** considerations about every aspect of how it is run, including the use of its information. Ethics are a set of principles that underpin how a business behaves; ethical and legal behaviour are not the same thing. A business that collects unnecessary data about its customers is acting illegally under the Data Protection Act; a business purchasing such data without knowing whether or not individuals had agreed to its sale would be acting unethically (the firm selling it would be breaking the Data Protection Act).

Staff behaviour

Many businesses have codes of practice governing staff behaviour when using the internet and company email. For example, some firms block shopping sites and eBay to prevent staff using them in work time. Many colleges have social media policies that forbid staff from being in contact with former students via sites such as Facebook – this would not be breaking the law but could be seen as inappropriate.

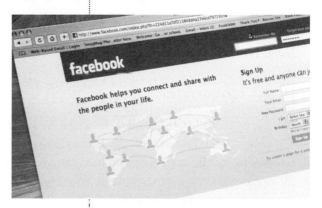

Information ownership

Policies on information ownership look at who owns an employee's ideas – the employee or the employer who paid the employee to have the ideas – and whether the employer owns the employee's thoughts or just their work. Many employees don't realise that their employer owns their ideas while they are under contract – an employee who has a great idea while at work and then sells it to another business is breaking the law.

Freedom of information

The Freedom of Information Act gives people the right to access information stored by public bodies. For example, if you felt that litter was a problem in your area, you could access the information held by the council about bin collections. This Act applies to all public bodies including the NHS, schools, the Houses of Parliament and the BBC.

Whistle-blowing

A **whistle-blowing** policy encourages employees to raise any serious concerns they may have about their employer within the business rather than externally. Often employees don't raise concerns about health and safety, staff bullying or fraud, etc. because they feel that doing so is disloyal to their manager and/or colleagues. Communication channels enable staff to raise their concerns and there is usually a named contact whose job it is to deal with these issues.

Discuss

A business can behave in a legal way and yet operate unethically. In groups, discuss, using examples, whether this statement is true.

? Did you know?

Mattel (the creators of Barbie) took legal action against one of its former employees, Carter Bryant, a designer who sold his idea for Bratz dolls to rival toy firm MGA Entertainment. Mattel claimed it should own Bratz because Bryant was working for Mattel when he came up with the idea. The case was settled for an undisclosed sum paid by Bryant to his former employers.

Key terms

Whistle blowing: raising concerns about wrongdoing in an organisation

? Did you know?

It was John Wick, a former SAS officer, who first blew the whistle on British MPs' expense claims. The scandal rocked parliament back in 2009. Former Labour MP Eric Illsley was the first to receive a jail sentence when found guilty of fiddling his expenses.

Operational issues related to the use of business information

P6 Operational issues

A business has to consider operational issues with regard to the use of information. By law a business has to protect the information it stores and needs to ensure it is secure by installing a firewall and virus protection. Systems also require backing up regularly and most companies back up all their data at least once a day

Health considerations

There are various health problems associated with the regular use of computers. These include back problems caused by sitting hunched at a computer for too long, eye strain from staring at computer screens for long periods and RSI (repetitive strain injury) due to repetitive movements of the hands and arms. To avoid these, the law states that employers must:

- provide employees with tiltable screens
- provide anti-glare screen filters
- provide adjustable chairs
- provide foot supports
- make sure lighting is suitable
- make sure workstations are not cramped
- plan work at a computer so that there are frequent breaks
- pay for appropriate eye and eyesight tests by an optician.

Continuance plans

A business should have in place continuance plans, which allow it to continue in the event of a critical incident. This could be a fire at the business property, damage to stock, the long-term illness of key staff or hackers attacking its IT systems. Incidents such as these can cost a business its customers and its reputation so a contingency plan that outlines how the business will continue is vital.

In December 2010 British airports came under harsh criticism when the UK was hit by heavy snow and services came to a standstill. Both disgruntled passengers and Airports Council International (ACI) complained that British airports were the weak link in the airline

Your assessment criteria:

P6 Explain the operational issues in relation to the use of business information.

M2 Analyse the legal, ethical and operational issues in relation to the use of business information, using appropriate examples

? Did you know?

'Monkey' is one of the most commonly hacked passwords.

Discuss

Discuss with the ICT staff how often the data in your school/college is backed up. Is it often enough?

Discuss

These health regulations do not apply to students in college. Do you think they should?

infrastructure. The airports were unable to cope with the snow and freezing temperatures and were criticised for failing to make plans for what do in the case of adverse weather conditions.

Technology

ICT comes at a cost and for businesses to make full use of the technology available they need to invest in resources and in development to ensure they do not get left behind. Due to the rapid rate at which technology evolves they need to spend money on trained staff and increasingly complex software.

Q | Research

Visit the Business Link website (www.businesslink.gov.uk). What should be included in a business continuity plan?

M2 ▶ Analysing legal, ethical and operational issues

A business has to ensure that its communication complies with both legal and ethical obligations and that the information It has is from a reliable source and is stored securely. It needs to ensure that it has considered all its operational issues, has staff that have been appropriately trained and has the hardware and software it needs to function. Not all businesses are effective in implementing these responsibilities.

Q | Research

Select a business you have studied for this unit and examine how effectively it deals with the legal requirements, ethical considerations and operational issues relating to its business information.

? | Did you know?

A survey commissioned by the Communications Management Association (CMA) revealed that:

- *one in three UK companies had been hacked*

- *44 per cent of British businesses don't have a website*

- *only 51 per cent of small businesses back up their data daily.*

Methods of communication

P7 ► Audience requirements

A business that is planning to communicate with its customers has to understand who those customers are, what their demographics are (see Segmentation in consumer markets in Unit 3, page 140) and what their requirements are. This can help a business to make sure that its communications are understood and are sent via the right method.

For example, if a business were trying to communicate with a 90-year-old woman who has never had or used a computer and who finds using the telephone a challenge, using email or the telephone would not meet her requirements. A business hoping to gain her attention should use a letter or leaflet.

Electronic methods of communication

Once the audience requirements have been established, a business then needs to select its communication method. Electronic methods have changed since the early days of fax machines, which were slow and expensive and often sent faxes that were impossible to read. Businesses now use methods such as:

- the internet
- touch screens
- DVD
- digital broadcasting
- text messaging
- WAP (Wireless Application Protocol).

A business's choice of electronic method will depend upon its own resources and those of its audience.

Your assessment criteria:

P7 Outline electronic and non-electronic methods for communicating business information, using examples for different types of audiences

🔑 Key terms

Demographics: *the characteristics of a group of people, including factors such as age, gender, income, religion, etc*

Spam: *unsolicited emails – direct mail by email*

WAP: *Wireless Application Protocol – a web browser for devices such as mobile phones which gives its users access to the internet and email*

❓ Did you know?

Approximately 247 billion emails are sent worldwide every day and it is estimated that 80 per cent of these are spam.

Non-electronic methods of communication

More traditional methods of communication are still widely used, either because of financial constraints (investment by the business in new technology may not be possible) or because these are the methods accepted by the audience. Letters, memorandums, newsletters, flyers, leaflets and invoices are used, and are often delivered through direct mail.

Key terms

Direct mail: advertising material sent through the post to prospective customers

Memorandums: short notes about something that needs to be remembered

Discuss

How much electronic communication do you receive in a day? How much non-electronic communication do you receive in a day?

Did you know?

Every person in Britain receives approximately 290 pieces of junk mail a year.

Did you know?

A BBC survey in 2008 found that:

- 70 per cent of those aged 65 or over had never been online

- a third of people aged 55–64 had never been online

- 93 per cent of those educated to degree level had internet access at home

- only 56 per cent of people with no formal qualifications had internet access at home

- 29 per cent of women in the UK had never used the internet

- 20 per cent of UK men had never used the internet.

Communication skills

P7 **Communicating effectively**

Part of a business's success in communicating with its customers will depend on the communication skills of its staff.

Figure 4.3 Communication skills

Skill	Explanation
Choosing the appropriate form of communication – formal or informal	Whether a message is informal or formal will depend upon the message and the audience. A nightclub offering free drinks to customers is likely to use an informal method of communication, e.g. a text message, whereas an insurance company with a special offer for over 60s is more likely to send a formal letter.
Using verbal and non-verbal communication	Verbal communication skills include speaking clearly and using the correct tone of voice; non-verbal communications include facial expressions and gestures – a sales person who looks bored and has their arms folded while talking to a customer about a 'great' offer is unlikely to convince the customer to buy.
Listening	Listening skills are as important as verbal skills – failing to listen to responses or requests from customers can mean that the message is misunderstood.
Understanding	The sender of the message has to understand what the message is in order for the receiver to understand it. A sales person who tries to explain APR (annual percentage rate of interest) when they have no idea what they are talking about will not be able to explain what the customer will be paying – and will be unlikely to make a sale.
Seeking clarification	This skill is very important when communicating with customers. A business has to ensure that: • it has understood what the customers need and want • the customer understands what the business does.
Responding to customer needs	Being swift to respond to customer needs gives a business a competitive advantage – Tesco responded to customer need during the recession by supplying a range of discount brands long before the other supermarkets.
Using eye contact	Someone who fails to make eye contact is perceived as untrustworthy. Businesses need their customers to trust them.
Using facial expressiveness	Your face often tells people more about what you are thinking than what you say – think about how you react if you taste something you don't like. Staff have to make sure their facial expression matches what they say.
Using body language	According to experts, 50 per cent of our communication is what we do, not what we say. If we stand hunched up, unable to make eye contact and shifting our weight from foot to foot, not only will we look uncomfortable but we will make other people uncomfortable and less likely to listen to us.

Figure 4.3 (continued)

Skill	Explanation
Using the appropriate level of professional language	Businesses need to remember that not everyone in their audience has the same technical understanding of their product or service. For example, a business selling digital cameras, should remember that some customers will know about resolutions and some will not.
Adapting communication techniques to audience requirements	By utilising good listening skills and questioning techniques a sales person can adapt their sales pitch according to the needs of the customer.
Using presentation skills	Giving a good presentation and holding the interest of the audience is a skill that requires practice. Getting a presentation wrong can result in losing business, particularly in sales pitches.
Inviting commitment to shared goals	This is a skill that many sales people employ – they make the customer believe that their mission is to give them a better deal on energy prices, car insurance, mortgage interest, etc. when really their goal is to make a sale. Making the customer believe you both have the same goal means they are more likely to buy.

Better interaction or flirting?

In 2010 the restaurant chain Pizza Express employed a former actor Karl James to train its staff in interaction skills to improve the way employees related to customers. Tabloid newspapers claimed the restaurant was providing staff with lessons in flirting in an attempt to boost sales and tips. Whether the chain had flirting or improved communication in mind when arranging the classes it is clear that improved communication with customers helps improve business performance.

Recent studies in the US identified that the root of every customer complaint is a lack of respect from staff and that two out of three people believe that sales staff don't care about them or their needs. A study into customer dissatisfaction about call centre staff found that the top cause of dissatisfaction was, rude staff, followed by 'poor attitude'.

 Discuss

What is the difference between interacting and flirting?

The effectiveness of business communication

D2 So, how did they do?

How effective are businesses at communicating with their customers? How much does this communication contribute to the success of the organisation?

Case study

IKEA is a global brand that was started in Sweden in 1943 by 17-year-old Ingvar Kamprad and now has stores in 38 countries worldwide. IKEA was built on the philosophy 'to create a better life for the many'. It refers to customers as visitors and is famous for its low-cost designs, which start with a selling price not a product. It is also famous for its retail concept, 'you do half, we do half', encouraging customers to serve themselves and then assemble the product when they get home. Stores throughout the world have the same layout and livery, although individual stores have some control over some of the room sets in order to appeal to their local market.

The company has a number of ways of communicating with its customers. It runs high-profile TV advertising campaigns, which give messages such as, 'Chuck out your chintz', 'Stop being so English' and 'Tidy up'. It has a free catalogue that is delivered to homes in the catchment area of stores and is available in store. There is also a family card scheme.

IKEA seems to have been unaffected by the economic downturn – its message about affordability seeming to have hit home with consumers. The company's only change has been to accommodate new customers who have downshifted from stores such as John Lewis to IKEA, and who may have struggled with the idea of 'doing half'.

The company has a strong ethical viewpoint. Family card holders are encouraged to repeat visit (and repeat purchase) as every swipe of the family card plants a tree. The company supports initiatives that benefit causes such as UNICEF, Save the Children

> **? Did you know?**
>
> *In 1991 Gerald Ratner, the chief executive of a major jewellery company, Ratner Group, was invited to speak to the Institute of Directors. In his speech, he joked about some of the company's products, referring to a sherry decanter being 'crap' and saying that some gold earrings were cheaper than a prawn sandwich but probably wouldn't last as long. His comments were quoted in the press and this communication nightmare nearly destroyed the company.*

and American Forests. For 4 years in a row, from 2007, IKEA was named one of the World's Most Ethical Companies by the Ethisphere Institute.

1. Ingvar Kamprad is fiercely proud of his Swedish roots. How is this patriotism communicated to customers?

2. The IKEA family card is not, as the name suggests, a loyalty card for families, but a card that enables all customers to become part of the IKEA family. What message does this give to customers?

 Research

How effective is IKEA in communicating with its customers? Have there been any documented operational issues? How does the company compare to the business you have been studying?

Case study

The launch of a new car requires a business to make full use of the communication methods that are available: print media, TV advertising, radio advertising, a slot on *Top Gear*, Facebook, Twitter, consumer test drives, etc. Back in the 1950s, the choice of business communication methods was a little more limited than it is today but when Ford launched the Edsel at that time, it did so through a campaign that involved the car being kept under wraps for months. In order to generate interest among consumers who were supposed to become desperate to get a first look at the new model, it was not even shown in the TV commercial. For months adverts appeared in newspapers and magazines proclaiming 'The Edsel is coming'. The company even created a 1-hour TV show, *The Edsel Show*, for the launch.

The hype worked and the business communication generated a huge amount of interest in the car, but the product failed to live up to the hype. Consumers and critics believed it to be ugly and over-priced. Ford failed to sell its target numbers and after 2 years the product was removed from the market.

In this case, the communication contributed to the product's failure. The advertising proclaimed, 'There has never been a car like the Edsel', and it transpired that there hadn't. The over-enthusiastic communication prior to the car's launch meant that the product failed to live up to consumers' expectations.

The moral of this story, it would appear, is not to communicate to customers what you can't deliver.

1. Communication can contribute to the success of a business/product. In this case, why was communication blamed for the product failure?

2. Why was Ford ineffective in communicating with its customers?

Assessment checklist

To achieve a pass grade, my portfolio must show that I can:

Assessment criteria	Description	✓
P1	Explain different types of business information, their sources and purposes	☐
P2	Present complex internal business information using three different methods appropriate to the user's needs	☐
P3	Produce corporate communications	☐
P4	Evaluate the external corporate communications of an existing product or service	☐
P5	Explain the legal and ethical issues in relation to the use of business information	☐
P6	Explain the operational issues in relation to the use of business information	☐
P7	Outline electronic and non-electronic methods for communicating business information, using examples for different types of audiences	☐

To achieve a merit grade, my portfolio must show that I can:

Assessment criteria	Description	✓
M1	Analyse different types of business information and their sources	☐
M2	Analyse the legal, ethical and operational issues in relation to the use of business information, using appropriate examples.	☐

To achieve a distinction grade, my portfolio must show that I can:

Assessment criteria	Description	✓
D1	Evaluate the appropriateness of business information used to make strategic decisions	☐
D2	Evaluate the effectiveness of business information and its communication as key contributors to the success of an organisation, using examples to illustrate your points	☐

9 | Creative product promotion

LO1 Know the constituents of the promotional mix

- ▶ What is the promotional mix?
- ▶ How does a company decide on the appropriate mix for its products/services?
- ▶ How do companies communicate effectively with their customers?
- ▶ How do customers respond to promotion?

LO2 Understand the role of promotion within the marketing mix

- ▶ What contribution can products and services make to promotion?
- ▶ How does the price help to promote products and services?
- ▶ How does the place help to promote products and services?
- ▶ How does the packaging help to promote products and services?
- ▶ How do people help to promote products and services?
- ▶ How do processes help to promote products and services?
- ▶ How does physical evidence help to promote products and services?
- ▶ What are promotional objectives and why are they important?
- ▶ What is branding and why is it valuable?

LO3 Understand the role of advertising agencies and the media

- ▶ Why employ advertising agencies?

- ▶ What types of media are available to use?

- ▶ How do businesses decide which media to use?

- ▶ What is the role of the internet in promoting products and services?

LO4 Be able to create a simple promotional campaign

- ▶ What is a campaign brief?

- ▶ What is a creative brief?

- ▶ What content should you choose?

- ▶ What are campaign tactics?

- ▶ How do you develop a promotion plan?

Promotional mix

It is not enough for companies only to consider three out of the four elements of the **marketing mix**. They may have good products, sold at the right prices and in the right places. However, they need to generate sales and hence profits by communicating effectively to their customers. This is what is known as promotion. A company will use a mix of promotional activities that it thinks will best suit its target customers.

Your assessment criteria:

P1 Describe the promotional mix used by two selected organisations for a selected product/service

P1 Promotional tools

The **promotional mix** is the blend of different types of activities and tools used by businesses to make potential customers aware of their products or services. Choosing the right mix of promotional tools can make or break an organisation. There is little purpose in having great products, at the right price and sold in the right place if nobody knows about them!

The purpose and objectives of the promotional mix include:

- increasing sales and market share

  explaining the uses of the product

- showing the product features that are better than the competition

- conveying a brand image

- promoting any new features of an existing product

- showing the benefits of the product.

There is a variety of different promotional tools available to organisations in order to achieve these objectives.

Advertising

Advertising involves communicating with customers using media such as television, newspapers, magazines, billboards, posters, radio and cinema. The purpose of advertising is to inform (provide information about a product) and persuade people to buy. For each advertising campaign a business has to decide the key message it wants to communicate to customers (what it wants to say) and the medium it will use (how it is going to get its message across). The most successful advertising campaigns are those that promote the uniqueness of products compared with their competitors. Advertising communicates to a large number of targeted customers. However, it is not personalised to

Key terms

Advertising: *communicating to a large number of customers, through media such as TV and radio, in order that customers prefer a particular product over the competition*

Marketing mix: *successful businesses have the best marketing mix by selling the right products, at the right price, in the right place and using the most suitable promotion (the 4Ps)*

Promotional mix: *all of the marketing communications that are used by a business, consisting of a blend of advertising, sales promotion, public relations, personal selling, sponsorship and direct marketing*

? Did you know?

An estimated $21 billion was spent on internet advertising in 2007.

individuals and it is difficult for an organisation to get feedback from its customers about its advertising.

Personal selling

Personal selling is verbal communication with potential customers about a product or service, with a view to making a sale. Its purpose is to inform customers about the products, demonstrate how products work and develop good customer relations. Often, it can involve building individual relationships with potential customers.

However, personal selling is very expensive as it involves employing many sales people to talk on an individual level to customers.

Discuss

In pairs, discuss possible advantages and disadvantages of firms using:

- *personal selling*

- *advertising*

as forms advertising of promotion.

Why do you think organisations choose to use these particular promotional tools?

Key terms

Personal selling: *verbal communication with potential customers about a product or service, with a view to making a sale*

Door-to-door selling can be very effective at increasing the sales of products that need to be demonstrated to customers.

P1 Promotional tools *continued*

Sales promotion

Sales promotion is the attempt to persuade customers to buy a product or service by offering them an incentive. Incentives can vary and include money-off coupons, discount vouchers, competitions, free gifts and loyalty cards points.

Sales promotions are often used for new products on the market to persuade customers to try the product in the hope that they will continue to use it once the promotion is over.

Public relations

The Institute of Public Relations defines **public relations** as follows: 'The planned and sustained effort to establish and maintain goodwill and mutual understanding between an organisation and its publics.' Public relations is generally the art of changing public opinion through a variety of different communications to customers. These can include press releases, promotional videos, competitions and prizes, celebrity endorsements, websites, direct mailings and community involvement programmes, to name a few.

Direct marketing

This is the building of a relationship between an organisation offering a product or service and a potential customer. The Institute of Direct Marketing defines **direct marketing** as: 'The planned recording, analysis and tracking of customer behaviour to develop relational marketing strategies.' Direct marketing consists of the following activities: direct response adverts, magazine inserts, direct mail, telemarketing and e-marketing.

Direct mail (also known as 'junk mail') is the most popular form of direct marketing. However, it is often dismissed by customers as it is usually wrongly targeted or of poor quality. Therefore, in order for it to be effective, it is important that direct mail has appealing designs and appropriate content, and that the organisation sending it has the contact details of the customers who they are trying to target.

Sponsorship

Sponsorship is when a business supports an event or whole organisation by giving money or other resources that are valued by that organisation. In return, the business receives advertising at the event, exposure to potential customers and benefits from the publicity for the event.

Your assessment criteria:

P1 Describe the promotional mix used by two selected organisations for a selected product/service

---

 Key terms

Direct marketing: building a relationship between an organisation offering a product or service and a potential customer

Public relations: the planned and sustained effort of changing public opinion about a business or product through a variety of different forms of communication to customers

Sales promotion: an attempt to persuade customers to buy a product or service by offering them an incentive (e.g. discounts, buy one get one free, etc.)

Sponsorship: when a business supports an event or whole organisation by giving money or other resources that are valued by that organisation

---

? Did you know?

It used to be legal to advertise tobacco to promote a product that kills half of its users! It is now illegal.

For example, The Premier League is sponsored by Barclays. This gives Barclays a powerful brand visibility worldwide.

Sponsorship is extremely popular among large companies that are seeking to create awareness or persuade their target audience to think positively about the organisation or its products. It also allows organisations access to very particular segments of the market, often in an environment where the customer is prone to be more receptive to the organisation.

Choosing promotional tools

An organisation must carefully select which forms of promotion it is going to use from the variety of tools available to it. The blend of promotion it chooses in order to convey the desired message and corporate image to its customers is an extremely important decision. It needs to ensure that the promotional tools it chooses present the organisation's selling messages to the maximum number of customers for the lowest cost.

As the economy and the market in which organisations work change, their promotional mix may also change. Therefore, companies need to continually monitor the response rates to their promotional activities so that they know which are the most effective. This is why companies often ask you, 'How did you hear about us?'

Q Research

For a product of your choice, find all examples that you can of the associated promotional mix and feed back to the rest of the class. Don't just focus on advertising – you must try to find examples from the whole promotional mix.

Q Research

In pairs, research the different tools the following organisations/products use in order to promote themselves:

- *Wimbledon All England Lawn Tennis Club*
- *Apple iPad*
- *Walkers crisps*
- *McDonald's.*

💬 Discuss

In your pair, discuss why the organisations chose this particular mix of promotional tools.

Barclays has sponsored the Premier League since 2004.

Decisions about the appropriate mix

The special thing about promotion is that it can be so heavily influenced by the other elements of the marketing mix. The product's features and benefits have to be promoted, the price will convey the quality of the product, and the place where it is to be bought from will also need to be promoted, whether this is done by the retailer or the producer.

Your assessment criteria:

M1 Explain how promotion is integrated with the rest of the marketing mix in a selected organisation to achieve its marketing aims and objectives

M1 Marketing aims and objectives

With so many promotional options to choose from, an organisation chooses the correct mix of promotional tools in order to achieve its **marketing aims and objectives**. These are those goals set by the marketing department, which must be achieved by the promotional methods it chooses.

Marketing aims and objectives must fit within the organisation's aims and objectives (see Figure 9.1).

Key terms

Marketing aims and objectives: the goals and targets set by the marketing department within an organisation to help the business to meet its overall business aims and objectives

Figure 9.1 How Coca-Cola's organisational aims and objectives could be translated into its marketing aims and objectives

Examples of what Coca-Cola's business aims and objectives might be	Examples of what Coca-Cola's marketing aims and objectives might be
• Maximising return to shareholders while being mindful of our overall responsibilities • Bringing to the world a portfolio of beverage brands that anticipate and satisfy people's desires and needs	• Increasing brand awareness • Greater understanding of customer needs • Development of new products • Re-launch of products

The promotional activities that Coca-Cola chooses have to ensure that it fulfils its marketing aims and objectives. Therefore, choosing the appropriate promotional mix is vital to the organisation's success.

In order to meet its marketing aims and objectives, there are many different elements that an organisation must consider when deciding on its promotional mix.

Did you know?

Coca-Cola spent approximately $2.6 billion on advertising in 2006.

Cost of the promotion versus the benefit

The promotion that an organisation chooses will not always bring in the desired amount of sales immediately. Therefore, an organisation considers how long it may take to achieve the desired number of sales before investing in the promotion. In other words, it looks at the promotion in the long term. The organisation may also consider promotion from a short-term point of view and only invest in it at certain times of year. For example, a stationery producer may invest heavily in promotion at the end of summer, ready for the start of the school year in September.

Target market and exposure to the media

An organisation invests in the promotional tools that will most effectively expose its products or services to its target market, rather than just opting for the cheapest form of promotion. For example, sponsorship may be an expensive option for a company like Nike, but the organisations and individuals it sponsors (e.g. Arsenal Football Club) means that it can communicate more effectively with its target customers.

Type of market in which the organisation operates

Organisations can either operate in business-to-consumer markets (b2c), i.e. they sell to the end consumers of products; or business-to-business markets (b2b), i.e. they sell to other businesses. The type of promotion chosen will depend on the type of market in which an organisation operates. Organisations that operate in a b2c market often use advertising, direct marketing and sales promotions, whereas organisations that operate in b2b markets often use personal selling and public relations activity. For example, Pfizer, which sells medication to doctors, employs staff to go to GP surgeries to personally sell the drugs and highlight their benefits over competing drugs.

Q Research

Choose four of your favourite companies (these could include football clubs) and find out who they sponsor. Explain why you think they sponsor that particular event/ organisation/person and how much (approximately) it costs them to do this.

Q Research

- *In pairs, research the aims and objectives of an organisation of your choice.*

- *Research the types of promotion it uses to promote a particular product.*

- *Try to come up with what you believe, from your research, would be its marketing aims and objectives.*

Coca-Cola's brand is worth an estimate $68.73 billion.

Appropriate mix, communications model and consumer response

M1 More factors affecting the mix

Market stability

If an organisation operates in a rapidly changing market (e.g. new technology), it may need to choose promotional activities that do not take a long time to prepare, such as a high-profile public relations campaign instead of a TV advert, which could take months. Alternatively, if the organisation operates in a stable market where products don't change that much over time, it may choose to try to minimise costs and use the same adverts year after year. Can you think of any adverts that you have seen on TV year after year?

Channel strategies

In order to decide on which promotional methods to use, organisations must consider the ways in which their target customers prefer to buy their products. For example, if most of their customers buy online, there is little point promoting their products through personal selling.

Branding, positioning and competition

Brand positioning is related to how the product appears in the minds of the customers, compared with the other products on the market. To be successful an organisation needs to consider what its competitors' promotions are and how this impacts on how it markets its own product.

Budget requirements

The marketing objectives of the promotion are set at the start of the year. The budget is then set in order for the promotion to achieve these objectives.

Timing requirements

Certain products are seasonal and sell much better at different times of the year, for example, ice cream in summer and children's toys at Christmas. Therefore, any promotional tools that an organisation agrees to invest in will be used at appropriate times of the year.

Your assessment criteria:

M1 Explain how promotion is integrated with the rest of the marketing mix in a selected organisation to achieve its marketing aims and objectives

Key terms

AIDA: an acronym for the four stages of the buying cycle: attention, interest, desire and action

Decode: understand the promotional message

Encoding: the way the sender sends a message in their promotion

Feedback: the communication a sender gets from a receiver about their promotion

Media choice: the choice of which type of promotion to use in order to communicate best with target customers

Message: the communication a sender makes to a receiver

Noise: a general term used to describe all of the marketing communications that people hear or see on a daily basis. A successful marketing campaign is one that can be heard over all the noise!

Sender/receiver: the organisation that is sending out a promotional message/the customer at whom the promotion is aimed

The communications model

In order for an organisation to select the most effective promotional mix, it must understand exactly what **message** it wants to send out to its target customers and how (**encoding**), to ensure that the target customers receive the message. This is what is known as the **sender/receiver** communication model. The receiver (i.e. the customer) must **decode** or understand the message from the sender (i.e. the organisation).

However, this model does not reflect reality. We see lots of promotion (otherwise known as marketing **noise**) on a daily basis, and we have to decide which adverts appeal to us the most. So organisations have to ensure that they develop promotional material and make the right **media choice** to cut through this noise and appeal to their target customers. Organisations must also get **feedback** on their promotional mix from their customers, so they know which forms of promotion are most effective.

Consumer response hierarchy

The purpose of promotion is essentially to create sales. Organisations consider how the different promotional methods work at different stages of the buying process. Promotion seeks to move a buyer through four distinct stages of the buying cycle, known as **AIDA**;

1. First, the promotion must get the target customer's *attention*, so must appeal to their needs and fit around their lifestyle.

2. This will make the customer *interested* in the product so that they research it and discount competitors' products.

3. They then have a *desire* to buy the product.

4. And finally, they take *action* and purchase the product.

If the promotion does not appeal to the target market, the customer is unlikely to follow these four stages and therefore will not purchase the product.

Q Research

Gather some different forms of advertising (clips of TV adverts, flyers or newspaper adverts). Explain how effectively the adverts have used AIDA. Describe how the adverts could be improved.

Q Research

- *Research the business aims and objectives of a company of your choice.*

- *Decide what its marketing aims and objectives could be, based on these overall business aims and objectives.*

- *What promotional mix would you choose for the company in order to best meet these marketing aims and objectives? Justify your decision.*

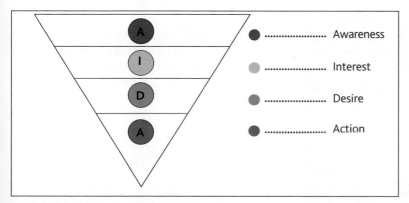

Figure 9.2 The AIDA communication model

Promotional mix and the role of promotion

The role of promotion is extremely important for any company. Even if an organisation has the best **products and services** sold at the best price and in the best place, if none of the target customers have heard about the product, it won't sell.

D1 Evaluating and justifying a promotional mix

In order to evaluate and justify the promotional mix used by an organisation in relation to its marketing objectives, it is necessary to research the promotional mix that the company has used in the past, and what its marketing aims and objectives were for that promotion.

In order to evaluate the promotional mix sufficiently, you will need to explain whether you believe the organisation has met those objectives or not and describe why you think is the case. It is also important to give a detailed description of any improvements the organisation could have made in order to achieve its objectives more effectively.

You will need to carry out detailed research to decide whether the promotional mix was a success and met the marketing objectives. You must also describe why you believe the organisation chose the particular promotional mix in order to achieve its objectives.

Your assessment criteria:

D1 Evaluate and justify the use of an appropriate promotional mix in relation to marketing objectives for the selected organisation

P2 Explain the role of promotion within the marketing mix for a selected product/service

 Key terms

Products and services: *goods that are either tangible (products) or intangible (services) offered to customers for sale*

 Discuss

In pairs, discuss the use of a promotional mix chosen by an organisation.

- *Do you think it has effectively met its objectives?*

- *Justify your answer and feed back to the rest of the class.*

? **Did you know?**

Global corporations spend approximately $620 billion each year to make their products seem desirable and get us to buy them.

P2 ▶ Products and services in the promotional mix

The reason that promotion is such an important part of a firm's success is that it can be heavily influenced by other elements of the marketing mix.

All of the elements of the marketing mix convey the same message to potential customers. For example, think of an iPhone advert – it shows customers exactly what the phone can do, promoting the *product's* benefits and features. The *price* is such that it gives the impression of quality and the *promotion* reinforces this quality message. The promotion must not contradict this message, for example, Apple is unlikely to produce direct mail to promote its latest iPhone! And the *place* where iPods are sold also communicates its quality and unique qualities (think of the Apple shops).

Many products and services exist within what is known as a product range. For example, Walkers has a range of crisps such as Walkers Crisps, Quavers and Doritos. Walkers chooses its promotion to best promote the product range, even though the different products are aimed to suit different market segments, different tastes and different price expectations.

The role of promotion is to convey the product range's features and benefits, and this is particularly important if the organisation is trying to promote a new product. Also, by promoting a range of products, the organisation is not only cutting costs, as it does not have to produce several different types of promotion, it is also establishing the corporate image and reputation in the minds of the customers by showing that all of its products are of a similar high quality. This often means that customers then choose to buy other products in the range based on the good name.

When an organisation has developed a new product, promotion plays a large role in launching it onto the market. This may be in the form of product or market trials (i.e. the organisation may choose to place the product in selected stores to test customer reactions to it) or sales promotions in order to tempt potential customers to purchase the product.

Discuss

• In groups, discuss any experiences you have had of market trials or sales promotions.

• Make a list of them and then decide why the organisation decided to use this form of promotion.

Did you know?

Walkers crisps and snacks are eaten by approximately 1 million people each day!

Products, services and price

P2 More about products and services

Promotion influences customers' perceptions of the quality of a product by showing them the features and communicating the quality, design and style of the product. In this way, the promotion often implies that if you were to buy the product then you would be perceived in the same way as the promotion. Often, organisations use promotion to show all of the different products in their range, and the variations they offer. For example, the Walkers adverts often promote several different flavours in a single advert.

A successful promotion is one that communicates the unique selling point (USP) of the product to the customer, i.e. the benefit that the product can offer compared with others on the market.

The timing of a promotion is key to the success of the product. This is especially true with seasonal products (such as Christmas decorations) or limited edition goods. If an organisation such as Sainsbury's advertised its Christmas products in July, the promotion would be ineffective as nobody would be inclined to buy Christmas products at that time. However, if the promotion were in October and November, it would be a lot more effective at increasing sales.

The quantity of promotional activity will contribute to the success of the promotion. It will depend on the amount of the product the organisation is expecting to sell. After employing Gary Lineker, Walkers increased its promotional activity and sold an extra 114 million packets in 2 years!

Promotion also serves to inform the customer of any associated services the product comes with. In most cases this is customer care, for example, a phone number to ring if you are pleased or, conversely, dissatisfied with the product (next time you eat a bag of crisps, have a look on the packaging for this). However, it could also be advertising other services, for example, iPod adverts also show the features of iTunes, the service offering alongside the product offering.

Price

Promotion plays a key role in informing the customer of the **price** being charged for a product. The price of a product or service often conveys a perception of quality – customers are prepared to pay more for a product that they perceive is of higher quality than other products on the market. In this way, the price also creates an overall image of the company.

Key terms

Price: the amount of money a product or service can be bought for

Gary Lineker in a Walkers advert

? Did you know?

There are 55 different varieties of Walkers crisps, and new lines are added to the range on a regular basis.

Promotional activity often reflects the prices charged for the product. It is often the case that organisations that sell higher quality products and services spend a lot more on their promotion than those that sell products and services of lower quality.

Price will be affected by:

- Costs – The costs of producing the product or service are the most important factor that will influence the price of a product or service. For example, if the cost of car parts increased, the selling price of the car would also have increase to compensate for this.

- Competitors' prices – An organisation will research the prices competitors are charging for similar goods and base their prices around these, so that they are competitive.

There are many different pricing strategies a firm can use to set its prices, including:

- competitor pricing – basing your price on your competitors' prices

- cost-plus pricing – setting the price by adding a fixed amount or percentage onto the cost of the product

- penetration pricing – setting a very low price in order to gain sales (penetrating the market)

- predatory pricing – setting a very low price in order to eliminate competitors

- price discrimination – setting different prices for the same good, e.g. peak and off-peak prices for train tickets

- price skimming – setting a high price before other competitors come into the market

- psychological pricing – setting a price just below a large number to make it seem cheaper, e.g. £9.99 instead of £10.

When customers purchase an iPhone (the product) they also use a service (iTunes).

Place, packaging, people and processes in promotion

P2 Place

The **place** is the location from which a product or service can be bought. This does not necessarily have to be a physical location – it could be via the internet, for example, or through the red button on your TV, over the phone or via a catalogue. These forms of 'place' are known as 'direct selling'. This means firms do not sell through retailers, but direct to the customer. Promotion plays a key role in informing customers where they can purchase the product or service.

When products are sold by retailers (e.g. Asda selling Heinz baked beans), the firm has to rely heavily on the retailer to promote its products effectively. This may be through the promotions that you see at the end of the aisle in supermarkets, or sales promotions that they offer, for example, 'Buy one get one free'. Retailers are able to offer such good sales promotions because they buy the products from wholesalers in bulk and then sell on individual products to customers, hence making a profit.

When retailers (e.g. supermarkets) are used to sell products, they are known as intermediaries. A firm such as Heinz must decide whether to use a push strategy, a pull strategy or a mix of the two when selling its products to intermediaries. A push strategy would be Heinz encouraging the supermarket (or intermediary/retailer) to buy its products, which it will then promote and sell to the end consumer. A pull strategy is Heinz encouraging consumers directly to buy its products, so that the supermarket (or intermediary/retailer) has to buy them to meet the demand from consumers.

Packaging

The **packaging** of products plays a vital role in the product element of the marketing mix. It promotes the product through its appearance and the messages it conveys to customers of quality.

The role of packaging is to establish a noticeable difference between products. It shows the distinctiveness of a product, which is important because there are so many competing products that organisations have to ensure that their products stand out from their competitors'. Walkers, for example, uses different-sized packaging (e.g. multipacks, 34.5g bags, Big Eat and share size) to

Your assessment criteria:

P2 Explain the role of promotion within the marketing mix for a selected product/service

Key terms

Packaging: *the materials in which the goods are presented to the customer*

Place: *the location from which goods and services can be bought*

Walkers have lots of different packaging to distinguish them from their competitors.

distinguish its products from the competition. Packaging can also play a role in revitalising a product without changing the product itself. For example, Walkers brought in foil packaging before its competitors. This benefited the customers as the functionality of the packaging meant that the product was fresher for longer.

People

The **people** who sell a service are largely responsible for its promotion. They are often seen to be the ambassadors for the service and are there to build relationships with the customers to encourage them to buy. The people selling the service must be trained to effectively promote the service and communicate up-to-date information to customers. Training and development is important in order that all sales people are giving customers the same information, so there is a consistency of image. If this is not the case, and customers receive different information from different members of staff, it can lead to confusion and frustration and ultimately to lack of sales.

Processes

The **processes** are the systems that are in place to assist an organisation in delivering a service. For example, banks send out credit cards automatically when their customers' old ones have expired. In order for this to happen, efficient processes have to be in place so that the expiry dates of credit cards are identified. This fosters customer loyalty and confidence in the company, which means customers are happy, and it creates and maintains a positive image.

 Case study

Burger King has launched its first UK Dessert Bar in Westfield shopping centre in London. It will only sell desserts.

The move comes as Burger King looks to offset flagging sales by diversifying its portfolio away from its core burger franchises.

1. Explain how diversifying into Dessert Bars will help Burger King to promote itself.

2. What role will the 'place' and 'people' have in helping Buger King to promote itself?

 Describe

Select five different products that you buy on a regular basis. Look at their packaging and describe:

- *what the packaging looks like*

- *how the packaging helps to promote the product.*

 Did you know?

The biggest difference between a top-performing sales person and a poor performer is listening skills.

 Key terms

People: *(only for services) the staff that have been employed in order to sell the service; these are seen as an essential part of the service offering*

Processes: *(only for services) the systems used to assist the organisation to deliver the service*

 Reflect

Next time you visit a shop, make a note of how the people and the processes help to promote the products.

Physical evidence and promotional objectives

P2 Physical evidence

Physical evidence allows the customer to make judgments about an organisation. If you walk into a restaurant and your expectations are met of a clean, friendly environment you will make perceptions based on your sight of the service. This promotes the service before the customer has actually experienced it. The colours, sounds, images and lighting are factors in creating the right ambience (i.e. types of physical evidence) for the customers and therefore promoting the service. The people delivering the service have also got to ensure that their tone of voice, language and appearance are appropriate for the service they are promoting.

🔑 Key terms

Physical evidence: *(only for services) the element of the services marketing mix that allows the customer to make a judgement on the service being delivered*

💬 Discuss

In groups, discuss any experiences you may have had (positive and negative) of:

- *sales staff (people)*
- *processes*
- *physical evidence in shops.*

What made them positive or negative experiences? How did they help to promote the organisation and products/services?

❓ Did you know?

Dissatisfied customers tell an average of ten other people about their bad experience; 12 per cent of customers will tell up to 20 people. Satisfied customers tell an average of five people about their positive experience. Bad news really does spread fast!

Apple Stores have sales staff especially trained to help with all your needs.

Promotional objectives

Organisations set **promotional objectives** to be met. These are the goals and targets that the promotion has to achieve, and they are usually related to the number of sales the company has experienced since starting a promotional campaign.

For a promotional campaign to work it must support the overall aims and vision/mission of the business. It is therefore important that the marketing department not only has departmental objectives, but also has objectives for what the promotional campaign must achieve for the organisation as a whole. Figure 9.3 shows how an organisation translates its promotional objectives from its corporate mission statement.

Figure 9.3 The meanings of the different levels of objectives within an organisation

Level	What does it mean?
Corporate mission statement	This is the overall vision of the company
Business aims and objectives	What has to be achieved to deliver the vision
Marketing objectives	The role the marketing department plays in contributing to the business aims and objectives
Promotional objectives	The promotional tactics that the marketing department will use

Examples of promotional objectives include:

- Raising awareness of product/service – The promotional activity should raises awareness of the product or the organisation in the minds of the consumers.

- Creating distinctive market presence – The promotional activity should help the product or organisation stand out in the minds of the consumers.

- Increasing market share – The promotional activity should help the organisation to capture a greater market share of the market. This means that sales and, thus, profits need to rise.

The promotional objectives must outline the target audience. These are the people or businesses the promotional campaign is aimed at and who are most likely to respond to the messages the promotional activity is conveying. The organisation must research the attitudes, interests, opinions, aspirations and demographics (such as age and gender) of the target audience and why they buy certain products, so it can tailor its product and promotional activity to customers' needs.

Branding

P2 The power of brands

Branding can be a significant promotional tool in itself. Strong brands identify one product from competing products that are very similar. Brands give organisations a separate identity and the promotion should convey the personality and values of the brand. In 2010, the world's most valued brand was Google Inc. for the fourth year running. Its brand value is estimated at $114 billion!

It has been especially important during the recent recession for organisations to invest heavily in their brands and promotional activity, as they want to retain their loyal customers. An organisation's brand value can, however, decrease if its products do not come up to scratch. In 2010, a number of Toyota cars were recalled due to mechanical faults, which resulted in the brand value dropping.

Equally important is the personality the brand conveys – the way it speaks and behaves to its customers in the organisation's promotional activity. The characteristics of the brand are communicated through all of the elements of the marketing mix, whether it be the people representing it or through the promotion and packaging. For example, the Diesel clothing brand demonstrates its personality by making the individual who wears it stand apart from the crowd. The promotional activity should express the personality traits of the target audience. For instance, Dove promotes its brand as honest, feminist and optimistic. By promoting the brand's personality the promotion ensures that the brand is unique and long lasting.

There are many benefits to the organisation of having a strong and valuable brand. These include:

- Being able to charge premium prices – Consumers will be more willing to pay more for Heinz baked beans than Asda's Smart Price baked beans. This is because the brand communicates quality and has a loyal customer base.

- Differentiating one organisation from another is key in markets where the products are similar.

- Promoting other products that the organisation sells – For example, if you like to use Dove soap, you may be more inclined to buy Dove deodorant and shower gel, as you trust the brand.

An organisation benefits from a strong brand when launching new products or trying to enter new markets. This is known as brand extension.

Your assessment criteria:

 P2 Explain the role of promotion within the marketing mix for a selected product/service

Key terms

Branding: this can be in the form of a name or symbol, for example, that helps to identify products or services from the competition

? Did you know?

When the brand Google was created in 1996 it was originally named 'Backrub'!

 Discuss

Why do you think we pay more for branded goods than non-branded goods?

Virgin is a good example of how brand extension can be applied to very different markets. You may not realise just how many different markets the Virgin brand extends to: aeroplanes, holidays, cruises, media, experience days, megastores, radio, mobile phones and drinks, to name a few!

Discuss

In groups, discuss why you think these brands have achieved such massive brand values. Make sure you mention the following in your discussions: products, prices, places, promotion, people, processes, physical evidence, objectives and branding.

Virgin's brand extensions

 Case study

In December 2010, Unilever bought the Radox and Brylcream brands for € 1.2 billion. Unilever wants to expand its home and personal care categories and plans to acquire a number of leading brands to fill the gaps in its portfolio.

1. How does acquiring these brands help Unilever to promote itself?

2. Why is it important to Unilever to increase its brand portfolio?

? | Did you know?

Richard Branson, the owner of the Virgin Group, has more than 200 entertainment, media and travel companies around the world. He has also registered the business name Virgin Interplanetary in case space travel becomes commercially viable!

The role of advertising agencies

Since the majority of organisations regard promotion as an important factor in their success, a large part of their budgets go on creating their promotional campaigns. For this reason, many organisations choose not to create the promotional campaigns themselves but to outsource them to specialist companies called advertising agencies.

Your assessment criteria:

P3 Explain the role of advertising agencies in the development of a successful promotional campaign

P3 What advertising agencies do

An **advertising agency** is an organisation that specialises in creating new ideas and designs for promotional campaigns. Agencies also book advertisement time and space, plan advertising campaigns and provide help and advice a client may need when it wants to enter and succeed in a chosen market.

There are many different services that advertising agencies offer to organisations who want them to produce their promotional campaigns. These include:

- Media planning – The agency chooses and arranges the communication channels which will be used for the promotional campaign to best meet the target audience's needs in the most cost-effective manner (i.e. deciding where adverts should be shown and then buying the media time on TV or space in magazines or on billboards).

- Advertisement design – The creative department creates promotional ideas through copywriting (the words in an advert), typography (type styles and layout) and graphic designs.

- Production – It produces the advertisement or TV commercial.

Advertising agencies advise on the costs options of all of the services they offer. Organisations may choose to carry out some of the work themselves and outsource only certain things to the advertising agency, to save money.

However, whether the promotional campaign is done by an advertising agency or **in house** by the organisation, all of the elements of the promotional campaign are co-ordinated and therefore consistent in their approach, so that the promotion is effective.

🔑 Key terms

Advertising agency: an organisation that specialises in creating new ideas and designs for promotional campaigns on behalf of other businesses

In house: within a company, e.g. producing a promotional campaign without using an advertising agency

🔍 Research

In pairs, think of some recent promotional campaigns that you have seen. Research which advertising agency created the campaign.

❓ Did you know?

George Reynell, an officer at the London Gazette, set up what is believed to be the first advertising agency in London in 1812.

🗂 Design

Create your own advert for a product of your choice. Explain why you chose each element of the advert and what you are trying to convey to customers.

Advertising agencies create new ideas and designs for promotional campaigns.

 ## Case study

The Government Cabinet Office's Efficiency Reform Group approved a second set of FAST stroke TV campaigns in December 2010 to run in March 2011. This was in response to the success of the first FAST stroke campaign that was commissioned in December 2008. Simon Burns (the Health Minister) said: 'The campaign successfully achieved a rapid change in behaviour – within a year, an estimated 9,864 more people reached hospital faster, 642 of whom were saved from death or serious disability... the evidence demonstrated that the campaign achieved a payback of £3.16 for every £1 spent!'

(Source: *Marketing*, 6 December 2010)

1. Why were the FAST stroke campaigns a success?

2. What role did advertising agencies have in ensuring the success of this campaign, do you think?

Types of media, selection and the internet

P4 Media

Media are the different ways that promotional messages are communicated to customers. The media planning department must decide on the types of media it wants to use. This will depend on the product, organisation and promotional objectives. Different types of media include:

- local – media shown in a certain area, e.g. a town. This could include an advert for a local radio station or newspaper, for example

- regional – media shown in a larger area, e.g. a county. This could include regional TV adverts, for example

- national – media shown across the whole country, e.g. a magazine advert

- international – media shown across many countries, e.g. adverts on the internet

- terrestrial – media only shown through an analogue aerial

- satellite – media shown through a satellite dish

- digital – media shown through a digital aerial

- internet – media shown on the internet

- specialist media – magazines and journals that specialise in a specific subject, e.g. *Play* is a specialist magazine for digital game players

Criteria for media selection

The media planning department has to consider various different factors when choosing the different types of media for a promotional campaign.

The first consideration is cost. The media planning department must balance the cost of the promotional campaign with the proportion of the target audience it is expected to reach. There is little point spending thousands on a promotional campaign if none of the target audience will see it. Honda reportedly spent $6.12 million on an advert for their new Honda Accord!

The second consideration is how best to achieve the promotional objectives. In order to meet the promotional objectives, the media planning team needs to have a clear idea of the target audience, and the type of media which is best at communicating the key messages

Key terms

Media: *all of the different ways that promotional messages are communicated to customers, including TV, magazines, radio, billboards and the internet*

? Did you know?

The average person in America spends 52 minutes a day reading a newspaper. Over 70 years, a typical person will spend a little less than 2 years reading a newspaper.

Q Research

Research how much the following companies spent in the last year on advertising their products:

- *Mercedes*

- *HMV*

- *JD Sports.*

to that audience. It may be the case that a black and white advert in a newspaper for donations for a charity will not evoke enough emotion compared with a TV advert.

The third consideration is the timing, circulation and readership of the form of media that is going to be used. For example, the media planning team would have to consider where the magazine is circulated and how many people read it before deciding on its appropriateness for the promotional campaign.

The role of the internet

The internet has been available to use in homes across the country for the last 15 years. However, it has had a massive impact on the way companies chose to promote themselves. First, it has removed the 'middle men', so organisations can promote themselves on their own websites. This is known as disintermediation. It has also enabled organisations to market their products and services directly to customers, making one-to-one communication between customers and companies easier. For example, if you have a problem with a product, you can contact the manufacturer directly via email rather than visiting the shop where you purchased it from. The development of mobile phones has also meant that the internet is available in the palms of most people's hands, making one-to-one communication by advertisers all the more easy.

The internet has had a massive impact on the way companies choose to promote themselves.

 Did you know?

Google Inc. generates profits from the advertising that is bought on its free-to-user email, online mapping, office productivity, social networking and video sharing services.

Discuss

In your pairs, discuss the following points about the research you did above:

- *why you both think it has been such a successful promotional campaign*

- *the role that the advertising agency played in creating the promotional campaign*

- *why the media that it used were chosen.*

 Discuss

Why do companies feel the need to advertise online?

The role of advertising agencies

Some companies decide to use advertising agencies when they want to create a new promotional campaign and others decide to create the promotional campaign in house. This means that the marketing department creates the promotional campaign without using specialists.

Some of the advantages and disadvantages of using advertising agencies over in-house are outlined in Figure 9.4.

Figure 9.4 The advantages and disadvantages of using advertising agencies for a promotional campaign vs. creating it in house

Advantages of using an advertising agency	Disadvantages of using an advertising agency	Advantages of creating it in house	Disadvantages of creating it in house
• The people who work in advertising agencies are professionals.	• Advertising agencies cost a lot of money, so only large companies with lots of money to spend on promotion will be able to afford them. Even a small advertising agency may charge £500 a day.	• It is cheaper to keep the work in house.	• An organisation needs a lot of resources to develop and implement a promotional campaign.
• In an advertising agency all of the elements of the promotional activity are coordinated, ensuring a consistent approach and therefore more effective promotion.	• A business may think that the market in which it operates is too complex for an agency to understand.	• Often, employees have targets to meet for their job to be secure and so they may be more concerned with achieving the right result for the campaign.	• If an in-house promotional campaign does not meet its objectives because of the inexperience of the in-house team it will be difficult to dismiss all of the staff.
• By employing an advertising agency, the organisation does not need any resources in house.	• Advertising agencies have lots of clients and therefore conflicting demands are likely to be made.	• A company working on an innovative product may want to limit the number of people who are aware of the product.	• The in-house team may find it difficult to keep generating creative ideas.

? Did you know?

Ancient Greeks and Romans used to advertise for their lost and found items on papyrus.

💬 Discuss

For the promotional campaign that you chose in the previous research activity, discuss the advantages and disadvantages of using an advertising agency.

There are several advantages to firms using advertising agencies.

 ## Case study

Simon Seeks, a travel reviews website, spent £2 million in December 2010 on a national TV campaign to earn customers' trust and promote itself to more customers. The campaign has been created by Space City Productions and the media has been handled by Mediacom North.

1. What are the advantages to Simon Seeks of using an advertising agency and a media agency?

2. What are the disadvantages to Simon Seeks of using an advertising agency and a media agency?

Promotional campaigns

When a promotional campaign is created it has to meet certain criteria. These include the promotional objectives, identifying the target market, identifying the promotional message, establishing the promotional budget and costs, choosing the promotional and media mix, etc.

P5 Campaign/creative brief

When a company wants to create a promotional campaign it will either use an advertising agency or create it in house. Whichever it chooses, it must set out clear guidelines on how the campaign should be developed. This should be done through a campaign/creative brief, which will include the following information:

- background to the proposed campaign, comments about the target market, explanation for the need for the promotional activity, how the promotional campaign is expected to contribute to the overall aims of the organisation

- objectives of the promotional campaign, i.e. what it is expected to achieve

- the target market that the promotional campaign is aimed at, i.e. age, gender, ethnicity, where they live, their jobs and other lifestyle factors

- customer benefits of the product and details of possible competitors

- description of the product details, its USP and how it is to be launched onto the market

- explanation of the budget for the promotional campaign

- timescale of the promotional campaign, i.e. how long is it going to last, the implications of this to the campaign.

Selection of content

A campaign/creative brief should carefully consider the content of the promotional campaign, i.e. what is going to be communicated to potential customers. This includes:

- features of the product or service

- performance of the product or service

- benefits to the customer of the product or service

🔑 Key terms

Campaign/creative brief: outlines the objectives of the promotional campaign and all of the possible ideas and plans that will need to be investigated in order to meet the objectives

? Did you know?

Wall painting promotions date back to 4000 BC.

Design

For a product of your choice, create your own campaign brief.

- quality of the product or service

- reliability of the product or service.

Campaign tactics

The campaign tactics need to be considered before producing the promotional plan. They should include:

- How is the campaign going to reach its target audience? This should include a description of the target audience.

- What media are going to be selected and why?

- What is the design of the promotional materials/images going to look like and why?

- What is the text going to look like?

- What are the objectives of the campaign?

- What is the budget for the campaign?

- What images are going to be used and why? (colour, impact of the images, style, if a TV advert the pace of the images)

- What other sensory dimensions will be included, e.g. sound, touch, etc?

- Will focus groups be used in order to research the campaign?

- Creation of storyboards, so that the stages of the campaign can be planned effectively. This may include a mock-up of the campaign (especially if a TV/radio advert), final proof, review, planning of the next stage of the promotional campaign.

It often takes several meeting with clients to decide on campaign tactics.

Creating your own promotional campaign

P5 The promotional plan

A **promotional plan** considers a number of factors for a promotional campaign. When producing a promotional plan it should follow a specific layout and content.

Steps in developing a promotional plan

1. Outline the objectives (from the campaign/creative brief) – The objectives must be clear and SMART and expressed as a numerical target with a time limit, e.g. raise brand awareness by 10 per cent by September. Without this information the eventual success of the promotional campaign could not be established.

2. Identify the target audience (from the campaign/creative brief) – Explain who is meant to 'hear' the promotional message. Customers can often be grouped together because they have something in common which makes them similar, e.g. women at work who have families – products that appeal to them would include anything that would save time.

3. Detail the promotional message – The promotional message will be created from the promotional objectives. By understanding what the campaign has got to achieve, you can create a message for the customers.

4. Determine the promotional budget – Before looking into the promotional mix for the campaign, it is important to establish how much money you have to spend and therefore what you can afford. You will need to calculate the costs of all elements of the promotional campaign.

5. Choose the promotion and media mix.

   a. What mix of promotion you are going to choose and why? You will need to decide on a mix of advertising, personal selling, sales promotions, publicity, public relations, etc. You will need to decide which best meets the needs of your target audience within the budget constraints.

   b. What mix of media are you going to choose? You will need to consider local, regional, national and international; and also the types of media, e.g. internet, terrestrial or satellite TV, radio, which magazines/newspapers. Why? Often the type of media you choose to use will depend on what you need to tell your customers. If there is a lot of detailed information, you may consider a print advertisement in a newspaper so the customer can get all of the necessary information.

Your assessment criteria:

P5 Design a promotional campaign for a given product/service to meet the needs of a given campaign/creative brief

 Key terms

Promotional plan: *a plan that considers a number of factors, such as choosing the promotional mix, timing and frequency, costs, mix of media and possible use of the internet*

 Design

Create a promotional plan for opening a new coffee bar. You have £10,000 to spend on promotion and the coffee bar will open in 3 months' time.

c. You will need to consider use of the internet. This may be in the form of banner advertising, website development, use of the internet for feedback from customers, etc.

6. Integration into the marketing mix – How does the promotional mix fit into the other elements of the promotional mix? How does the promotion best reflect the product, price and place?

7. Frequency and timing of the promotion.

a. A promotional campaign should not be seen as a one-off burst of promotional activity. It should be viewed as a long-term investment in the product and should last as long as the product.

b. When the product has been launched, the promotion should be in short bursts, but in the long term the promotion will have to be repeated so that all customers get the messages – they may have missed it first time around!

c. You will need to consider which elements of the promotional mix will be done at the same time, e.g. sales promotions may be used at the same time as a TV/radio advert. Advertising would raise awareness and the sales promotions would cement a sale.

d. The time of year the promotional campaign in launched is also important. Customers need to be in the right frame of mind to buy.

8. Evaluation of the promotional plan – This needs to be completed once the promotional campaign has finished. A campaign is only successful if it has achieved its objectives. Objectives can usually be measured by the number of sales or increase in profits the company has achieved. Evaluation is necessary so that the campaign can be improved in the future. An evaluation includes:

a. strengths and weaknesses of the campaign

b. how effective the campaign was in meeting its aims and objectives. How could it have been more effective?

Did you know?

In the Middle Ages most people could not read, so shopkeepers began using signs with simple images to advertise their businesses.

Discuss

Choose a promotion that has caught your attention recently. For the promotion you have chosen:

- *Discuss all of the elements that would have had to be considered in creating the promotional plan.*

- *Decide what you think the objectives would have been, its target audience and how much you think it cost.*

- *What other elements of the promotional and media mix were used?*

Promotional plans are necessary for effective promotional campaigns.

Existing marketing campaigns

M3 Providing a rationale

In order to achieve M3, a **rationale** must be provided as to why a promotional campaign has been produced. This means explaining why the company thought it was necessary to produce a promotional campaign. A promotional campaign must be chosen and then the following points about is should be discussed:

- Why was the promotional campaign necessary?

- What are the promotional objectives of the campaign?

- Why is the promotional campaign expected to achieve the promotional objectives?

- It may be a good idea for you to choose a promotional campaign that you know well and like. Ensure that you find lots of information about the campaign, including which advertising agency produced it, the cost of the campaign and the expected increase in sales from the campaign.

Alesha Dixon, the new face of Bacardi's promotional campaign

Your assessment criteria:

M3 Provide a rationale for a promotional campaign

D2 Evaluate an existing national marketing campaign

Key terms

Rationale: the fundamental reasons why a promotional campaign has been produced

Research

Research Bacardi's recent promotional campaign for their winter cocktails, featuring Alesha Dixon.

- *Why do you think this promotional campaign was necessary?*

- *What were the campaign's objectives?*

- *Do you think it achieved its objectives?*

D2 Evaluating an existing marketing campaign

In order to **evaluate** an existing marketing campaign, the following steps need to be taken:

• Choose an existing national marketing campaign.

• Research and describe the objectives of the campaign.

• Describe how the marketing campaign has achieved its objectives. Why?

• Describe any aspects of the campaign that you believe have not met the objectives. Why?

• Suggest any recommendations that could be made to improve the promotional campaign.

• It is important to back up any recommendations and research with quotes from valid sources. Make sure you make notes of the sources as you go along.

Key terms

Evaluate: describe what is good and what it not so good, along with evidence and research and making recommendations for improvement

Discuss

In groups, decide on an existing national marketing campaign that you are all familiar with. Discuss what you believe are the objectives of the campaign, whether you think they have been achieved and how it could be improved.

Facebook only started making a profit in 2009. Enormous expenses and growing databases pushed Facebook investors to reinvent their advertising market.

Assessment checklist

To achieve a pass grade, my portfolio of evidence must show that I can:

Assessment criteria	Description	✓
P1	Describe the promotional mix used by two selected organisations for a selected product/service	☐
P2	Explain the role of promotion within the marketing mix for a selected product/service	☐
P3	Explain the role of advertising agencies in the development of a successful promotional campaign	☐
P4	Explain the reasons behind the choice of media in a successful promotional campaign	☐
P5	Design a promotional campaign for a given product/ service to meet the needs of a given campaign/creative brief	☐

To achieve a merit grade, my portfolio of evidence must show that I can:

Assessment criteria	Description	✓
M1	Explain how promotion is integrated with the rest of the marketing mix in a selected organisation to achieve its marketing aims and objectives	☐
M2	Explain the advantages and disadvantages of using professional agencies in ensuring promotional success	☐
M3	Provide a rationale for a promotional campaign	☐

To achieve a distinction grade, my portfolio of evidence must show that I can:

Assessment criteria	Description	✓
D1	Evaluate and justify the use of an appropriate promotional mix in relation to marketing objectives for the selected organisation	☐
D2	Evaluate an existing, national marketing campaign	☐

10 | Market research in business

LO1 Understand the main types of market research used to make marketing decisions

- ▸ What is primary research?
- ▸ What is secondary research?
- ▸ Qualitative or quantitative?
- ▸ What is the strategy?

LO2 Be able to plan research

- ▸ Stages for researching
- ▸ What's the objective?

LO3 Be able to carry out research

- ▸ Census vs. sample
- ▸ What is a questionnaire?
- ▸ What is a survey?
- ▸ What is the difference?

LO4 Be able to interpret research findings

- ▸ Stats, stats and more stats
- ▸ Presentations and diagrams
- ▸ What are your limitations?

Primary research

All businesses need to undertake market research in order to find out about their customers, their competitors and the market. There are two types of market research: primary and secondary. Primary research is carried out first hand by an organisation when it wants to find out something specific. Primary research can be costly and time consuming. Secondary research has already been carried out by somebody else for another reason and the information is in the public domain.

P1 Observation

Observation is carried out simply by watching customer behaviour. There is no interaction between the researcher and the customer – no questions are asked and therefore the researcher cannot understand why a customer is behaving in a certain way. For this reason, observation is usually carried out alongside other types of primary research. Observation has one major benefit in that the behaviour that the researcher is observing is not in any way distorted as the researcher is not influencing the customer and actual behaviour is being recorded.

The most common type of observation is carried out by mystery shoppers, who go into organisations such as restaurants, cinemas and shops, and pretend to be a customer, while observing the service, the layout, etc. They then write a report on what they have observed and this is given to the organisation.

Figure 10.1: Observation as a method of primary research

Fitness for purpose	Used when customer behaviour is to be analysed and can be used to give quantitative data
Cost	Inexpensive once cameras, etc. are installed
Accuracy	Accurate as respondents are not influenced by the researcher
Time	Replaying tapes to analyse behaviour can be a time-consuming exercise
Validity	Valid as respondents are not influenced by the researcher. However, the researcher's interpretation could be inaccurate
Response rate	Excellent as respondents may not even know they are participating

Key terms

Observation: a method of primary research that involves watching customer behaviour

? Did you know?

Toy companies use observation as a primary research method. They observe which toys the children play with the most.

Experimentation

Experimentation is used to gain information on certain products and customer behaviour. An experiment usually involves the organisation creating a situation in which the researcher can change certain elements while keeping other things the same and then measure the effects. For example, when United Fruits was considering replacing its Gros Michel variety of banana with the Valery variety, a simple experiment was first carried out to see if customers were aware of the difference. In selected retail outlets, the two varieties were switched on different days of the week and sales data was then examined to determine what effect the variety had on sales. In this case, the variety of banana was being changed while keeping everything else the same. The results were that switching the bananas had no effect on sales and United Fruit was therefore able to replace Gros Michel bananas with Valery bananas.

Key terms

Experimentation: a method of primary research that involves trying out tests to gain information on products and customer behaviour

Research

Do some research to find out which other companies have used experimentation to gain primary data about their products/services.

Figure 10.2: Experimentation as a method of primary research

Fitness for purpose	Used for information on products and customer behaviour and provides quantitative data
Cost	Expensive – needs careful planning and monitoring
Accuracy	May be difficult to identify what factors are affecting customer behaviour
Time	Can be time-consuming as experiment may not provide results quickly
Validity	Validity maybe compromised if respondents know they are being watched and therefore change their behaviour
Response rate	Good as respondents may not even know they are participating. However, if they are aware, response rate can decline as it may be difficult to recruit and keep them over a period of time

Surveys

Surveys are carried out with chosen individuals who are asked questions about their behaviour. The individuals chosen are referred to as respondents. Surveys may be carried out in a number of different ways:

- Face-to-face – The researcher and the respondent speak face to face. These surveys are very expensive to carry out and people are usually unwilling to co-operate. One of the drawbacks is the possibility of the researcher picking a certain type of respondent, which will mean that the results are biased. The advantages include the possibility of using products in the surveys and the ability to encourage respondents to expand their answers. There is also little time wasted when interviewing respondents face to face.

Key terms

Respondent: the individual chosen to answer survey questions

Survey: a questionnaire that is completed by respondents either by post, over the telephone, face to face or via email

- By post – The surveys are posted to respondents, who answer the questions on the survey and post it back to the organisation. A prize or present is usually offered for completion of the survey. The advantage of postal surveys is their low cost; however, this is counter-balanced by the low response rate.

- By email – The surveys are sent to respondents via email. These are fast and cheap, but the response rates are low as respondents are very wary of completing surveys online due to fear of receiving spam mail and lack of confidentiality.

- By telephone – The researcher asks respondents survey questions over the telephone. These are best used for a national survey. The questions are usually short and therefore the surveys are short and cheap and the answers can be immediately analysed. However, they tend to have low response rates, customers' phone numbers can change and customers are wary of being sold products under the guise of a survey.

Figure 10.3: Surveys as a method of primary research

Fitness for purpose	Can be used to collect data from certain respondents and for consumer research; provides qualitative and quantitative data
Cost	Inexpensive but face to face can be expensive
Accuracy	Have elements of inaccuracy as in face-to-face surveys respondents can be chosen which makes the results biased and respondents can be influenced by the researcher
Time	Can take a long time to complete face-to-face surveys and to get postal returns
Validity	Validity can be compromised as respondents can be influenced by the researcher or may not understand the questions
Response rate	Fairly low, especially for postal surveys

E-marketing research

E-marketing research usually comes in the form of web surveys. There are two types of web survey: standard surveys (which are electronic but look similar to paper surveys) and interactive surveys. The questions on interactive surveys appear on the screen one at a time and depend on the respondent's answer to the previous question. E-marketing research is carried out to gain feedback on web services and web usage.

Figure 10.4: E-marketing research as a method of primary research

Fitness for purpose	Can be used for feedback on web services and usage
Cost	Inexpensive
Accuracy	Accurate as respondents are not influenced by the researcher
Time	Quick
Validity	Valid as respondents are not influenced by the researcher
Response rate	Fairly low

Focus groups

Focus groups are selected groups of (usually between eight and ten) people who are used for in-depth interviews and discussions. The aim of using a focus group is to discover the respondents' detailed opinions and attitudes about products, concepts, organisations, competitors, advertising, etc. Respondents are encouraged to discuss all ideas in depth with each other.

Key terms

Focus group: a selected group of people used for in-depth interviews and discussions

Design

Design a survey gathering data on the use of the school/college canteen.

Figure 10.5: Focus groups as a method of primary research

Fitness for purpose	Can be used for in-depth discussions on products, organisations, competitors advertising, etc.; provides qualitative data
Cost	Expensive as the focus groups may need to meet several times to get consistent views
Accuracy	Can be slightly inaccurate as respondents can be influenced by other respondents
Time	Can be time consuming to recruit people and analyse results
Validity	Validity can be compromised as respondents can be influenced by other respondents; however, a moderator can ensure all points are covered in detail
Response rate	Excellent as people tend to talk freely

P1 Panels

A **panel** is a group of respondents who provide information over a period of time. Respondents may be asked to complete surveys or a diary or may be interviewed. Panels provide information on changes in households, organisations, products and individuals over time. Panels may be used to identify changes in the market (e.g. whether customers are buying more fruit and vegetables over time), consumer attitudes to a product (e.g. whether customers like the new packaging) or customer behaviour (e.g. whether customers have bought more products since the new advertising campaign).

There are, however, many issues to be considered before using panel research:

- It is very difficult to get a broad range of people to complete the panels as usually only people who are interested in the products take part.

- It is difficult to retain respondents for the entire time that the panel is used.

- For consistency, when people no longer want to take part they must be replaced with similar people.

- Panellists may complete the diaries, etc. incorrectly.

Figure 10.6: Panels as a method of primary research

Fitness for purpose	Can be used to monitor consumer behaviour over time
Cost	Inexpensive
Accuracy	Accurate as respondents are not influenced by the researcher but respondents need to be trusted to complete the surveys correctly
Time	Can be time consuming
Validity	Validity can be compromised if respondents do not complete the surveys properly
Response rate	Fairly low

Your assessment criteria:

 P1 Describe types of market research

 Key terms

Panel: a group of respondents who provide information over a period of time

Field trials

A **field trial** involves testing a product over a period of time. For example, if Sony were to bring out a new television, the company might want to test it over a period of time to ensure that customers are able to use it and that the product meets the intended specification. Respondents give feedback on the strengths and the weaknesses of the product. Field trials are expensive to organise and respondents often drop out of the trial because they are unhappy or have lost interest in the product.

Figure 10.7: Field trials as a method of primary research

Fitness for purpose	Can be used for feedback on certain products; provides qualitative and quantitative data
Cost	Expensive to recruit respondents and train them
Accuracy	Accuracy may be compromised as respondents may change their behaviour because they know it is being analysed
Time	Can be time consuming
Validity	Validity can be compromised if respondents are unhappy with the product or poor records are kept; otherwise excellent
Response rate	Good to poor as respondents can get bored

Piloting

Piloting involves giving a questionnaire to certain respondents in order to identify and correct design flaws in a product. Usually only a few people complete a pilot, so it is important that these respondents reflect the needs of the whole group.

Figure 10.8: Piloting as a method of primary research

Fitness for purpose	Can be used for identifying and correcting design flaws
Cost	Inexpensive
Accuracy	Accuracy can be compromised if only a few people complete the pilot
Time	Can be time consuming
Validity	Validity is compromised if only a small sample of respondents complete the pilot
Response rate	Good to poor

Key terms

Field trial: the testing of a product over a period of time

Piloting: the giving of a questionnaire to certain respondents in order to identify and correct design flaws in products

 Reflect

Reflect on the relative merits and drawbacks of each type of primary research method.

Secondary research

Secondary research is research that has already been carried out by another organisation for a different project. Secondary research can be useful for identifying market trends and for understanding the bigger picture in relation to any primary research. It can be used to compare research in order to check its validity and can provide data that an organisation is unable to collect itself.

Your assessment criteria:

P1 Describe types of market research

P1 Internal sources of secondary research

Internal sources of information are held by the organisation that carried out the research. There are various types of internal research.

- Data records – organisations hold data records that contain market research information such as where customers are located geographically, what products are purchased, when they were bought and how much was spent. These data records enable organisations to send promotional material to customers and informs decisions about opening branches in new areas, which products to buy more of, which products to put on sales promotions and amending discount schemes according to peaks in demand.

- Loyalty schemes – These record details of all card-holders' purchases, how often they visit stores, which stores they visit, how often they buy certain products and whether advertising influences when they buy certain products. Examples include Sainsbury's Nectar card and Boots' Advantage card.

- EPOS (Electronic Point of Sale) – These are usually used in retail in the form of a scanner that scans bar codes. They give the organisation information about payment, stock, products and prices. Organisations can collect information regarding store sales, product sales by region or sales of certain product categories. This can reveal changes in purchasing behaviour according to the store or the product.

- Website monitoring – This is used by e-commerce organisations. It monitors which web pages are used, which search engines are used to find the organisation's site and when websites are used. For example, when customers log on to a site such as www.amazon.co.uk, Amazon monitors not only what you buy but also the products that you look at. Therefore, compared to high street retailers, web traders have more insight into their customers as they know how many 'window shoppers' they have as well as how many customers.

Key terms

EPOS (Electronic Point of Sale): a computerised system for recording sales

Loyalty schemes: schemes to keep the business of existing customers, which provide the organisation with details about card holders

Research

Research companies' loyalty schemes.

- *What are the advantages to the company and the customers of loyalty schemes?*

- *What are the disadvantages to the company and the customers of loyalty schemes?*

- E-transactions – Web traders have a wealth of information about their customers, including their name, address, email address and often credit card details. High street retailers are not privy to this information. Web traders are able to recommend products to customers based on their past purchases. For example, Amazon recommends products to you and also reminds you of products you have looked at in the past.

- Accounting records – The accounts departments of an organisation has records of all purchases and customers. This information can be valuable for market research as it can help to build up a picture of the type of customer that the business attracts.

- Production information and sales figures – The products that an organisation produces and then sells are a good indication of what its customers want, although this information is not very specific to each customer.

- Sales personnel – The sales staff within an organisation are the people who get to know their customers the best as they are the ones who build relationships with the customers. Sales staff are therefore often the best source of information regarding an organisation's customers, competitors' promotional activities, competitors' pricing, the after-sales service offered by similar organisations and market trends that customers are buying into.

 Discuss

In groups, discuss the sorts of market information you believe sales personnel would know that could be useful to the organisation. Compare your answers with another group.

Sales personnel are often a rich source of market information.

P1 Internal sources of secondary research continued

Delphi technique – this technique is used by large firms to gather information and views about the future. An independent person gathers together important people (usually directors) within an organisation and asks them independently for their views on the organisation's future according to their area of specialism. Any extreme views are discarded and the consensus view on the firm's future is communicated back to the directors.

A Delphi panel could be made up of:

- the marketing director who believes that the majority of the business's customers are under the age of 25

- the production director and research and development director who believe that new production techniques and technologies will change the way products are made and delivered

- the sales director who believes that more people are buying healthier foods.

These opinions would be used to make general future plans. Even if none of the opinions turned out to be correct, at least the firm would have considered all the possibilities.

External sources of secondary research

Secondary research is also available from outside the organisation. External sources of secondary research include:

- The internet – The internet has become one of the most widely used sources of external secondary information. Search engines such as www.google.com, www.ask.com and www.bing.com are used to find valuable sources of marketing information. However, researchers have to be wary of where the information has come from – it is important to look at the source of the website to ensure that the information on the site is valid.

- Government statistics – The government regularly commissions research which is then published by the Office of National Statistics (ONS) on www.statistics.gov.uk. Government reports include market research on population growth, employment statistics, social trends, expenditure, economic trends and regional trends.

 Key terms

Delphi technique: a technique used to gather a consensus of views on the future of an organisation

 Discuss

A census was carried out in March 2011 about all members of the UK population.

- *What are the advantages of the Office of National Statistics carrying out a census?*

- *What are the disadvantages of the Office of National Statistics carrying out a census?*

- Libraries – Libraries hold a wealth of information including company reports, newspapers, companies' financial information, databases, market research reports and reference books.

- Universities – Universities hold the same information as a local library but also have trade journals, which are industry specific and include articles written by academics based on research. Universities also publish their own research and often specialise in specific industries.

- Company reports – Companies have to produce financial reports about their organisation every year. These reports include important information about profits, sales, future growth and their management teams. This information has to be sent to Companies House (www.companieshouse.gov.uk) and is accessible to the public. It can be very useful for organisations to gain the company reports of their competitors in order to gauge what their future developments are. Company reports can also be accessed at www.ftannualreports.com.

- Specialist agencies – Specialist market research agencies, such as Mintel (www.mintel.com), Datastream (www.datastream.com) and Dun and Bradstreet (www.dnb.co.uk) produce reports on markets and products and then sell them to organisations that have an interest in those markets or products. They are very expensive because they are very detailed and relate to specific industries

- Trade journals – These can be found in university libraries. They provide a wealth of information about market and industry trends and developments, and new products and services. A list of the different trade magazines can be found online at Yahoo Directory at the following address:
http://dir.yahoo.com/Business_and_Economy/Business_to_Business/News_and_Media/Magazines/Trade_Magazines/

Key terms

Specialist agencies: market research companies that provide business information about other businesses

Trade journals: specialist magazines about a particular industry that include articles based on research

Research

Go to www.statistics.gov.uk and try to find reports about an industry that interests you.

External secondary research

Choosing a research method

P1 Making a decision

There are many sources of secondary market research, so it is important to select the one that is most relevant to your needs.

The main criterion for selecting a particular type of market research is its validity. You may come across research that answers your market research question exactly, but this does not mean that the research is accurate and reliable. When considering a piece of secondary research, ask the following questions:

- Has the research has been undertaken by a specialist in the field?

- Is the cost of acquiring the research affordable/reasonable?

- Has the research has been conducted in the recent past (not more than 5 years ago)?

- Is the research unbiased?

- Can the research be backed up by other sources?

If the answer to any of the above questions is 'no' then, generally speaking, the data should not be used and it may be wise to conduct your own primary research.

The use of ICT

Market research existed long before ICT was invented, but it took a lot longer to carry out, analyse and gain access to. Businesses can now access market research from many internal and external sources. Techniques such as EPOS mean that market information is available incredibly quickly and huge databases of information can be gathered and stored. The data can be easily analysed on spreadsheets so that trends and patterns can be identified quickly, accurately and efficiently.

Types of research

There are various different types of research.

- **Quantitative research** produces figures. For example, you might research the number of sales of a certain product within an industry, or how much the economy has grown as a percentage over a period of time. Both primary and secondary research can be quantitative.

Your assessment criteria:

P1 Describe types of market research

P2 Explain how different market research methods have been used to make a marketing decision within a selected situation or business

Key terms

Quantitative research: research that produces information in the form of figures

- **Qualitative research** provides data on emotions and opinions. For example, you might research why people buy certain products, their opinions on brands or their thoughts on advertising campaigns. Both primary and secondary research can be qualitative.

Key terms

Qualitative research: research that produces information about opinions and emotions

- Triangulation involves using different methods of market research to research the same thing. This increases the validity of the results by cross-checking the data.

- Strategic research is carried out in order to find out information that is needed to make big decisions within an organisation that may have long-term consequences.

- Technical research is used to find out the impact of decisions that have been made within an organisation. For example, if an organisation has just started selling online, technical research may be carried out to find the impact that this has had on sales.

Quantitative research provides figures.

- Databank research is the process of collecting and updating information that an organisation collects.

Discuss

In pairs, discuss the appropriateness of organisations using both quantitative and qualitative research.

- Continuous research is research that is carried out to produce continuous results and data. This is usually done so that trends and patterns can be analysed over time and so that organisations can spot small changes in the market before they become large changes. Therefore, the organisation can implement changes in their strategies before the changes occur on a large scale.

- Ad hoc research is research that is completed as a one off. It is usually carried out at short notice when the organisation has not seen the need to carry out research into the issue previously.

You may decide to research a small high street shop that has just started selling a new product range.

P2 ▸ Choosing an organisation

In order to complete P2, you will need to research an organisation that has recently made an important marketing decision, such as launching a new product or new sales promotions, changing its advertising strategy or starting to trade online. You need to study the market research that was done before this marketing decision was made. You must describe the qualitative and quantitative research that has been undertaken and explain how this helped the business to reach its decision.

Research

In pairs, research possible organisations that you could use to investigate the market research that has been undertaken in order to make a marketing decision.

Market research planning and objectives

P3 ▶ Making a plan

Your assessment criteria:

P3 Plan market research for a selected product/ service using appropriate methods of data collection

Before you start your market research, there are several stages that you must work through in order for your research to be effective, accurate and valid.

Stage 1 – Creating the research brief

This should outline why the research is needed, explain how the data will help important decisions to be made and ensure that the results of the research will be available ready for any important decisions that are to be made. A typical outline for a research brief is shown in Figure 10.9.

Figure 10.9: An outline research brief

Research brief
1. Background to the company (industry, market, products and services)
2. The research project (why it is being undertaken, what decisions will be influenced by the research)
3. Objectives (what information is required, what data will be qualitative and what will be quantitative)
4. Research methods (secondary research or primary or both, sampling methods and options)
5. Reporting and presentation (what type of report will be written, any meetings that may be needed during the course of the research)
6. Timing (timescales for research completion, the budget available to complete the research)

Stage 2 – Defining the issue and setting the objectives

It is very important for organisations to truly understand what research needs to be undertaken as it is an expensive mistake to undertake inappropriate research. Therefore the issue that is being researched has to be described and the reasons behind this issue need to be explored. Once the issue to be researched has been clarified, then the objectives need to be set. These objectives should be SMART (see Unit 3, page 109) and should outline exactly what the research is planning to discover.

Stage 3 – Planning the data to be collected

It is important to establish what research has already been carried out recently within the organisation as there is little point carrying out research that has already been undertaken. The organisation needs to decide what data is to be collected, how is it going to be collected, who is going to collect it and when it is to be collected.

Stage 4 – Forecasting

There are two different ways to plan and forecast the research project: a **Gantt chart** or **critical path analysis**. A Gantt chart is a diagram of how the project will be completed, as shown in Figure 10.10.

Figure 10.10: A Gantt chart

Task to be completed	Task start date	Task end date	Week 1	Week 2	Week 3	Week 4	Week 5	Week 6
Identify target audience	28/01/2011	04/02/2011						
Prepare questions for questionnaire	28/01/2011	11/02/2011						
Produce questionnaire	11/02/2011	18/02/2011						
Distribute questionnaire	18/02/2011	25/02/2011						
Analyse results	25/02/2011	11/03/2011						

Critical path analysis divides the research project into all possible parts, including different options, and predicts how long it will take to complete each part. It is then possible to choose the fastest way to complete the whole project.

Stage 5 – Collecting the data

Decisions need to be made as to how the data will be collected, who will collect it and how the results will be recorded and stored. It is also necessary to collect primary and secondary, internal and external and qualitative and quantitative data and to explain the reasons how the project will benefit from each of these. Details about the target population also need to be described, including all demographic information.

Key terms

Critical path analysis: *a way of planning and forecasting your market research by dividing the research into parts and calculating how long each part will take and then choosing the fastest methods to get to the desired outcome*

Gantt chart: *a table or flowchart that enables the timings of each element of a research project to be seen diagrammatically*

P3 ▶ Making a plan *continued*

Stage 6 – Analysing and evaluating the data

Analysis of quantitative data produces statistics so that trends and patterns can be seen. This type of data is usually entered into a spreadsheet so that tables and charts can be used to illustrate patterns and trends diagrammatically. Analysis of qualitative data on the other hand is usually done through looking at customers' comments (either verbal or written).

Stage 7 – Presenting the findings

The results of the research need to be presented, either in a written report or in a verbal presentation. The presentation needs to be accurate and detailed in order for the organisation to benefit from the research findings.

Stage 8 – Making recommendations

Recommendations need to be made about how the issues raised can be dealt with. These recommendations should be backed up by the research in both qualitative and quantitative formats.

Stage 9 – Re-evaluating the marketing activities

Once the findings have been presented and recommendations have been made, the research should enable the organisation to re-evaluate its marketing activity and make the necessary changes.

PESTLE analysis

Market research is often undertaken because an organisation wants to understand more about the external factors that are affecting its business. The acronym used to describe the external factors that can affect a business is PESTLE. Figure 10.11 shows the research that an organisation may undertake as part of a **PESTLE analysis**.

 Discuss

Discuss all of the steps that you need to undertake in order to complete your research project.

 Design

Design a Gantt chart to show how long each task is going to take.

 Key terms

PESTLE analysis: an analysis of the Political, Economic, Social, Technological, Legal and Environmental factors that can affect a business

Figure 10.11 Possible research content related to PESTLE

External factor	Possible research content
Political	What political decisions may affect the business in the long run? For example, adopting the Euro or changing import or export taxes
Economic	What decisions relating to the economy may affect the business? For example, changes to interest rates, inflation rates, VAT
Social	What trends have emerged meaning that more people are more or less likely to buy the business's products?
Technological	What new technology has evolved which could positively impact the business?
Legal	Have any laws been passed which could positively or negatively affect the business?
Environmental	Have customers' needs to live in a more environmentally friendly manner affected the business or what new product developments could come from this?

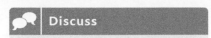

Discuss

In pairs, discuss the external factors that could affect the research project that you will undertake

The contents of the budget is an external factor that affects businesses.

M1 Research content and methods

A business's research objectives will affect what is researched (the research content) and how the research is carried out (the research methods).

Your assessment criteria:

M1 Explain, with examples, how different market research methods are appropriate to assist different marketing situations

Figure 10.12: Research objectives, research content and research methods

Research objectives	Research content	Possible research method
Customer behaviour	What prices tempt customers to buy the product? How important are sales promotions to customers? What customer service levels do customers expect?	Primary research – qualitative data
Buying patterns	When do customers buy the product the most? Is this related to seasons or sales promotions? Are buying patterns different in different stores across the country?	Secondary research – forecast sales by location and time period Primary research – quantitative sales figures
Consumer preferences	Which products do customers prefer? Why? How do customers prefer to purchase products? Where do they prefer to buy the products from?	Secondary research – specialist agency reports (product growth and trends, payment method trends, etc.)
Customer satisfaction	Do the products have all of the features that customers want and need? Is customer service effective? Are the purchasing methods effective?	Primary research – qualitative (opinions and suggestions for improvement) and quantitative (sales returns and complaints figures)
Sales trends	Which products are growing in sales? Which stores are experiencing more sales?	Secondary research – market trends Primary research – sales figures by region
Brand awareness	Do customers know the brand? What does the brand mean to customers?	Primary research – qualitative (opinions and emotions connected to the brand)

Q Research

Research the types of research methods you could use in order to best answer your research objectives.

Q Research

Research the buying patterns of your potential customers.

Figure 10.12 (continued)

Advertising awareness	Do customers understand and respond to the key advertising messages? Are customers aware of the product benefits? Are they aware of where to purchase the product?	Primary research – qualitative and quantitative (sales figures during advertising promotion periods)
Product development success	What are competitors launching? What are these sales like? Which product sales are growing? Which products are failing?	Secondary research – company reports and trade journals (competitor success) Primary research – sale figures and trends
New product opportunities	Which existing products could be revamped or have their packaging changed? Which new target markets could be exploited?	Secondary research – specialist agency reports on customer and market trends Primary research – customer suggestions
Changes in the market	What changes in customer needs have developed? Do customers now prefer to buy online?	Secondary research – specialist agency reports Primary research – customer tastes
Emergence of new markets	Where are the growing markets? What are the customers' tastes and how can these be exploited? Which products will best suit these markets? What pricing and advertising will best suit these markets?	Secondary research – market data and trends and competitor analysis in the potential market
Competitor activities	How well are competitors doing? What are their products? How effective is their marketing? How effective is their packaging and pricing? How effectively do they respond to market changes?	Secondary research – company reports, trade journals and statistics

Discuss

Discuss your research objectives with a partner.

Emergence of new markets – China has the fastest growing construction market in the world.

Probability sampling

P4 ▶ What is sampling?

In the UK, a census is carried out every 10 years. This involves asking everyone in the country a series of questions. Contacting everyone in the population is costly and time consuming, so most market research chooses a sample of people to represent the group that is being researched. The sample should reflect the views of the whole group. Choosing this sample is called sampling.

Generally speaking, the larger the sample size, the higher the research costs. Therefore, when deciding on appropriate sample sizes, the budget should be taken into account. Researchers may decide on an appropriate sample size by looking at similar research projects or may rely on previous experience. However, the most unbiased and valid method of choosing a sample size is to use statistics. This is a guaranteed method of getting a random sample that should truly represent the population being studied. Using statistical methods to select sample sizes means that researchers can calculate the accuracy of and the level of confidence in the research. For example, a researcher may have a high degree of confidence (85 per cent) in research that shows that the average teenager sleeps for 6 hours on week nights, with an accuracy of plus or minus 1 hour.

Choosing your sample size statistically can be done by one of two methods: probability sampling and non-probability sampling.

Probability sampling

This method systematically selects people to sample, and can be undertaken in a number of ways:

- Random sampling – This is when all members of the population have an equal chance of being selected. It is like a raffle – everybody who has a ticket has an equal chance of winning a prize. Random sampling is perfect for projects where the population being researched is not large.

- Systematic random sampling – This is similar to random sampling but does not need to identify every member of the population and is therefore considered easier. This method selects random numbers from a population. For example, if there were 100 students in your school, every 3rd student could be chosen, starting from student number 8.

 Your assessment criteria:

P4 Conduct primary and secondary research for a selected product/ service making use of identifiable sampling techniques

 Key terms

Probability sampling: a method of selecting respondents that uses some form of random selection

Research

Research the advantages and disadvantages of the following sampling techniques:

- *random sampling*
- *systematic random sampling*
- *stratified random sampling*
- *multi stage sampling*
- *cluster sampling.*

- Stratified random sampling – This method takes into account the fact that some customers are more important than others and weighs up how important particular customers are. For example, in a school, 200 students from Years 7 and 8 used the canteen and spent a total of £1000 per week; 150 students from Years 9 and 10 used the canteen and spent a total of £1000 per week and 100 students from Years 11, 12 and 13 used the canteen and spent a total of £2000 per week. A sample of 200 students chosen randomly would not represent the whole market. To make the sample representative, the bigger spenders (those in Years 11, 12 and 13) should make up half of the sample as they spend half of the total sales. Similarly, Years 7 and 8 and Years 9 and 10 should make up a quarter of the sample each.

- Multi stage sampling – This method samples respondents randomly but is not as expensive as random sampling. For example, in a school, random sampling would list every student in the school and pick names at random. Multi stage sampling could start by taking all students who arrive at school before 8.10am in the morning (first stage), then those students who have a middle name (second stage), and then those students who have blonde hair (third stage). This would give you your sample. This is a silly example, but it shows how random the process can be. Organisations can use this method on a geographical basis, selecting certain regions, then certain towns within those regions, and then the households on certain streets within those towns.

- Cluster sampling – This method involves dividing the population into groups that represent the population. For example, in a school you could divide the population up

Students can be sampled in a variety of ways.

into five students from every year (five from Year 7, five from Year 8 and so on). Those students would then be grouped and they would make up one cluster. Everybody would then be in similar clusters, each representing a sample of the population. Some of these clusters would then be sampled in a random way.

> **Discuss**
>
> *Discuss the appropriateness of the different methods of probability sampling for your research project.*

Non-probability sampling

P4 Non-probability sampling

Generally speaking, **non-probability sampling** produces the best results, but it is expensive and time consuming. It is used when random sampling is not possible. There are various different types of non-probability random sampling:

- Quota sampling – This is when samples of a whole market are selected to reflect the whole market. Quota sampling is usually done by dividing the market up into age groups so that the characteristics of the sample reflect the whole population. Quotas are usually chosen from small geographical areas, which make the research relatively inexpensive.

- Convenience sampling – This is when the researcher chooses the sample simply for convenience. For example, when you are stopped in the high street by a researcher, you are chosen just because you happen to be walking past the researcher. As long as the respondents chosen seem to be representative of the target market, the method is seen as valid.

- Observation – This involves observing respondents (usually by CCTV) who use a particular organisation. It involves collecting behavioural data and is usually accurate as the respondents generally do not know they are being observed.

- Focus group – This involves gathering together a small group of people who are representative of the population to discuss certain issues about their behaviours, product usage, etc. Respondents are chosen according to their ability to discuss the topic.

- Judgement sampling – This involves the researcher using their judgement to select respondents to interview based on whether their views are thought to reflect the whole population. Important members of a sample are chosen as their opinions are seen to have more weight than the opinions of others.

The implications of different samples

When deciding whether to use probability or non-probability sampling, the following issues need to be taken into consideration:

- Probability sampling means that the results of your research will be clear and there is no doubt as to whether the sample is representative of the population. The research can therefore be used to project results. However, selection is expensive and time consuming.

Your assessment criteria:

P4 Conduct primary and secondary research for a selected product/ service making use of identifiable sampling techniques

Key terms

Non-probability sampling: a method of selecting respondents that does not involve random selection

Research

Research the advantages and disadvantages of the following sampling techniques:

- *quota sampling*
- *convenience sampling*
- *observation*
- *focus groups*
- *judgement sampling.*

- Non-probability sampling is cheaper but the samples are not guaranteed to represent the population as sample sizes tend to be a lot smaller. On the plus side, in-depth views can be sought and the researcher can target respondents whom they deem to be important.

When choosing which sampling method to use, the cost and accuracy of each method should be taken into account.

Discuss

In groups, discuss the appropriateness of non-probability sampling methods for your research project.

Figure 10.13: The cost and accuracy of various sampling methods

Sampling method	Cost	Accuracy
Probability sampling		
Random	Very expensive	Excellent
Systematic random	Very expensive	Excellent
Stratified random	Very expensive	Good
Multi stage	Costly	Good
Cluster	Costly	Good
Non-probability sampling		
Quota	Costly	Good
Convenience	Cheap	Not very good
Observation	Costly to buy necessary equipment but thereafter fairly cheap	Acceptable
Focus group	Very expensive	Acceptable
Judgement	Costly	Acceptable

Observation is costly.

Questionnaires

P4 | Questionnaire design

Questionnaires are used to ask a series of questions of respondents. They are used in telephone interviews and one-to-one interviews and can be sent out in the post. The design of a questionnaire, no matter how basic, is crucial in order to gain accurate information. The content and phrasing of the questions, the layout and sequence of the questionnaire and the way in which respondents answer the questions all have a bearing on the accuracy of the results. Generally, effective questionnaires have certain common elements:

- an introductory short sentence that explains why the questionnaire is being carried out.

- an example question and answer that shows respondents how to complete the questionnaire

- concise questions that do not use slang or acronyms

- questions that are all directly linked to the research project

- no questions that might not be understood by some people

- questions that are easy to answer (this improves the completion rate of your questionnaire).

Questionnaires should be as short as possible – a maximum of 30 questions (to avoid losing the attention of the respondent). The 'skip to question xx' option can be used to shorten the questionnaire for eligible respondents.

The questions can be factual or can ask for opinions or the reasons why the respondents behave in a certain way. Factual questions usually relate to age, gender, address, etc. Opinions are the respondents' thoughts, feelings, emotions and attitudes about certain issues or products. Questions that ask respondents why they behave in a certain way (e.g. why they buy their food shopping from Asda) are important as they give the researcher an insight into the motivations of their respondents. Organisations may use this sort of data to create advertising campaigns or sales promotions. Factual data is the most reliable data; opinions and motivations are subjective and may not be as reliable as the respondent may be trying to tell the researcher what they think he or she wants to hear. However, they are extremely valuable in getting to know customers' thoughts on certain issues.

Your assessment criteria:

P4 Conduct primary and secondary research for a selected product/ service making use of identifiable sampling techniques

Questions

The order in which the questions appear – their sequencing – is important. The first few questions should be the most interesting in order to gain the respondent's attention. The questions should be in a logical order as the issues raised in one question could influence how the respondent answers subsequent questions. General questions should be asked first, followed by more specific questions.

There are several different types of questions that can be used:

- **Dichotomous** – These 'closed' questions give the respondent a choice of two answers – yes or no (usually). These questions are useful as the respondent clearly knows the purpose of the question and there will be one answer that is right for the respondent. They are useful to the researcher because if a respondent answers 'no' to a question to which the researcher only wants respondents who answer 'yes', there is no need for the researcher to ask the respondent any further questions.

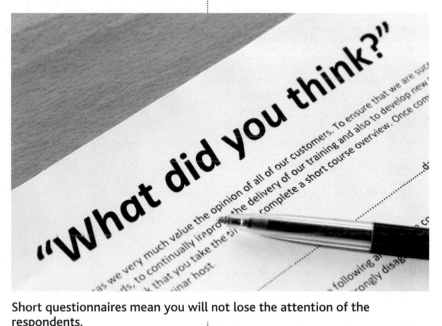

Short questionnaires mean you will not lose the attention of the respondents.

- Multiple choice – These offer the respondent a few different answers to choose from. These are sometimes difficult to design as you have to think of all the possibilities, though 'other' can be used.

- Scaled – These use a scale or rating as an answer to a particular question. For example, 'on a scale of 1 – 5 (where 1 is not important and 5 is very important) rate how important completing your BTEC Business coursework is.' This is known as a **semantic differential scale**. Other scaled questions ask the respondent to circle whether they strongly agree, agree, neither agree nor disagree, disagree or strongly disagree with a statement. This is known as a **Likert scale**.

- Open ended – Respondents have to answer these questions in a sentence and they therefore usually relate to opinions, thoughts, behaviours or motivations. These questions can lead to an endless variety of answers, which can be difficult to analyse. They are generally used where the researcher is not sure what the possible answers could be to a certain question.

 Design

Design a questionnaire that aims to find out students' thoughts on a recent issue. Use all of the types of question listed on this page.

 Key terms

Dichotomous questions: *closed questions to which respondents can only answer yes or no*

Likert scale: *a scale on which respondents circle strongly agree, agree, neither agree nor disagree, disagree or strongly disagree in response to a question*

Semantic differential scale: *a scale on which respondents circle a number according to how they feel about a certain statement*

Surveys

P4 ▶ What is a survey?

A **survey** is the whole process of designing a research project, producing research objectives, choosing sampling methods and collecting and analysing data. Some people use the words 'survey' and 'questionnaire' as if they were the same thing, but a questionnaire is just one method of data collection and therefore just part of a survey.

A survey should outline *what* is being researched, *where* the research is taking place and *why*, *when* it is taking place and *why* and finally *how* it is taking place.

A questionnaire is a form of data collection.

🔑 Key terms

Survey: *the process of a research project*

✍ Describe

Describe to your partner the difference between a survey and a questionnaire. Once you are clear on the difference, find five people over the next week (outside of your class) who do not know the difference and explain it to them.

M2 ▶ Bias, relevance and response rate

When deciding which form of data collection to choose, there are several issues that need to be considered.

Bias

Bias is the tendency of respondents to have a one-sided perspective on an issue. A good research project aims to reduce bias so that the results are not influenced in such a way as to produce a certain result. Bias can affect the validity and reliability of your results and therefore affect decisions that are made as a result of the research. There are a number of ways in which the bias in your data collection methods can be reduced.

If interviews are being held or questionnaires read to respondents, the interviewer can have a major impact on the respondents. The interviewer's facial expressions, tone of voice, body language and style of dress can generate a degree of bias. Although some of these are out of the interviewer's control, dressing and speaking in a neutral manner and avoiding using body language can reduce bias.

Pilot testing your questionnaires on colleagues is a good idea.

The questions that are asked of respondents (whether on paper or verbal) can be biased and therefore this has to be identified and reduced. Questions such as 'Some people believe that not charging tuition fees is wrong. What do you think?' are biased. The question should be rephrased as 'What is your opinion about tuition fees?'.

The order of questions can influence respondents and therefore needs careful consideration. General questions should be asked before specific questions, positive before negative and behaviour questions before attitude questions.

Certain methods of data collection may also make respondents feel that they should give an answer that is socially acceptable and not necessarily true. For example, respondents are not likely to tell you that they seek power and status or are jealous of somebody else's spending power. Most people want to conform to the social norm and this can create bias. Questions should be asked in such a way that respondents do not feel that they have to answer in a certain way. Making data collection anonymous can help to overcome this problem.

Relevance

It is important that respondents are only asked relevant questions and therefore, where possible, skip questions should be used. For example, if you are asking students about canteen food, the first question could be 'Do you buy your lunch from the canteen?' If they answer 'no', any questions regarding the choice and quality of the food can be skipped.

Response

It is important for the **response rate** to your research project to be as high as possible. Response rates can be increased by ensuring that the data collection method is short, easy to understand, interesting and quick to complete. Personal touches such as a message from the researcher for a postal questionnaire or an introduction by the researcher for a verbal questionnaire can also help.

It is always a good idea to test your questionnaire out on a few respondents before using it in your research project. This pilot stage should reveal any big problems and enable you to rectify any errors.

 Key terms

Response rate: *the number of respondents who participated in a research project compared to the total population of the sample*

 Discuss

Discuss with a partner the possible methods of data collection you could use. Once these have been decided, research together how the possibilities of bias can be reduced and response and relevance increased.

Interpreting your results

P5 ▸ Statistical procedures

Interpreting your results and presenting them in either a written report or verbal presentation is the last and one of the most important steps in your research project. The interpretation and presentation should both be carried out in way that is both clear and relevant to the organisation. Several statistical procedures are used in order to draw conclusions from the results collected:

- **Arithmetic mean** – the average. To find the arithmetic mean of a set of numbers, the numbers are added together and then divided by the number of numbers.

    For example, the numbers of students visiting the school canteen every day for a week: 60, 56, 60, 88, 96

    $$\text{arithmetic mean} = \frac{\text{sum of the numbers}}{\text{number of numbers}}$$

    $$= \frac{(60 + 56 + 60 + 88 + 96)}{5}$$

    $$= \frac{360}{5}$$

    $$= 72 \text{ students per day}$$

- **Median** – the middle value of a set of numbers. To find the median, place the numbers in order and then find the middle value.

    For example, the numbers of students visiting the school canteen every day for a week: 60, 56, 60, 88, 96

    numbers in order: 56, 60, 60, 88, 96

    median = middle value = 60 students per day

If there is an even number of values in the set, take the middle two numbers, add them together and divide by 2.

    For example, the number of customers purchasing items in a shop over a 6-day period: 45, 32, 39, 41, 57, 102

    numbers in order: 32, 39, 41, 45, 57, 102

    take the two middle values and add them together: 41 + 45 = 96

    divide them by 2 = 48

    median = 48 students per day

 Key terms

Arithmetic mean: *the average of a set of values*

Median: *the middle number of a set of values*

• **Mode** – the most popular number in a set of values. This is a very valuable statistic for organisations as it highlights the popular price (for example) that customers prefer to pay, which the arithmetic mean and median fail to highlight.

> For example, the numbers of students visiting the school canteen every day for a week: 60, 56, 60, 88, 96
>
> mode = most popular number = 60 students per day

It is possible to have more than one mode if two numbers are equally the most popular of a set of values.

• **Range** – the spread of a set of numbers. This is found by calculating the difference between the largest number and the smallest number.

> For example, the numbers of students visiting the school canteen every day for a week: 60, 56, 60, 88, 96
>
> largest number = 96
> smallest number = 56
>
> range　= largest number – smallest number
>
> = 96 – 56
>
> = 40

Organisations may use this to find out the range of prices for their products. It can be used to highlight the range of prices from their basic products to their premium products.

• **Inter-quartile range** – This is calculated in order to reduce the impact of any extreme numbers (either small or large). It divides the data into quarters (hence the word quartile) and then ignores the first and last quartiles, only taking into account the middle (or 2nd and 3rd) quartiles. This is done is by drawing a cumulative frequency curve. The data is divided into quarters and the inter-quartile range is then calculated. For example, the numbers of students visiting the school canteen every day for a week: 60, 56, 60, 88, 96.

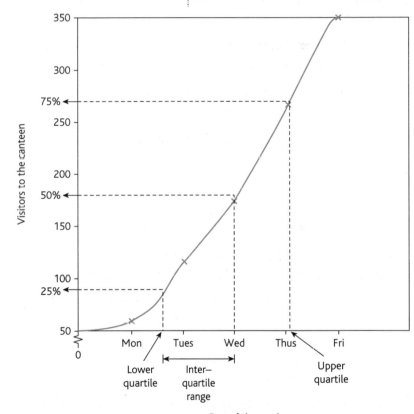

Figure 10.14: **Cumulative frequency chart showing the inter-quartile range**

Presenting your findings

In order to achieve P5, you need to present your research findings diagrammatically, graphically, verbally or in writing.

P5 Scatter diagrams

Scatter diagrams are graphs that are used to plot two different sets of data in order to compare them and to see if there is a correlation or a relationship between the two. When there is a relationship between two sets of data and they are both going in the same direction, for example if both variables are increasing, it is called a positive correlation. For example, sales of food in the canteen increase when the school spends more money on the quality of the food. This is shown in Figure 10.15.

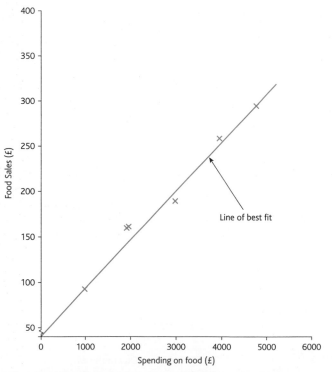

Figure 10.15: A scatter diagram showing a positive correlation between increased spending on food and sales

When there is a relationship between two sets of data, but they are going in opposite directions, for example, as one variable increases, the other variable decreases, this is known as negative correlation. For example, as the caterer sells more expensive food, the number of complaints about the food falls. This is shown in Figure 10.16.

When there is no relationship between the two sets of data, for example, the spending in the canteen and the number of BTEC National Business reports handed in on time, there is said to be no correlation. This is shown in Figure 10.17.

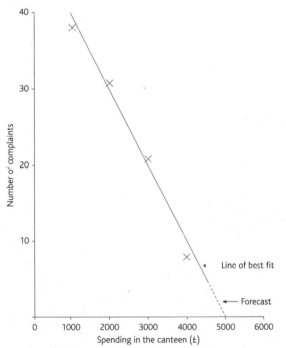

Figure 10.16: A scatter diagram showing a negative correlation between an increase in the quality of the food and a fall in the number of complaints

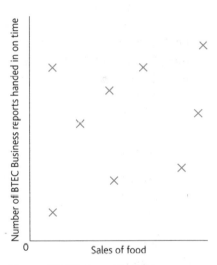

Figure 10.17: A scatter diagram showing no correlation between the sales of food in the canteen and the number of BTEC Business reports handed in on time

Times series

A times series is used when data is measured at successive points in time. The data can be recorded on a weekly, monthly or annual (yearly) basis. The time is usually on the horizontal axis, with the variable on the vertical. Where there is a relationship between the time and the variable, the graph can be used to predict what will happen in the future. Figure 10.18 shows a times series for the sales of food in the canteen over a month.

Food sales

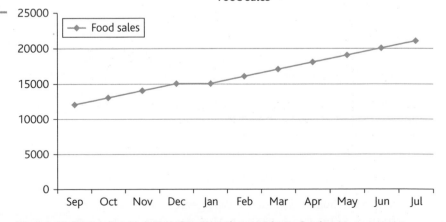

Figure 10.18: A times series showing the number of sales in a canteen over a year

P5   Trends

When interpreting research data, it is very useful to spot **trends** in that data. This means identifying a general direction or tendency of the data to rise, fall or remain the same over a period of time. Trends are usually shown in a line graph. These are sometimes shown on the news to indicate how the economy has grown or shrunk over the past few years. Often, there are fluctuations in the line graph (shown by jagged rises and falls) and in this case, a line of best fit is used to show the general direction of the trend.

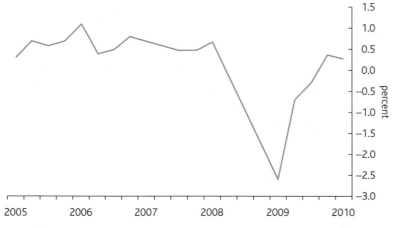

Figure 10.19: A line graph showing how the economy has changed over time

Spreadsheets

Spreadsheets (like those on Microsoft Excel) enable you to illustrate business trends and statistics in a diagrammatic form. Bar charts, pie charts and scatter diagrams can all be created by using spreadsheets.

Oral report

Most people find it more difficult to give an **oral report** than a written one because of their nerves. Therefore, if you decide to present your findings verbally, you must carefully plan everything you are going to say. Using software such as Microsoft PowerPoint will make your presentation look professional. Your oral report should follow the same sequence as a written report:

- introduction (introduce yourself; explain the format of the presentation, the reasons for the study and the objectives)

- research methodology (describe the research methodology, data collection method, sampling technique, timescale and budget)

Your assessment criteria:

P5   CInterpret findings from the research presenting them clearly in an appropriate format

🔑 **Key terms**

Trend: *the general direction where data appears to rise, fall or stay the same*

Spreadsheets can be used to quickly illustrate research data.

🔑 **Key terms**

Oral report: *a report that is delivered verbally to an audience*

- findings (describe your findings and how they link to your objectives – put your findings in the order of the objectives as this is easier to understand; show graphs and tables along with statistical techniques)

- conclusions and recommendations (explain the key points that have come from your findings, the implications for decision-making and your recommendations for improvements)

- questions (invite questions and comments from the audience).

Follow these basic steps to ensure your oral presentation is as good as possible:

- Practise beforehand.

- Ensure all technology is working beforehand.

- Use eye contact.

- Do not read everything off the screen (make notes that back up what is on the screen).

- Vary the tone and pitch of your voice to keep your audience interested.

- Project your voice so everybody can hear you.

- Check the audience's understanding throughout the presentation.

- Provide handouts.

- Stay calm.

Written reports

Formal reports have a set format, which should be adhered to:

- Title page – Title of the report, who the report is written for, name of the author/researcher.

- Table of contents – List the information contained in the report in the order it will be found.

- Executive summary – One page overview of the important information contained in the report.

- Introduction – Brief overview of the problem being addressed, background information to understand the reasoning and the need for the report.

- Secondary research conducted with reasons for using the chosen data – The relevance of the secondary research to the research should be highlighted.

- Primary research methods that were used – Where, how and from whom, along with reasons for using these methods; sampling techniques, data collection methods, characteristics and size of sample should also be explained.

💬 **Discuss**

In pairs, discuss whether you will choose to present your findings in an oral or a written report. Explain your reasons.

What are the advantages and disadvantages of each form of reporting?

Visual aids serve to communicate information in a diagrammatic form.

P5 ▸ Written reports *continued*

- Data analysis – Brief overview of the methods used, reasons why they were appropriate, outcomes of the analysis, significance of the results.

- Research findings – The main body of the report and the actual results of your research: a detailed presentation of your interpretation of the statistics found relating to the research project and analysis of the data collection.

- Conclusions and recommendations – Conclusions are broad generalisations that focus on addressing the research questions; they should be in the order of your research objectives. Recommendations are your choices for strategies based on the conclusions that you have made.

- Appendices – This section should include all the supporting information from your research project that you did not include in the main body of your report, e.g. surveys, calculations, complex secondary research tables.

Informal written reports have fewer sections, but should include an introduction, findings, conclusion and recommendations.

In both oral and written reports, visual aids should be used to communicate information in a diagrammatic form to the reader or audience. Computer graphics, graphs, charts and tables are concise and effective ways of summarising information and keeping the reader or audience interested. However, do not overdo the visual aids as they then lose their impact. Choose them carefully, ensuring that each one serves a real purpose.

Audience

Always be mindful of your audience when writing your report, whether it is to be presented in written or oral form. A report that is too long will lose the interest of the reader or audience and will therefore devalue the results of the report. The report should be clear and should taken into account the fact that the audience or readers may not have any previous knowledge of the research. Even if the reader goes back to the report in a month's time, they should still find it easy to understand. The report should be interesting to read or listen to. Using diagrams to present some of the information can help to make the report both clear and interesting but you must ensure that the information that you present is effective. There is little point, for example, in

> **Your assessment criteria:**
>
> **P5** Interpret findings from the research presenting them clearly in an appropriate format

Keeping your audience interested is essential.

producing quality tables and charts but with little explanation as to what they mean and their relevance to the research objectives. Also, if too many charts and tables are used, the information that they are there to present may get lost among all of the visual aids.

Conclusions and recommendations

You must ensure that the information that you present is of good quality as this will affect your conclusions and recommendations. The research findings must also be relevant and closely linked to the objectives. The conclusions of your research should draw some general concepts from the specific findings of your research and should focus on the original questions around which the research was planned. The recommendations should be based on these conclusions and are your chosen tactics. Do not draw any conclusions or make any recommendations that your research cannot clearly support. It is essential that your recommendations are realistic as unrealistic recommendations will mean that all of the work, time and money that have gone into the research will have been wasted.

Presentation

The quality of your presentation is also dependent on the facilities that you have at your disposal. Producing a written report on a scrap piece of paper with scruffy handwriting is going to devalue the report. Ensure you have the facilities available to produce an informative and professional piece of research. If you are producing an oral report, equipment such as a projector (for a PowerPoint presentation) must be checked beforehand so that they are in full working order. This will avoid any embarrassing and unprofessional mishaps.

Check that equipment is working before you present your report.

 Design

Design a checklist of all of the facilities you will need to produce both a written and an oral report.

Charts and graphs

Charts and graphs can display information in a very concise and effective way. They can also serve to break up endless pages of writing.

Your assessment criteria:

P5 Interpret findings from the research presenting them clearly in an appropriate format

P5 Bar charts

A **bar chart** is a series of bars (either horizontal or vertical) representing the values of different items. The bars in bar charts should have gaps between them. They are used to compare totals side by side. Figure 10.20 shows the total number of different ice creams sold in a particular location in June, July and August.

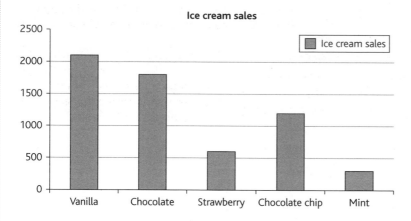

Figure 10.20 A bar chart showing the different flavours of ice cream sold in June, July and August

Key terms

Bar chart: a series of bars (horizontal or vertical) representing the values of different items

Pictogram: a type of bar chart that uses pictures instead of bars

Pie chart: a circular chart divided into segments

Pictograms

A **pictogram** is a type of bar chart that uses pictures instead of bars. For example, if you were to draw a pictogram of the number of ice creams sold in the months of June, July and August, you may draw ice creams to represent the numbers sold (see Figure 10.21).

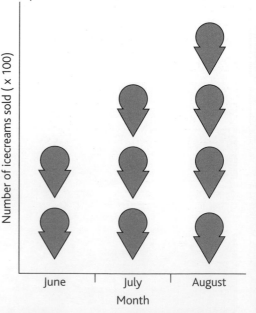

Figure 10.21: A pictogram showing the number of ice creams sold in June, July and August

Pie charts

A **pie chart** is a circular chart divided into segments. Each segment represents the value of an item. Each segment is the same percentage of the circle as the item is of the total of all the items.

For example, a pie chart could be drawn showing the percentages of the different flavours of ice cream that were sold in June, July and August

(see Figure 10.22).

Histograms and frequency curves

A **histogram** can look very similar to a bar chart, but a histogram has no gaps between the bars. A histogram is a diagrammatical representation of a frequency distribution table. A histogram shows the cumulative values in the table and therefore the width and area of the bars can vary. A point is drawn at the mid point of each bar on the histogram and a line is drawn joining all of the mid points together – this is the frequency curve. Figure 10.23 shows the number of ice creams bought per order per customer in June, July and August, and Figure 10.24 shows this information in the form of a histogram and frequency curve.

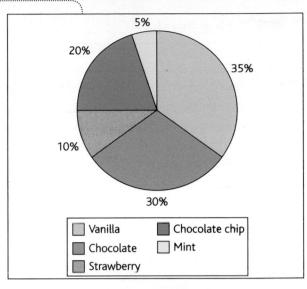

Figure 10.22 A pie chart showing the different flavours of ice cream sold in June, July and August

Key terms
Histogram: a diagrammatical representation of a frequency distribution table

Figure 10.23: A frequency distribution table for the number of ice creams bought per order per customer in June, July and August

Size of the Ice cream order	Frequency
Less than 3	80
3 and less than 5	70
5 and less than 7	50
7 and less than 10	20

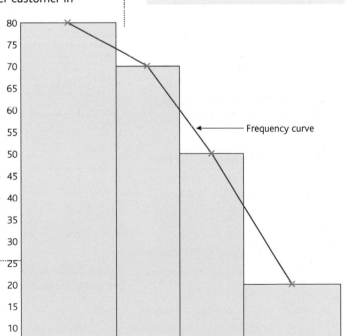

Figure 10.24: A histogram with frequency curve showing the number of ice creams bought per order per customer in June, July and August

P5 Line graphs

Your assessment criteria:

P5 Interpret findings from the research presenting them clearly in an appropriate format

A **line graph** uses a line to connect data points and show a change in data over a period of time. It might show, for example, how sales rise and fall over the period of a year. Usually, the period of time is shown along the horizontal axis and the variable (for example the number of ice creams sold) on the vertical axis. Figure 10.25 shows the number of ice cream sales in June, July and August in the form of a line graph.

Key terms

Line graph: a graph that uses a line to connect data points and show a change in data over time

Scattergram: also called a scatter diagram, a diagrammatical representation of two different variables, showing the relationship between the two

Ice cream sales

[line graph with y-axis from 0 to 3000 in increments of 500, x-axis showing June, July, August. Legend: Ice cream sales. Points approximately at June 1500, July 1850, August 2650]

Figure 10.25 A line graph showing the ice cream sales in June, July and August

Scattergrams

A **scattergram** is a diagrammatical representation of two different variables. Each variable is plotted on a different axis and the points are made on the chart. It is known as a scattergram because the points are scattered; however, a trend can usually be seen. Scattergrams are often used by market researchers as they show trends and the relationship between two different variables (for example, the amount spent on a new advertising campaign and the resultant increase

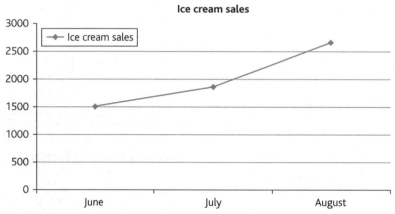

Figure 10.26 A scattergram showing the relationship between the temperature and sales of ice creams

in sales). Figure 10.26 shows a scattergram of the relationship between the temperature of the day and the sales of ice creams.

Choosing the best statistical techniques

It is important to choose the right statistical technique for your data. Figure 10.27 explains what each technique is designed to do.

Figure 10.27: The appropriateness of various statistical techniques

Statistical technique	is good for:
Bar chart	• comparing totals • comparing sales figures in different years
Frequency curve and histogram	• comparing purchases by customers or sales teams • comparing the time spent on certain behaviours by customers • comparing checkout times • comparing sales according to price ranges
Line graph	• showing values rising and falling over time • showing interest rates, unemployment figures, exchange rates, population change and employment rates
Pie chart	• comparing market segments and sales
Scattergram	• comparing two variables, such as advertising and sales, queues and complaints, number of sales staff working and sales

Interpreting the results

When examining and interpreting the results of your research project you should ask the following questions:

• What do the statistics tell you about the characteristics of the market?

• What is the significance of the data?

• What is the relevance of the data?

• What trends have emerged?

• How does this affect the organisation?

Design

Design three of the following for your research project:

- *pictogram*
- *bar chart*
- *pie chart*
- *histogram and frequency curve*
- *line graph*
- *scattergram.*

Explain your reasons for choosing those particular three.

Discuss

In pairs, discuss the appropriateness of each of the statistical techniques.

M3 Analysing and recommending

In order to achieve M3, you need to present your research findings with comments on their implications for the organisation you are researching. You then need to make recommendations as to how the marketing strategies of the organisation could be improved or implemented.

D2 The limitations of your research

When evaluating your research, it important to be aware of its limitations. You can assume that there is going to be some degree of error in your results as the sample size was probably quite small. No research project is ever 100 per cent accurate because of the limitations that can affect the results:

- Excess of information in customer databases – Nowadays, databases can hold so much information that it has to be filtered down to what is deemed relevant. This can be difficult to do. However, the fact that there is so much information means that the reliability and validity of the information can often be verified through different sources.

- E-business feedback overload – E-businesses have several ways that customers can give feedback on their experiences. This is all qualitative data that needs to be analysed. This can mean that there is too much information, which can result in the data being underused and therefore useless. The decisions that should be based on this feedback therefore get lost.

- The reliability and accuracy of the sample – Your sample should be as representative as possible of the population being researched. The way in which it is selected must reflect this. Sampling error is defined as the difference between the results from your sample and the actual results from the whole population. All sampling methods include some degree of sampling error, but your aim should be to minimise this by choosing the most appropriate methods for your research project.

Your assessment criteria:

M3 Analyse the research findings and make recommendations on how marketing strategies could be adapted or implemented

D1 Evaluate the market research method used by a selected organisation

D2 Evaluate the findings from the research undertaken

Discuss

In a group of no more than three, explain your research projects to each other. Discuss the implications of your research findings for the organisation. Each member of the group should come up with at least one recommendation for the other members' research projects.

- Bias – Although bias can be reduced (see pages 244–5), there will always be a degree of bias. Interviewer bias occurs if the interviewer has to explain questions to the respondents, as this introduces the interviewer's interpretation. Similarly, interviewers may tend to approach only those respondents that look happy and attractive. Bias can also occur in questionnaires.

- Subjectivity – In focus groups, the interviewer or moderator is usually responsible for the collection of the qualitative data. Their choice of data to use, interpret and analyse is subjective. Subjectivity is less of a problem with quantitative data, although the interpretations, conclusions, recommendations and implications can still be subjective.

 Discuss

In pairs, discuss the limitations of your research.

D1 A selected organisation's marketing research methods

In order to achieve D1, you need to evaluate the research method used by an organisation (this could be one that you have looked at for previous grading criteria). You may, for example, have recently been stopped in the street by a researcher working for a particular organisation, or you may be aware from internet research of an organisation that uses focus groups or mystery shoppers. You need to explain the appropriateness of the method, its limitations and how the results are used for decision-making within the organisation. You need to make justified recommendations (backed up with examples and sources) for improvements in the way the organisation should conduct its market research.

 Research

Research the market research methods used by a number of different organisations.

Assessment checklist

To achieve a pass grade, my portfolio of evidence must show that I can:

Assessment criteria	Description	✓
P1	Describe types of market research	☐
P2	Explain how different market research methods have been used to make a marketing decision within a selected situation or business	☐
P3	Plan market research for a selected product/service using appropriate methods of data collection	☐
P4	Conduct primary and secondary research for a selected product/service making use of identifiable sampling techniques	☐
P5	DInterpret findings from the research presenting them clearly in an appropriate format.	☐

To achieve a merit grade, my portfolio of evidence must show that I can:

Assessment criteria	Description	✓
M1	Explain, with examples, how different market research methods are appropriate to assist different marketing situations	☐
M2	Explain the reasons for choosing the particular method of data collection for a selected product/service	☐
M3	Analyse the research findings and make recommendations on how marketing strategies could be adapted or implemented.	☐
M4		☐
M5		☐

To achieve a distinction grade, my portfolio of evidence must show that I can:

Assessment criteria	Description	✓
D1	Evaluate the market research method used by a selected organisation	☐
D2	Evaluate the findings from the research undertaken.	☐

LO1 Know what role internet marketing has within a modern marketing context

▶ What is modern marketing and how does it affect you?

▶ How has internet marketing changed the way we do business?

LO2 Understand the benefits of internet marketing to customers

▶ Personalising and customising

▶ Reaching far and wide

LO3 Understand the opportunities offered to businesses by internet marketing

▶ Getting more bargaining power

▶ Information overload

▶ Building relationships

▶ Being efficient

LO4 Understand the challenges faced by businesses using internet marketing

▶ What are the challenges?

▶ Market feedback overload

▶ When businesses get it wrong

The 7Ps

P1 ▶ The marketing mix

The role of marketing in the modern world is to find out the needs and wants of the target audience and to strive to meet these by providing products and services to meet the audience's requirements. Marketing has been an important part of businesses for years, long before the internet came along. Businesses have always had to think about whether their products and services meet the requirements of their customers. If they do not do this, people will stop buying their products. Internet marketing is based on the basic principles of the marketing mix. Before looking at the unique features of internet marketing, it is necessary to revisit the marketing mix (the 4Ps): product, price, place and promotion.

Product

A product is the physical offering to a customer which meets their needs and requirements. When products are being developed, some basic questions have to be asked:

- What are the customers' needs?
- What product will meet those needs?
- Who are the customers?
- What are the product features?

Price

The price is the amount paid for the product or service. The price depends on the target market for the product. Pricing can affect the sort of customer who will buy the product, how much of it will be sold and the image of the product. A marketer can use different pricing strategies according to the business's aims and objectives. The different pricing strategies are:

- competitor pricing basing the product prices on what competitors are charging
- destructive pricing setting a price that will drive competitors out of the market
- discriminatory pricing having different prices for different customers
- penetration pricing setting a price that will penetrate a market initially
- skimming the market setting a high price because the product is unique.

Place

Place is the location from which a product is sold. This does not necessarily have to be a physical location, such as a shop on the local high street. It can also be the internet, the TV 'red button' and teletext, to name but a few. Place also takes into account how the product is distributed, from manufacturer to distribution centres and warehouses to wholesalers and retailers.

Promotion

The promotion of products and services makes customers aware of the benefits of the products and services. Promotion includes advertising and sales promotions. It means that customers become aware of products and services that are available to them and which they otherwise may not have heard about.

The extended marketing mix

Over the years, the UK has become what is known as a service economy. This means that it produces more services than products, and chooses to buy many products from foreign companies. Marketing a service is different from marketing a product because people are closely involved in the selling of services, and there are also processes involved and a physical place (evidence) where the customers purchase the service. The extended marketing mix therefore includes: people, processes and physical evidence.

People

The satisfaction of the customers depends on the services that they receive from the people delivering the service. These people include waitresses in restaurants, tellers in banks and teachers in schools.

People who sell services are an important factor in the marketing of the service.

Processes

The processes involved in service delivery can include self-service counters in supermarkets or cafés or the filing and processing of forms in banks. The effectiveness of these services affects what the customers think of the service and therefore whether they continue to purchase it or not.

Physical evidence

This is the environment in which the service is delivered. Even though services themselves are not physical products, the environment in which the service is delivered can be used to entice a customer to purchase the service. For example, people often look in a hairdresser's window to see what the salon looks like before deciding whether to have their hair cut there.

 Design

Design, on an A3 piece of paper, either a shop or a bank where the extended marketing mix has been put into practice.

Modern marketing

Marketing involves more than just the 4Ps or 7Ps; it is a whole way of doing business. The growth of the internet has meant that businesses have changed the way that they market their products and services. They can now build closer relationships with customers via **relationship marketing**, identify new product and market developments and use the internet to ensure they achieve their objectives.

Your assessment criteria:

P1 Describe the role internet marketing has within a modern marketing context

P1 Relationship marketing

Businesses must build relationships with their customers to ensure that they continue to purchase goods and services from them. It is a lot more expensive for a business to use marketing to gain new customers than it is to keep their existing customers happy. The internet has helped tremendously in ensuring that relationships with customers are built and that they last. The internet allows customers to customise the products they buy, for example by designing their own kitchen online.

🔑 Key terms

Relationship marketing: *the building of relationships between the business and the customer in order to better meet the customer's needs*

Online kitchen design, fitted kitchen design, bedroom design

OnlineKitchen&BedroomDesign

HOME
ONLINE DESIGN
KITCHENS
BEDROOMS
LINKS
CONTACT US

Welcome to the online kitchen and bedroom design web site where you can design your own kitchen, free of charge, using a powerful online CAD kitchen design package to design your new fitted kitchen without committing yourself to being chased to death to buy a new fitted kitchen or fitted bedroom from the web site operator (**read more about online design packages**)

Before you start to design, you will need to measure your kitchen or bedroom to produce a rough sketch floor plan and you will need to mark in the position and sizes of your doors and windows. Then click on **online design** to start the kitchen CAD design programme, or go to **useful tips for bedroom design**. Tips for kitchen design are to be found once you start the design package but if you are going to attempt a design initially without the online cad design package, click here for useful tips for kitchen design.

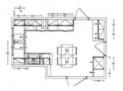

Whichever way you decide to proceed, whenever you are ready, we will take over the design task for you, at no cost and with no obligation to buy anything from us. Once the design stage is completed, we will price your fitted kitchen or fitted bedroom using professional quality, colour co-ordinated kitchen cabinets or fitted bedroom furniture and stunning kitchen or bedroom doors of your choice. And because everything comes direct from the factory with low internet overheads, you can be sure the price will be right

Websites such as www.onlinekitchendesign enable customers to customise and design their own kitchens.

The internet enables customers to get exactly the product that they want. This helps to build a relationship between the customer and the business. Communication and feedback between customer and business is more flexible as a result of emails, feedback and 'contact us' pages on websites. Businesses can also analyse customer feedback in order to improve their services and better relate to their customers.

❓ Did you know?

Online businesses are increasingly using social media sites, such as Facebook, to build relationships with customers and make their businesses grow further.

New opportunities

Use of the internet can mean rapid changes to the way a company does business. It exposes the company to more customers and markets in a way quite unlike anything it will probably have experienced previously. The internet can expand businesses faster than they anticipate and can be a significant help in achieving their aims and objectives. The internet can facilitate:

- Market development – Internet businesses can reach new markets (including overseas markets) due to the low cost of internet advertising.

- Market penetration – Internet businesses can increase their market share by offering better customer services and increased promotion in the markets that they are already in.

- Product development – An internet business can develop new products to be sold over the web.

Improved technology

The use of telecommunications within computer networks has meant that the internet is becoming ever more powerful and faster. We are able to access more information on the World Wide Web at a greater speed than was ever possible before. This has opened doors for some internet businesses as they can upload more information onto their websites for their customer. In October 2010 Virgin Media announced that it was to take pre-registration details for its new 100Mb broadband.

New objectives

When a business decides to launch online, it will set new objectives in order to achieve its overall aims. Businesses normally expect to do more business once they are online and so their objectives should be in line with this – and they should still be SMART. A business's objectives could therefore be to increase internet revenue by x%, to make cost savings of x%, to increase customer retention by x% or to increase sales in a certain market by x%. Whatever they may be, the objectives must address the fact that once the business is online, it suddenly becomes a bigger business. The internet also enables a business to gain accurate measurements of its objectives by measuring how the website is performing.

 Describe

In groups, describe the advantages and disadvantages of a business starting to trade on the internet. Feed back your answers to the rest of the class.

In 2010 Virgin started to take pre-registration details for its faster 100Mb broadband.

Technology-enabled segmentation and targeting

P1 Segmentation

When a business sells products and services, it has to ensure that they meet the needs of the target audience; otherwise it will not sell anything. However, we do not all want to buy the same things. For example, one consumer may buy trainers for running and be willing to pay £200 for them; another consumer may buy trainers for fashion purposes and therefore the style and price will be different.

The marketing department in a business has to make sense of all the groupings that exist within the markets in which it operates – this is called segmentation. By segmenting a market, and then researching the various needs and preferences of each segment, the marketing department is able to see the unique characteristics of a particular segment, make products specifically to suit its needs and market the products using tactics (from the marketing mix) that will appeal to that segment.

Internet businesses use a variety of methods to segment their market:

- Demographical – This is when a business segments a market depending on the make-up of the population. This could relate to income, age, educational attainment or employment status, for example.

- Psychographic – This is the segmenting of a market using the personal characteristics of consumers. For example, some consumers use the internet for social reasons; others for research, reading the news online and accessing information; others use internet banking and comparison websites. Businesses need to be aware of the reasons why consumers use the internet so that they can tailor their websites to suit those needs and preferences.

- Economic – When an internet business is looking at expanding into different countries, it is useful for it to look at the wealth and the extent of e-commerce in the country. This sort of information is available at www.eiu.com.

- Usage based – This is when an internet business segments its market depending on the amount that the internet is being used in different parts of the world. In some countries internet usage is high; in other countries this is not the case. Internet businesses use this sort of information to give them an understanding of how to target their customers. This information is gathered from companies such as Nielsen NetRatings and www.clickz.com.

Key terms

E-commerce: *buying and selling online*

Segmentation: *the different groupings within a market that have similar characteristics*

Research

In pairs, research internet usage by country.

- *What does this tell you about each of the countries that you have researched?*

- *How would an internet business use this sort of information?*

b2b, b2c and c2c

E-commerce involves interactions taking place between different users of the internet. Some online businesses buy from and sell to other businesses, not consumers. These are known as business-to-business (b2b) transactions; for example, a business purchasing raw materials from another business. The most popular type of e-commerce is businesses selling to private individuals; for example, individuals buy clothes online from businesses. These types of transactions are known as business-to-consumer (b2c). The internet has also enabled consumer-to-consumer (c2c) transactions through auction websites such as eBay.

Disintermediation

Goods bought from a high street retailer have had a long journey to reach that retailer. For example, when you buy an item of clothing, the fabric has been transported from the plant to a manufacturer who produced the item of clothing, then on to a warehouse before being purchased by a retailer and ending up in a shop. This is known as a supply chain and the manufacturer, the warehouse, the retailer and the customer are all intermediaries, meaning they all either move, store or package the items. Internet businesses sometimes have no need for all these links in the chain as consumers can buy directly from the source. This is known as disintermediation. A prime example of this is consumers purchasing flights online instead of going to a travel agent.

Direct market communications

The internet allows businesses to communicate directly with the consumer instead of producing adverts. Online businesses send **direct marketing communication** to customers via email, promoting sales, discounts, etc.

An example of disintermediation is a consumer buying flights directly from an airline website.

P2 Individualisation of market attention

When you go online, you decide which websites to visit and are not pushed into visiting particular sites. This is why the internet is known as a pull medium. You make a personal choice and therefore a one-to-one relationship can be built between you and the company. Online businesses are aware of this and will personalise webpages to suit each individual user.

Mass customisation

Just as the internet can enable one-to-one relationships between customers and businesses, it can also enable businesses to customise products to suit their customers. Mass customisation means that products can be adapted to meet each customer's individual needs, so no two items are the same.

Mass customisation uses some of the techniques of mass production; for example, in the case of a watch, the internal mechanism is the same for all products. However, a wide variety of personalised options can also be offered to customers. For example, if you decide to buy a Swatch, the basic watch mechanism is the same no matter which watch you choose, but there are thousands of different options in terms of colours, straps, etc. Even a traditional mass production manufacturer such as BMW now boasts that no two of its new cars are the same.

Mass customisation was used, for example, by Levi Strauss in 1994 with its Original Spin jeans for women. Customers were measured in the stores and their details were sent electronically to then factory. The customised jeans were then cut and mailed to the customer.

The internet has increased the possibilities for mass customisation. For example, Dell established its leadership of the PC market by allowing customers to assemble their own PCs online. The company puts together the components as requested at the last minute before delivery. Ford likewise allows its customers to build a vehicle from online options.

The internet has meant mass customisation has become more widely available.

Your assessment criteria:

P2 Describe how selected organisations use internet marketing

Key terms

Mass customisation: large-scale production of products that are customised to suit individual customers' tastes and preferences

More information

The internet allows customers to research the products that they want to buy without having to visit a number of different shops. Customers are therefore able to save both time and money. There are also websites that compare different products, for example www.comparethemarket.com and www.uswitch.com

Wider and more distant markets

The internet is available all over the world, making it easier for us all to buy and sell products and communicate with people no matter what country they live in. As usage of the internet continues to grow in all countries, businesses are able to access customers in countries and markets that they could never have reached if the internet was not available to them.

Product impact

Some customers do not like the fact that they cannot physically see and feel products that they buy online. Internet businesses have therefore tried to overcome this by offering extra information to increase the impact of the product. This includes detailed product information, reviews from and lists of previous customers, warranties and expert advice.

 Discuss

In groups, discuss the advantages of using comparison websites, such as www.comparethemarket.com. Why do some firms, such as Direct Line, choose not to advertise on comparison websites?

? **Did you know?**

Dell was one of the first businesses to introduce mass customisation on the internet.

 Case study

Money Maxim (www.moneymaxim.co.uk) is a price comparison website on which customers can compare utilities, personal finance and insurance services. The business aims to deliver a service to customers that is independent and is paid commission when visitors to the website take out policies with companies that are featured. Money Maxim prides itself on the personalised service it offers to customers compared to other major price comparison websites.

1. Why do customers choose to use price comparison websites?

2. How do smaller price comparison websites such as Money Maxim compete against large online sites such as www.comparethemarket.com and www.uswitch.com?

Online activities, effectiveness and communication

P2 Enhanced products and services

The internet has brought about an increase in customer support and customer reviews. Customers can now research the details and prices of traditional products and services on the internet. The internet has also brought about a total change to the traditional music and games market. Music and games can now be purchased and stored online so that there is no longer a need for a physical product. iTunes offers music as a service rather than a physical product and the increase in the popularity of apps means that games no longer needs to be a physical product either.

Online and offline

Some internet businesses have only ever existed online and have never had physical shops for customers to visit. Some high street retailers now also sell online, for example Marks and Spencer, Sainsbury's and Debenhams. A few online retailers started life as high street retailers but are now only available online, such as Dixons.

Market effectiveness

The internet gives retailers the opportunity to have a much bigger effect on their market than was previously possible. Online retailers can build one-to-one relationships with their customers by personalising the webpages of customers who have registered on their website. For example, eBay personalises webpages to suit individual customers, displaying information about previous items that they have looked at, recommending items and reminding them about the end times of certain auctions.

An online business can also monitor its customers' activity in terms of the products they have viewed and bought. This then allows them to recommend products and prompt their customers to review products, building upon the one-to-one relationship. These relationships allow businesses to understand their customers more and therefore target them more effectively.

Your assessment criteria:

P2 Describe how selected organisations use internet marketing

Research

Make of list of your ten favourite shops on the high street. Research them and then describe their online presence. Do they sell products online or just offer information? What are the benefits of selling online and offline?

? Did you know?

iTunes was first launched in 2001.

Discuss

In groups, discuss the following quote: 'Companies must learn to operate as if the world were one large market – ignoring superficial regional and national differences... The global competitor will seek constantly to standardizes his offering everywhere.' (Theodore Levitt, 1983)
Do you agree or disagree? What are the advantages and disadvantages of ignoring cultural and linguistic differences?

Discuss

In groups, discuss the advantages to online retailers of personalising webpages. Are there any disadvantages?

Music can now be bought online as a service rather than a physical product.

 ## Case study

Jenny has a business selling jewellery – Jen's Jewels. She pays rent for a shop in her local high street. Trade has not been going well recently due to the economic downturn and she is struggling to pay the rent. She has been considering the possibility of trading solely online. She has consulted a web designer who has advised her to set up the website so that payments can be made online and so that customers have to log in to create their own personalised webpages. This will be a lot more costly than simply having a website that allows customers to browse the products and then purchase them over the telephone.

1. What are the benefits of personalising webpages for customers?
2. What are the drawbacks of personalising webpages for customers?
3. What are the benefits of offering payment online to customers?
4. What are the drawbacks of offering payment online to customers?

Research

In pairs, research any other products that have changed due to the internet, in that they no longer have to be physical products and are now available online.

The benefits of internet marketing

P3 Benefits to customers

Internet marketing offers a number of benefits to customers.

- Opportunities to compare and select providers and gain increased bargaining power – The internet allows customers to research products from different suppliers, easily and quickly comparing their specifications and prices. Comparison websites such as www.kelkoo.com and www.letsbuyit.com also allow consumers to compare prices, giving them much greater bargaining power. There are also instances where the internet provides the opportunity for customers to set their own prices, for example at www.priceline.co.uk and at online auctions such as www.ebay.co.uk where consumers are able to place bids after viewing the item and its minimum reserve.

- Availability of more comprehensive and up-to-date product information – The internet allows sellers to provide detailed product information (largely to compensate for the fact that customers cannot touch, smell and physically see the products). This is the case in b2c and b2b websites. For example, www.airclic.com is a b2b website that offers potential buyers essential product information tailored to the industry in which the buyer operates.

- Opportunities for lower costs – Customers can take advantage of lower costs by using the internet to make real-time cost savings. This occurs in internet auctions where the website constantly updates the prices when bids are made and stops bids when the time for the auction has expired. This is known as dynamic pricing. There is also the opportunity for greater supply convenience through the responsiveness of transaction facilities. This is most popular when buying airline flights, for example at www.ryanair.com. When few seats on the flight have been sold, prices are low to encourage people to buy; however, as the time of the flight gets closer, and there are fewer seats available, prices increase. The website responds immediately to changes in the market.

- Immediate online sales and customer service – The internet offers the opportunity for customers to make immediate purchases, usually with the reassurance of a confirmation and updates on delivery via email (e.g. at www.amazon.co.uk). The internet also offers unrivalled customer service because websites are available 24 hours a day, with FAQ areas and 'About us' and 'Contact us' links. Buying online also means that customers do not have to travel anywhere to purchase goods and do not risk any unsatisfying sales experiences. If customers are unhappy with the level of service that they have received online, they can make their

Your assessment criteria:

P3 Explain the benefits to customers of a business using internet marketing

M1 Analyse the benefits of internet marketing to customers

Research

Think of two products you would like to buy. Research them using a comparison website.

- *What are the advantages of using comparison websites?*

- *Would you use them again? Why?*

Key terms

Dynamic pricing: prices that change online according to market conditions

Did you know?

The original name for Amazon was Cadabra.

complaint online. They can share their experiences with other customers and get a collective view, for example at www.grumbletext.co.uk.

- Pooling of customer experiences – The internet offers customers the opportunity to air their views in chat rooms. The benefit of this is that customers' views are pooled together and potential customers can see all of the reviews for the product or service. However, this is only available in c2c markets.

- Better prices and no sales pressure – Online customers often benefit from lower prices due to the removal of the middle men (the intermediaries). They are therefore buying directly from the seller. Customers can find buying online more relaxing as no pushy sales techniques can be used.

- Easier to cancel, quicker and more flexible – Customers often find it easier to cancel orders online as they are not embarrassed by having to speak to anyone face to face. The internet shopping experience is also quicker and available 24 hours a day, giving customers more leisure time and more flexibility.

The internet enables customers to make online complaints.

> **💬 Discuss**
>
> *In groups, discuss the benefits to customers of buying goods and services online.*

M1 ▶ Analysing the benefits

In order to analyse the benefits to customers of internet marketing, it is necessary to explain the benefits and compare them with the benefits of offline shopping. You need to analyse areas such as the greater freedom of choice offered by internet marketing, the benefits of price and product comparison sites, the benefits of personalised market attention and the benefits of dynamic pricing which does not exist in offline marketing.

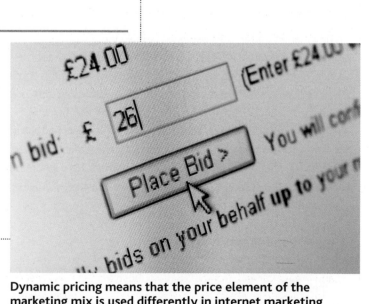

Dynamic pricing means that the price element of the marketing mix is used differently in internet marketing compared to more traditional offline marketing.

The benefits for businesses

 P4 **Building relationships**

When a business, whether it is in a b2b or a b2c market, decides to start trading online, a whole host of new communications become available. As long as it has a well planned website where its products and services are presented clearly and the product information is extensive, it can gather a plethora of information about its customers including their names, addresses, postcodes, telephone numbers and email addresses. The business can then build a database of customers and personalise their webpages according to their previous purchase history. For example, Amazon recommends products to its customers, showing what other customers who have made similar choices have bought, and reviews each of its products. This allows more frequent and individualised communications from the business in the form of emails about promotions, product launches, new services and special offers that may be of interest to the customer. This is how relationships are built.

Businesses also find it easier to alter adverts online as once an alteration has been made, it is only a click away from being shared with the customer. This is quicker and cheaper than changing physical adverts, which then have to be reprinted and displayed. The internet also allows companies to respond quickly to changes in market needs as online stock-holding information can be used to buy in more of the product in good time compared with an offline business that may require longer to register the change.

In b2b markets, businesses also need to build these sorts of relationships through effective communications online. The success of a b2b relationship depends primarily on the communications between the two businesses. If these are good and the relationship lasts long term, the transactions that are made between the two become quicker and records of the transactions are more reliable and accurate. Businesses often use 'customer relationship management' software in order to handle their customers efficiently. This software automates a sales response, responds to customers' queries, manages emails and sends out direct mail.

Customised buyer menus

A customised buyer menu recommends purchases to customers based on their previous transactions, allows them to track current transactions and see their purchase history. When a customer goes onto a business's website, the business has that customer's full attention at least in the initial seconds. It is therefore vital that the website is appealing and relevant to

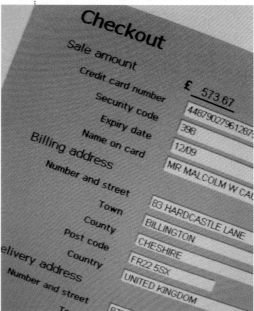

Amazon uses purchase histories to build relationships with customers.

Your assessment criteria:

P4 Describe the benefits and opportunities to the business of using internet marketing within the marketing mix of a selected business

Key terms

Purchase history: *the record of all of the products/services bought by a particular customer*

the customer in order for them to use it effectively. For this reason, when a customer registers with a site, the business records the customer's purchases and creates customised menus to suit the customer's next visit. This means that the business can respond more accurately to the customer's needs and wants.

Product development opportunities

An internet business can also use information to identify product development opportunities. The business can gather information about its products and services by asking customers to leave feedback about the product or service they have received. Also, businesses can buy marketing research information from similar businesses online. In addition, the internet allows customers to buy from firms that they would never have been able to buy from previously. Some online b2b firms will sell online to private customers, opening up a new segment of the market to them.

Sales opportunities

Internet businesses also benefit from the opportunities for immediate sales of products such as banking and insurance policies. These types of products can be bought within minutes, offering immediate peace of mind to customers. Online businesses can also offer substitute forms of certain products such as music, films and radio and TV programmes. By using online forms of these products, customers have the flexibility of watching or listening at their leisure. Businesses can also benefit from offering marketing information in the form of podcasts. For example, the BBC offers podcasts of news summaries and programmes, which viewers can download at any time.

Podcasts are a way of offering marketing information to customers.

⚷ Key terms

Podcasts: *small multimedia files that are downloaded from the internet*

🔍 Research

Research other websites that use purchase history to build relationships with customers. What benefits and opportunities does this give to the businesses?

Making the internet work for businesses

P4 ▸ Opportunities online

Expanding an offline business into new markets is a very costly exercise. For a start, new premises have to be bought, new staff have to be hired and more advertising is required. However, online businesses can expand into new markets relatively cheaply. An online business can reach wide geographic areas, generating new sales through exporting. However, expanding a business online can still be difficult; many businesses are not profitable when they first decide to start trading abroad due to exporting, packaging, customer service and delivery costs.

Small online businesses can trade with relatively low costs and compete with much larger firms. To customers looking at a website, a small business can appear to be operating on exactly the same scale as a much larger firm. The internet also offers businesses the opportunity to show customers some of their products and services 'virtually'. Some estate agents and kitchen design companies offer virtual tours of houses and kitchen designs – customers can 'walk through' computer-generated images that are uploaded onto the site.

The internet offers customers access to services and products 24 hours a day, 7 days a week. For example, customers can carry out online banking without visiting a branch. When banks decided to offer online services to customers, they still kept their branches on the high street. This is known as 'bricks and clicks' – the bank has a brick building in the high street but also offers services at the click of a mouse. Other firms that operate like this are retailers such as B&Q, Next and Marks and Spencer. Some firms operate only as 'clicks' companies – they do not have a branch or store to visit (e.g., Amazon and Dixons).

Some companies that started life as 'bricks' companies, such as Tesco, then developed into 'bricks and clicks' companies, offering products online. The internet has also given Tesco the opportunity of **market diversification** into insurance and banking, which would perhaps not have been so easy to offer had the company not been trading online.

Your assessment criteria:

P4 Describe the benefits and opportunities to the business of using internet marketing within the marketing mix of a selected business

P5 Explain how internet marketing has made a selected business more efficient, effective and successful

🔑 Key terms

Market diversification: expanding a business by offering new products and services

🔍 Research

In pairs, research other' bricks and clicks' companies. What market diversification opportunities has the internet allowed them to explore?

The internet has offered companies like Tesco the opportunity for market diversification.

P5 Business efficiency

By going online, a business can become more efficient, effective and therefore successful. This can happen in several different ways:

- Using the internet to manage the supply chain – All businesses in b2b markets are part of a supply chain. A business is both a buyer and a supplier – it buys from one business and sells to another. For example, a business that makes calculators will buy (or procure) the components from a number of other companies, make the calculator and then sell it to retail outlets such as WHSmith. For businesses working within a supply chain, a high level of communication is required in order for the supplies to get to the relevant companies on time. The internet allows companies to manage the supply chain more efficiently and effectively, creating an electronic link to coordinate the shipping of products, negotiate with suppliers and track orders, etc. The internet allows all of the people involved in this supply chain to share relevant information and specify their requirements. Being electronically connected to all other suppliers and buyers in the supply chain offers businesses opportunities to be more informed, efficient, effective and competitive.

- Using electronic communications to reduce staff costs – Using the internet means that not as many staff are needed to act as communicators with other businesses, as fewer people are needed to manage online communication via the web. This reduces a business's costs as fewer staff have to be employed.

 Design

In groups, pick a product with which you are familiar. Design the supply chain for the product, from the suppliers to the customer. Explain, at each link in the chain, how the internet is used to make the links within the supply chain more effective and efficient.

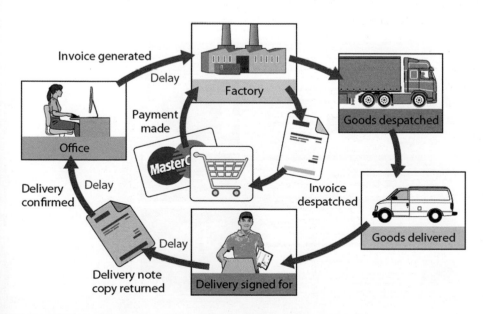

There are a number of inevitable delays within a conventional supply chain.

P5 Business opportunities

By going online, a business can become more efficient, effective and therefore successful. This is because the internet offers a business the opportunity to:

- Increase sales from existing customers – An offline business may choose to start trading online as it sees opportunities to improve its sales in the markets in which it already operates.

- Enter completely new markets – The internet provides a cheaper and more effective way of penetrating markets.

- Monitor competitor activity – The internet holds a wealth of information for customers, but also for businesses. They can use to it to monitor what their competitors are doing and check customer trends and developments in order to develop new products and services.

- Advertise online – This means that a business can reach a far greater audience for a lower cost than by using traditional promotional methods.

Internet advertising

Online advertising has become big business and is a vital part of all successful advertising campaigns. Banner ads are probably the most popular form of internet advertising. These are small rectangular advertisements on websites that, once clicked on, take the internet user to the advertiser company's website.

Search engines are another way for customers to find out about a business. When a customer types in a vague description of the type of company they are looking for, thousands of companies' websites can be suggested. For example, if you type 'bed and breakfast, Pattingham' into a search engine such as www.google.co.uk, a host of websites are listed. Businesses pay to be sponsored links so that their businesses show up on the first page of these lists.

Banner ads are probably the most popular form of internet advertising.

? Did you know?

The first formal advertising on the internet happened in October 1994 on Hotwired, when AT&T launched a banner campaign on the site.

Links also offer businesses low cost methods of getting traffic to their websites. There are two different types of links:

- **Affiliate links** – A link to one business is placed on another site in return for money. The money received depends on how many times the link is clicked on.

- **Reciprocal links** – These are two-way links between two businesses.
  No payment is made between the two.

Web portals are links pages where information is presented from a range of sources. They are similar to search engines but also offer services such as email, news, stock prices and entertainment. An example is www.yahoo.com.

Web portals offer businesses the opportunity to attract more traffic to their websites.

 ## Case study

Online advertising is essential for any online business to be successful. There are many different types of internet advertising, including banner ads, search engines and links. However, some online businesses choose to advertise through PPC (Pay Per Click). This is when the websites only pay the host when their ad is clicked on.

This can have many benefits for online businesses.

PPC advertising can give the online business immediate results compared to search engine optimisation as the PPC advert will be on the search engine website as soon as it has been made. The placement of the PPC advert on the search engine depends on how much the online business pays (the further towards the top or the side of the search engine website, the more expensive it is). However, it can be argued that PPC allows online businesses to control the amount of money they spend. For example, it is possible for an online firm to choose to spend only £20 per day on advertising for a particular product.

PPC advertising is also useful for online businesses that want to specifically target customers in other countries. It is possible to place a PPC advert with a specification that is for web browsers in Spain, for example. Similarly, if an online business only wants to advertise in peak seasons, or at certain times of the year, the ad can be customised to run only at these particular times.

1. What are the benefits of PPC advertising?

2. Compare and contrast PPC advertising with one other form of internet advertising.

 Key terms

Affiliate links: hyperlinks that direct potential customers from one site to another – payment is made for 'click through' sales

Reciprocal links: links between two websites

Web portals: sites or systems that give access to information from a variety of sources

 Discuss

In groups, discuss the opportunities that are available to internet businesses to become more efficient, effective and successful.

Challenges of internet marketing

While the internet offers lots of benefits to businesses, it also creates its fair share of challenges. A business must look at the value that being online adds; if it fails to add value, the strategy that was used to initiate internet trading must have been poorly thought out or inappropriate for that business.

There are several challenges that face businesses using internet marketing. These include:

- Disintermediation – There are benefits to disintermediation (see page 269), but it also presents some challenges to businesses. Some internet businesses now sell directly to the customer (e.g. www.dell.com). Retailers who previously sold their products may object to business being taken away from them and refuse to sell the products in future.

- Channel conflict – When a business starts distributing products online, this can threaten relationships that have been built up in the past with existing distributors. Businesses must be aware of their **core competence** (i.e. what they do best) and therefore focus on developing this and developing the necessary relationships with other businesses in order for their core competence to develop. Argos, for example, realises that its competence is providing catalogue orders to customers and therefore outsourced their order calls during the Christmas period to a call-centre company called beCogent.

- Low customer confidence in payment security – Customers are often concerned about paying for goods over the internet, especially in the light of news stories about identity fraud and hacking. This means that many people refuse to buy online for fear of their card details being used fraudulently. Businesses therefore need to reassure their customers with regards to security and costs.

- Higher reliability expectations – Due to the flexibility that the internet offers to customers, they have begun to expect more from online businesses in terms of reliability and speed of service. The challenge for online businesses is then to not let their customers down. An online company can invest heavily in creating an easy-to-use, informative, secure, personalised and competitive website, but if the company cannot meet customer expectations, the investment has been wasted. Online businesses need to manage customer expectations with realistic promises and do so profitably.

Your assessment criteria:

P6 Explain the challenges of globalisation facing a selected business when using the internet as a marketing tool

Key terms

Channel conflict: when a business starts trading online and threatens existing relationships with businesses within its supply chain

Core competence: what a business does best

Discuss

In pairs, discuss the benefits and drawbacks of paying for goods online.

- An overload of market feedback – Many online businesses want to continue to improve their customer service in order to stay competitive. To do this, they need to know how well they are doing and therefore collect customer feedback from webpages and 'Contact us' links. However, sometimes a company receives so much information, due to the ease with which customers can leave feedback, that it is too much for the company to process. Similarly, most websites ask a customer to register before purchasing goods in order that the business can deliver them a personalised service. However, when registered customers are asked to leave lots of personal details, such as name, address, email address, telephone number, the company needs very sophisticated and expensive databases in order to process all of this data (as individual and group customer profiles) and use it effectively to market its products in the future.

- Complex analysis – There is little point an online business receiving market feedback from its customers if the information gathered is not analysed. When a company has too much information, it can sometimes require analysis that is too complex and therefore not always understood.

- Revising marketing goals in line with the capacity to process feedback – The amount of market feedback that online businesses receive (and hopefully process effectively) means that they also have to reassess their marketing goals in order to meet the changing needs of their customers. If a business is not able to process the information, its marketing goals will not be inline with its customers' needs.

Businesses can sometimes receive too much information.

 Discuss

In groups, discuss the benefits and drawbacks of online businesses having market feedback.

Discuss

In groups, discuss how online businesses can overcome the challenges of market feedback overload.

P6 More challenges

- Keeping pace with market and technological change – In an increasingly technological age, businesses are under growing pressure to innovate in everything they do and in all markets. Businesses need constantly to accommodate new ways of working, with new technologies and providing faster and more efficient products. Speed is everything and this adds pressure to the daily running of a business.

- Ensuring maximum access via ISPs and search engines – Businesses and private customers must ensure that they receive a satisfactory level of service from their ISP. The speed and reliability of access is crucial. Search engines are also very important to the success of a website as the majority of web users use search engines to find websites. A company's website must be registered on the search engine and preferably be elevated in the search engine's listings.

- Security of site information and payment systems – Viruses and hackers, etc. are a constant threat to internet security and mean that customers and businesses are continually trying to increase their security online. Customers need to be reassured that the payment system used by the website is secure. Similarly, information on a website needs to be protected as part of a business's e-business strategy. There are three different ways of protecting website information:

  - authentication – customers must identify themselves through a username and password

  - authorisation – identifying who has access to information, ensuring a policy is set up to protect the information and ensuring it is centrally controlled and monitored

  - encryption – the changing of data into a format that nobody else understands unless they have a 'key'. Personal information, prices, contracts and research should all be encrypted.

- Linguistic/cultural sensitivity – As the internet continues to grow worldwide, it is becoming increasingly important to ensure that websites are understood by all nationalities, especially if the business is aiming to expand into new markets. Businesses need to be careful when translating from one language to another as mishaps can cost the business. Cultural differences should also be considered. For example, when Disney

Key terms

ISP: *Internet Service Provider – company that offers an internet connection*

In Italy, Schweppes Tonic Water was translated incorrectly as Schweppes Toilet Water.

opened Euro Disney it did not take into consideration the cultural differences between Europeans and Americans. It built the restaurants too small, not realising that Europeans like to sit down for mealtimes; the rides were not sufficiently weatherproof; American-style service was not welcomed and the French felt that the uniform guidelines stripped them of their individualism. Similarly, when Kellogg's promoted its products in India, it found (and is still finding) it difficult to overcome the culture of eating hot vegetables in the morning.

- Additional legal complexity – When customers buy products over the internet from abroad (e.g. from Australia) and the product is faulty, there is an issue as to which legal and taxation system applies to the product (e.g. Australia's or the UK's). When a business sets up a website to sell in other countries, it must satisfy all of the legal requirements that exist in those countries, which can add extra costs to the business.

M2 ▶ Analysing

In order to complete M2, you need to choose an online company and analyse the opportunities and challenges that it faces or has faced and those faced by its customers. You need to consider all of elements of the marketing mix including product, pricing, placement and promotion.

D1 ▶ Evaluating

In order to complete D1, you need to review the information that you have presented about the online business chosen in M2. You must outline your own views, based on judgements and backed up with research. You must judge whether the performance of

Kellogg's faced challenges when promoting its products in India.

your selected business could be enhanced through integrating internet marketing into its overall marketing strategy, despite any challenges that you have identified. You will need to explore the principles, benefits, opportunities and challenges of internet marketing and weigh up any opposing considerations before reaching a final supported viewpoint.

Q | Research

Research examples of cultural or linguistic insensitivities that have occurred when businesses have entered into other markets.

Q | Research

Research online companies that you could investigate and analyse for M2. Make a list of all of the opportunities and challenges they have faced.

 Discuss

In groups, discuss one of the companies that you have chosen and the opportunities and challenges that it has faced. Discuss whether you believe internet marketing has met customers' needs. Back up any viewpoints in your discussion with facts.

Assessment checklist

To achieve a pass grade, my portfolio of evidence must show that I can:

Assessment criteria	Description	✓
P1	Describe the role internet marketing has within a modern marketing context	☐
P2	Describe how selected organisations use internet marketing	☐
P3	Explain the benefits to customers of a business using internet marketing	☐
P4	Describe the benefits and opportunities to the business of using internet marketing within the marketing mix of a selected business	☐
P5	Explain how internet marketing has made a selected business more efficient, effective and successful	☐
P6	Explain the challenges of globalisation facing a selected business when using the internet as a marketing tool	☐

To achieve a merit grade, my portfolio of evidence must show that I can:

Assessment criteria	Description	✓
M1	Analyse the benefits of internet marketing to customers	☐
M2	Analyse the marketing opportunities and challenges faced by a selected business when using internet marketing	☐

To achieve a distinction grade, my portfolio of evidence must show that I can:

Assessment criteria	Description	✓
D1	Evaluate the effectiveness of internet marketing in meeting customer needs for a selected business	☐

15 | Development planning for a career in business

LO1 Know how to access career-related information

▸ There's so much information out there – How do you know where to start looking for career-related information?

▸ What types of information do you need?

LO2 Be able to develop a personal career development plan

▸ Think about where you want to be in 2 to 5 years' time.

▸ How are you going to get to where you want to be in life?

▸ What targets will you set and how are you going to make sure you achieve them?

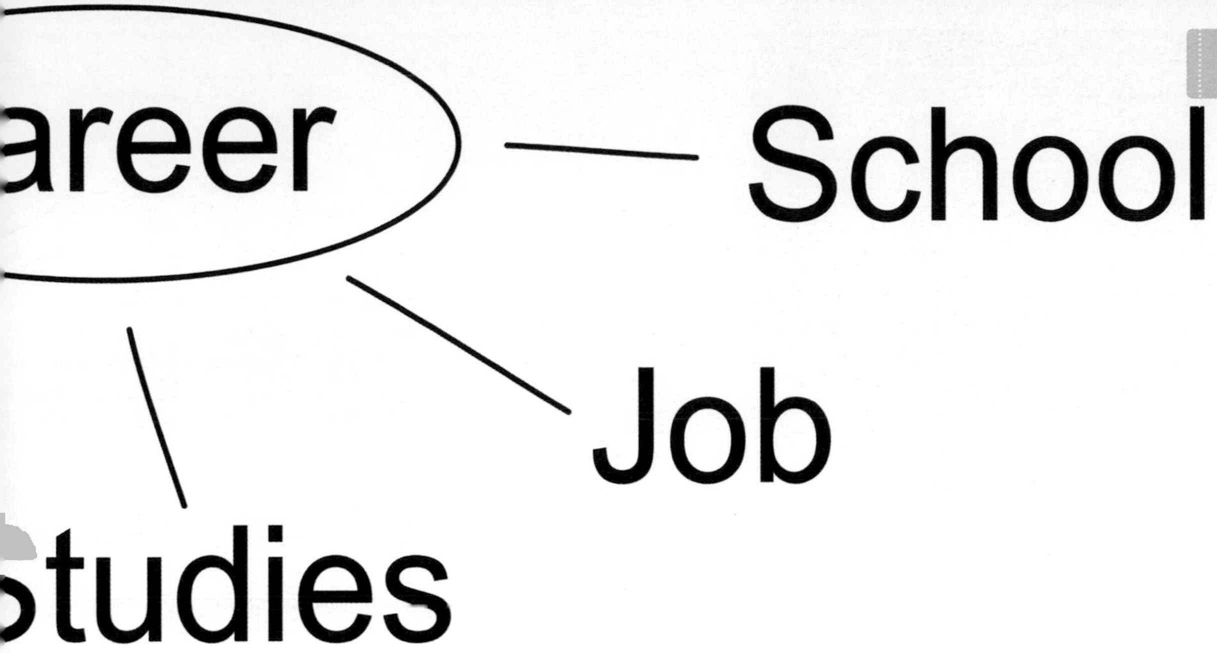

areer —— School

Job

tudies

LO3 Be able to develop a range of transferable business skills at the appropriate level	LO4 Understand methods of professional development and training
▸ What skills do you have that make you more employable?	▸ How do you ensure you continue to develop professionally?
▸ What level of qualifications do you want to achieve?	

When deciding on your next step after your school-based education, it is necessary to research all of the different options.

P1 Where to look

There are several agencies, some government run and others not, that offer careers-related advice and help. It is not their job to tell you what career to go into but by learning about your skills and interests, they can suggest careers which may interest you and tell you what you need to do to move towards a career in that area. Career advice should enable you to make the right decisions and to avoid making mistakes. In order to complete P1, you should research your future career by looking at all or some of the following services:

Connexions offers advice on careers, learning, health, housing, etc.

- Connexions (www.connexions-direct.com) is an organisation that offers advice on careers, learning, health, housing, leisure, work, money, relationships and travel for 13–19 year olds in the UK. It offers careers resources and advice on post-16 choices.

- Skills Funding Agency (www.skillsfundingagency. bis.gov.uk) is a government agency that ensures that adults can gain access to training so that they can succeed in their careers and therefore play a significant role in our economy. It also advertises job vacancies and gives advice to employers on how best to support and nurture the skills of their employees.

- Young People's Learning Agency (www.ypla.gov.uk) is a government agency that provides funding to support young learners aged 16–19. Job vacancies are posted on the website and there is also a wealth of information about financial support for students' education.

- Job Centres (http://jobseekers.direct.gov.uk and www.jobcentreonline. com) are government centres that advertise job opportunities and vacancies. They help potential employees get back to work and give them advice on how to apply for jobs. They support employers by offering advice on the different programmes they offer.

- Prospects (www.prospects.ac.uk) is a graduate careers website which advertises both jobs and courses.

Careers services are available at most schools, colleges and universities. They offer personal advice and career support and usually have databases of jobs and course vacancies. Your school/college or local library or careers service may have access to CASCAID's Kudos software. This software guides you through questions, asks about your qualifications and suggests types of career that may interest you.

Career and recruitment fairs are exhibitions at which employers, schools, universities and colleges display information and meet potential students and employees. To find a careers fair in your area go to www.careerfairs.com A visiting speaker may come to your school or college to tell you about careers-related information on a specific company or industry or how to apply for courses and/or jobs.

🔍 Research

- *Research careers or recruitment fairs that are happening in your local area.*

- *Book an appointment with your careers service in school/college.*

If you know the company you would like to work for, a good place to start looking for career-related information is on its website. The majority of companies provide information on vacancies and application procedures. An organisation's website will also tell you a lot about the company, enabling you to judge whether it really is a company you would like to work for. Similarly, the Human Resources department – the department that recruits, selects and retains employees – can supply you with information about jobs available and how to apply.

If you have been on work experience (usually in year 10 and year 12) you will have a good insight into the company that you worked for, and if you are looking to start a career in the same area, it makes sense to contact the company for advice.

It may also be useful to look in newspapers as they often advertise job vacancies, training and educational courses. Similarly, if you know the industry you would like to have a career in, trade or specialist journals often advertise job vacancies in the industry.

A typical careers fair

If you are looking into applying for universities and colleges, you should request a prospectus from college or university websites or from your local careers service. These are full of information about the campus, the courses offered and the entry requirements.

Qualifications and training

P1 ▶ Qualifications

There are many benefits to the organisation of having a strong and valuable brand. These include:

- HNDs (Higher National Diplomas) – work-based higher education qualifications. These are vocational qualifications that are designed to equip you with the skills necessary to carry out a particular job. For more information on HNDs go to www.direct.gov.uk and search for HND.

- Degrees – level 6 academic qualifications. These are offered by universities in many different subjects. Degrees are necessary to gain entry into certain careers but not all. It is important to research the type of degree you would like to study. For information about all different types of degrees and universities in the UK go to www.ucas.ac.uk.

- Foundation Degrees – higher education qualifications that combine workplace learning and academic study. They have often been designed with the help of employers, colleges and universities that specialise in that industry. They are designed to equip people for a certain kind of job but also give you the general skills for any type of job. For more information on Foundation Degrees go to www.direct.gov.uk and search for Foundation Degree.

- National Vocational Qualifications (NVQs) – qualifications based on a certain type of job. They are competence related, i.e. based on your ability to carry out the job. They can be studied as part of an apprenticeship or while at work or college. For more information on NVQs go to www.direct.gov.uk and search for NVQ.

- Vocational Qualifications (VQs) – qualifications specifically about a particular type of work (you are studying for one now). BTECs, City and Guilds and OCR Nationals are all vocational qualifications. They are work related and allow you to learn in more detail about a particular type of work or industry. For more information on VQs go to www.direct.gov.uk and search for VQ.

- Occupational Qualifications – cover the skills and competencies that you need to know in order to carry out a specific job, for example

> **Research**
>
> *On your own, look at all of the different types of qualifications that you could complete. Which ones interest you the most and why?*

UCAS provides a wealth of information about degrees and universities.

> **? Did you know?**
>
> *In 2008/09 89.9 per cent of graduates went on to employment or further study.*

plumbing. They are based on national standards and are usually assessed in the workplace. You can undergo occupation qualifications when you are already working full time or when you are at school or college with a work placement or part-time job. There are no age limits or special entry requirements.

- General Qualifications – cover GCSEs (General Certificate of Secondary Education) and GCE A-levels (General Certificate of Education Advanced Level). These are academic qualifications that are on a specific subject and a generally taken in a range of subjects by 14–19 year olds in the UK. GCSEs are usually the minimum requirement in order to get onto an A-level course.

Training

Most careers also offer training once you have gained a job. There are several methods of undertaking learning and training. In certain careers you may undertake on-the-job training where you are trained in the workplace, using the tools and documents that trainees would use when they are fully trained. Off-the-job training takes place away from the workplace and usually means that the training is not directly related to the production line in the company. E-learning is another method of training where the employee uses a computer in order to carry out training. The training is delivered via the internet, audio or video tape, satellite TV or CD-Rom.

Discuss

In pairs, pretend one of you is a careers advisor and the other is a student visiting the careers advisor. As the careers advisor, you must advise the student on all of the sources and types of information you think would be relevant to them. Once you have completed the task, swap roles.

A student undertaking training

Creating a career plan

Creating a career plan is an important step as you come closer to finishing your vocational qualification. It takes you from choosing your occupation through the steps to being employed and reaching your short-, medium- and long-term career goals.

Your assessment criteria:

P2 Complete a career plan identifying your development needs

P2 Personal SWOT analysis

A **personal SWOT analysis** enables you to identify your Strengths, such as your qualifications, knowledge, skills and experience, that may be valuable in your chosen employment. You should then identify your Weaknesses, which may include gaps in your qualifications, knowledge or experience, weak points in your personality and financial constraints. The purpose of identifying these is so that you can plan how to overcome them. The next step is identifying any Opportunities that are open to you that could be used to your advantage at present or in the near future. These could include job vacancies, sponsorship or financial incentives if you are looking at gaining extra qualifications or gaps in the marketplace that you could exploit, given your skills. The last aspect of SWOT is identifying any Threats that may be of a disadvantage to you. These may include potential financial problems, unfavourable changes in the economy or changes in the marketplace that may mean your skills and knowledge become outdated.

Use the questions in Figure 15.1 to help you complete a personal SWOT analysis.

Key terms

Personal SWOT analysis: an analysis of yourself identifying your strengths, weaknesses, opportunities and threats

Did you know?

Organisations also complete SWOTs to analyse their business.

Figure 15.1 How to complete a personal SWOT analysis

Strengths What are your positive aspects?	Weaknesses What are your negative aspects?
• What qualifications do you have?	• Are there any gaps in your qualifications?
• What work experience do you have?	• Are there any gaps in your knowledge?
• What specialist knowledge do you have?	• Are there any gaps in your experience?
• What skills do you have?	• Do you have any financial difficulties?
• What are the positive aspects of your personality?	• What are the weak points in your personality?
• What motivates you?	• What circumstances make you feel unhappy or frustrated?
• Do you have any other strengths?	• Do you have any other limitations?

Figure 15.1 (continued)

Opportunities What aspects at present or in the near future could you use to your advantage?	Threats What aspects at present or in the near future may be a disadvantage to you?
• Are there any job vacancies that are available to you?	• Do you have any potential financial problems?
• Are there any gaps in the marketplace you could exploit?	• Is there any competition from rivals?
• Are there any scholarships or bursaries available to you?	• Are there any unfavourable conditions in the economy?
	• Are there any changes in the marketplace that could mean that your skills and knowledge become out of date?

Short-term career goals

Once you have identified your strengths, weaknesses, opportunities and threats, you need to identify your **short-term career goals**. This means thinking about where you would like to be in 2 years' time. You need to consider how you are going to get there and consider any weaknesses or threats that have been identified that may prevent you from achieving your short-term career goals. You will also need to consider what you are going to do in order to convert your weaknesses and threats into strengths and opportunities.

Medium-term career goals

Your **medium-term career goals** are concerned with where you would like to be in 5 years' time. You need to think about how you are going to get there, perhaps what extra skills, experience, knowledge and qualifications you may have or need to gain and also how your job may change in the next 5 years.

Discuss

In groups, take it in turns to discuss your strengths, weaknesses, opportunities and threats. You may be surprised by what others have to say.

Design

Design a career goal map for your partner. Look at the goals your partner has set for you. Do you agree with them?

Key terms

Medium-term personal career goals: what you would like to achieve in your career within the next 5 years

Short-term personal career goals: what you would like to achieve in your career within the next 2 years

Did you know?

SWOT analysis was created by Albert Humphrey.

295

Creating a Curriculum Vitae

 P2 **Summarising your experience, qualifications and skills**

A **Curriculum Vitae (CV)** is a written description of your educational history, work experience and skills. It is a formal document which is needed when you apply for certain jobs. It should summarise all of your qualifications, work experience and training. It is important to update your CV every time you achieve something, whether it is a new qualification or training or an award. Your CV should sell you and your skills and qualities to a potential employer.

 Case study

When Michael first applied for jobs, he wrote what he thought was a brilliant CV. He really sold himself, or so he thought. However, after not getting any invitations to interviews, he started to wonder where he was going wrong. He decided to take his CV to his local careers advisor. She pointed out the mistakes in his CV. She listed them as follows:

- too long
- too many sentences
- no expertise/skills section
- not targeted at the role being applied for
- no personal profile
- too much detail in the education section
- no achievements section
- too much use of 'I'.

For each of the points listed above, advise Michael on how to overcome these common problems.

 Your assessment criteria:

P2 Complete a career plan identifying your development needs

 Key terms

Curriculum Vitae (CV): *a written description summarising your education, work experience, skills and knowledge*

Discuss

- *In groups, take it in turns to talk about what you could include in your CV.*
- *Ask each person in the group to give you another example of what could be included in your CV.*

? | **Did you know?**

If you have even one spelling mistake in your CV, a potential employer will probably throw the CV straight in the bin. They have to start shortlisting somehow!

Curriculum Vitae
Wendy Goodwin
223 Sedgley Road
Lanesfield
Telephone (01456) 789000 or 07777 655544
Email: wendygoodwin@thebestCV.co.uk

Date of Birth: 24 August 1991   Nationality: British

Personal Profile
I consider myself to be a very motivated individual. I have recently started my degree in Business at London University. I have also worked as a valuable member of a team at Pizza Express for the last 3 years. I have worked my way up to team leader and have gained several skills in doing so. I am an excellent team player, I understand how to manage people with differing personalities, I can set and achieve targets and I always strive to make the customer as happy as possible. I am now looking for my next challenge in an office environment. I would like to gain experience in the field of Human Resources as I am keen to specialise in this as part of my degree. Becoming a HR administrator would mean that I would be using my customer-facing skills, while working in a team and meeting company targets.

Education and Qualifications

2010–2013	University of London, BSC Business, (Predicted 2:1)
	Modules studied include HR in the workplace, Business to Business Marketing and Finance.
2008–2010	Mudley 6th Form College
	BTEC Business (Distinction)
	BTEC ICT (Merit)
	A-Level Law (B)
2003–2008	Mudley Girls High School
	GCSEs – 6 GCSEs including Maths and English

Work Experience

June 2010– April 2011	Pizza Express, Team Leader
	Main responsibilities included managing a team of five waiting staff, meeting and greeting customers, managing customer complaints and serving tables.
	Skills gained include team-working skills, problem-solving skills and excellent time management.
July 2008–Mar 2010	Staples Stationery, cashier
	Main responsibilities included working on the tills and shelf stacking.
	Skills gained included excellent communication skills, interpersonal skills and problem solving.

Skills

I speak French
IT skills including the confident use of Word, Excel, Access and Publisher

Interests and Activities
During my gap year I travelled around Europe which greatly helped my daily communication skills and French language skills through meeting a variety of people. I also enjoy playing netball and basketball on a regular basis. Playing these sports has meant that I have kept physically fit and am capable of working with other people in order to achieve a common goal.

References

Available on request

Figure 15.2 Example of a CV

Carrying out a skills audit

P3 Identifying gaps

Your next important step is to carry out a **skills audit**. A skills audit helps you to identify the skills and strengths that you have, and the skills and strengths that you need in order to achieve your short- and medium-term career objectives. Once you have researched and chosen a career you should have also worked out the skills and qualifications that you require.

The skills that you do not yet possess will be identified in your skills audit; this is otherwise known as your **skills gap**. Once you have identified your skills gap, you should plan how you are going to fill the gap – what are you going to do in order to gain those skills.

You may also find that you are lacking certain qualifications. This is known as your **qualifications gap**. You will then need to create a **qualifications map** of how you are going to gain these qualifications, from where, how much they will cost and when you are planning to complete them.

Your assessment criteria:

P3 Carry out a skills audit to identify skills gaps

 Key terms

Qualifications gap: a detailed list of all of the qualifications that you need to gain in order to achieve your short- and medium-term career goals

Qualifications map: a plan for how you are going to fill your qualifications gap

Skills audit: an analysis of all of your skills and strengths

Skills gap: any skills you can identify that you may need in order to achieve your short- and long-term career goals

Figure 15.3 An example of a skills audit

Skills	Where the skills have been developed
Communication and literacy skills	Good use of written English gained from producing a range of reports and essays.
	Always have corrections to the structure of my work and therefore I will make arrangements to talk to the teacher about how this can be improved.
	During my BTEC Business I have completed many presentations. I prefer, however, making individual presentations rather than group ones as I feel more in control. I plan to organise groups better and practise taking part in group presentations.
	Clear communication is very important between me, other colleagues and my boss. My interpersonal skills are also developing rapidly as I am dealing with more and more customers.
	I plan to go to the careers centre at college in order to improve my interview techniques.
Team-working skills	I have played lots of football for my school team. I have also completed my Duke of Edinburgh Bronze Award where we had to complete a group expedition. We had to work closely as a group in order to plan and undertake the expedition. In groups I always strive to make a positive contribution.
	I need to develop my leadership and organisation skills. I may organise an event within my college.

Figure 15.3 (continued)

Skills	Where the skills have been developed
Organisation and independent learning skills	I am self-motivated when I am undertaking a task that I enjoy. However, I am trying to develop my time-management skills as I rarely hand my coursework in on time. I therefore need to improve the preparation that I do. I have had a couple of different jobs in local stores over the last 2 years. In these I was expected to take responsibility and act on my own initiative.
ICT skills	I am very confident using Word and Excel as I use them on a regular basis. However, I am not so confident with Access, PowerPoint or Publisher. I am planning to sign up to a free computer class after college in order to improve these skills. I am very confident using email as I use it to keep in touch with friends and family.
Numerical skills	GCSE Maths grade C and I am confident using basic maths skills including graphs and charts and some statistical techniques such as mean, mode and median. I am not so confident with mental arithmetic and this could cause problems in the future if I need to add up customers' orders.
Research and problem-solving skills	Whenever a problem arises I take time out to think of a solution. I try not to panic but think logically about how it can be solved. During my Duke of Edinburgh expedition we came across problems as a group and individually that needed solving. I therefore have a good knowledge of the processes you need to undertake in order to solve a problem. I do lot of online research on a weekly basis for my BTEC Business coursework. However, I need to join my local library in order to prepare myself for university so that I can learn how to use online library catalogues.

Discussing your skills can be a valuable exercise.

 Discuss

- *In groups of three or four, discuss each other's strengths in terms of skills and suggest to each other how these could be improved.*

- *When you go home, ask your friends and family if they agree with this assessment of your skills and how they could be improved.*

Target setting

 M1 A personal development plan

Creating your own **personal development plan** helps you to reflect on what you need to do in order to stay on track to achieve your short- and medium-term career goals.

First, you should write a description of the development needs you have identified by carrying out your personal SWOT and skills audit. These may include enhancing your computer skills by completing a course at college or developing your interview techniques by visiting your career centre. You then need to write down in detail how you are going to maintain the correct level of skills; this could be by continuing to practise them. For example, if you need to maintain good levels of oral communication you may need to continue practising speaking in front of audiences and could offer to do a presentation at college. You may also have identified **training requirements**.

You should also describe how and when you are going to review your development plan. This means you will need to set yourself **timescales** of when you are planning to develop your skills and deadlines by which you should have completed the work. Remember that these deadlines must fit with the timings of your short- and medium-term career goals.

Your assessment criteria:

M1 Assess methods of achieving development needs within the timeframe of the career plan

P4 Create SMART targets for the career plan

Key terms

Personal development plan: a plan of how to meet your development needs in order to achieve your short- and medium-term career goals

Timescales: periods of time within which you must gain or maintain your development needs

Training requirements: any training you may need in order to meet your development needs

Creating a personal development plan

Discuss

Discuss in groups of three or four how you will go about creating your personal development plan.

- *What development needs have you identified?*

- *How will you meet those needs?*

- *How do these fit in with the timescales of your career goals?*

P4 SMART targets

The most effective short- and medium-term career goals are SMART – Specific, Measurable, Achievable, Realistic and Time related. An example of a **SMART target** is: to become finance assistant with an accounting firm and achieve 50 per cent in all of the modules in my CIMA qualification in the next 2 years. This objective is:

- specific in that it details exactly what has to be done

- measurable because a pass mark percentage has been included

- achievable as long as the individual is dedicated and self motivated to achieve it

- realistic if it is calculated that it is possible to attain

- time related as the length of time in which it should be achieved is stated.

Mapping your progress

Once you have set and ensured that your short- and medium-term career goals and your development goals are SMART, it is important that you map your progress against these targets. This entails making notes of anything that you are doing, planned or otherwise, that means you are working towards achieving them. All of your achievements from now on until you achieve your goals must be recorded as a way of proving that you have achieved these goals.

Did you know?

SMART was invented by George Doran, Arthur Miller and James Cunningham.

Key terms

SMART targets: targets that are Specific, Measurable, Achievable, Realistic and Time related

Discuss

- Discuss with a partner the importance of having SMART targets.

- Attempt to work out together how your short-term, medium-term and development goals can be made SMART.

Specific – targets have to be detailed.

Measurable – targets have to include a measurable figure.

Achievable – everybody needs to be committed to achieving the target.

Realistic – targets have to be possible to attain.

Time related – a length of time should be added.

Figure 15.4 SMART targets

M2 > Progress towards targets

It important to set yourself targets, but it is even more important to achieve them. You therefore need to ensure that you continually **evaluate** your **progress** towards them and audit that progress. This means reflecting on what has gone well and what has not gone so well.

Adjusting targets and reassessing objectives

No one expects you to come up with perfect career goals first time round. It may be that your interests change as you study or work more, or you may decide to become even more ambitious. **Adjusting targets** that you have set is an important step in ensuring that you meet your desired career goals. After adjusting your targets it may also be necessary to **reassess the objectives** that you set in your personal development plan. If you adjust your career goals, your development objectives may also change. You must ensure that all of your adjustments and reassessments are still SMART.

Responding to feedback

In order to be successful in life, it is essential to listen to people – especially those who know what they are talking about. Your tutor, career advisor, family or friends may look at your targets and give you feedback on whether they are suitable for you. You may have been too hard on yourself and be expecting too much, or you may have been too easy on yourself and need pushing a little more. **Respond** to this **feedback** by using it to adjust your targets and reassess your objectives.

Getting feedback from a tutor, career advisor, family or friends is very helpful.

Your assessment criteria:

M2   Monitor and audit progress towards targets using appropriate success criteria

D1   Evaluate the distance travelled in achieving the planned objectives of the career plan

Key terms

Adjusting targets: *changing your career goals in order to reflect the present situation*

Evaluating progress: *judging what has gone well and what has not gone so well in relation to progress towards your career goals and development plan*

Reassessing objectives: *reflecting on the objectives set in your personal development plan to assess whether they are still valid for the adjusted targets*

Responding to feedback: *gaining insight from others regarding the progress and adjustments you have made and feeding this back into your personal development plan*

Discuss

Discuss your targets with your teacher, friends and family. Ensure to write down any feedback they give you.

D1 How far have you travelled?

Once you have made a career plan it is important to evaluate how far you have got at any given time towards achieving the objectives. This is not an exercise that needs to be done only once; it is something that you will need to do at least annually during your working life.

In order to evaluate how far you have travelled from when you set your objectives to the present time, you need to look at what you have done to date and whether it is what you set out to achieve in the timeframe. If you have achieved your objectives, you need to look at how and why you achieved them.

If you did not meet your objectives, you need to ask yourself what you need to do in order to meet them and how you can readjust your targets in order to reach your objectives by the next deadline. You also need to explain why you have not reached your objectives.

This process of self-assessment is also known as **lifelong learning**. It is the process of constantly updating your achievements in order to continue bettering yourself and striving to achieve all your personal and professional goals. Lifelong learning is taken extremely seriously in the world of work with yearly appraisals taking place to ensure that you are travelling well through your career objectives.

Discuss

In pairs, discuss how far you think you have 'travelled' towards achieving your targets. Be sure to justify your thoughts.

Key terms

Lifelong learning: continuous updating of skills, knowledge, abilities and qualifications

How far have you travelled towards achieving your goals?

Developing transferable business skills

P5 Transferable business skills

Your assessment criteria:

 P5 Demonstrate transferable business skills

Transferable business skills include all of those skills that are necessary in all types of jobs, whatever field you choose to go into. They may be skills that you have already demonstrated, but they may also be skills that you have never used before and which therefore require some practice.

Skills for life are the skills that you will need throughout your personal and professional life. These include:

- Communication skills – the ability to share or exchange information or ideas with others. This includes knowing when it is appropriate to use formal language (e.g. in letters, interviews and presentations) and when it is acceptable to use informal language (e.g. text messages, conversations and some emails). Non-verbal communication includes written communication, either on paper or screen. Verbal communication uses the human voice – presentations, interviews, telephone calls and video conferencing. Body language and the ability to listen are also valuable communication skills.

- ICT skills – these are becoming increasingly important in our personal and professional lives and include the ability to use programmes such as Word, Excel, PowerPoint and Access, and to email and research online.

- Numeracy skills – these include the ability to do mental arithmetic and to use statistical techniques and basic mathematical functions. A grade C in Maths GCSE is a minimum requirement for the majority of jobs.

Wider transferable skills include the functional skills that are necessary to participate in life, education and work, such as literacy, numeracy and ICT. The importance of numeracy and ICT skills has been outlined above. Literacy skills are those needed in order to be able to read and write, including the ability to structure sentences, phrases and paragraphs correctly and to ensure your spellings are accurate.

Vocational skills are the practical and manual skills that you need in order to do your job. You are learning vocational skills through your BTEC National Business qualification. This qualification is all about preparing you for a career in business and is therefore teaching you how to write reports, undertake presentations, communicate effectively and be prepared for interviews.

 Key terms

Skills for life: the skills you will need throughout your personal and professional life, including communication, ICT and numeracy skills

Vocational skills: the practical and manual skills you need in order to do your specific job

Wider transferable skills: these include the functional skills that are necessary to participate in life, education and work, such as literacy, numeracy and ICT skills

Technical skills are the specific knowledge that you need for your career. They may include the ability to use graphic design software if your chosen career is in marketing and advertising or your ability to use certain machinery if you are choosing a career in engineering. If technical skills are necessary for your career, you will usually have on-the-job training while at work. There are lots of colleges that offer short courses on specific computer programmes if you have identified these as a necessary step in gaining a job.

Work-related skills are the skills that employers are looking for in candidates when offering them a job. They are generally those skills that you have never been taught. These include creative problem solving, leadership, taking the initiative and team working. All of these are important in gaining and maintaining a job. You may find that you are asked in interviews or job application forms to give an example of when you have displayed these skills.

Research

Research the sorts of skills that you will need in order to do your chosen career. Feed these back to the rest of the class.

Key terms

Technical skills: the specific knowledge that you need for your career

Work-related skills: skills that employers are looking for in candidates when offering them a job, including creative problem solving, leadership, taking the initiative and team working

Skills for life

P5 ▸ Research skills

You will often be given a question or assignment that you will need to research in order to complete. Being able to research effectively does not mean simply typing the word or phrase into a search engine and trawling through the numerous links. The following are a few tips for improving your **research skills**:

- Know exactly what you want to find out. This may sound silly, but you need to be very specific about your research otherwise you will find lots of irrelevant information. You need to keep your research focused and not get sidetracked, printing off hundreds of pieces of what you think is research. Make a list of four or five questions you want answered and focus on these.

- Do not just rely on the internet. Although lots of us use the internet as our first point of call, books can be just as useful. You do not need to read every single book that is mildly related to what you have to research – use the index to find out if the book includes anything related to your topic.

- Do not believe everything you read online. The web address (URL) gives clues about the information. If it ends in .edu or ac.uk it means that it is an education site and therefore valid. Other professional domains include .gov and .org. If the web address ends in .com or .co.uk, the information could be valid but be cautious – check the author of the site and compare the information with that on other sites.

- The internet sometimes offers too much information. Your aim when researching should therefore be to get the most relevant pages to the top of the results list. Look on the internet for a guide to using search engines – you'll be amazed at how much easier it can be to get the information you want.

- Remember to include a bibliography or webography for all research that you use in an assignment. Get into the habit of noting the URL of any website you use, along with the author, title, place of publication, publisher and date of publication with page numbers for any books that you use.

Time-management skills

In order to meet deadlines you need good **time-management skills**. The art to effective time management is planning. Ensure that you make plans of when you are going to complete certain tasks and make sure

Your assessment criteria:

P5 Demonstrate transferable business skills

Key terms

Research skills: the ability to find out valid and useful information and use it for your own purposes

Time-management skills: the ability to manage your time effectively so that you meet deadlines

Research

Using the tips on the left, research the qualifications that you could do after completing your BTEC Nationals. This may be a degree or apprenticeship. Start by writing a list of four or five questions to which you want the answers.

Design

In groups, imagine that you have a friend who is not very good at doing research. Design a guide that shows them what to do.

they are completed by your deadline. Also, ensure that the tasks that you agree to complete are within your limits. You need to get to know what you can achieve and be ready to tell someone (*not* the day before the final deadline) if you are struggling. These skills are important at college and school, but are vital in the workplace. If you demonstrate an inability to get things done at work you will find yourself without a workplace to go to.

Research skills are valuable in education and at work.

 ## Case study

? | Did you know?

The average person uses 13 different methods to control and manage their time.

Steven is studying BTEC National Business at his local college. His assignment is due on Tuesday, so he started it last Thursday evening after dinner.

He decided to work in his bedroom. His football kit was on his desk, so he put his laptop on his bed. He spent a while looking for the lead to plug in his laptop and then began to read the assignment. He discovered that he needed some notes he had left at college. He decided he would get the notes the next day and therefore began by reading the textbook. After a quarter of an hour of reading, his friend Henry rang. He asked whether Steven wanted to go and watch their local football team. Steven decided to continue work on the assignment on Saturday. Saturday was very busy. His friend David rang to ask whether Steven would be available to play five-a-side football that afternoon. His team won their game and they all went to the pub to celebrate. By the time Steven got home, it was too late to start work.

On Sunday Steven helped his dad with the gardening and visited his niece and nephew in the afternoon. He started the assignment after dinner. He still didn't have his notes, and the assignment was proving to be harder than he thought. He started to think that he wouldn't get the assignment finished on time. He'd have to do some quick work on Monday and Tuesday evenings. It wouldn't be his best work, of course, but that couldn't be helped.

1. Identify and list Steven's time-management problems.

2. List and explain five strategies that Steven could use to overcome his time-management problems.

Gaining qualifications and evaluating your development

In your career plan and qualifications map, you will have identified the qualifications you are going to need in order to get your desired job. It is important to assess, therefore, what transferable business skills you are going to need in order to gain these qualifications.

Your assessment criteria:

M3 Assess ways of achieving the level and types of transferable business skills needed for the career plan

D2 Evaluate own development of transferable business skills

M3 Qualifications

No matter what **level of qualification** you are studying or wanting to study, certain transferable skills are necessary. You will need to research into the level of qualification you want to achieve (and outline this in your career plan and qualifications map) and then assess which transferable business skills are necessary in order to achieve this. You should be able to justify why you believe these skills are necessary in order to gain the qualification.

Qualifications range from levels 1 to 8 in the **Credit Framework**. You are currently working on a level 3.

Key terms

Credit Framework: otherwise known as the QCF (Qualifications Credit Framework), this is an easy-to-understand framework that explains the level of qualifications, how they compare to each other, the measure of the qualifications and how students can progress to the next level

Level of qualification: qualifications range from level 1 (equivalent to GCSE Grades D–G) to level 8 (equivalent to a doctorate)

Figure 15.5 Qualifications Credit Framework (QCF)

QCF level	Qualification title (examples)	Equivalent to
1	Level 1 BTEC Certificates and Awards	GCSE (D–G)
2	• Level 2 BTEC Diploma • Level 2 BTEC Extended Certificate • Level 2 BTEC Certificate	• 4 GCSEs (A–C) • 2 GCSEs (A–C) • 1 GCSE (A–C)
3	• Level 3 BTEC Extended Diploma • Level 3 BTEC Diploma • Level 3 BTEC Subsidiary Diploma • Level 3 BTEC Certificate	• 3 GCE A-levels • 2 GCE A-levels • 1 GCE A-level • 1 GCE A-level
4	Level 4 Higher National Certificate	Certificate of Higher Education
5	Level 5 Higher National Diploma	Diploma of Higher Education/Foundation Degree
6	BTEC Advanced Professional Diplomas, Certificates and Awards	Bachelor degree
7	BTEC Advanced Professional Diplomas, Certificates and Awards	Masters degree/Postgraduate diploma
8	Specialist Awards	Doctorate

What qualifications do you want to achieve?

 Research

Research what level of qualification you would like to aim for. Look into

- *where you could study it*
- *how much it would cost*
- *how long it would take to complete.*

 Discuss

Discuss with a partner or group how you think you have done to date with developing your transferable business skills. Get your peers' thoughts on how well you have done and how they think you could improve. Add these to your evaluation.

D2 Evaluating yourself

In order to evaluate yourself it is important to know what you have done to date, whether you have stayed on track and what you need to do in order to improve.

In order to evaluate the development of your transferable business skills, you will need to reflect on:

- which skills you have worked on and how
- why these skills are necessary to achieve your goals
- what other skills you need to develop
- how you are going to do this
- what you would have done differently if you were to repeat the exercise.

We all learn from our experiences and self-evaluation is a valuable process that can help us to continually improve.

 Key terms

Evaluate: *to judge how well something has gone, what could have gone better and how it could be improved next time*

Take time to evaluate yourself carefully.

Continuing professional development

Continuing professional development (CPD) means developing and improving the quality of your work in your profession. It is essential to ensure that you gain more knowledge and skills and therefore improve the way in which you perform. Part of your teachers'/ lecturers' CPD involves being observed by another member of staff, who then gives them feedback on how they can improve their teaching so that your lessons become even better.

Your assessment criteria:

P6 Discuss methods of continuing professional development and training relevant to the career plan

P6 Forms of CPD

There are many different forms of CPD that you will come across during your career. The various types of CPD are outlined below and on pages 312–313:

Induction training

The training that you are given when you first start a job is called induction training. It helps new employees to reach the level of performance that is expected of them. It may involve learning how to use certain facilities/ machines in the organisation and meeting key employees in order to understand the culture of the organisation. It is crucial in making new members of staff aware of the expectations and targets of the organisation.

Performance appraisal

A performance appraisal is the process by which a manager examines and evaluates the work of an employee by comparing it to targets or standards already set. The manager gives feedback to the employee on their performance (usually over the last year) and gives them new targets and ideas on how to improve. Performance appraisals usually determine whether the employee needs more training, is ready to be promoted and/or is due to receive a bonus.

On-the-job training

On-the-job training takes place at work while the employee is still carrying out their job. Usually an experienced employee trains a less experienced member of staff. It is based on the principle of learning by doing.

? | Did you know?

With 16 per cent employee participation, on-the-job training is the second most attended form of vocational training in the European Union.

Q | Research

For a career of your choice, research the types of on-the-job training, off-the-job training, training programmes and education you may have to complete.

On-the-job training

Off-the-job training

Off-the-job training takes place away from the employee's job, usually at a training centre or college. It usually involves lectures, case studies and role plays, and is usually delivered by a professional lecturer.

Graduate training programmes

These are the training schemes that are available to graduates (students who have completed their degree) and usually allow the graduate to experience many if not all aspects and roles within the organisation. Graduate training programmes tend to last approximately 1 year but this depends on the employer. They usually involve some on-the-job and off-the-job training.

Management education

Management education is the teaching of the theories and processes of a business. It is usually specific to an organisation and offered to an employee who has secured a job as a manager. It involves the teaching of planning, organising, staffing and leading a team of employees.

Management training

Management training is designed to improve leadership, supervision, planning and staffing skills. It may also involve training on how to build positive relationships with employees and how to handle stress. Usually, organisations provide their own management training, although it is also available outside of organisations in the form of workshops and courses.

Management training

P6 ▸ Forms of CPD *continued*

Coaching and mentoring

There is often confusion between coaching and mentoring as both are the development of a one-to-one relationship in which the coach or mentor supports the employee. However, there are some very distinct differences. The focus of the relationship for a mentor is the mentee, whereas the focus of the relationship for the coach is the *performance* of the coachee. A mentor is usually a sounding board for the mentee where there is no specific agenda to discuss, whereas the coach will always have specific topics to discuss with the coachee. The role of a mentor is to teach the mentee how to handle certain situations, whereas the role of the coach is to improve the performance of the coachee. Coaching and mentoring take place in many organisations with the intention of improving the focus, experience and education of the recipient.

Projects

Employees are usually put onto certain projects that their managers have felt will help them to improve and learn new skills. Often, employees are put together on projects with people they do not know so that they can develop a wider knowledge of the culture of the organisation and improve their team-working skills.

A student undertaking e-learning

Secondments

A secondment is when an employee is temporarily transferred to another department, usually within the same organisation for a specified period of time. This may be because the employee wants to learn new skills and experience, or may, in some cases be because their existing department has a temporary lack of need for them.

Shadowing

Shadowing involves an employee learning about a job by walking through the day of a more experienced employee. Shadowing is temporary and usually unpaid and allows the employee to learn about an area of interest within the organisation. It enables the employee to witness first hand the experience of the job, the skills involved and the potential career options.

Your assessment criteria:

P6 Discuss methods of continuing professional development and training relevant to the career plan

? Did you know?

In 2007, US organisations spent $134.39 billion on employee learning and development.

 Design

Design a training dictionary describing all of the types of training you have learnt about.

E-learning

This method of learning involves the employee using a computer in order to carry out training. The training is delivered via the internet, satellite TV or CD-Rom.

Discuss

Discuss with a partner which types of CPD you think you will come across in your chosen career. Explain why you think this.

Vocational and professional courses

A vocational course is one in which the student learns about a particular type of job along with the practical skills that are needed to undertake that job. You are currently on a vocational course where you are being taught the practical side of a career in business. Professional courses are usually seen as academic and are usually related to learning in more detail about a profession. For example, employees who gain jobs in finance, often have to undertake a professional course known as CIMA (from the Chartered Institute of Management Accountants) or ACA (from the Association of Chartered Accountants). These courses aid them with the professional knowledge needed to undertake their job effectively.

Job rotation

This is when an employee is moved between different departments, functions or roles within an organisation. The aim of job rotation is to expose the employees to the different types of jobs in the organisation so that they can gain experience and a wider variety of skills.

Retraining

Retraining involves an employee undergoing training that they have already done in order to update their knowledge or skills.

Lifelong learning

Lifelong learning is the process of constantly updating your achievements.

Shadowing an experienced member of staff

It is the notion that we never stop learning and therefore always need to learn new skills and knowledge so that we can progress and develop to achieve our goals.

Assessment checklist

To achieve a pass grade, my portfolio of evidence must show that I can:

Assessment criteria	Description	✓
P1	Identify sources of information related to the career path	☐
P2	Complete a career plan identifying their development needs	☐
P3	Carry out a skills audit to identify skills gaps	☐
P4	Create SMART targets for the career plan	☐
P5	Demonstrate transferable business skills	☐
P6	Discuss methods of continuing professional development and training relevant to the career plan	☐

To achieve a merit grade, my portfolio of evidence must show that I can:

Assessment Criteria	Description	✓
M1	Assess methods of achieving development needs within the timeframe of the career plan	☐
M2	Monitor and audit progress towards targets using appropriate success criteria	☐
M3	Assess ways of achieving the level and types of transferable business skills needed for the career plan	☐

To achieve a distinction grade, my portfolio of evidence must show that I can:

Assessment criteria	Description	✓
D1	Evaluate the distance travelled in achieving the planned objectives of the career plan	☐
D2	Evaluate own development of transferable business skills	☐

18 | Managing a business event

LO2 Be able to plan a business event

- ▸ What are the different types of event that need planning?
- ▸ What arrangements will you need to make?
- ▸ How will you choose a venue?
- ▸ What resources will you need?
- ▸ How will you schedule everything?

LO1 Understand the role of an event organiser

- ▸ What skills will you need to plan an event?
- ▸ What is the role of an event organiser?

LO3 Be able to run a business event

- ▸ What activities will happen on the day?
- ▸ How will you ensure everybody and everything is safe and secure?
- ▸ What support will you offer?
- ▸ How will you troubleshoot?

LO4 Be able to follow up after a business event

- ▸ What happens after the event?
- ▸ How will you evaluate the event?
- ▸ What information do you need and how will you get it?

P1 ► The skills required

You may have attended big events in the past – music festivals or exhibitions. These events don't just happen; they have to be meticulously planned by event organisers to ensure they are successful. This planning requires a number of skills.

Communication skills

Event organisers have to meet with lots of people to discuss the plans for an event and therefore need the ability to talk and listen to people. Communication skills are needed throughout the process, from the initial meeting with the client to find out their requirements for the event through to instructing colleagues on how to set up the event, and talking to customers to evaluate the event. Communication skills are also important when coordinating venue management, caterers, stand designers, contractors and equipment hire.

Interpersonal skills

Event organisers need to interact and deal with people effectively. They need to work well with colleagues to ensure that the event runs smoothly and the client needs to feel comfortable approaching the event organiser so that planning can be organised to their specification. Interpersonal skills may also be required to secure speakers or special guests.

Time-management skills

Event organisers need good time-management skills. They must ensure that all of the necessary planning is done prior to the event and be able to work well under pressure and to tight deadlines.

Problem-solving skills

Event organisers need the ability to solve problems efficiently and effectively in order that everything goes to plan. This may involve being diplomatic when dealing with people or being creative in their outlook to solve problems such as coordinating suppliers, dealing with client queries and troubleshooting on the day of the event.

Your assessment criteria:

P1 ► Describe the skills required of an event organiser

? | Did you know?

In 2011 there were 339 courses on offer in the UK for event management.

 Discuss

Discuss how good you think you are at each of the skills described on these pages. Be prepared to justify your answers.

Negotiation skills

Negotiation is the process of discussing a problematic issue with a view to finding a solution. Effective negotiation involves the ability to compromise. Event organisers need negotiation skills when agreeing and managing the budget, talking to suppliers and planning room layouts. These skills may also be required when talking to clients whose ideas about a potential event are too outrageous!

Planning skills

All events start out as a plan with deadlines. The skill of the event organiser is to ensure that the plan takes hold and works with as few problems as possible. Event organisers use their planning skills to produce timelines, book venues and source suppliers, understand and adhere to legal obligations, coordinate and brief staff at the event and create and monitor the budget. Contingency planning involves thinking through the solutions to any problems that may arise.

Resource-management skills

Event organisers need to make effective and efficient use of all the resources available to them. This requires resource-management skills. The resources can include money, staff and time, as well as any contacts they may have in order to identify opportunities for events.

Monitoring skills

Event organisers should monitor all the planning leading up to and during an event to ensure its smooth running. Monitoring skills are also used to ensure that insurance, legal and health and safety obligations are adhered to.

Evaluation skills

After every event, the event organiser needs to evaluate the event so that they know what has gone well and what has not gone so well. These evaluation skills enable event organisers to continually improve the quality of the events and the service they offer to clients. Feedback from attendees of an event should help the organiser to see what needs to be improved.

> **? Did you know?**
>
> *You can do degrees and foundation degrees in event management.*

> **Q Research**
>
> *In pairs, research any event-organising jobs that are available in your area. Access the person specification for the job and highlight all the skills that are necessary to do the job.*

An event organiser should make regular contact with clients before an event to make sure all their needs are met.

The role of an event organiser

Organising an event, whether large or small, means taking responsibility for a number of jobs.

Organising

The event organiser should ensure that the venue is booked, the location of the venue is suitable (e.g. has good transport links and is large enough to hold the expected number of people) and the catering is organised.

Planning and reserving facilities

The event organiser needs to have planned what and who is needed and to have reserved these in advance. This may mean booking portable toilets for a festival or guest speakers for a conference.

Setting up the programme

The event organiser must set up the programme for the event. This means planning what is going to happen, where and when, and ensuring that the attendees are aware of this. The programme may be in the form of a leaflet given to attendees or could be a poster placed around the venue. The timings for the programme must also be organised.

Preparing and distributing supporting documents

Supporting documents are all the documents produced in order for the event to run smoothly. These may include a timeline of what needs to be done and by when, minutes of meetings, insurance forms and health and safety guidelines.

Adhering to organisational procedures and legal requirements

Event organisers must adhere to procedures laid down by the venue owners and to laws relating to their event.

Limits of the role

Event organisers inevitably encounter problems during the planning, running and evaluation of events that cannot be solved or overcome. It is, however, their role to ensure that they work to the specification of the event as best they can.

Key terms

Programme: a schedule of what is to be done

Discuss

In groups, discuss an event that you have attended recently.

- *Explain the role that you think the event organiser played in the running of the event.*

- *What do you think the limits of the role were in this case? Justify your answer.*

M1 Organisational procedures

Venue owners may have requirements in place to ensure that nobody is harmed at an event and the venue is left as it was found. These organisational procedures may cover where to enter and exit the event; traffic arrangements for staff and attendees; what to do in an emergency, including fire safety and emergency routes; insurance; first aid and provision for litter. This information should be made available to all partners, staff and event attendees.

Legal requirements

Event organisers must adhere to current legal requirements when organising an event. These include:

- Health and Safety Act 1974 – The purpose of this act is to ensure that employers carry out general duties to ensure the safeguarding of employees, themselves and members of the public. This includes completing risk assessments, implementing health and safety measures, appointing competent people to ensure these are put in place, setting up emergency procedures and providing information and training to employees.

- Premises licences – The event organiser should apply for a premises licence if alcohol is to be sold, if there is to be regulated entertainment and/or if there are to be late night refreshments.

- Food Safety Act 1990 – The purpose of this act is to ensure that any food served or sold does not harm anybody and is of a quality that the customer would expect. It should also ensure that the advertising of food is not misleading.

Consumer protection laws

Event organisers must adhere to consumer protection laws. These are in place to protect the consumer and ensure that any goods sold are fit for purpose and not defective in any way.

Contracts and agreements

Event organisers set up standard form contracts and agreements for employers, staff, exhibitors, partners and suppliers. A contract is set up between two parties, does not allow for negotiation and ensures that signatories adhere to those obligations set out in the contract.

Continually communicating with staff at an event helps to ensure there are no problems.

Types of event and prior arrangements

In order for an event to be successful it must be planned effectively. Without planning, the event would simply not happen. A lot of work has to be done before an event and a plan provides a schedule for the work to be done.

Your assessment criteria:

P3 Prepare a plan for a business event

P3 What sort of event?

There are several different types of events, including:

- routine events – happen on a regular basis and the specification usually stays the same, e.g. meetings

- non-routine events – are usually one-off events that do not happen frequently, e.g. wedding receptions

- formal events – include meetings, conferences and staff training sessions

- informal events – include exhibitions and trade fair stands.

Before the event

Many things need to be arranged prior to an event taking place. The event organiser usually starts by meeting the client to clarify the **purpose of the event**. Establishing the purpose of the event helps to ensure that the event is geared to please the target customers. A brief is then drawn up explaining:

- what needs to happen before, during and after the event

- the type of event

- the size of the event

- the target audience

- the numbers attending

- the responsibilities of key staff

- any procedures that need to be followed during the event.

The **budget** needs to be discussed with the client and monitored during the whole process. The budget is calculated by analysing the costs of everything that needs to be bought in order for the event to be a success. The event should not go over the planned budget.

? Did you know?

It takes 9 years to plan for the Olympic Games.

🔑 Key terms

Budget: *the amount of money available to spend on an event*

Purpose of the event: *why the event is taking place*

 Design

Design a budget for your event.

The supporting documents, which may include agendas of meetings and relevant meeting papers, need to be distributed to staff, partners and exhibitors to ensure everybody involved in the event is consulted and the planning is exact. Communication should be clear and accurate and any instructions or alterations in arrangements need to be shared with everyone involved.

Another key planning task is to secure an appropriate venue. It must be convenient for all attendees, with good transport links. It should also be able to hold the number of people expected to attend.

Being able to schedule everything when planning the event is fundamental to a successful event. Software such as Microsoft Outlook can be a valuable tool to ensure that timings for jobs are planned prior to and after the event. The event organiser must take on the liaison role and communicate with everybody effectively so that diaries are updated with any changes, and any alterations to the availability of resources are communicated to all involved.

When scheduling jobs to be done before, during and after the event, the organiser must take care and use their experience in allocating the times to undertake each job. They must consider the travel involved for people to get to the event, any rest periods they may need during the event and any time for preparation before the event, for example, time for exhibitors to set up their exhibitions. It may also be necessary to book travel for people, for example to provide minibuses from train stations if the budget will allow and it is deemed necessary. All travel documentation should be sent out to those who need it, flights and accommodation must be booked, return journeys checked and any other potential problems, such as language barriers, should be addressed.

It is always a good idea to be over-prepared for an event and all plans should be confirmed in good time.

Design

Design a schedule for all of the jobs that you believe will need to be carried out before the event.

Discuss

In groups, discuss what planning needs to be done for your event. How will you delegate jobs? Ensure you consider all of the points in your schedule (above).

Planning for the event is crucial to its success.

Choosing a venue

Points to consider

Choosing the venue for an event can be one of the most important factors to its success. There are many things to consider when choosing the right venue.

Location

Where the venue is situated is an important consideration. It must be convenient for all the attendees to get to.

Size

The venue must be able to hold the anticipated number of attendees and have the correct number of facilities for them.

Advance notice or booking

Some venues get booked up very quickly and therefore securing your chosen venue in time is an important factor. Careful and early planning should avoid disappointment.

Hotels are popular choices for events because of the facilities they offer.

Facilities

The facilities that a venue offers need to be assessed. Your requirements will depend on the target audience. For example, if a lot of elderly people are expected to attend an event, the venue must have few or no stairs. Parking should also be assessed prior to an event if it is deemed important. As many people travel by car to events, adequate and convenient parking can be a priority. Catering access and cooking and serving facilities also need to be assessed if the event is to provide refreshments for attendees.

Delegates

The number and type of delegates is an important consideration. The chosen venue will need to be able to hold the expected number of delegates and be a suitable venue for them. If an event is for children, for example, a conference centre would not perhaps be a wise choice.

Special requirements

Some or all of the attendees may have special requirements, such as dietary (e.g. vegetarian or Halal) or access related (disabled toilets, exits and entrances on one level). Whatever the requirements may be, it is important to find these out prior to booking the venue so that a venue can be chosen that meets these needs.

Venue checklist

Before choosing and booking a venue, it is useful to create a venue checklist for a desired venue to ensure that everybody's needs are catered for.

Resources

The resources that the venue offers should also be considered before booking a venue. The room or rooms where the event is to take place should be assessed in terms of size, appropriate layout (e.g. a boardroom or a theatre) and correct equipment (e.g. overhead projectors, flip charts and paper). The venue should also be assessed to determine whether the necessary equipment and materials (e.g. display stands and literature for the stands) can be delivered, hired and/or provided and will fit. Refreshments should also be considered in terms of whether they can be provided by the venue or whether alternative arrangements can be made.

? Did you know?

There are around 23,000 conference centres in the UK.

Key terms

Facilities: the features, equipment and services offered

Venue checklist: a list of all the factors that a venue must have

Q Research

In groups, research all of the conference centres in your local area. For each conference centre, list the advantages and disadvantages with regards to your event.

Decide which of the conference centres would be your ideal choice and explain your answer. Research how much it would cost to hold your event at your chosen conference centre and whether it is available on the date you require.

Discuss

In groups, discuss possible venues for your business event. Create a checklist that lists everything the venue needs to offer in order for the event to be a success.

Conference centres are popular choices for business events due to their size, facilities and transport links.

Running and evaluating an event

D1 Evaluating an event

As part of your **evaluation** of an event that you have attended, for example. a career fair, a revision conference or a meeting within college, you will need to explain what was good and what was not so good about the way the event was managed, and justify your answers. You should consider how well the event was run, the resources that were used, the planning of the event and the choice of venue.

Students running a business event

P5 Running an event

As part of running an event — whether it is a presentation, group activity or workshop — you need to consider health, safety and security, and provide other forms of support.

Health, safety and security

When running an event, health, safety and security should always be a priority, and certain procedures therefore have to take place. All staff should be made aware of the emergency procedures prior to the event and clear and sufficient signage needs to be in place for delegates in case of an emergency. Delegates should be told about any housekeeping arrangements. The security of materials and equipment should also be considered, as should the confidentiality of any information that is shared and communication that takes place.

Your assessment criteria:

D1 Evaluate the management of a business event making recommendations for future improvements

P5 Provide support for the running of an event

M2 Analyse the arrangements made by an event organiser to plan a business event

🔑 Key terms

Evaluation: *a judgement as to the quality of something by describing what has gone well, what has not gone so well and what could be done differently next time, with justifications*

Health, safety and security: *the protection of people, buildings, materials and equipment*

💬 Discuss

Discuss the different ways in which you could evaluate your event. Ensure you discuss the pros and cons of each method.

Event support

During the running of an event, certain support measures need to be in place. This event support may include note-/minute-taking, manning stands, ensuring screenings between stands are sufficient, putting up displays and ensuring the delegates have the right papers and are aware of the location of the conference room and facilities (this could either be done in person or with signage or both). Someone should also be in charge of recording attendance and cancellations.

Recording attendance provides information about the success of the event.

Key terms

Event support: practical help during the running of the event, such as note-taking, ushering delegates and recording attendance

Discuss

In groups, discuss what event support and health, safety and security issues you will need to consider during your event. Delegate jobs to people in your group.

M2 Analysing the planning

Prior to your event taking place, you need to analyse all of the arrangements that have been made during the planning of the event. You may need to look at minutes of meetings that you have had in order to do this effectively.

You will need to analyse what has gone well with the planning of the event, what has not gone so well and what you would do differently if you were to plan the event again. You must justify all of your analysis with examples of what has taken place to date.

It is important to plan effectively before your event takes place.

Discuss

In your groups, decide what has gone well so far and what you could have improved on. Make sure everyone makes at least one point at it is valuable to get everyone's opinion regarding the planning of the event.

Dealing with problems

P6 What could go wrong?

No event goes completely to plan and therefore it is important to consider potential problems before they occur. Putting in place certain plans will enable you to **troubleshoot** more effectively during the running of an event.

Liaison with delegates

Not only is it important to meet delegates as they arrive at an event, but it can also be helpful to contact them prior to the event to ensure that they do not have any problems, queries or special requirements. In this way, unforeseen problems can be tackled prior to the event.

Revision of event outcomes

After planning an event, certain issues may arise that alter the outcome of the event. This information should be communicated to all staff and partners, and if necessary to the delegates.

Arising issues

Certain problems may arise during the event that you will need to plan for. These may include the following:

- Non-attendance of delegates – you will need to put in place procedures for how to tackle the non-attendance of delegates. However, it is always good practice to send a courtesy email or text with the information from the event.

- Last-minute photocopying – it may be necessary to do last-minute jobs at the event, such as photocopying. You should therefore consider where and how you to accommodate this. Remember, it is always wise to have spares of everything.

- Inadequate room or facilities – you may find that more people attend than you were expecting and therefore the room that you had planned to use is not large enough. Consider how you would overcome this problem. You should also check and double check the facilities in the room, ensuring that there are enough chairs and that the projector is working, for example.

Your assessment criteria:

 P6 Produce guidelines for dealing with problems

 Key terms

Troubleshoot: solve problems as they occur

Q Research

Research online for examples of contingency plans. What is the purpose of creating a contingency plan?

? Did you know?

When we don't have any problems, the human mind has a tendency to create extra ones!

It is important to record all the attendees at your event.

- Non-delivery of resources – you need to consider the possibility that any resources that you have ordered may not be delivered on time; this could include refreshments, catering or information packs, for example. You will need to think about how you will overcome these problems if they do occur.

It is always best to be prepared for any problems that you can foresee and to consider all problems, no matter how ridiculous they may seem. Planning for how you would overcome these problems should they occur is known as **contingency planning**.

Last-minute photocopying could be a reality.

 Key terms

Contingency planning: setting up plans and possible solutions regarding problems that may occur in the future

 Design

Design a contingency plan for your event.

? **Did you know?**

There is a popular saying: a problem shared is a problem halved.

 Discuss

In groups, discuss what possible problems may occur during your event and how you could overcome them.

After the event

After the event, there is still plenty to be done – your job as an event organiser does not end when the last person leaves.

Your assessment criteria:

 P7 Carry out follow-up activities after a business event

M3 Evaluate how a business event can inform future planning

P7 Vacating the event

When **vacating** the event, there are lots of jobs to be done to ensure your event is an overall success. These include:

- Leaving the venue clean and tidy – It is important to ensure that someone (or all of you) is responsible for tidying up after the event and leaving the venue as clean and tidy as you found it. All litter must be picked up and all equipment should be put away.

- Returning or securing equipment – All equipment must be locked away securely and/or returned to its owner to ensure it is not damaged or stolen. Again, someone should be given this responsibility.

Reconciliation of accounts to budget

After the event, you will know the total final cost of the event. A vital task is the **reconciliation of accounts to budget**. This will enable you to see whether the event has been financially viable and whether you overspent, stayed within your budget or underspent. You will also be able to calculate whether you have made a profit or a loss or broken even. Reconciling the final cost with the budget is essential – it shows where money was saved and spent and therefore informs any future planning of similar events.

Key terms

Reconciliation of accounts to budget: *comparing the final costs with the original budget to calculate whether you have overspent, underspent or stayed within your budget*

Vacating: *leaving*

It is important to tidy up after an event.

Discuss

In groups, discuss what jobs will need to be done after the event and choose people who are going to be responsible for these jobs.

M3 Evaluating the event

After the event, an evaluation is necessary as it informs any future events in order that they are also successful. Firstly, it is important to debrief all staff about the event, discussing what went well during the event and what they believe could have been improved. This can be done as a question and answer session to ensure that a detailed evaluation is undertaken.

It is also a good idea to hand out **questionnaires** to delegates to find out their thoughts about the event. You should delegate this responsibility to someone along with the collection of competed questionnaires. The questionnaire could be made up of simple yes or no answers; a scale, rating certain elements of the event on a scale from 1–5; or open-ended questions asking for opinions. In designing the questionnaire, you must bear in mind the delegates and their ability to complete it. The questionnaire must be delivered to delegates in the most convenient way possible and should not take too long to complete as this will reduce the number of respondents. If you are handing the questionnaire out in person, it's a good idea to have pens available. You may choose to email the questionnaire, but you may not get a good response rate. Offering a small bribe for people to complete the questionnaires may be worth considering.

When evaluating your event, you will need to explain any problems that you encountered, why these problems occurred, what the **solutions** were and what you would do if you were to plan a similar event to ensure these problems did not occur again. It is also important to describe any lessons that you have learned from planning and running the event.

Completed questionnaires are a vital source of feedback.

Discuss

In groups, discuss what sort of questionnaires you would like to design for your delegates to complete. Have a look at some examples online. Consider how many questions to use, what they should ask and how they should be answered.

Evaluating an event

Reviewing the success of your event is an important step. It will help you to decide whether or not this is a career you may like to go into. Event organisers should review the success of their events in order to know what worked and what should be done differently at the next event. There are many ways that the success of an event can be measured.

P8 Circulation of materials

After the event, circulating materials is a necessary step in evaluation. There are several different types of material that can be circulated. These include:

- **Meeting minutes** – Minutes are the notes that are taken during a meeting to summarise what was said, what jobs were given to people and when they are supposed to be completed By reviewing minutes of meetings it is possible to review what jobs were done well and by whom and what jobs were perhaps not done so well and how they could have been done better.

- Evaluation forms/questionnaires – These give the delegates' perspective on how well the event went. It is a good idea to include a question about how they think the event could be improved.

- Post-event papers – Any other materials that have been given to delegates can also provide information. For example, travel cost forms will tell you how delegates travelled to the event.

In order to review the success of the event, all those who attended should be questioned as to its success. Therefore, it is a good idea to form a circulation list – a list of people (perhaps delegates and staff) who attended the event along with their contact details. Evaluation forms or questionnaires can then be posted, or evaluative questions could be asked over the telephone.

 Key terms

Circulation lists: lists of people who attended the event with the contact details so that forms can be sent to them

Meeting minutes: notes taken during a meeting, summarising what was discussed and by whom, what jobs are to be done by whom and when

Discuss

Discuss in your groups how you plan to compile a circulation list, how you will find out the contact details of all parties and how you will contact them after the event.

Completed questionnaires provide essential feedback.

D2 Evaluating the feedback

Collecting the feedback from an event can sometimes be the hardest job of all. Ensure that you have put in place easy ways for the delegates to give you the feedback. For example, ensure there are pens available and staff around to collect completed questionnaires, and perhaps offer a bribe for completing the questionnaire.

The feedback you receive about your event may come in the form of delegates talking to you and in the answers you receive from your questionnaires/evaluation forms. Whatever form the feedback takes, it needs to be evaluated. A good way of doing this is by completing pie charts and/or bar graphs based on the questions asked in the evaluation forms.

Graphics that show the results of your questionnaire make it easier to make judgements about the event. Your evaluation should comment on what went well in the planning and running of the event as well as after the event, what did not go so well and what you would do differently next time. Ensure that you justify each of your points with examples, figures or quotes from your feedback.

Graphics help with the evaluation of an event.

? | Did you know?

There are over 300 functions in Microsoft Excel.

Design

In pairs, create an 'idiots' guide to creating graphs and bar charts in Microsoft Excel'. You should include how to create the charts from start to finish. Pretend that the person reading your guide has never used Excel before. You must include instructions on how to:

- *create a pie chart*
- *create a bar graph*
- *enlarge your graphs*
- *export your graphs into a Word document.*

Q | Research

Research all of the different ways you could evaluate a questionnaire. Consider how you may use these methods in your evaluation.

Assessment checklist

To achieve a pass grade, my portfolio of evidence must show that I can:

Assessment criteria	Description	✓
P1	Describe the skills required of an event organiser	☐
P2	Explain the role of an event organiser	☐
P3	Prepare a plan for a business event	☐
P4	Arrange and organise a venue for a business event, ensuring health and safety requirements are met	☐
P5	Provide support for the running of an event	☐
P6	Produce guidelines for dealing with problems	☐
P7	Carry out follow-up activities after a business event	☐
P8	Review the success of the business event	☐

To achieve a merit grade, my portfolio of evidence must show that I can:

Assessment criteria	Description	✓
M1	Assess the importance of meeting organisational and legal requirements when planning a business event	☐
M2	Analyse the arrangements made by an event organiser to plan a business event	☐
M3	Evaluate how a business event can inform future planning	☐

To achieve a distinction grade, my portfolio of evidence must show that I can:

Assessment criteria	Description	✓
D1	Evaluate the management of a business event making recommendations for future improvements	☐
D2	Evaluate feedback from delegates participating in the event	☐

34 | Website design strategy

LO1 Know the purposes of a range of websites

- ▶ The difference between b2b and b2c websites
- ▶ The difference between commercial and non-commercial websites
- ▶ Identifying a website's target group
- ▶ The place of a website in the marketing mix and the promotion mix
- ▶ How technology can change how a website is used

LO2 Understand the main elements in web design for usability and visual appeal

- ▶ Usability as a key component of a site's success
- ▶ Making sites easy to navigate and up keeping them up to date
- ▶ Respect for users' privacy
- ▶ The Disability Discrimination Act
- ▶ Combining visual appeal with the need for speed and information

LO3 Be able to plan the development of a website for an organisation

- ▶ Identifying the business strategy, customers, customers' expectations and competitors' actions
- ▶ The functions of a site
- ▶ Personalising the web experience
- ▶ Identifying the resources required and the associated cost
- ▶ Evaluating the site before its launch
- ▶ Considerations for a website launch

Purposes of websites

P1 Commercial purposes

The primary aim of a commercial website is to make a sale. This may be to another business (for a **b2b** business) or to a member of the public (for a **b2c** business).

Some b2c businesses use direct sales models on their websites, which allow for both delivery and transactions online. For example, customers on www.play.com wanting to purchase an album can buy the MP3 version and download it immediately after making a payment, or can buy the CD, which is then delivered by post.

Not all websites have the facility to make online purchases. Some businesses use their website as a brochure – a pre-sales model. For example, the website for the wedding make-up business Elle Au Naturel (www.elleaunaturel.com) acts as an online brochure. Customers wanting to make a booking must contact the company via email.

Some businesses use their site for post-sales support with online manuals, warranties and a technical support team available to answer queries either via email or live web chat.

Not all sites are directly related to sales revenue and may instead focus upon corporate communication and public relations. Many businesses also use Twitter and Facebook for these purposes. It is also common for business websites to include a section for press articles about the company and testimonials.

Your assessment criteria:

| P1 | Describe how three contrasting organisations use their websites for business purposes |

🔑 Key terms

b2b (business to business): a business that sells to other businesses

b2c (business to consumer): a business that sells to members of the public

❓ Did you know?

The percentage of internet users purchasing goods and services online is 85%.

🔍 Research

Visit www.elleaunaturel.com. The site is clearly aimed at promoting the business to potential customers through its galleries, the information about its staff and services and press articles.

Non-commercial purposes

The web is the ideal place to promote your business's activities, which may not always be commercial. Central and local government, social enterprises, charities and campaigning groups all have websites.

Political parties have websites to encourage people to join their party, to enable people to make donations and to persuade people to vote for them. Charity websites give information about their cause and explain how people can get involved. Some websites collect data from visitors about their opinions to help formulate campaigns.

Sites such as HM Revenue and Customs (www.hmrc.gov.uk) are operational in that they allow users to make tax return submissions and to calculate their statutory maternity leave, PAYE, National Insurance, corporation tax, etc. Other government sites allow users to buy their car tax disc, register for a European Health Insurance Card (EHIC) and buy a TV licence.

Research

Visit the website for the charity Shelter (www.shelter.org.uk). What information does the site offer? What do you think are the website's purposes?

Business online is not just about shopping!

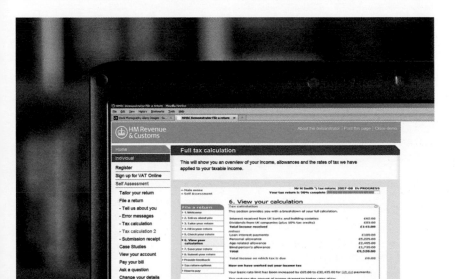

Tax returns are one of the many purposes of the HM Revenue and Customs website.

Research

Visit the website www.hmrc.gov.uk. What do you think its purposes are?

M1 ► Key marketing concepts

A website's success in achieving its business purpose (commercial or non-commercial) depends on whether it has been designed to meet the requirements of its audience. A website therefore has to be designed with the end user in mind. A business uses the information it has about segmentation of the market (according to gender, income, age, etc.) to identify a target group. It will then plan its **marketing mix** around the characteristics of this target group – where they live, how they shop, whether they prefer to shop online or visit a retail premises. Websites such as www.play.com and www.amazon.co.uk use the web as the place element of their marketing mix as they have no other premises.

A business will also consider the place of the website in the **promotion mix**, and its importance within this mix. It may also use other websites, such as Twitter and Facebook, to promote its site.

(See Unit 3, pages 104–161 for more details on key marketing concepts.)

Your assessment criteria:

M1 Analyse how a selected website has been designed to meet the requirements of its target audience

🔑 Key terms

Marketing mix: *an integrated strategy for marketing a product, which normally includes price, product, promotion and place*

Promotion mix: *an integrated strategy for promoting a product, which normally includes advertising, sales promotions, public relations and personal selling*

📋 Case study

Elle Au Naturel is a wedding hair and make-up business, based in Surrey but offering a service across the UK. The wedding market is largely segmented by social class/income. The average wedding in the UK costs £15,000–25,000 and the average spend on hair and beauty is £170. Elle Au Naturel charges £250 for hair and make-up for the bride, which means that its target customer has an above average budget.

The business uses this information and targets its customers in terms of the style and design of its site. The muted colours, font style and use of images all suggest that the business is aimed at a discerning clientele.

The website is the most important element of the company's promotional mix. The business used to run a monthly advert in one of the best-selling wedding magazines but stopped doing this 2 years ago and found that it had no impact on bookings. Most bookings come from recommendations from previous customers or via a Google search.

1 Elle Au Naturel does not have a Facebook page or a Twitter account. Why do you think the business does not promote itself through social networking sites?

Current and future developments

When planning a website a business needs to be aware of both current and future developments that may impact on site traffic and usage. In 2010, 73 per cent of homes in the UK had an internet connection and broadband is continuing to be extended across the country.

Increased use of mobile internet connections has led to more users accessing the internet via their phones. This means that businesses need to be aware of download times and the use of images on their websites.

When planning a website, scalability is important. Redesigning a site every time a new product or service is added takes time and costs money. Websites should therefore be planned and designed so that changes can be made without requiring a relaunch or a redesign of the site, both of which are expensive. At the same time, the site should not look empty in order to allow for future changes as this can affect the site image.

In 2010 Selfridges had to relaunch its website. The new design includes 'rooms' for each department, is fully transactional and has a 'wish room' feature. Each page also has a pop-out information desk that provides product details and delivery information. This is the store's first fully transactional website, making the company a latecomer to this type of site. Its original site did not have the scalablity to adapt to the demands of today's online customer so an expensive redesign and relaunch was required.

Many retailers now have apps to make shopping online even easier.

Usability

Usability is key to a website's success. The main factors affecting usability are:

- navigation
- language
- efficiency
- accuracy
- speed of response
- respect for privacy.

If a website is planned with these factors in mind, its users should be content and therefore make full use of the website – through to the purchase of a product or retrieval of information. Usability is important in building the users' trust in the website and customer loyalty. The various factors in the usability of the site (and the design of the site – see pages 344–5) are important at a user's first visit and subsequent visits as trust needs to be built and then sustained. A website should also remain up to date in order to build trust with users. Out-of-date information, products that are out of stock and a website that was last updated 6 months ago don't build confidence in the business.

Navigation

The primary purpose of many commercial websites is to make a sale and therefore a profit. It is therefore essential that customers can easily navigate from the home page to the products/services they need in order to complete a sales transaction. The frustration felt by a user when they are unable to do this means they are unlikely to visit the site again. If the site is slow to load, requires plug-ins or has links that don't work then the customer is likely to leave.

Language

The tone and style of language used on the website needs to be suited to the target audience. The text must also be legible and a suitable font should be used.

Efficiency

The efficiency of a website should be looked at from the perspective of the user. The business should look at how many clicks it takes to get to the information or outcome that the customer needs. It should also consider whether the customer is getting value in terms of the time they need to spend on the website.

Your assessment criteria:

P2 Explain the usability features of the websites of three contrasting organisations

Key terms

Usability: how easy a website is to use

Discuss

In groups, discuss instances when you have visited a website only to quickly navigate away without meeting your purpose. (Maybe you planned on making a purchase but registering with the site took too long or required too much information or the site was too complex and you couldn't find the product you were looking for.) Which sites do you regularly use? What makes them usable?

Discuss

In 2010, Facebook had more than 500 million active users, 50 per cent of whom log on to Facebook on any given day. The average user has 130 friends.

Discuss how usability has allowed Facebook to achieve this level of loyalty.

Accuracy

It is essential that all the information given on the website is accurate. The website should also deliver on its promises – if it states that delivery will be in 3–5 days then the business needs to make sure that this happens.

Speed of response

The planning of a website should take into account how important it is to the customer to have instant access. Some customers prefer to meander through a site. For example, customers of Elle Au Naturel probably spend some time on the site to get inspiration for their own wedding and to feel comfortable and build a relationship with a member of staff prior to booking. Customers on a supermarket shopping site usually just want to complete their weekly shop in the minimum amount of time and with the minimum amount of effort. A customer completing an enquiry form expects a fast response. Failure to respond quickly makes a business look unreliable.

Websites don't always work as well as they are supposed to. A site that uses multimedia, complicated graphics and a large number of images can slow down the response speed. Some users have a slow connection to the internet or an old PC with a slow processor. Internet bottlenecks can also occur – you have no doubt experienced this at college when a whole class is accessing the same sites for coursework and the server cannot handle the amount of traffic.

Have you visited a website looking for one thing and come away with another? Shopping sites usually enable you to complete a purchase in as short a time as possible and keep your focus on the items you are shopping for. Some websites, however, offer additional suggestions in an attempt to **upsell** while you are visiting. Amazon, for example, shows its customers the items other people bought when they made the same purchase.

Respect for privacy

A business must comply with the Data Protection Act when collecting information from customers and should not request information that is irrelevant or intrusive. For example, asking for a person's annual earnings is necessary if the person is applying for a bank loan via a website or filling in a tax return on the Inland Revenue's website. A retailer, however, should not ask for this information when a new customer registers (unless that customer is completing a credit agreement). Most websites display a privacy statement.

Key terms

Upsell: *a sales technique to induce the customer to buy extra or more expensive items*

Did you know?

In December 2010 the websites for Mastercard and Visa were both subject to denial-of-service attacks (DDoS). These attacks overrun websites with traffic and transaction requests until they are unable to manage. In this case the attacks were carried out by supporters of the WikiLeaks founder who at the time had been arrested. The assaults caused problems for banks, retailers and shoppers in the busy run-up to Christmas.

Research

What is the privacy policy of your college?

Privacy Policy

This privacy policy sets out how Elle Au Naturel uses and protects any information that you give Elle Au Naturel when you use this website.

Elle Au Naturel is committed to ensuring that your privacy is protected. Should we ask you to provide certain information by which you can be identified when using this website, then you can be assured that it will only be used in accordance with this privacy statement.

Elle Au Naturel may change this policy from time to time by updating this page. You should check this page from time to time to ensure that you are happy with any changes. This policy is effective from 25.11.2010.

What we collect

We may collect the following information:

- name and job title
- contact information including email address
- demographic information such as postcode, preferences and interests
- other information relevant to customer surveys and/or offers

What we do with the information we gather

We require this information to understand your needs and provide you with a better service, and in particular for the following reasons:

- Internal record keeping.
- We may use the information to improve our products and services.
- We may periodically send promotional emails about new products, special offers or other information which we think you may find interesting using the email address which you have provided.
- From time to time, we may also use your information to contact you for market research purposes.
- We may contact you by email, phone, fax or mail. We may use the information to customise the website according to your interests.

Design and accessibility

Design considerations

When designing a website, a business has to balance its own aims with the needs of its customers and the budget it has for the site.

When you visit a website, what is the first thing you notice:

• the company name or logo?

• the background colour?

• the text colour or font?

• the images?

How important is the visual appeal of the site to you, the customer?

User paths

For a business, its website is its online shop. It is important that the customer doesn't walk in and then walk straight back out again. In much the same way as retailers entice customers into their shops and then persuade them to buy, a website has to entice customers into the virtual shop and persuade them to make a transaction.

In a shop, the retailer will direct the customer to walk down certain aisles and past certain products and will position special offers at the end of each aisle. A website also has paths to guide the user through the site to make a purchase and will try to persuade users to make impulse buys.

A retailer wants to lead a customer to a transaction quickly and easily.

 Discuss

Visit the Tesco website, www.tesco.com, to look at the different paths a customer can take depending on their aim. Discuss how the site guides the user through the e-store.

Ranking of information

Information on websites is usually ranked. A search for a CD on Amazon, for example, will bring up an image of the product and information about the price, delivery times, stock and special offers. This is then followed by 'frequently bought together', which shows what other customers bought at the same time as the CD you are looking at, then product details, track listings, a product description, tags to allow users to join in discussions related to the band and then customer reviews. Customer reviews are highly valued by prospective customers as they may offer objectivity.

Search engines

Most of us now find information on the web via a search engine, so businesses have to make sure that their website will show up in searches. This is called optimisation. Website design has to include features that will show up in a search index. For example, a video clip on a home page that uses the text 'enter site' will only appear on an index as 'enter site' and not what the site is about.

Businesses often find that there are conflicts between aspects of usability and having a visually appealing site. Graphics, multimedia and images can lead to a site being slow, whereas a fast, optimised site can lead to a high search engine ranking and a quick response to customer searches but a visually uninspiring experience for the user.

Accessibility

The Disability Discrimination Act 1985 made it an offence to discriminate against people due to a disability. The Equality Act 2010 largely replaced this Act and requires 'reasonable adjustments' to be made to provide the disabled with a service that is generally available. This includes access to everyday services such as websites.

The Act requires that websites are accessible for users who are visually impaired and those who are unable to use a mouse (sometimes voice text is required). As yet, no firms have been prosecuted for failing to have a website that does not conform with the Act, but the Act is relatively new so there could well be prosecutions in the future.

The charity Add International (www.add.org.uk) has a feature on its website that enables users to change the website to text only, to change the background, text colours and font size to improve readability. Users can also select a sitemap to make navigation easier.

 Discuss

Why are more and more retailers using customer reviews as a feature on their websites? What are the risks involved in including this information?

? Did you know?

The verb 'to google' was added to the Oxford English Dictionary in 2006.

 Discuss

Which is the worst website you have ever visited? Why?

Key terms

Optimisation: *maximising a website's position in searches by search engines to ensure that the site is near the top of the search list*

 Research

Visit the website www.add.org.uk and change the font and colours. How does it alter the readability of the site?

Visual appeal and designing a website

P3 Visual appeal

There are a number of ways of improving the visual appeal of a website:

- Colours, font and graphics – these can be used to reflect a business's brand and livery.

- Page transitions – this is the way that the user moves from one page to another. The Barbie website, for example, uses images as buttons and has multimedia on its transitions.

- Unified style – many commercial sites have a unified style, which means that all the webpages use the same layout and colours. This gives the site a professional image.

- Consistency – a consistent design means that users know what to expect from the site, how to navigate from page to page and how to use the information and make a purchase.

- Consistency with brand image – a customer of Barclays bank expects the website to have the same corporate image as a branch. The site is a virtual branch of the bank and not only reflects the company's logo and livery but also has images that tie in with the current advertising campaign.

- White space – reading on a computer puts a strain on a user's eyes. White space is important as it makes reading online easier and helps text and graphics to stand out.

- Appeal to target group – the design of a website must take into account its target group. For example, the Barbie website is pink and has links to fashion tips and games such as Pet World and Dolls of the World, whereas the Manchester United website has information about matches, tickets and soccer schools.

- Multimedia – using multimedia on a website has both advantages and disadvantages. It affects access times to the site and makes accessibility (see opposite) much more difficult but some users (particularly children) will expect it.

Your assessment criteria:

P3 Describe how the websites of three organisations have been designed to appeal visually to their users

P4 Design a website for a specified organisation to meet stated purposes for a defined target group

D1 Evaluate the extent to which the design of a selected website helps the originating organisation to meet its objectives

🔍 Research

Visit the following websites:

- *www.barclays.co.uk*
- *www.uk.barbie.com*
- *www.greenpeace.org.uk*

How do they use colour? Is it to reflect their brand or to appeal to their users?

P4 Designing a website for an organisation

The website that you design must be for a specific organisation and must appeal to a defined target group.

When planning a website, you must consider the organisation that the website is representing (a b2b or a b2c company, a public service, etc.), the purpose of the website, the organisation's strategy and the part the website will play in achieving this strategy.

Consideration needs to be given to:

• Business objectives – does the company aim to increase sales/profits, move into new markets, raise the profile of a cause?

• Marketing objectives – these could be related to increasing market share, increasing promotional awareness (e.g. Greenpeace using its website to campaign for sustainable tuna fishing).

• Customer profiles – who are the typical customers of the business? What are their expectations of the website? For example, children expect a site to be interactive and use multimedia and Flash animations, whereas users of the NHS website want to be able to access to services and information about illnesses quickly.

• Users' experience/technical environment – do users of the site have the technology and the skills needed to access the site?

• Competitors' websites – what do the competitors' websites look like? How are they structured? How do they use colour and images? How easy are they to navigate?

D1 Meeting objectives

A website is part of a business's overall strategy and has a part to play in helping that business to meet its objectives.

For example, one of Tesco's strategies, as stated on the Tesco plc website, is to be as strong in non-food as in food. The company wants to make more sales and have a larger share of the non-food market. Its website has been a key part of its strategy in achieving this goal. It is not possible for Tesco's stores to stock all the non-food items that it sells, but its online shopping site has allowed the company to increase its non-food sales.

? Did you know?

The five most annoying things users cite about web designs are:

• music

• mouse over ads

• Flash animations

• pop ups

• load time and page speed.

Q Research

Visit www.tesco.com. Is it easy to navigate to the non-food items from the home page? How do you find the products you are looking for? What information is provided? Do you think the site is helping Tesco to achieve its target of increasing non-food sales? How could it be improved?

Designing a website

P4 Functions of the site

When planning a website, you must consider the functions that are required. Many retail websites have a search function to allow customers to find a product quickly instead of having to trawl through a particular category. Links to further information may also be needed. The NHS website, for example, has links to clinical trials that users may want to take part in.

Some websites require users to be registered. If customers are making a purchase, they need to provide payment and delivery information. Registering saves customers time when they visit the site again and also gives the business a database of customers it can contact with future marketing offers. Other sites that may require registration are discussion forums and social networks.

A 'Help 'facility allows customers to gain more information from the business. Some sites have a live help function that is available during certain hours; others have a help page answering frequently asked questions or have a pop up that gives extra information.

Most commercial websites aim for customers to make a purchase. This requires a transaction, which users expect to be secure. Businesses should be open about the arrangements on their site and the security level offered.

Security is a primary consideration for both shoppers and retailers.

Your assessment criteria:

P4 Design a website for a specified organisation to meet stated purposes for a defined target group

Completing a transaction requires payment and the payment options, such as a credit or debit card or a service, such as PayPal or WorldPay, should therefore be considered. Businesses have obligations to keep their users' financial data secure.

A website may require background functions such as a database to store information about customers who have registered with the site. A database such as Microsoft Access may be sufficient for a small business.

Personalisation

One of the advantages the high street has over a web business is the face-to-face contact with customers: 'Hello, Miss Harwood, how was your holiday?', 'We have just got these new shoes in and they are in your size, I thought of you when they came in...'. Knowing your customers and personalising your service is a way of encouraging customer loyalty and generating repeat business. So, how can the web compete? Some sites use prompts such as 'Remember me?' or 'Save my password', which give the website the capability to pre-fill your user name and complete part of the information needed for a transaction. Some websites use cookies, which are a way of transferring information from one web session to another. A cookie allows a user to be identified and to continue from the point where they last left the site. Cookies allow sites to be more personalised as they recognise the user.

Personalisation can benefit both the user and the business. Collecting information about users' buying patterns and interests allows a business to make personal recommendations. Amazon does this to good effect. The company has a record of all the books a customer has purchased from the site in the past and uses this to make recommendations based on the authors and subjects they have shown an interest in. The system also looks at who else has bought the same books as the customer and what else they have bought and will then recommend items based on the

Amazon provides a high level of personalisation to encourage repeat business.

purchase patterns of other customers in the database. Key to this level of personalisation is the use of customer databases. This service can generate more sales and lead to repeat business and customer loyalty. This can be beneficial to customers because it saves them time and effort and makes the transaction process easier.

Key terms

Cookies: *files stored on your computer that keep track of your browsing on a particular website*

P4 Resources required

An essential part of planning a website is identifying the resources required by the business. These include:

• the domain name – the address for the website

• software options – will the business use an online 'shop' package or develop its own software?

• security measures – what does the site need to be secure?

The hosting of a website can be done by the business itself but most small businesses do not have the resources or time available to maintain the site and therefore use an internet service provider (ISP). The ISP is responsible for providing the business with a connection to the internet and hosts the website either through a **shared server** or a **dedicated server**. The advantages of using an ISP are that it saves the business the expense of buying its own server, and usually offers very fast internet connection and security, such as virus protection. The drawback is often the cost.

In order to choose how to connect to the internet, a business has to consider:

• the costs involved in buying the equipment and hosting themselves versus the cost of an ISP host

• security issues

• maintenance of the site.

The site can be created by the business itself using web authoring tools such as Dreamweaver. These simplify the process and are ideal for people with no knowledge of HTML. Graphics and tables can be inserted and the pages can be seen as they are created. The program is expensive to buy, however, and some web designers don't like taking over sites that have been created in this way, so if the business expands and needs a larger site, a re-launch could be necessary.

Typical costs of developing a small website

The costs of developing a website vary enormously. For example, Mini Movers (see Unit 4, page 169) got its domain name from Getting British Business Online (www.gbbo.co.uk) – a joint initiative from Google, Enterprise UK, BT and e-skills UK set up to help British businesses get their first website online. Under this initiative businesses get a free domain name and a free website for 2 years. When a friend of the owner of Mini Movers offered to host the site and relaunch it, the new design cost £175 (£100 for professional photographs and £75 to host the site for 12 months; the design and construction costs were free). Elle Au Naturel paid £1,200 for the relaunch of its website.

Research

Visit www.123-reg.co.uk. How much would a suitable domain name be for your chosen business?

Key terms

Dedicated server: *a computer program that provides services to other programs within a network*

HTML (hypertext mark-up language): *the code used to create webpages*

Shared server: *a server that is used to host several websites*

Assessing a website

For a website to be successful it must serve the organisation and help it to meet the business objectives while appealing to the target audience.

? | **Did you know?**

Research by Jupiter Research found that only 14 per cent of customers were influenced by personal recommendations on websites to make a purchase.

 Case study

The Elle Au Naturel website was relaunched in 2010. The company wanted to use its site to expand the business's client base across the UK. When the business first started 13 years previously, the owner of the company did the make-up and hair for every client and employed freelancers to help her when needed. This was no longer possible as during the summer the company sometimes had eight weddings per weekend. The owner, however, wanted to maintain the close relationships she had established with clients and demonstrate through the website the talents of all the staff.

The business had also diversified and now offered other services such as hairdressing, hair extensions, manicures, pedicures and make-up lessons and the sale of organic make-up products from Australia.

The website is key to the company's promotion mix as the primary means of promoting the business. The site is optimised to ensure its ranking on search engines. Most of the company's enquiries now come via the site or through personal recommendations and the company no longer advertises in bridal magazines.

Since the relaunch of the website, enquiries have increased by around 20 per cent and bookings for 2011 are 10 per cent up on the previous year. The new services offered have received more interest and sales of products have also increased.

1. Based on the information in the case study, does the new website for Elle Au Naturel (www.elleaunaturel.com) serve both the business and its target customers?

P5 Evaluating the design

When evaluating the design of a website, the business owner is the obvious place to start but the opinions of target customers should also be considered. Questions should also be asked about whether the site is fit for purpose and meets the design brief.

To achieve P5 you need to draw up plans for the evaluation of your own website design and should give thought to user acceptance testing, the website's use in a range of technical environments and accessibility.

User acceptance testing

The users of the site will be the business owners and staff and the customers. Acceptance of the site means that the target customers visit the site and use it for its intended purpose, that the business is happy that the site fits in with its business image and brand and promotes its business objectives and that it works.

? Did you know?

In 2004, two US travel firms (priceline.com and ramada.com) were prosecuted for failing to make their websites accessible to blind and partially sighted people. Priceline was fined $40,000 and Ramada $37,500 and they were both ordered to make the necessary accessibility adjustments to their sites.

As yet there have been no prosecutions in the UK under accessibility but the law changed in 2010 so British firms could find themselves in the dock if they fail to make their sites accessible.

All aspects of a website are scrutinised prior to its launch.

Use in a range of technical environments

In order to meet all its users' needs, the website should perform with different web browsers and different connectivity. Images should ideally be GIFs or JPEGs as PNGs can be incompatible with Internet Explorer. As more and more people are now accessing the web via WAPs, the site needs to be readable on a phone screen. Connectivity also varies depending on how users are connected to the internet (this could be through a LAN, a modem or directly from their computer). Speeds vary and it should be possible to download the site through all different types of connection without users becoming frustrated due to lengthy loading times. Users also have different levels of technical expertise and all of them need to be able to navigate their way around the site.

Accessibility testing

You need to consider how accessible the site is for disabled users. Since the introduction of the Equality Act, websites must be designed to enhance accessibility for all users including disabled customers. There are over 8 million people registered as disabled in the UK and many of these will use the internet, so it is important their needs are considered in the design of a website.

Research

Visit www.tesco.com and evaluate how easy is it to navigate.

* *How many clicks does it take to buy an item (e.g. a bike for yourself costing under £200)?*

* *How accessible is the site? Can you easily follow the instructions on the site to change the text size, colour and background colour?*

* *Compare the Tesco site to one of its rivals, e.g. Asda, Morrions or Sainsbury's.*

* *Which site do you think has the best design? Why?*

Planning the launch

P6 · Considerations for the launch

There are a number of issues that need to be taken into consideration when launching a small website.

Maintenance and updates

All websites require maintenance and updating over time. For example, the company may move premises or change staff and need to update the contact information, products may change seasonally, graphics may date or the addition of new pages may mean that old links don't work logically.

Owners often want to update their sites themselves, and training to do this should be included in the planned launch. Other owners prefer to outsource this. Depending on the size of the site, maintenance costs vary enormously (starts from around £12 a month).

Customer feedback

Consideration should be given as to how customers will contact the business – staff may have business email addresses or communication may be via an online feedback form. The business should also think about how this feedback will be collected and acted upon.

Promotion

Once a website has been designed and is ready to launch it has to be promoted to ensure customers can find it. In much the same way as a high street business will use its shop window to attract customers and may give out flyers with a map to show where it is, a website needs to guide customers to its location. Attracting traffic to the site is one way of attracting sales.

Businesses can do this by registering with an internet directory such as Foogle (via www.google.co.uk/addurl). Once registered, the site needs to be recognised on search engines. Submitting a site map to Google webmaster helps achieve this and site optimisation should be considered to ensure a high ranking on searches.

All employees' business cards and email signatures should include the web address and all publicity material should direct people to the site.

Key terms

Outsource: to contract out a role or service rather than employing a member of staff to do it

Traffic: visitors to the site

Research

Google your college. How high does it rank in the search results?

Security of ICT systems

The security of data (such as customer details and payment details) should be considered. If the business is using ISP hosting, security is the ISP's responsibility. The security on the site should be communicated to users at the launch. The site has to comply with laws such as the Data Protection Act and should have a privacy policy. The payment system should keep financial data secure.

Business continuity plans

A small business launching its first website should have plans for the future. These should incorporate how future changes in the business can be added to the site without requiring a relaunch.

M3 Appropriateness of plans for launch

The launch of the Mini Movers website was done on a shoestring and with the help of favours. As a result, there was no formal handover at the launch and consideration had not been given to accessibility or business continuity. On the week of the launch the owner was interviewed on the radio and there was a feature about the business in *Lancashire Life* magazine. This meant that a press page was needed on the website that hadn't been planned for. The ISP host was responsible for security, but as no transactions took place, this area was not a concern .

Flyers and a Twitter account were used to promote the launch of the business and direct traffic to the website. When customers began ringing to register, the owner was so excited that she failed to ask how they had found out about the company's classes so was unable to identify if the website had met her aim.

 Discuss

How appropriate do you think the launch of the Mini Movers website was?

D2 Making recommendations

The Mini Movers website launch was somewhat haphazard, as is often the case when relying on favours, and was not as successful as it could have been. The original plans were to have four classes every Saturday and later to expand provision into a new area on Sundays, but the business had only two classes for the first term and only one of these classes was full.

A better launch plan could have improved the effectiveness of the website in attracting customers and helping to fill the classes.

 Discuss

• *Make justified recommendations about how the website launch for Mini Movers could have been improved.*

• *Visit the website www.minimoversdance.co.uk and discuss how the design of the site could be improved.*

Assessment checklist

To achieve a pass grade, my portfolio of evidence must show that I can:

Assessment criteria	Description	✓
P1	Describe how three contrasting organisations use their websites for business purposes	☐
P2	Explain the usability features of the websites of three contrasting organisations	☐
P3	Describe how the websites of three organisations have been designed to appeal visually to their users	☐
P4	Design a website for a specified organisation to meet stated purposes for a defined target group	☐
P5	Draw up plans to assess the design of a website aimed at meeting a specified purpose	☐
P6	Draw up a plan for the launch of a website for a specified organisation	☐

To achieve a merit grade, my portfolio of evidence must show that I can:

Assessment criteria	Description	✓
M1	Analyse how a selected website has been designed to meet the requirements of its target audience	☐
M2	Assess how own website design contributes to fulfilling the organisation's purpose through meeting the requirements of the target audience	☐
M3	Explain the appropriateness of the plan for the launch of a website for a specified organisation	☐

To achieve a distinction grade, my portfolio of evidence must show that I can:

Assessment criteria	Description	✓
D1	Evaluate the extent to which the design of a selected website helps the originating organisation to meet its objectives	☐
D2	Make justified recommendations for how a website design and launch plan could be improved	☐

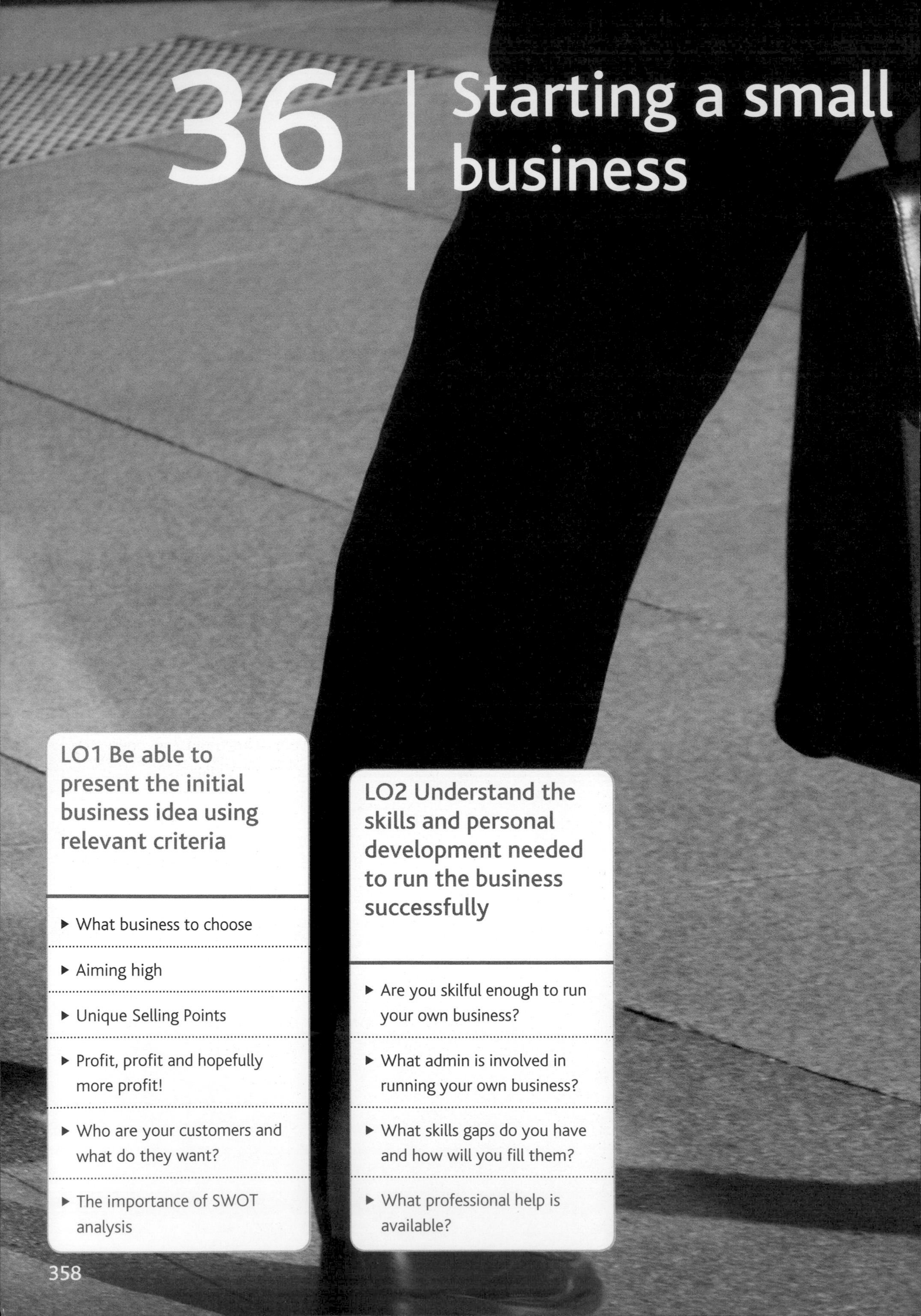

36 | Starting a small business

LO1 Be able to present the initial business idea using relevant criteria

- ▶ What business to choose
- ▶ Aiming high
- ▶ Unique Selling Points
- ▶ Profit, profit and hopefully more profit!
- ▶ Who are your customers and what do they want?
- ▶ The importance of SWOT analysis

LO2 Understand the skills and personal development needed to run the business successfully

- ▶ Are you skilful enough to run your own business?
- ▶ What admin is involved in running your own business?
- ▶ What skills gaps do you have and how will you fill them?
- ▶ What professional help is available?

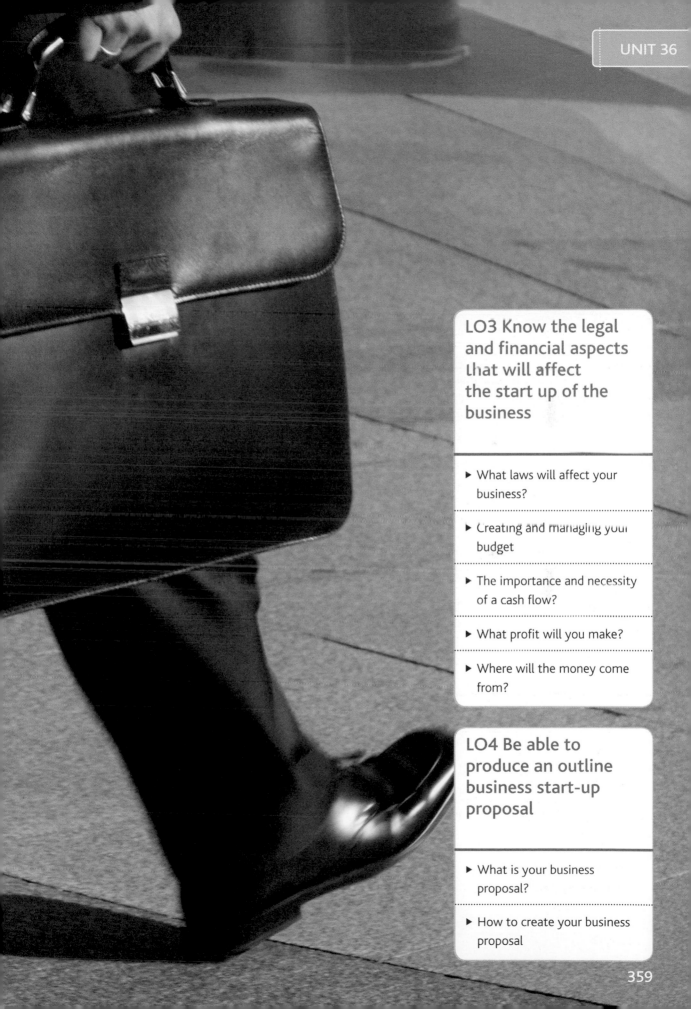

LO3 Know the legal and financial aspects that will affect the start up of the business

▶ What laws will affect your business?

▶ Creating and managing your budget

▶ The importance and necessity of a cash flow?

▶ What profit will you make?

▶ Where will the money come from?

LO4 Be able to produce an outline business start-up proposal

▶ What is your business proposal?

▶ How to create your business proposal

The initial business idea

In order to start this unit, you need to decide on a product or a service that you would like to sell. This can be a difficult task. You may decide to copy and modify an existing product, develop a product that interests you or come up with an innovative idea that fills a gap in the market.

P1 Type of business

Once you have decided on your product or service, you have to decide what type of business you want:

* Starting a new business – if you have an innovative idea or are adapting an idea from a product that is already on the market you may well start a new business. This takes a lot of work and is very risky, but can be extremely rewarding.

* Purchasing an existing business – the advantages of this option include the fact that you will have an existing reputation and existing customers, it will be quick to start trading, it is usually less risky than setting up a new business and it can be easier to raise finance. The disadvantages are that existing customers may not stay with your business, the business may not be right for you and purchasing an existing business usually costs more than starting a new one.

* Buying a franchise – when a small business buys the right to use a larger firm's name and products, the small business becomes known as the franchisee. You have to invest a certain amount of money (usually thousands of pounds) in order to buy the right to use the larger company's names and products. The larger company (the franchisor) helps the smaller company with training, the name and all equipment and resources. Well-known franchises include Domino's, Burger King and McDonald's

Figure 36.1: The advantages and disadvantages of buying a franchise

Advantages	Disadvantages
• You get the rewards of running your own business.	• You have not got complete control over the running of the business.
• There is security in numbers – there are a lot of other franchises to talk to if you need help.	• A fraction of the profits go to the franchisor.
• There is security in size – there is less chance of a large company failing.	• You are very restricted in terms of the products you sell and the prices.
• The name and products are already established.	• The raw materials have to be bought from the franchisor.
• Training and uniforms are supplied.	• Not all frachises are successful.
• Resources are supplied for fitting out the shop	• The shop layout is designed by the franchisor.
• Advertising is national and supplied when you purchase the franchise	

Aims and objectives

Once you have decided on the type of business that you want to set up, you need to determine your aims and objectives.

Aims are broad and general statements of the long-term purpose of the business. An example of an aim for a joinery company might be:

- to supply from stock nationwide the small builder's routine bathroom and kitchen requirements, assuring no-call-back quality and best local price.

Objectives are short-term goals that help the business to achieve its aim. Objectives have to be SMART (Specific, Measurable, Achievable, Realistic and Time related). An example of the same joinery company's objectives might be:

- supplying 99 per cent of our kitchens and joinery at the cheapest price available
- delivering 99 per cent of our kitchens and joinery within 1 week
- ensuring all customers are happy with the service provided.

Business planning

When taking on a large venture like a new business, planning is essential to ensure success. Creating a business plan is important because it:

- enables you to think everything through – what needs to be bought, possible problems, possible sales, all the costs involved
- shows bank managers that you are serious about setting up the business – they will therefore be more willing to lend you money.

Bank managers will be more willing to lend money if you have a business plan.

You, your product, your competition and the business environment

P1 ▶ Preparing for business

Before setting up your business, there are a number of issues that require careful consideration. You need to think about your motivation and suitability for the role of business owner, the suitability of your product for the market and the bigger picture of the environment in which you will be starting a business.

You

Starting up your own business takes a lot of time and effort, which has implications for your personal and social life. Running the business may mean that you often have to work evenings and weekends to catch up on paperwork, make orders and talk to suppliers. You need to consider whether you are up for the job.

You may choose to explain why you would like to set up your own business in your plan. People set up their own business for a number of reasons:

- for personal pleasure
- to boost their self esteem
- to work for themselves and make all the decisions

- for independence and to be their own boss
- for a sense of power
- for a sense of personal achievement through making the business successful.

Your product

Your product or service needs to have something that no other product or service offers. This is its **Unique Selling Point (USP)** and is what attracts your customers. You also need to consider how many people are likely to want to buy your product (see Identifying your target market, page 364). There is little point starting a business and selling your products if you are not going to make a profit. Before you set up your business, you should carry out the necessary calculations to ensure that you will be profitable by producing a break-even analysis, a budget, a profit and loss and a cash flow forecast (see pages 386–9).

Your competition

In order to be successful, you need to outperform the competition – have the competitive edge. You therefore need to do a lot of research into who your competitors are and what they are offering to customers.

 Key terms

Unique Selling Point (USP): *what makes your product different from competitors' products*

 Discuss

When supermarkets decide to locate a store in a neighbourhood, it is important that it outperforms its competition. Pretend you work for your nearest large supermarket, and answer the following questions:

- *Who are your competitors?*
- *Where are they located?*
- *What are their strengths and weaknesses?*
- *What are their sales?*
- *What products do they offer?*
- *How do their products compare to yours?*
- *What prices do they charge?*
- *What is their marketing strategy and advertising strategy?*
- *What do they do better than you?*

The business environment

It is important for new and existing business to be knowledgeable about the trends that are taking place in the business world. These external influences can present both opportunities and problems. At this planning stage, it is important to consider all of the external influences – local, national, international and commercial – that could affect your business. A PESTLE analysis looks at the Political, Economic, Social, Technological, Legal and Environmental influences of which you should be aware.

Figure 36.2 A PESTLE analysis

External influences	Questions to ask	Area of influence
Political	How stable is the government at this time?	National
	Is the country in which you are operating likely to go to war?	National and international
	Are there any new tax policies that may affect your business?	National
Economic	What are the current interest rates and how could this affect your business?	National
	What is the current rate of inflation and how could this affect your business?	National
	What are the current levels of employment and unemployment?	Local and national
	What are current retail sales trends?	Commercial
	What is the availability of credit for customers like?	Commercial
	What is the average income of your customers?	National
	What is current customer confidence like?	National
Social	What are current education levels like?	Local and national
	What are the current crime statistics?	Local and national
	What changes are occurring in the population?	National
	What trends are there in customers' lifestyles?	National
Technological	Is there new machinery available that may help your business?	Commercial
	How could ICT help your business?	Commercial
Legal	What employment laws may affect your business?	National
	What health and safety legislation will affect your business?	National
	Will competition law affect your business?	National
Environmental	How will you dispose of waste?	Local
	How will you manage any pollution that you create?	Local
	What would your local community's views be of your products/services?	Local

Your customers and your sales

P2 | Identifying your target market

In order to have a successful business, it is vital that you identify your **target market** – your customers – and establish that they want to buy your products. This means carrying out some market research.

- Decide on your market research objectives – what do you want to find out?

- Create a research brief and proposal – outline the methods you will use and why.

- Create a research plan – outline which primary and secondary research methods you will use and why.

- Collect the market research data.

- Analyse and evaluate the market research data – what are the key points that you have found out from your research?

There are two different types of market research that you will need to carry out:

- primary research – methods include conducting surveys and questionnaires, focus groups (in depth-discussions), observations (watching how customers behave) and field trials (testing your product on customers)

- secondary (published research) – research that has already been carried out and published by somebody else. It is usually data that will tell you about the trends in the market. You can find secondary research:

    - on the internet

    - in libraries

    - in company reports

    - in trade journals

    - at www.statistics.gov.uk

    - from Mintel, Datastream and Dun and Bradstreet.

Sales forecasts

To get an idea of how many of your product you are going to sell you should prepare **sales forecasts**. These are estimates, but if you carry

Your assessment criteria:

P2 Explain how to identify the target market

Key terms

Sales forecast: *working out what your possible sales may be before you start trading*

Target market: *the segment of the market that you are marketing your products to*

out high-quality primary research they can be fairly accurate. In order to make your sales forecasts as accurate as possible, you should explore the following:

- What sort of customers are likely to buy your products?

- Would they consider buying products from your company?

- How much would they be prepared to pay for your products?

- How often would they buy your products?

- Are they more likely to buy the products at certain times of the year? If so, when?

Even after you have collated answers to all of these questions, there is still an element of guesswork involved when trying to work out your sales forecast. It is always good practice to underestimate your sales, especially in the first couple of months of trading; you can always build your sales after your initial trading period.

Predicting customers' actions and choices

It is very difficult to predict customers' actions and choices. People are impulsive and therefore trying to foresee what their behaviour may be is a very inexact science. The only way of having a rough idea of what customers' actions and choices may be is to try to cover appropriate questions in your primary market research. Philip Kotler identified seven inputs which tempt customers into buying products or services. These inputs prompt customers into certain outputs (their choices). This is known as his black box model (see Figure 36.3).

Asking potential customers questions regarding the inputs in Kotler's black box model should give you a better idea of their likely choices relating to the sales of products and therefore the effects on your business.

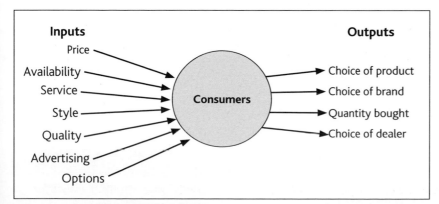

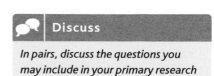

Discuss

In pairs, discuss the questions you may include in your primary research questionnaire.

Figure 36.3: Philip Kotler's black box model

Your competition and your market

P2 Competition

P2 Competition

One of the most important factors in your business's long-term survival is the presence of competitors in the market in which you are operating. As part of your primary research you need to determine who your competitors are and where they are situated. You need answers to the following questions:

- Who are your competitors?
- How many are there?
- How good is their advertising and marketing?

- How are you going to gain a market share?
- How strong are your competitors?
- How might they react to you coming into the market?

A walk around the area in which you are planning to open your business can be useful, along with looking on the internet (for example on www.yell.com) to identify any more competitors.

Strengths and weaknesses

In order to ensure the success of your business, you need to identify the strengths and weaknesses of the business. A **SWOT analysis** enables you to identify your internal strengths and weaknesses, and the opportunities and threats that are external to your business. A detailed SWOT analysis helps you to exploit your strengths and opportunities and try to overcome your weaknesses and any threats that you identify.

You can complete a detailed SWOT analysis by answering each of the questions in Figure 36.4.

Market trends

In order for your business plan to be taken seriously, you will have to analyse any market trends that are occurring in the industry that you are planning to enter. To learn about the market trends in your chosen industry, you should ask particular questions in your primary research, including:

- What is the history of customers buying products similar to what you are offering?
- How could your products in this market be developed?

Your assessment criteria:

 P2 Explain how to identify the target market

 Key terms

SWOT analysis: *a strategic planning method used to evaluate the Strengths, Weaknesses, Opportunities and Threats involved in a project or a business*

 Design

Design your own SWOT analysis for your proposed business.

Secondary research can also be very useful when trying to establish market trends. It can, however, be hard to find. You should try to analyse competitors' and market sales as a whole by looking at sites such as www.statistics.gov.uk and local company reports.

Figure 36.4 A SWOT analysis

Strengths (internal)	Weaknesses (internal)
• What are the advantages of setting up the business?	• What are the disadvantages of setting up the business?
• What are your capabilities?	• What gaps do you have in your skills?
• What are your competitive advantages?	• Do you lack a reputation?
• What are the USPs of your products?	• Do you lack competitive strength?
• What resources do you have (assets and people)?	• Do you lack finances?
• What experience and knowledge do you have?	• What are your time pressures?
• What finances can you input into the business?	• What are your distractions?
• What are the likely returns on your investment?	• Is there a lack of commitment or leadership?
• What marketing will you carry out? Who will you target? How will you make people aware of your products?	• Do you lack experience?
• What is innovative about your business?	• Do you lack qualifications?
• What is your location?	
• What are your prices? What is the quality of your products? How are you ensuring value for money?	
• What qualifications do you have?	
• What IT facilities do you have available?	
Opportunities (external)	**Threats (external)**
• Are there any market developments to exploit?	• Are there any issues with regards to politics, law and the environment?
• Are any of your competitors vulnerable?	• What are your competitors' intentions?
• Are there any lifestyle or market trends to exploit?	• Are there new developments in technology that you cannot take advantage of?
• Are there any new technologies to exploit?	• How will you sustain your internal strengths?
• Are there any new markets to enter?	• Are there any obstacles to overcome?
• Are there any niche target markets?	• Are your finances sustainable?
• Are there any new USPs to gain?	
• Do you have any business already established?	
• Do you have lots of market research and information?	
• Is there any scope for partnerships?	

Identifying your target market

In order to achieve M1, you will need to explain the methods that you used in P2 to identify your target market and explain why they were suitable.

M1 Primary research

Your primary research may have included doing an observation; for example, watching customers in competitors' shops. If you chose this method, you will need to explain why. It may be that you chose it because the location of your competitor is local and therefore it was convenient for you to visit.

If you wrote a survey, again you will need to explain why. It is important that you explain what questions you asked in your survey and why you felt it was necessary to ask these questions. You will also need to explain the layout of your questionnaire – open-ended questions, closed questions, a scale or multiple choice – and the reasons for your choice. You should also explain how you decided who to give the questionnaire to, how you ensured that they completed the questionnaire and how easy it was for you to access these potential customers. You may have decided to complete a survey over the telephone or face to face. If you chose one of these methods, you need to explain why you chose it.

Setting up a focus group is an effective way of gathering the opinions of your target market. If you decided to carry out a focus group, you will need to explain why you felt this was necessary, how you chose your participants, when the focus group was held, where it was held and provide a summary of what was discussed.

You may have chosen to carry out a field trial. This would have entailed you giving a sample of your product to customers for them to test. If you used this method, you will need to explain why you chose it, how you developed a product for customers to test, how you chose the customers, how you ensured that they used the product effectively and how you gained feedback.

It is always best to use at least two of the methods of primary research as this enables you to gather more accurate results. If you have used more than one method, you will need to explain why you decided on the mix of methods.

The benefits of primary research are:

• Direct contact with your potential customers

• Research that is tailored to meet your exact needs and is therefore specific and detailed

Your assessment criteria:

 M1 Explain methods used to identify the target market for the proposed business

 Key terms

Primary research: the collection of data that does not already exist

 Design

Design the following:

• a preliminary survey for finding out about your potential customers

• a plan for a focus group for your potential customers

• a plan for a field trial of your product/service.

• Answers that are confidential and therefore provide you with an insider's view of the market that your competitors do not have.

The drawbacks of primary research include the following:

• It is time consuming

• It is expensive

• You have to analyse all of the data

Secondary research.

You also need to explain your choices of secondary (or published) research. Your reasons may include the ease of access to the research, the time that was available to you and the accuracy of the published research.

The benefits of secondary (published) research are:

• It is usually pretty quick to find.

• All of the analysis is done for you.

• No data collection is necessary.

• You can gain information on larger scale studies.

• It is very useful for collecting data on market and industry trends.

The drawbacks of secondary research include:

• The research may not be very specific to your needs.

• The quality of the research may not be very good.

• The research may be out of date.

Once you have explained why you used each method and its benefits and drawbacks, you should also explain the effect on your business of gaining all this information and how you will attempt to overcome the drawbacks of each type of research.

Key terms

Secondary (or published) research: research that is already compiled and analysed for you

Reflect

Next time you visit a shop, make a note of how the people and the processes help to promote the products.

Primary research is extremely useful for getting to know your target market.

P3 Your own contribution

Starting your own business is very tough. People who do so often have little time to themselves and often lose money in the short term. However, it can be very rewarding and there are obvious benefits to being your own boss.

The success of your business depends on the skills that you have and the skills that you are prepared to develop. It may also mean relying on the skills of others as it may not be possible for you to have all of the skills required to run your own business.

Each business is different and therefore requires the owner to have a different skills set. The skills required depend on your individual business, but there are a number of skills that are common to most businesses.

Skills relating to your products and services

If you are planning on making your own products, it is important for you to have the necessary technical and operational skills to make them. There is little point in starting a business making clothes if you do not know how to use a sewing machine. Even if you are not planning to make your own products and are going to buy them from a manufacturer, you will still need a detailed knowledge of the product so that you can negotiate with your suppliers and talk to your customers with confidence.

Management skills

In order to be a good manager you need specific skills. These include the ability to interact well with people and effectively influence and lead your employees. You also need to be creative and able to come up with new ideas and solve problems quickly and effectively (be able to think on your feet). The ability to make decisions is also an important attribute as is a detailed knowledge of your products and your customers.

Skills relating to recording and checking the performance of your business

When you run your own business, you need the ability to monitor everything that is going on and to rectify anything that is going wrong. Monitoring the performance of a business starts with the setting of standards of performance that all the employees should follow. Your performance standards should relate back to your aims and objectives and should be explained to all employees so that you are all working towards the same goal. You then need to be able to measure the performance of your business. The performance of your business depends on the sales, how many products you have produced, the cost of raw materials and how much cash you have got left to reinvest into your business. These performance indicators should be compared to the performance standards that were set and any remedial action should be identified and carried out.

Personal selling skills

Your customers will not always come knocking on your door and therefore you may need to improve your personal selling skills in order to tempt customers to buy your products. Selling requires good interpersonal and communication skills, the ability to identify customers' wants and needs, the ability to persuade them to buy, good knowledge of products, the ability to listen and the ability to spot signs from the customer that mean they are interested.

Personal selling skills are important in tempting customers to buy.

Case study

Major's Fish Restaurant is in Bilston, a small town outside Birmingham. The restaurant's primary product is takeaway cod and chips, but kebabs, sausages, pies and hot and cold drinks are also sold. The large eat-in restaurant is open for breakfast, lunch and dinner. Major's was started 30 years ago by Major Spencer and his wife, Olive. Major is a sole trader, which means that he controls the business completely and any profit he retains (after taxes such as VAT and income tax have been deducted) is his income. Being a sole trader has advantages. Major keeps the profits and has complete control over the running of the restaurant, but it is very hard work.

'I get up early to go to the shop to cut fish and peel potatoes. I make sure there are enough products to sell throughout the day. I contact suppliers and have to go to the cash and carry to get stocks of drinks, etc. I employ 20 staff. Our eat-in restaurant is getting more popular and therefore I need help preparing the food and serving the customers. However, I am often required to serve too. I hardly have any spare time as we are open from 7am till 11pm. The weekends are our busiest time as not only do we serve hundreds of customers, but Olive and I also have to do the staff wages and other administration tasks.'

1. What are the benefits to Major of having his own business?

2. What are the drawbacks for Major of having his own business?

3. What skills do Major and his wife have that make their business so successful?

 Discuss

Write down the skills you believe you possess. Swap your answers with a friend and ask them to make constructive comments on your skills base. Discuss how you could each improve your skills set.

What have you got to offer?

P3 ▸ Administration skills

Technical and operational skills are central to the success of your business, but administrative skills are also vital. You need to keep up-to-date records of all your business dealings, record details of sales and ensure you know when you need to order more products so that customers are not disappointed. Good administration skills require consistency, organisation and an eye for detail. Essential administration tasks include:

- writing letters

- producing invoices, order forms, receipts and reminders for payment

- managing budgets

- carrying out research

- organising customer information.

Your assessment criteria:

> **P3** Describe the skills needed to run the business successfully and what areas require further personal development

Administration skills are central to the success of a business.

Previous experience

The business that you have chosen to set up is likely to be in an area where you have experience – whether as a hobby or an interest or because you have worked in a similar business. This experience will be extremely useful when setting up and running your own business. It is important that you outline your previous experience in your business plan and explain the relevance of your experience to your business.

Personal strengths and weaknesses

Although you have already completed a SWOT for your business (see page 366), it is also important to do a personal SWOT analysis to identify your strengths and weaknesses, opportunities and threats. Your business should be built around your strengths and the opportunities that are available to you and you should work towards overcoming your weaknesses and any threats that you identify.

Key terms

Personal SWOT analysis: an analysis of yourself identifying Strengths, Weaknesses, Opportunities and Threats

Skills gap: any skills you can identify that you may need in order to achieve your short- and long-term career goals

Figure 36.5: A personal SWOT analysis

Strengths What are your positive aspects?	Weaknesses What are your negative aspects?
• What qualifications do you have? • What work experience do you have? • What specialist knowledge do you have? • What skills do you have? • What are the positive aspects of your personality? • What motivates you? • Do you have any other strengths?	• Are there any gaps in your qualifications? • Are there any gaps in your knowledge? • Are there any gaps in your experience? • Do you have any financial difficulties? • What are the weak points of your personality? • What circumstances make you feel unhappy or frustrated? • Do you have any other limitations?
Opportunities What aspects at present or in the near future could you use to your advantage?	Threats What aspects at present or in the near future may be a disadvantage to you?
• Are there any gaps in the one word: marketplace that you could exploit? • Are there any scholarships or bursaries available to you?	• Do you have any potential financial problems? • Is there any competition from rivals? • Are there any unfavourable conditions in the economy? • Are there any changes in the one word: marketplace which could mean that your skills and knowledge become out of date?

Identifying your skills gap

As a result of your SWOT analysis, you may find that you are lacking certain skills – that you have a **skills gap**. Once you have identified a skills gap it is important to plan how you are going to 'fill' the gap. What are you going to do in order to gain those skills? This can be done by completing a skills audit, as shown in Figure 36.6.

 Discuss

In groups, discuss the skills that each of you possesses, where you gained these skills and what skills you do not have and how you are going to develop them.

If necessary, research the ways in which you could develop the skills that you do not have.

Figure 36.6: A skills audit

Skills	Do I have the skills? If yes – where have they been developed? If no – how they will be developed?
Technical and operational skills, relating to: • products and services • management • recording and checking the performance of the business	
Personal selling	
Administration	

Developing your skills

P3 Professional help

It is not always possible to have all of the skills needed to run your own business. It may therefore be necessary to seek **professional help**. Be wary, however, as this is often costly. Professional help can include:

- accountants – to advise on financial matters and prepare financial statements (costly but vital for tax purposes)

- solicitors – to advise on legal matters relating to your business

- consultants – to provide business advice and guidance relating to cost cutting, expansion, development and rectifying problems

- Business Link (www.businesslink.gov.uk) – a government-run organisation that provides advice and support for new businesses.

Training

When you completed your skills audit and personal SWOT analysis, you may have identified skills that you do not yet possess. One way of overcoming these skills shortages is to go on a training course. Training courses come in all shapes and sizes and are on offer at colleges and through private organisations. You should research the training courses available to you in terms of their accessibility, cost and the length of time they take to complete.

Planning and timescales

Having identified your skills gap, you should plan carefully how you intend to fill it. You will need to research the timescale involved in acquiring the new skills and whether this will fit into the planned opening of your new venture. Thorough planning should also ensure that you stay on track.

Key terms

Professional help: the use of experts to advise and help in the setting up and running of a new business

Professional help is costly but sometimes necessary.

Research

Research the relative merits and drawbacks of using professional help.

M2 ▶ Analysing your personal development needs

In order to analyse your personal development needs, you will have to look at each of the skills that you have or do not yet have and explain in detail why that skill is necessary to the success of your business. You will also need to explain the timescales involved in gaining new skills and why these timescales are appropriate.

In order to complete M2, it is a good idea to draw up an action plan of how you will address all of your skills gaps and explain how filling each gap will specifically help the running of the business. You will finally need to explain how you will monitor that you are gaining your skills and how you will check that you have successfully acquired the skills.

Gaining skills through training courses can be invaluable to the success of your business.

Case study

Gaining professional help and training for setting up your own business can be central to your success. Organisations such as The Prince's Trust offer a range of programmes including training, personal development, business start-up support, mentoring and advice for youths. The aim of The Prince's Trust is to help disadvantaged young people in the UK by offering assistance in a number of practical ways, for example:

- personal development courses.

- cash awards of up to £500 with advice and support.

- low-interest loans and grants to support business start-ups.
  The Prince's Trust has helped over 60,000 young people to set up their own businesses. After 12 months, 96 per cent of those supported by the business programme were still self-employed or still in employment.

1. What are the advantages of using professional help such as that offered by The Prince's Trust?

2. Research The Prince's Trust (www.princes-trust.org.uk) to see if it could help you with your business start-up.

Discuss

In pairs, discuss why it is necessary for you to complete the training that you have outlined in your skills audit.

P4 Legal status

When starting a new business, there are many legal issues that will affect how you can run the business. The first thing that you need to decide is the legal status of your business. There are several options available to you.

Sole trader

A **sole trader** is a business owned by just one person. The advantages of this type of ownership are:

Advantages	Disadvantages
• You have complete control over the business.	• You cannot take a holiday very easily as you are the business.
• It is cheap and easy to start up.	• You have unlimited liability (see opposite).
• You get to keep all of the profit.	
• You do not have to send your accounts to Companies House and therefore your affairs are private.	

Partnership

A **partnership** is a business owned by at least two people who have shared responsibility for the running of the business:

Advantages	Disadvantages
• More money can be invested into the business.	• Partners may fall out or disagree.
• The responsibility is shared	• The partnership would no longer exist if one of the partners were to leave.
• You can go on holiday as the other partner can cover for you.	• You have unlimited liability (see opposite).
• There is more knowledge and expertise available..	• You have to share the profits.

Your assessment criteria:

P4 Describe the legal and financial aspects that will affect the start up of the business

Key terms

Sole trader: a business that is owned by one person

Partnership: a business that is owned by at least two people who share responsibility for the running of the business

Limited companies

A **limited company** is a business that is owned by its shareholders:

Advantages	Disadvantages
• You have limited liability (see below).	• The business's financial information is in the public domain as accounts have to go to Companies House.
• The company can continue trading even if a shareholder dies.	• Profits have to be shared among the shareholders.
• There is the opportunity for more investment in the firm through more shareholders.	• It is expensive to set up.
	• Decision-making is slow as all shareholders have to agree.

Cooperatives

A **cooperative** is a business that is owned and run by the people who benefit from the service that the business provides. The people are called members and the profits are shared among them:

Advantages	Disadvantages
• The business is equally owned by its members.	• Everybody has equal liability if the business were to fail.
• Employees usually own a part of the business.	• It is difficult for members to influence business decisions and decision-making is usually a slow process.
• It involves fair voting systems.	

Legal liabilities

Depending on the type of business you decide to set up, your legal liability will differ. Legal liability refers to whether or not you are liable to pay for the debts of your business. There are two types of legal liability: limited and unlimited.

Limited liability means that if the business were to fail and therefore have debts to pay, then the shareholders (or members) would only lose the money that they invested in the shares of the business – the amount of money they lose is limited to what they have invested into the company. Under no circumstances would the shareholders have to use any of their personal assets to pay for the debts of the company.

Unlimited liability means that if the business were to fail and therefore debts had to be paid, the owners of the business would have to use their own personal possessions (for example, their house) to pay for those debts. The amount of money they could lose is unlimited.

Key terms

Limited company: *a business that is owned by shareholders*

Cooperative: *a business that is owned and run for the benefit of those using the service it provides*

Key terms

Limited liability: *if the business fails, the shareholders only lose what they invested in the business*

Unlimited liability: *If the business fails, the owners are personally responsible – all debts are paid for from the sale of their personal possessions*

Discuss

In groups, discuss the relative merits and drawbacks of each type of ownership.

Which do you think your business should be and why?

SPRAKE & KINGSLEY
SOLICITORS TO THE WAVENEY VALLEY SINCE 1790

Partnerships have unlimited liability.

Trading terms and conditions

It is important that you let your customers know the conditions under which they are buying your products or services. You should outline these terms in order to protect your company from any unreasonable claims by customers. The trading terms and conditions should cover details about price, payment and delivery arrangements, if relevant. It is good practice to state your trading terms and conditions in writing and place them where customers can see them.

Trading standards

The Trading Standards Institute (TSI) is a not-for-profit professional body that aims to protect consumers from unreasonable business traders and illegal trading through campaigns, educational activity and political lobbying. TSI is the professional body for Trading Standards professionals throughout the UK. Its members are employed by local authorities in Trading Standards Services that are authorised to enforce a wide range of consumer and other trading laws. For example, the TSI it helps to ensure that when you go to a shop you are not sold fake goods and when you buy a car that the miles on the clock have not been tampered with. Look at the Trading Standards website (www.tradingstandards.gov.uk) to research how trading standards legislation could affect the running of your business. The website also offers help and advice on how to set up a new business.

Licences

Some types of business require a licence in order to trade legally, for example childminders, nursing homes, theatres, hairdressers, taxis and pet shops. You need to research whether your business will need a licence. The costs of a licence should to be taken into consideration in your start-up costs.

Record keeping

Legally, you must keep records of certain aspects of your business, such as:

- wages and salaries – records of the wages and salaries paid to you and employees

- cash book – a record of all of the money coming in and going out of the business, including all payments by cheque and credit and debit cards

- petty cash – records of any small items that you buy with cash for the business

- sales and purchase ledgers – a record of all of your sales and everything that you have purchased for the business

Your assessment criteria:

P4 Describe the legal and financial aspects that will affect the start up of the business

Key terms

Trading Standards Institute (TSI): a not-for-profit membership organisation and professional body that aims to protect customers from rogue traders through its members who are employed as Trading Standards Professionals within local authorities

The Trading Standards Institute aims to protect customers against rogue traders.

Research

Over the next week, go into shops and look out for their trading terms and conditions. Make a note of what they cover and how they are worded and displayed.

- minutes of meetings – records of any meetings that you have with staff or customers (so that action points can be taken from them and the outcomes of decision-making processes can be referred back to)

- stock records – records of everything that is bought in as stock or raw materials (if you don't do this you will not know when to order more stock)

- accident records – in 1995, a new law came into force requiring all businesses to keep a record of all accidents and injuries that occur on their premises (the records must be kept for 3 years).

Resolving problems

Legally, you are obliged to provide certain documents for your business that outline what to do when problems occur. These include:

- a grievance policy – the policy staff can follow if they feel they have been treated unfairly while at work. This must be a written document and be given to all staff.

- disciplinary policy – the policy that the business will follow if a member of staff behaves inappropriately. It should outline what is expected of staff and what sort of behaviour is regarded as inappropriate and the steps that will be taken if a member of staff behaves in this manner. This must be a written document and be given to all staff.

National and local laws

There are many laws that you have to comply with when setting up a new business and it is down to you as the owner to find out which laws affect you. It is a legal requirement to take out certain forms of insurance, depending on the nature of your business. These may include:

- Buildings and contents insurance – this protects the building in which the business operates and the contents that the business owns within that building in case they are damaged or stolen.

- Owner's liability insurance – this protects the business if anybody entering its premises were to get injured.

- Product liability insurance – this protects the business if one of its products were to injure somebody.

- Keyman insurance – this covers the business against losses as the result of something happening to a key person in the business (for example someone whose expertise the business relies upon).

- Public liability insurance – this protects the business if one of its employees injures somebody or damages property while at work.

> **Q | Research**
>
> *Over the next week, research any cases of rogue traders. You may do this on the internet, or by watching programmes such as Watchdog. Feed back your findings to the rest of the class.*

P4 Regulations and bylaws

Legally, firms also need to adhere to several regulations; again it is your responsibility as a business owner to know which affect your business. Some of the more common regulations include:

- Data protection – if you store information about your customers you have to abide by the Data Protection Act 1998.

- Distance selling – if you decide to sell your products over the internet or phone, you must provide written details of the order to customers and a period of time during which they can cancel their order (7 days).

- E-commerce regulations – if you decide to sell your products over the internet you will need to abide by these regulations.

- Fire regulations – you have to adhere to certain fire regulations that relate to business premises.

- Health and safety – you are responsible for the health and safety of yourself, your employees and anybody else who visits your premises. By law, you have to carry out a risk assessment which outlines how safe your premises are. You also need to have a written health and safety policy.

- Planning permission – if you want to extend or build your own premises or change the use of your premises, you will need to seek approval from your local council.

Bylaws are local laws that are made by local government; it is your responsibility as a business owner to know which bylaws affect your business.

Staff

As a business owner, you may need to employ members of staff. All employees need to have a contract of employment. This has to be given to them within 2 months of starting work. It outlines the job, when employment started, payment, hours of work, holidays, sick pay, notice period, etc.

You have a legal responsibility to pay your employees. You must:

- provide them with a pay slip

- comply with national minimum wage

- make statutory payments for maternity, paternity, sick pay, etc.

You also have a responsibility to outline their hours of work (if the employee is over 18 years old) as set out in the working time regulations. Employees:

- must have 4 weeks of holiday per year

- cannot work more than 6 days per week

- must have a 20-minute break every 6 hours of work

- must work no more than a 48-hour week.

Business owners also have the duty and responsibility not to discriminate against employees and customers. This includes taking reasonable steps to ensure access for disabled people and ensure that disabled employees able to work effectively for you. It also means that you cannot discriminate on grounds of gender, sexual orientation, race, religion or age.

Regulatory bodies

The UK government and certain industries have set up organisations that set standards to which business must adhere. The **regulatory bodies** include:

- Office of Fair Trading – monitors business activity to ensure it is fair and competitive.

- Financial Services Authority – regulates banks, building societies and insurance companies.

- Food Standards Agency – ensures certain standards are met when businesses prepare food.

Sources of advice

There is lots of help out there when setting up your own business. Sources include:

- Business Link (www.businesslink.gov.uk)

- British Chambers of Commerce (www.britishchambers.org.uk)

- Department for Business, Innovation and Skills (www.bis.gov.uk)

- Federation of Small Businesses (www.fsb.org.uk)

- National Enterprise Network (www.nfea.com).

Key terms

Regulatory body: government-run organisations that set standards in certain industries

Research

On your own, research which laws and regulations will affect your business.

Business Link offers advice on setting up your own business.

Budgets and costs

Budgets

One of the many reasons people decide to set up their own businesses is because they believe they can make money. However, to start with, you may not make any money at all and you may even find you are losing money. It is important, therefore, to complete a personal survival budget in which you work out how much money you need in order not to go into debt.

Figure 36.7: A personal survival budget

Estimated yearly expenditure (£)	Estimated yearly income (£)
Rent	Earned income
Food	Benefits
Clothing	
Savings	
Car	
Loan	
Mobile phone	
Socialising	
Total	**Total**

Your assessment criteria:

P4 Describe the legal and financial aspects that will affect the start up of the business

? | **Did you know?**

Asking 'How much does it cost to set up a business?' is like asking 'How long is a piece of string?' However, preparing for typical expenditure is a good place to start.

Q | **Research**

Research potential locations for your business, investigating the advantages and disadvantages of each site.

It is essential to choose a location for your business that is near your customers.

Costs

There are considerable costs involved in starting up and then running a business. It is important, therefore, to consider the various financial aspects of the undertaking.

Premises

Location is an extremely important factor in the success of your business. You should look at the various possible locations for your premises and consider the following questions:

- Are your customers nearby?
- Are your competitors nearby?
- Is it easily accessible?
- What is the area like?
- What are rent or purchase costs?
- Are there storage facilities?

Equipment and supplies

Before starting your business, you will need to buy lots of equipment and supplies. In order to plan these costs, you will need to complete a **capital needs breakdown.**

Key terms

Capital needs breakdown: *a breakdown of all the costs you need to spend on equipment, supplies and fittings in order to start your business*

Figure 36.8: A capital needs breakdown

Fittings (£)	Equipment (£)	Supplies (£)
Storage	Cash till	Raw materials
Shelving	Lights	Stationery
Signs	IT equipment	Uniforms
Counter		
Total:	**Total:**	**Total:**

P4 Costs *continued*

Running costs

Running costs are the costs involved in the day-to-day running of your business, such as gas and electricity, insurance, rent and stock purchases. These should all be considered when putting together your cash flow forecast (see pages 386–7).

Staff

Employing staff is a costly business – they all need paying. There are also legal requirements with which you need to comply:

* They must be paid at least the minimum wage.

* You will need to pay National Insurance.

* You may wish to contribute to pension schemes.

Pricing

You will need to decide on the pricing of your products. Your options include:

* Cost-plus pricing – this involves calculating how much it costs to make your products and then adding a percentage on top of that (your profit margin). For example, if it costs you £1 to make a product and you decide to add a profit percentage of 50 per cent then you would sell your product for £1.50. However, if you choose this type of pricing, calculating the costs is not always easy, as it is difficult to allocate costs such as gas and electricity to the price of making one product. It can also be difficult to calculate the costs of providing a service.

* Demand-orientated pricing – this involves deciding on the price of your product depending on the demand for it (but obviously still covering your costs). There are a number of types of demand-orientated pricing:

  * competition pricing – setting your prices to match your competitors

  * penetration pricing – setting a low price in order to attract people to buy a new product – it is hoped they will like it and continue to buy it, even when the price rises

  * promotional pricing – dropping the price of a product for which the demand is declining in order to attract interest

  * skimming – setting a high price for a new product in order to maximise profits – this is usually used when the owner is very confident about the success of your product and is often used with technology products, such as the iPhone, where prices are high to start with, but may be lowered once the initial demand falls.

Skimming is used to charge high prices to start with when demand is high.

 Discuss

Discuss which pricing policies you will choose and explain your reasons for doing so.

 ## Case study

Cathy has just set up her own cake-making business. She employs staff to make the cakes and has bought equipment for making the cakes and a van to deliver the cakes to customers. She has found that there are lots of start-up and running costs. Start-up costs are generally those one-off costs that need to be paid to start up the business. Running costs are those that need to be paid on a day-to-day basis.

Cathy has found out that her running costs can be divided into direct costs and indirect costs. Direct costs are the costs that are directly related to the production of her cakes. Indirect costs (otherwise known as overheads) are those that she would still need to pay whether the business was making 10 cakes or 1000 cakes.

1. Give some examples of Cathy's start-up costs and her running costs.
2. Give some examples of Cathy's direct costs and her indirect costs.
3. Why is it important to identify your costs before setting up and running your own business?

Financial planning

P4 Break-even point

Break even is the point at which sales revenue covers all of the business's costs. At this point, the business has not made a profit or a loss, but simply broken even. Businesses need to know how many of their product they need to sell in order to cover their costs, as any product they sell after this will be making a profit.

In order to calculate the **break-even point**, you firstly have to calculate the contribution per unit – how much each individual product contributes towards covering the costs of the business.

These costs can be broken down into two main types:

- Fixed costs – costs that do not change no matter how many of the product you sell. For example, the amount of rent the business has to pay stays the same whether they sell 2 products a week or 2000 products a week.

- Variable costs – costs that do change depending on how many of the product is sold. For example, the more products you make and therefore sell, the more raw materials you will need to buy.

You need to add together all of your fixed costs (giving you the total fixed costs) and all of your variable costs (giving you the total variable costs). You then need to know how much your variable costs are per product you make (the variable cost per unit). In order to do this you need to divide your total variable costs by the number of products made.

Once you have those two figures (total fixed costs and variable costs per unit) you can calculate the break-even point.

$$\text{break even} = \frac{\text{total fixed cost}}{\text{unit contribution}}$$

unit contribution = the selling price of one of your products – the variable cost per unit

For example, imagine you are starting a cake-making business. Figure 36.9 shows how to calculate the break-even point.

Cash flow forecast

In order to prepare a **cash flow forecast** you need to have an idea of how many products you plan to sell in your first year of trading. This should come from your market research. A cash flow forecast considers all of your expenses (what you are spending) and income (the money that is coming into the business) over a period of a year.

A cash flow forecast enables a business to plan ahead for times in the year when it may not have a lot of money. Figure 36.10 on page 388 shows a cash flow forecast for Designer's Closet, a business selling designer clothes.

Figure 36.9: Calculating the break-even point

Total fixed costs per year = £10,000

Total variable costs per year = £8000

Number of cakes made per year = 4000

Selling price per cake = £25

First, calculate your variable cost per unit $= \dfrac{\text{total variable costs}}{\text{number of cakes made}}$

$= \dfrac{8000}{400}$

$= 20$

Then calculate your unit contribution $= \text{selling price} - \text{variable cost per unit}$

$= 25 - 20$

$= 5$

You can then calculate the break-even point $= \dfrac{\text{total fixed costs}}{\text{unit contribution}}$

$= \dfrac{10000}{5}$

$= 2000$

The company needs to sell 2000 cakes per year before it starts to make a profit.

Forecasted profit and loss account and balance sheet

Once you have completed a cash flow, it is then possible to produce a **profit and loss account** and **balance sheet** to show projected levels of profits. Alongside the information from the cash flow forecast, a little more information is required:

- Designer's Closet expects to finish the year with stocks of £2000 (estimated).

- Designer's Closet will **depreciate** its fixtures and fittings at a rate of 10 per cent per year.

- Designer's Closet will depreciate its equipment at a rate of 20 per cent per year.

 Key terms

Depreciate: to reduce the value of an asset over a specified number of years to allow for age, wear, etc.

Balance sheet: a financial summary of the assets, liabilities and equities of a business as of a certain date

Profit and loss account: statement showing a business's projected profit or loss

 Design

Design a cash flow forecast, a profit and loss account and a balance sheet for your business.

P4 Cash flow forecast

Figure 36.10: A cash flow forecast for Designer's Closet

	Jan (£)	Feb (£)	Mar (£)	April (£)	May (£)	June (£)	July (£)	Aug (£)	Sept (£)	Oct (£)	Nov (£)	Dec (£)	Totals (£)
Balance brought forward (B/F)	0	-4660	-4018	-1648	-1238	-1428	-908	1652	2412	3332	2942	5902	0
Income													
Owner's capital	1000	0	0	0	0	0	0	0	0	0	0	0	1000
Bank loan	2000	0	0	0	0	0	0	0	0	0	0	0	2000
Cash sales	1000	2000	3500	3000	2000	3000	3000	3250	3200	2100	3000	3500	32550
Credit sales	0	50	500	1000	1000	1000	1000	1000	1000	1000	1500	1800	10850
Total receipts	4000	2050	4000	4000	3000	4000	4000	4250	4200	3100	4500	5300	46400
Total cash available	4000	-2610	-18	2352	1762	2572	3092	5902	6612	6432	7442	11202	48740
Expenses													
Initial stock purchases	2000	0	0	0	0	0	0	0	0	0	0	0	2000
Cash purchases	2000	250	400	400	2000	250	250	250	2000	250	250	250	8550
Credit purchases	0	0	0	2000	0	2000	0	2000	0	2000	0	2000	10000
Sales returns	0	0	0	0	50	50	50	50	50	50	50	50	400
Gas and electricity	60	60	60	60	60	60	60	60	60	60	60	60	720
Fixtures and fittings	2000	0	0	0	0	0	0	0	0	0	0	0	2000
Equipment	1500	0	0	0	0	0	0	0	0	0	0	0	1500
Owner's drawings	100	100	100	100	100	100	100	100	100	100	100	100	1200
Advertising	150	150	200	200	150	150	150	200	200	200	250	250	2250
Insurance	30	30	30	30	30	30	30	30	30	30	30	30	360
Rent	400	400	400	400	400	400	400	400	400	400	400	400	4800
Wages	400	400	400	400	400	400	400	400	400	400	400	400	4800
Overdraft interest	20	18	0	0	0	0	0	0	0	0	0	0	38
Bank loan interest	0	0	40	0	0	40	0	0	40	0	0	40	160
Total payments	8660	1408	1630	3590	3190	3480	1440	3490	3280	3490	1540	3580	38778
Balance carried forward (C/F)	-4660	-4018	-1648	-1238	-1428	-908	1652	2412	3332	2942	5902	7622	7622

Annotations:

- This is the total that is earned or spent when you add all the months together.
- This should be the amount B/F at the start of the year.
- Total = 2000 (Jan) + 2000 (Feb) + 4000 (Mar) + 4000 (Mar) …
- This figure should equal the figure for the Dec balance C/F total figure.
- This figure should equal the total figure for the balance C/F figure.
- You may expect sales to increase in certain months due to demand increasing. For example, if this business was an Easter egg maker, demand in March and April would increase.
- The amount in the bank account at the start of the year (the opening balance)
- All of the income items added together
- The B/F for this month is the C/F from the previous month.
- Balance brought forward for that month plus total receipts
- In order to calculate your gas and electricity, divide your bill for the year by 12.
- This is how much you draw out for yourself.
- Total of all payments for that month
- C/F = total cash available – total payments. This is the amount that you have left at the end of the month. It is normal to make a loss in your first few months (even years) of trading.

Figure 36.11: A forecasted profit and loss account for Designer's Closet for year ended 31 December 2011

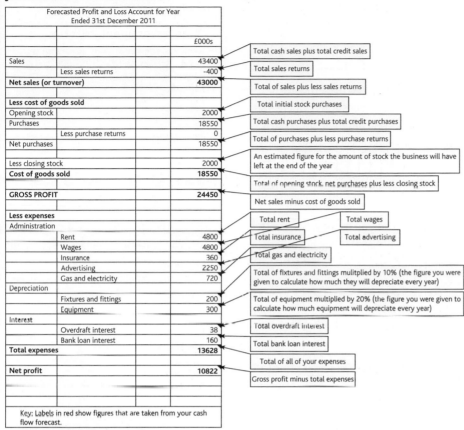

Forecasted Profit and Loss Account for Year Ended 31st December 2011				
			£000s	
Sales			43400	Total cash sales plus total credit sales
	Less sales returns		-400	Total sales returns
Net sales (or turnover)			43000	Total of sales plus less sales returns
Less cost of goods sold				
Opening stock			2000	Total initial stock purchases
Purchases			18550	Total cash purchases plus total credit purchases
	Less purchase returns		0	Total of purchases plus less purchase returns
Net purchases			18550	
				An estimated figure for the amount of stock the business will have left at the end of the year
Less closing stock			2000	
Cost of goods sold			18550	Total of opening stock, net purchases plus less closing stock
GROSS PROFIT			24450	Net sales minus cost of goods sold
Less expenses				Total rent Total wages
Administration				
	Rent		4800	Total insurance Total advertising
	Wages		4800	
	Insurance		360	Total gas and electricity
	Advertising		2250	
	Gas and electricity		720	Total of fixtures and fittings mulitplied by 10% (the figure you were given to calculate how much they will depreciate every year)
Depreciation				
	Fixtures and fittings		200	Total of equipment multiplied by 20% (the figure you were given to calculate how much equipment will depreciate every year)
	Equipment		300	
Interest				
	Overdraft interest		38	Total overdraft interest
	Bank loan interest		160	Total bank loan interest
Total expenses			13628	Total of all of your expenses
Net profit			10822	Gross profit minus total expenses

Key: Labels in red show figures that are taken from your cash flow forecast.

Figure 36.12: A forecasted balance sheet for Designer's Closet as at the end of December 2011

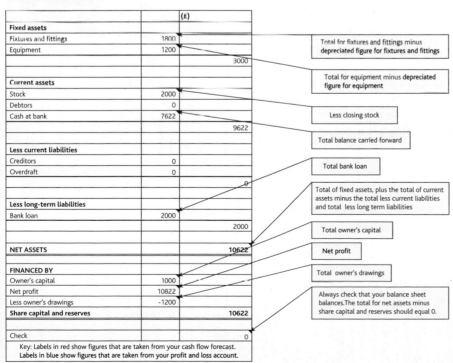

		(£)	
Fixed assets			
Fixtures and fittings	1800		Total for fixtures and fittings minus depreciated figure for fixtures and fittings
Equipment	1200		
		3000	Total for equipment minus depreciated figure for equipment
Current assets			
Stock	2000		Less closing stock
Debtors	0		
Cash at bank	7622		
		9622	Total balance carried forward
Less current liabilities			
Creditors	0		Total bank loan
Overdraft	0		
		0	Total of fixed assets, plus the total of current assets minus the total less current liabilities and total less long term liabilities
Less long-term liabilities			
Bank loan	2000		
		2000	Total owner's capital
NET ASSETS		10622	Net profit
FINANCED BY			Total owner's drawings
Owner's capital	1000		
Net profit	10822		Always check that your balance sheet balances. The total for net assets minus share capital and reserves should equal 0.
Less owner's drawings	-1200		
Share capital and reserves		10622	
Check		0	

Key: Labels in red show figures that are taken from your cash flow forecast. Labels in blue show figures that are taken from your profit and loss account.

P4 Sources of finance

No matter what sort of business you are planning, you need money to invest in the business to get it started. The difficult question is where you are going to get the money from. There are several different sources of finance.

Your own savings

You can use money that you have saved yourself to invest in your business. This will persuade other people to lend you money. Banks often match what you have invested as they believe that this will encourage you to work harder to make the business succeed.

Grants and sponsorship

Grants are sums of money that you do not have to pay back. There are various grants available, such as:

- Regional Selective Assistance – this is a grant that encourages firms that already exist to relocate or expand in certain 'assisted areas' of the UK.

- EU convergence region funding – this grant is available in certain parts of the UK to bring employment and economic development to the area.

- The Prince's Trust – this charity aims to support young people (aged 14–30) to set up their own businesses. It particularly aims to help disadvantaged youngsters who cannot raise finances from other sources. It offers low interest loans, grants in special circumstances, advice, mentoring, support and training.

Friends and family

Friends or family may be interested in lending you money and often do not charge interest.

Bank loans

Getting a bank loan is a necessity for a lot of people when setting up their own business. To get a loan from the bank you will need a faultless business plan and to have invested some of your own money into the business. Banks often lend money over a long period of time so that you can buy capital items, such as equipment. You have to pay interest on money that you borrow from a bank.

Your assessment criteria:

P4 Describe the legal and financial aspects that will affect the start up of the business

M3 Assess the implications of the legal and financial aspects that will affect the start up of the business

🔑 Key terms

Sources of finance: the different options available to you to finance the start up of your business

Accurate financial records have to be available for inspection by HMRC.

Overdrafts

An overdraft is a withdrawal from a bank account that exceeds the amount of money in the account. An overdraft can be very costly as banks usually charge high interest rates for overdraft facilities. Overdrafts should only really be used as a short-term measure when you have cash-flow problems and should not be used to buy capital items.

Mortgages

A mortgage is a big loan that is used to buy property. A typical loan lasts 25 years and is always secured on the property being purchased.

Leasing

This is similar to renting. Some businesses use leasing to avoid buying expensive equipment and to keep their cash flow healthy. There are two different types of leasing:

- Leaseback – the business owns a piece of equipment and sells it to a leasing firm. The business then leases back the equipment from the leasing firm.

- Direct lease – the business decides it wants to lease a certain piece of equipment. The leasing firm buys the equipment and then leases it to the business for a period of time. Once the lease period is over the piece of equipment goes back to the leasing firm.

Record keeping

It is essential that you keep accurate financial records for your business as these are used to justify all income and expenditure to HMRC (Her Majesty's Revenue and Customs) – the taxman.

Employing an accountant can ensure your record keeping is accurate.

 Discuss

In pairs, discuss the sources of finance that are available to you. Outline the pros and cons of each.

M3 ▶ Assessing the legal and financial aspects

In order to achieve M3, you must look at all the legal and financial aspects discussed in P4 and assess how they will impact on your business. You should explain all of the procedures that you need to put in place to meet these legal and financial requirements.

 Discuss

In pairs, discuss the legal and financial aspects that will impact on your business.

Business planning

Figure 36.13: Essential parts of your business plan

1. Executive summary.	2. General company description
• What will your product be? • Who will your customers be? • Who are the owners? • What do you think the future holds for your business and your industry? • Make it enthusiastic, professional, complete, and concise. • Write this section last.	• What business will you be in? What will you do? • What is your mission statement? • What are your company goals and objectives? • To whom will you market your products? • Describe your industry. • Describe your most important company strengths and core competencies. • What is the company's legal form of ownership?
3. Products and services	**4. Marketing**
• Describe, in depth, your products or services. • What factors will give you competitive advantages or disadvantages? • What are the pricing structures of your products or services? • What are your plans for customer service?	• Describe what market research was undertaken. • Describe your industry (market share, size, target market, trends, growth, barriers to entry). • Include a PESTLE analysis. • Describe your customers' demographic profile. • Describe your competition (direct and indirect). • Include a competition analysis. • What is your niche? • What is your promotional strategy? • What is your promotional budget? • What is your location?

5. Operational plan	**6. Management and organisation**
• Describe your production methods.	• Who will manage the business on a day-to-day basis?
• Describe the requirements of the location (space, storage, etc.).	• Outline that person's experience.
• What are your business hours?	• Outline that person's competencies.
• What legal aspects affect your business?	
• How many employees will you have?	
• Where and how will you find the right employees?	
• What will you pay your employees?	
• Describe your training methods and requirements.	
• Who will be your suppliers?	
• How will you organise delivery?	
• What will your costs be?	

7. Personal financial statement	**8. Financial plan**
• Include a personal survival budget.	• Include a break-even calculation.
	• Include a cash flow forecast.
	• Include a forecasted profit and loss account.
	• Include a forecasted balance sheet.
	• Outline your plans for growth and development.
	• Outline any contingency planning.

Banks offer advice on starting your own business.

 Research

Research business plan templates you could use. Explain the benefits and drawbacks of each template that you find.

D1 ▸ Professional looking and accurate

In order to achieve D1, your proposal needs to cover all of the elements outlined for P5 and also be a professional-looking document that is fluent in its descriptions with all data accurate and referenced.

 Design

Design a template for your business plan.

Assessment checklist

To achieve a pass grade, my portfolio of evidence must show that I can:

Assessment criteria	Description	✓
P1	Present the initial business idea using relevant criteria	☐
P2	Explain how to identify the target market	☐
P3	Describe the skills needed to run the business successfully and what areas require further personal development	☐
P4	Describe the legal and financial aspects that will affect the start up of the business	☐
P5	Produce a proposal containing the essential information for the start up of a business	☐

To achieve a merit grade, my portfolio of evidence must show that I can:

Assessment criteria	Description	✓
M1	Explain methods used to identify the target market for the proposed business	☐
M2	Analyse the personal development needed to run the business successfully	☐
M3	Assess the implications of the legal and financial aspects that will affect the start up of the business	☐

To achieve a distinction grade, my portfolio of evidence must show that I can:

Assessment criteria	Description	✓
D1	Present a comprehensive business proposal that addresses all relevant aspects of business start up	☐

37 | Understanding business ethics

LO1 Understand the meaning and importance of ethics in the business world

- ▶ What are business ethics?

- ▶ Making the right decisions

- ▶ How do businesses ensure they are ethical?

LO2 Understand the implications of businesses operating ethically

- ▶ Should stakeholders care?

- ▶ What happens when stakeholders disagree?

- ▶ Who puts pressure on businesses to be ethical?

LO3 Know the social implications of business ethics

▸ Bribery, corruption and discrimination

▸ Animal testing, spamming and shills

▸ What laws are in place to stop poor ethical practices?

LO4 Understand ethical concerns facing different communities

▸ Who puts pressure on governments and companies?

▸ Globalisation, outsourcing and Fair Trade

▸ The environment, child labour and cultural imperialism

In the business of being ethical

All organisations are in business for a reason, whether it is a private business operating for a profit, a public organisation delivering a service or a charity raising funds. However, organisations do not always make good decisions; some organisations make poor decisions which affect the staff, customers or perhaps the local people. For this reason, **business ethics** are important.

P1 What are business ethics?

Organisations are in business to achieve their corporate aims and objectives. In order for them to achieve their aims and objectives, they have to make decisions about their marketing, products, finances, locations and staff. These decisions are also related to their **operational activities**. A business's operational activity is anything that a business does in order to achieve its aims and objectives. Companies such as House of Fraser, Waitrose and JJB Sports are all in the retail sector and their operational activities revolve around selling their products, buying from their suppliers, delivering goods to their shops and promoting their products.

In order to carry out its operational activities and achieve its aims and objectives, is it ethical for a company to buy its supplies from a factory that uses child labour or a factory that produces high levels of carbon emissions that are damaging our planet or that disposes of its waste in such a way that pollutes our seas? Just as we are expected to behave responsibly, so are businesses.

If a business is ethical it focuses on making a helpful input into society and the local community. An example of an ethical company is Ben and Jerry's, which aims to 'make the best possible ice cream in the nicest possible way'. The company states on its website that: 'It's not only the mixing in the best ingredients that's important to us, our suppliers are too' (www.benjerry.co.uk/ourvalues). The company's **ethical activities** are as important as making a quality product and, for this reason, it sources its ingredients from producers and suppliers who share its values.

The **values of businesses** are those things that they believe are important. Just as we have values that mean we treat people with respect, so should businesses. Businesses are made up of people and it is these people's **individual ethical behaviour** that can determine the ethics of the business. It is the responsibility of managers within these businesses to ensure that their staff behaves ethically. Values also affect certain professionals. **Professional ethics** refers to the values that doctors, nurses

Key terms

Business ethics: *the examination of what is right and wrong in relation to business activities*

Ethical activities: *things that businesses do that are morally right*

Individual ethical behaviour: *the moral behaviour of individuals*

Operational activities: *things that a business does in order to achieve its aims and objectives*

Values of businesses: *the things that a business believes are important*

Did you know?

Ben and Jerry's donates 7.5 per cent of its pre-tax profits to charity.

and lawyers, etc. have. There are codes of ethics in these professions that ensure that the reputation of each profession is upheld. For example, when you visit a doctor, he or she is not allowed to discuss your diagnosis with anybody else without your consent. A doctor who breaks this rule of confidentiality can be banned from practising medicine.

Ben and Jerry's prides itself on being an ethical business.

Case study

In May 2009, some doctors in South Africa went on strike and this raised the important question as to whether it is professionally ethical for them to do so. If doctors are on strike, patients' well-being could be endangered. Some patient deaths in South Africa at this time have been attributed to the lack of care available during the strike. However, the striking doctors insisted that they were striking in order to improve long-term patient care.

1. Do you think it is unethical for doctors to strike? Explain your answer.

2. Do you think there are any alternative methods that doctors could use in order to get their point across?

Key terms

Professional ethics: the values that certain jobs (such as doctors, lawyers, nurses and accountants) involve

Research

In pairs, research three other ethical businesses that pride themselves on their values.

For each of these businesses describe their business ethics, their ethical activities and their business values.

Did you know?

Codes of practice are in place to ensure professionals continue to be ethical.

Ethical issues

Making the right decisions

All businesses can be ethical, whatever their size. For sole traders this may mean ensuring they recycle all their paper, which is very easy to manage. However, as businesses get bigger (public limited companies, for example) it becomes more difficult to ensure that everybody is playing their part in being ethical. The directors must therefore make policies and decisions to ensure that all parties are being as ethical as possible. This is part of **corporate governance**.

Businesses do not just try to be ethical within themselves, but also in their local communities and in the wider world. This is known as **corporate social responsibility (CSR)**. In the UK, all businesses are encouraged to practise CSR: 'to address... challenges based on their core competences wherever they operate – locally, regionally and internationally.' (*Corporate Social Responsibility, A Government update*, www.bis.gov.uk)

Even football clubs recognise the importance of corporate social responsibility. Manchester United's CSR, for example, involves working with the local community around its sites, charity organisations in the UK, and its global charity partner UNICEF.

Many businesses' ethical values revolve around the environment. There has been and still is a lot of press coverage about carbon footprints and we are more conscious than ever of the need to look after the environment. Every time you travel in an aeroplane you are adding hugely to your carbon footprint. Airline companies are therefore aware of their need to be more environmentally friendly because of the impact they have on global warming. British Airways was the first airline to have a voluntary carbon-offsetting scheme. Every time a passenger books a flight on www.ba.com, the carbon dioxide that the flight will produce is calculated along with the cost of the carbon per tonne at the time. The passenger can then make a payment that helps to fund hydroelectric power plants and wind farms.

The rate at which we are burning oil and coal and running petrol engines means that we have strengthened the greenhouse effect, which many people believe is leading to an unsustainable increase in the temperature of the Earth. In order to improve our Earth's **sustainability** we should limit our use of fuels, recycle, etc.

Your assessment criteria:

 P1 Explain the ethical issues a business needs to consider in its operational activities

---

🔑 **Key terms**

Corporate governance: *policies and decisions that directors of companies make that affect the ways companies operate*

Corporate social responsibility (CSR): *the concept of a business acting with concern for the community and the environment*

Sustainability: (environmental) *the ability to cause little or no damage to the environment and therefore allow it to continue for a long time*

🔍 **Research**

In pairs, think of three or four companies with which you are both familiar. Research their CSR policies.

When people think about ethical issues relating to business, they often think about **human rights**, about child labour, low wages and 'sweat factories'. These are issues that businesses have to consider when choosing suppliers. It may be that the supplies they get from third world countries are much cheaper than those from other countries; however, they need to consider whether this is because they are paying low wages (for example) and whether this is ethically right. In the UK, there are laws to ensure that our human rights are protected. For example, it is illegal to treat people differently based on their gender, race, ability or sexuality. This is not always the case in other countries. There is no minimum wage in some countries, meaning that workers can be paid very little. It is up to the businesses that buy the products to ensure the workers are being paid fairly. This is known as **Fair Trade**. In 2006, Sainsbury's and Waitrose decided to sell only Fair Trade bananas to protect the farmers who were the only losers of the price war that was (and still is) raging between the major UK supermarkets.

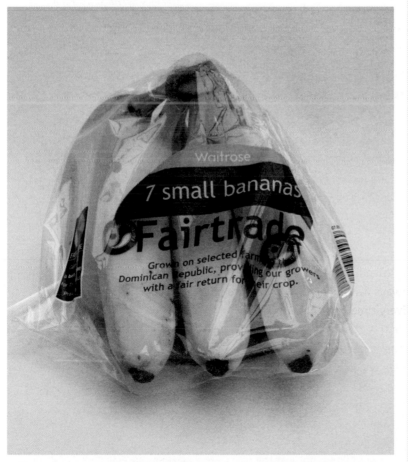

Fair Trade ensures that farmers are paid a fixed price for their produce.

 Key terms

Fair Trade: *a system that ensures producers are paid fairly for their products, bringing about the social, environmental and economic development of communities*

Human rights: *the basic rights that all individuals are entitled to as human beings*

? **Did you know?**

The Race Relations Act was established by parliament in 1976. In 2006, additional legislation was passed, the Race and Religious Hatred Act, which includes the additional offence of inciting religious hatred.

 Discuss

In groups of three or four, discuss the advantages and disadvantages of supermarkets only supplying Fair Trade produce.

Ensure you talk about:

• *prices*

• *ethics*

• *supply of goods.*

P1 > Ethical practice

Businesses need to ensure that they are not corrupt. **Corruption** means gaining advantage through illegal or immoral means. Corruption comes in many forms; for example, there have been stories over the years of police corruption, of police taking money from criminals in return for guarantees that they will not to be prosecuted. This is an example of serious corruption. Businesses have to ensure they are doing all they can in order to minimise corruptive practices in their organisation.

At the other end of the spectrum, businesses need to **trade fairly**. The Office of Fair Trading (www.oft.gov.uk) ensures that there is enough competition between fair trading businesses so that consumers get choice. Fair Trade means that:

- consumers can guarantee that the products they buy are of satisfactory quality

- competition between organisations is open and fair

- all businesses are open in their dealings.

In order to be ethical, businesses also need to comply with various laws – to show **legal and regulatory compliance**. This is so that consumers, employees and businesses are protected.

Consumer Protection law (Consumer Protection Act 1987, Sales of Goods Act 1979 and the Trades Description Act 1968) ensures that businesses do not describe goods in a misleading manner or overcharge for products. Consumers have rights, and businesses must respect these.

Employment law protects employees against being treated unfairly by their employers. The Sex Discrimination Act 1975, the Equal Pay Act 1970 and the Employment Protection Act 1975 ensure that all staff are dealt with in a fair way. Employees are also protected by the Health and Safety Act 1974. This law ensures that employees are not exposed to any risk or danger.

Ethical issues can also arise within a business's practices. They can arise due to the pressures that managers are under to meet aims and objectives, which sometimes mean that managers do not fully comply with health and safety laws. The **working conditions** that employees work in are also regulated by law. Working conditions do not just cover pay but also working hours, harassment, discrimination and holiday entitlement. Individuals also have ethical responsibilities, not just the business. It is the responsibility of the human resources department within a business to ensure that employees are following its ethical guidelines.

Your assessment criteria:

P1 > Explain the ethical issues a business needs to consider in its operational activities

Key terms

Corruption: gaining advantage through illegal or immoral means

Legal and regulatory compliance: when businesses obey the laws and rule of the country

Trade fairly: operate in an open manner, with fair competition, to sell goods of a satisfactory quality

Working conditions: the environment in which employees work

? Did you know?

Nike, the trainer manufacturer, has operations in Indonesia, Vietnam and China. Workers there get paid on average $2 a day.

The Office of Fair Trading ensures that there is enough competition between fair trading businesses so that consumers get choice.

 Case study

A woman who was employed in the office of a boat company for a number of years decided to seek employment with the same company as a deck-hand and wanted to gain a captain's licence. She alleged she was made to feel unwelcome by her male co-workers who said that the work was too heavy and dirty for her. Due to the recession, some of the company's services had to be axed, meaning that the company had to reduce the work hours for deck-hands. As a consequence, the woman's hours were cut and she suffered a loss of training and career opportunities.

She complained to the company that the male staff's hours were not cut by as much as hers and that her aspiration to be a captain had been seriously jeopardised.

The company acknowledged that the comments about the work being too heavy and dirty for her were made, and that this may have influenced the distribution of work. The complaint was settled by the company paying her compensation of £12,000, giving her a written apology and agreeing to undertake training on anti-discrimination.

1. What ethical issues are raised in this case?

2. Why is it important for anti-discrimination laws to be in place?

Stakeholders and ethics

P2 > Stakeholders and shareholders

Stakeholders are people who have an interest in a business. These people can include owners, employees, customers, suppliers, competitors and citizens.

Shareholders are the owners of a business as they own shares in the business. If a business is performing well, the value of the shares increase and therefore the value of the business also increases. The value of the business depends on the decisions that are made within the business. These decisions need to take into account short-term profit and long-term security.

Employees have an interest in a business's activities because the business pays their wages and dictates their working conditions. Employees add value to the firm by helping to provide products and services to customers. It is in a business's best interest to look after their employees and offer them good working conditions and benefits. Employers now compete to be the best firm to work for. Price Waterhouse Coopers has been voted *The Times* Employer of the Year for 7 years running.

Customers are important stakeholders as they purchase the goods and services that businesses offer. Customers will only purchase goods and services if they are satisfied with the product, they see it as value for money and it fulfils their needs. Businesses therefore need to keep customers satisfied by continuing to serve their customers' needs.

Suppliers sell their goods to other businesses. If the businesses that they sell to are not doing very well, the suppliers will be affected as their goods may no longer be required. Often there is a whole chain of suppliers that can be affected if a business fails to perform.

The existence of competitors can affect the success of other businesses. Businesses keep a watchful eye on other businesses in an attempt to outdo each other. Competitors can therefore have a considerable impact on the activities of businesses.

Citizens are the people who live in the community where businesses operate. They should therefore be considered when major business decisions are made. Many businesses now include doing good work in the community in their mission statement. This is included in their public relations activities. Businesses can affect the natural local environment, for example by expanding their site and devastating the local wildlife. Potential effects such as these should be looked at alongside the benefits

---

Your assessment criteria:

 P2 Explain the implications for the business and stakeholders of a business operating ethically

 Key terms

Shareholders: those who own shares in a business

Stakeholders: those who have an interest in a business

 Did you know?

You are a stakeholder in all of the businesses in your local area as what they do affects you.

 Design

In pairs, design a diagram of all of the stakeholders in your school or college. Explain why you believe they are stakeholders and what interest they have in the school/college.

of an expansion, such as the creation of jobs and effect on the prosperity of the area.

Different groups of stakeholders do not always have the same interests in a business and this can cause conflict. This is known as **conflicts of interest**. A business often has to balance these various interests in an attempt to make all stakeholders as happy as possible. It is often the case that stakeholders disagree.

If a business has launched a new product that is selling well, the shareholders will be happy as they will be getting a good return on their investment and employees will be happy as they job is more likely to be secure; however, citizens may not be happy if, for example, the business is doing so well that it wants to expand the premises and build on local land.

Key terms

Conflicts of interest: when the interests of the stakeholders do not agree

Businesses are now in competition to be the best employer.

Case study

As the Chinese economy started to grow in the mid-1990s, the Chinese government was keen to invite car manufacturers to make a car that was suitable for Chinese families. China has a population of around 1.3 billion and it is estimated that in the next 40 years between 200 and 300 million new vehicles will be purchased by Chinese citizens.

In China, owning a car is a huge status symbol and this has spurred 30 million Chinese citizens to take driving lessons, even though there are currently only 10 million vehicles in the country. Environmentalists are extremely concerned that in the future China could be consuming twice the amount of oil that the USA currently consumes and if China were to have as many cars on the road per person as Germany, the world would contain twice as many cars as it currently does.

1. List all of the stakeholders in this case study.

2. What are the interests of all of the stakeholders that you have identified?

3. What ethical issues arise in the case study?

4. What are the conflicts of interest between each of the stakeholders?

Did you know?

There are two types of stakeholder – primary and secondary.

Research

Research at least three companies in the press that have had recent conflicts of interest between their different stakeholder groups.

- *Why have these conflicts happened?*

- *What has the company done to resolve them?*

405

The implications of businesses operating ethically

 P2 The implications of ethical behaviour

With the immense growth of the internet, the world has become a much smaller place. News of something that has happened anywhere in the world can be transmitted to us all in a matter of seconds. It is no wonder, therefore, that businesses have become increasingly concerned about their behaviour. Many businesses have adapted their behaviour and now take their ethical responsibilities very seriously. This is often communicated through their mission statements. Nestlé's mission statement, for example, reads: 'our fundamental approach to business has been the creation of long-term sustainable value for our consumers, customers, employees, shareholders and society as a whole. The Nestlé Corporate Business Principles lay out our basic responsibilities to these stakeholders and openly state that we favour long-term business development over short-term profit. They include all nine principles of the UN Global Compact regarding labour standards, human rights, and the environment.' (www.nestle.co.uk/AboutNestle/OurResponsibility/)

Most businesses have established corporate social responsibility (CSR) programmes in response to **ethical pressures**. Since being taken over by Kraft, Cadbury has continued to take its CSR very seriously. Cadbury has set up the Cadbury Cocoa Partnership and Fair Trade programmes. The company's website states, 'To us, a delicious world is about living well and taking care of each other today, while being vigilant about the tomorrow that we'll leave for the next generations.' (www.kraftfoodscompany.com/Responsibility/)

Many businesses now ensure that they implement ethical practices. McDonald's, for example, once notorious for its unhealthy menu, has taken massive steps to promote healthier eating. Its website (www.mcdonalds.co.uk) lets you calculate how many calories are in each of its meals and gives guidance on how to follow a balanced diet.

Pressure groups

While many businesses now take their ethical responsibilities very seriously, there are still some that are damaging our planet through environmental or human neglect. This affects all of us as we are all stakeholders in the welfare of our planet. People who want to raise awareness of a particular issue sometimes form a **pressure group** in order to put pressure on businesses to act responsibly. Environmental pressure groups include:

• Friends of the Earth

Your assessment criteria:

P2 Explain the implications for the business and stakeholders of a business operating ethically

 Key terms

Ethical pressures: *the growing pressure put on businesses to take account of ethical concerns*

Pressure group: *a voluntary sector organisation that exists to raise awareness about certain issues in the hope that the government/businesses will take positive action*

- Environmental Justice Foundation

- Greenpeace.

Other pressure groups include:

- PETA – People for the Ethical Treatment of Animals (animal welfare)

- Amnesty International (human rights)

- Christian Aid (international development)

- Internet Watch Foundation (internet safety).

Pressure groups attract vast amounts of media attention and governments always need to listen to public opinion, which is often voiced through pressure groups. The public image of a business is very important as bad public opinion can have a huge impact on sales.

Ethical practices can make a real difference to a business's competitiveness. Ben and Jerry's, for example, has built its business on being ethical. The company has grown up in a world that is becoming more socially responsible, which has had a positive effect on its competitiveness and its reputation. Consumers feel they are doing the right thing by purchasing Ben and Jerry's products, and so the company is able to charge a premium for its products. Being ethical is also a competitive advantage for businesses as consumers trust ethical businesses more than those that are not seen as ethical and and are therefore more inclined to purchase their products. This adds value to ethical businesses.

There are other, less obvious benefits to ethical business practices. For example, reducing energy consumption cuts costs and makes companies more competitive. Also, being an ethical company could mean that the employees are happier and feel that they are doing a worthwhile job, lowering labour turnover and therefore saving the business the expense of employing new staff.

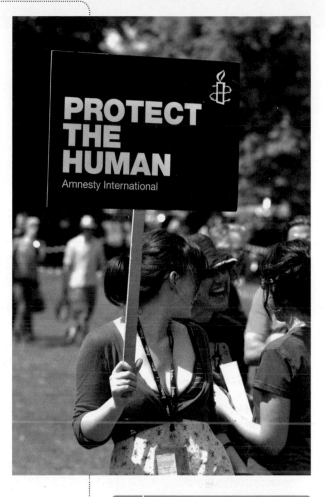

Q Research

In groups, research the above named pressure groups and answer the following questions:

- *What is a pressure group?*

- *Why do pressure groups exist?*

- *What does this particular pressure group campaign against?*

- *Has the work of this group made a difference in your opinion? Explain your answer.*

List some more pressure groups that you have found and explain what they campaign for.

The implications of ethical trade

Ethical trade

Ethical trade takes into consideration the conditions and practices that occur throughout the supply chain of a given business. In the past, Primark has been criticised for its use of unethical trading practices in Asian countries. It has now, however, appointed an ethical trade manager in Bangladesh, China and India, and has ethical trade policies and practices and delivers awareness-raising training to buying staff and suppliers. Its suppliers are expected to sign a **code of practice**, which ensures there is no use of child labour and that employment and health and safety law are adhered to.

Ethical trade has been proven to increase profits. A study undertaken by the Institute of Business Ethics showed that, between 1997 and 2001, those companies with an unambiguous commitment to being ethical produced 18 per cent higher profit/turnover ratios than those that did not.

Adhering to laws on health and safety, employment and the environment are not just a UK obligation. The UK is part of a union of countries known as the European Union (EU). As these countries trade with each other and the rest of the world, it is vital that there are laws regarding ethics within the EU. There would be little point having laws regarding, for example, the amount of pollution a business can produce in the UK, if the business could simply move its plant to Spain and continue to create pollution. Laws regarding employment are also EU wide. A 1993 EU directive states that no one should work more than a 48-hour week and that everyone is entitled to rest periods and breaks and a minimum of 4 weeks' paid leave per year. (In the UK, employees can opt to work for more than 48 hours per week, but this must be recorded in a form that is available for the authorities.)

The UN Declaration of Human Rights states that everybody has the right to work in favourable conditions and have protection against unemployment. They also have the right to equal pay for equal work, fair pay so that they can provide sufficiently for their families and the right to join a trade union to protect their employment interest. In January 1999, the UN initiated the **UN Global Compact** for businesses to work to a core set of values in

Key terms

Code of practice: *rules set out by a business to ensure ethical practices*

Ethical trade: *applying ethical practices at all levels of a business's supply chain*

UN Declaration on Human Rights: *a document aimed at creating a better world, based on fairness and justice*

UN Global Compact: *an initiative to encourage the world's leading business people to have shared values and principles*

The UN is an intergovernmental organisation that campaigns for human rights across the globe.

the areas of human rights, labour standards and environmental practices. Given the massive growth of economies in countries such as India and China in recent years, it is essential that workers in these countries are protected from damaging working conditions and we are all protected from unnecessary environmental damage.

 Discuss

In groups discuss the need for overseeing bodies such as the UN. Why is it important that they exist?

Better ethics

In order to achieve M1, you must select a business and assess how its operations could be improved. In order to assess the business's current operations, you can use the issues that you have described for P1 and P2 and assess what the business is doing currently that is ethical and then describe what is not so ethical, why it is not so ethical and how this could be improved. You will also need to explain how or if the business could deal with its operations in a better way.

 Discuss

In groups, discuss some businesses that you know of that have highly ethical operations. Explain why they are so important to the company.

A poor standard in working conditions is a major ethical concern for a number of global companies.

The ethics of finance and production

The activities of a business do not just affect the business itself; they affect the whole of society. These are the **social implications** of a business. Different areas of business can have different effects on society.

P3 Ethics in finance

The global financial crisis of the early 21st century was caused by banks lending money to customers who could not afford to repay the loan. For this reason and because there is so much scope for malpractice, the financial sector is more highly regulated than ever. Financial malpractice can include:

Bribery – This is the giving of money in return for an unfair advantage, and is a form of corruption. An example of bribery is a director giving money to shareholders in return for their votes.

Executive pay – This can, in some cases, be seen as an ethical issue if the top executives in a company are being paid too highly in relation to the effort that they put into their jobs. In response to the publication of the massive bonuses given to some bankers in the City of London, a number of businesses have decided to make public the earnings of their most highly paid employees. Government organisations, where the wages are paid by British taxpayers, have published this information in a bid for more openness. For example, in November 2009, the BBC published the earnings of its top 100 decision-makers.

Insider trading – This is the illegal use of information by stockbrokers to influence the price of shares. For example, if a stockbroker knows in advance that a company is being sold on the stock market they could buy shares in that company at a cheap price and, once the company is sold, sell them at a large profit. This is unethical and is detected by the Securities and Investment Board in the UK.

Lobbying – This is when businesses approach MPs in order to gain information or request that they take certain action. It is legal to lobby; however, if a business bribes the MP into taking certain action it is corruption.

Your assessment criteria:

P3 Describe the social implications of business ethics facing a selected business in its different areas of activity

Key terms

Bribery: *the giving of money in return for an unfair advantage*

Insider trading: *the illegal use of information by stockbrokers to influence the price of shares*

Lobbying: *the act of businesses approaching MPs to gain information or request certain action*

Social implications: *the effects on the whole of society of a business's actions*

? Did you know?

Bribery is known as a 'white collar' crime.

Q Research

In pairs, research recent cases of bribery, inflated executive pay, insider trading and lobbying. Present your cases to the rest of the class.

Ethics in production

Ethics can be an issue in the area of production for some businesses. For food producers, the issue of genetically modified (GM) food is an ongoing ethical debate. Genetically modified food is made from crops that have been artificially changed at a genetic level. Campaigners and scientists argue about the potential damage to our health of eating GM foods, the mixing of different species in the external environment and the fact that there has been no long-term testing to see if GM foods are dangerous.

Similarly, ethics in production exist with regard to animal testing. Around 2.8 million animals are tested on each year as part of the development of products from cosmetics to drugs. All human medical treatments are tested on animals as part of their development, and the ethical issue lies around the value of human life in relation to animal life and the suffering that the animals could experience during testing.

The final issue that exists in the ethics of production is planned obsolescence. This is the deliberate development of products that will need replacing after a certain amount of time. This is usually the case with appliances such as washing machines, etc.

Certain products that you buy may have been tested on animals.

? Did you know?

Of all the animals that are used for animal testing, around 50 per cent of them die 2–3 weeks after being tested.

💬 Discuss

In groups, discuss the pros and cons of animal testing.

The ethics of human resource management, sales and marketing and intellectual property

P3 Ethics in human resource management

There are several laws that exist in the UK to protect workers in their employment. Employees cannot be discriminated against on the basis of their gender, colour, sexuality or ability/disability. All employees should be employed on their own merits. Breaking these laws is both illegal and unethical. For example, some female workers in investment banks have claimed that their male counterparts have been paid higher bonuses for doing the same jobs.

Another issue in human resource management is the surveillance of workers. Watching employees using CCTV cameras or randomly checking their emails raises important ethical issues of privacy.

Ethics in sales and marketing

In sales and marketing, businesses have been known to use unethical means to make sales. These methods can include:

Green washing – The increasing pressure for businesses to be more environmentally friendly can give rise to businesses engaging in green washing, i.e. taking action to appear to be greener than they really are.

Shills – There are many websites on which customers can post recommendations and comments with regards to products and services, for example www.tripadvisor.com. These do, however, provide scope for businesses to be unethical and post false recommendations for their own products and services, pretending to be satisfied customers. People who do this are known as shills.

Spamming – This is when businesses send the same email to thousands of different email addresses. The emails are sometimes referred to as spam or junk mail.

Ethics in intellectual property

There are laws to ensure that people who create their own products or services are protected from people copying them. The owner of intellectual property controls the use of the product or service and is rewarded for the use of the product or service. The reason for protecting products and services in this way is so that people are encouraged to

Your assessment criteria:

P3 Describe the social implications of business ethics facing a selected business in its different areas of activity

 Key terms

Green washing: when companies pretend that they are greener than they really are

Intellectual property: something produced by the mind that has commercial value

Shills: people who are employed to write good (false) reviews about a company's products or services

Spamming: the sending of emails to thousands of users

 Discuss

In groups, discuss the pros and cons of software piracy and peer-to-peer file sharing.

be creative and innovative and continue to invent such products and services. Intellectual property laws protect creativity in the following ways:

- Software piracy – People should not copy software that someone else has created; instead they should buy a licence to use the software while not owning it.

- Counterfeiting – Counterfeit goods are made to look like the real product when in fact they are not. This happens with money and all manner of goods such as T-shirts, software, electronics and handbags. Counterfeit goods try to reap the advantages of the value of the real product.

- Peer-to-peer file sharing – This is the transferring of files from one computer to another, which is legal as long as the file has not been copyrighted. When a file has been copyrighted, however, it is illegal to share it. This has often been the case when people have shared their music with other internet users. Individuals or businesses copyright such material so that the time, money and resources that they have invested in creating the music are protected so that they can make money from its use and continue making music. This not only applies to music, but also to software.

Free music downloading is an ethical debate.

Global, corporate and individual implications

M2 ▶ The global implications

If businesses were allowed to operate exactly as they wanted, it is possible that we would all suffer. Business activity has **global implications** in terms of its effect on the environment. An increased level of pollutants entering the atmosphere threatens to hasten climate change. Unless businesses act now to become greener, the impact on the global environment could be deadly.

The corporate implications

Business ethics have various **corporate implications**. It is becoming increasingly important for businesses to be ethical as consumers become more aware of our planet's needs. Businesses draw up corporate social responsibility policies and procedures with which their staff must comply and which are designed to keep their stakeholders happy. Businesses also have to adhere to various laws, including anti-discrimination laws (such as the Sex Discrimination Act and the Disability Discrimination Act), health and safety laws (such as the Health and Safety at Work Act), consumer protection laws (such as the Sales of Goods Act and the Trades Descriptions Act) and laws regarding pollution, planning and waste. Businesses have to show legal compliance so that we are all protected, and to protect themselves from fines and penalties.

The individual implications

Business ethics have **individual implications** for both employees and consumers. Employees are affected by business ethics through the company's legal compliance with anti-discrimination laws and health and safety laws. This means that individuals are employed depending on their ability to do the job and not on their colour, gender, race or ability/disability. Employers also have to ensure that their employees are safe at work and not exposed to any unnecessary risks. Employees are also affected by business ethics through the company's corporate social responsibility (CSR) programmes. KPMG, one of the world's largest accounting firms, has CSR days when the employees help the local community by, for example, painting a school fence or clearing parkland.

As a consumer, individuals are also protected by business ethics through companies' legal compliance with certain laws such as the Sales of Goods Act and the Trade Descriptions Act. These laws ensure that products are safe, do what they are advertised to do, are of satisfactory

---

Your assessment criteria:

M2 Assess the social implications of business ethics facing a selected business in its different areas of activity

D1 Evaluate the impact of a selected business's ethical behaviour on stakeholders and the business

🔑 Key terms

Corporate implications: the effects on businesses

Global implications: the effects on the world and the environment

Individual implications: the effects on individual people

❓ Did you know?

According to USA Today, *83 per cent of people will trust a company more if it is socially responsible.*

quality and will not cause harm by their use. Individuals are also affected by business ethics in the environment in which they live. We are protected from breathing in excess pollutants in the atmosphere, have green fields for wildlife as the building of houses is restricted by planning laws and fines are in place to prevent unlawful waste disposal.

Laws now exist to limit the amount of pollution that factories can produce.

? Did you know?

According to a MonsterTRAK Recruitment survey, 90 per cent of young professionals would prefer to work for an environmentally friendly employer.

Q Research

In groups of two or three, research the laws that protect you on a daily basis. Feed back your thoughts to the rest of the class.

Q Research

In groups, research all of the stakeholders that would be affected by the ethical operations in the company that you discussed in the activity above.

- *What are their conflicts of interest?*

- *Why is it important for businesses to attempt to keep all of their stakeholders happy?*

D1 ▶ The impact of ethical behaviour

In order to achieve D1, you must focus on one business and evaluate the impact of the business's ethical behaviour on as many stakeholders as possible (see Figure 37.1 below). You should also evaluate any ethical issues that you have not covered in M1. You need to back up your views with research and make sure you source all of your research.

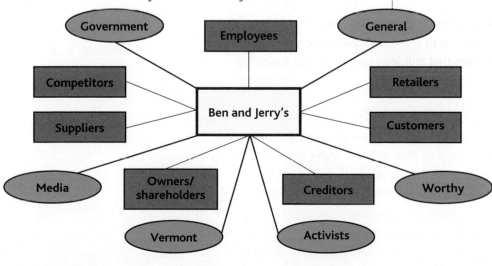

Figure 37.1 Stakeholder map

Communities and their ethical concerns

P4 The communities

We all belong to a number of different communities::

- the local area in which we live
- the area of the country in which we live
- the country in which we live
- the world in which we live.

As a result of the internet, cheaper flights and common currencies (such as the Euro), it is often said that the world is getting smaller, which means that we are becoming increasingly interconnected and are rapidly becoming one large community.

Local communities

It used to be the case that an average high street was home to small, local shops, each owned by one family. As time has gone on, large multinational companies have moved into our high streets and changed the way we shop. The presence of Starbucks and McDonald's, etc. in our local communities has a massive impact, putting local shopkeepers out of business, but creating jobs and bringing cash into the area.

Historically, some local communities were formed around certain trades. For example, the North of England used to be home to huge coal mines. The miners worked and lived in the local community, which was therefore affected by the environmental damage caused by the mines (including slag heaps and damage to coasts) and health complications of working in the mines. When companies choose to invest in a **local community**, the concerns and implications of the local community have to be taken into account.

Regional and national communities

Regional communities can be affected if there is catastrophic event such as the Aberfan mining disaster in 1966 in South Wales where a slag heap (from the coal mines) collapsed into homes and a school killing over 100 people. This had obvious effects on the local community; however, it also affected the region when ethical questions were raised. When the majority of UK coal mines closed following a national move away from the use of coal to alternative fuels, this had huge a impact on not only

? | Did you know?

Mining kills and injures more people than any other industry.

⚷ | Key terms

Local community: the local area in which a given person lives or company is situated

the local areas, but also the regional communities and the national communities as unemployment rose and crime increased.

Global communities

Certain issues affect us all as global citizens, regardless of where we live in the world. These issues are often environmental. In order to protect the environment in which we all live and to ensure we do not cause unnecessary and premature damage to our planet, certain pressure groups have formed. Pressure groups work to force governments to take action on certain issues and make the public more aware of these issues. Two very well known environmental pressure groups are Greenpeace and Friends of the Earth. Greenpeace is committed to stopping climate change which is caused by the burning of fossil fuels. It puts pressure on businesses that use dirty sources of energy and promotes the use of renewable energy, such as solar and wind power. Friends of the Earth works in local communities and also for the global community. There are over 200 local Friends of the Earth groups and more than 70 Friends of the Earth international groups. It is the only environmental pressure group that has this power. Friends of the Earth is committed to finding solutions to all environmental problems and providing information and tools to help people act in a more environmentally friendly manner.

Greenpeace and Friends of the Earth put pressure on governments to change policies and make the public aware of environmental issues.

Key terms

Global community: the world in which we live

National community: the country in which a given person lives or company is situated

Regional community: the area of the country in which a given person lives or company is situated

Did you know?

Greenpeace was first founded to oppose the USA testing nuclear devices in Alaska.

Research

In groups, research any environmental disasters that have occurred in your local or regional community in the last 100 years. Explain what the disaster was and how it affected the local and regional community in which you live.

The impact of overseeing bodies

P4 Overseeing bodies

An **overseeing body** monitors the actions of businesses, checking to see whether what they do can be judged to be ethical.

The UK government has passed laws and tries to implement codes of practice for the promotion of all sorts of ethical activities. It oversees:

- laws in the workplace (such as the Disability Discrimination Act, the Sex Discrimination Act, the Health and Safety at Work Act)

- laws relating to buying products (such as the Consumer Protection Act and the Trade Descriptions Act)

- laws protecting us from being provided with polluted water and air, etc.

- regulatory bodies (government owned) to protect us from unethical treatment in finance (www.fsa.gov.uk), food (www.food.gov.uk) and the advertising we see (www.asa.org.uk).

The UK government also backs the reduction of the rate of climate change by being a supporter of the Kyoto Agreement.

Several ethical issues do not affect just one country, but affect a number of countries. There is therefore a need for organisations to oversee the activities of businesses all around the world.

The **United Nations (UN)** is made up of 192 countries and is committed to maintaining harmony and avoiding war. The UN issued the Declaration of Human Rights and the UN Global Compact to ensure that we are all entitled to certain standards in employment and life and to eliminate the exploitation of vulnerable people by multinational corporations.

The **European Union (EU)** is made up of 27 countries. It makes intergovernmental decisions that are negotiated by the member states and passes laws that affect all of its members. The governments then work together to implement the laws. The EU also promotes the movement of people across all member states. In order to join the EU, countries have to meet certain conditions including respecting human rights, allowing its citizens to vote, having a properly working economy and abiding by laws set by the EU. Some people are pro Europe and want the UK to integrate further into Europe by using the Euro; other people are against being part of the EU (Eurosceptics).

Your assessment criteria:

P4 Examine the ethical concerns of the communities in which a selected business operates

Key terms

European Union (EU): *27 countries across Europe that are economically and politically united*

Overseeing body: *an overseeing body is an organisation that monitors the actions of businesses*

United Nations (UN): *an organisation that promotes peace around the world*

? Did you know?

The UN officially came into existence on 24 October 1945.

Design

Individually, design a new flag for the UN and one for the EU. Explain your designs and how they reflect the aims of both of the bodies.

The **World Trade Organisation (WTO)** is a global organisation that promotes free trade between all of its 153 member states. It does this by trying to get countries to eliminate their import taxes and other barriers to free international trade.

The **World Health Organisation (WHO)** is a sub division of the UN that promotes the well-being of people across the world. This includes their physical, mental and social health. The WHO also researches into health promotion, monitors global health and attempts to coordinate health policies between the different countries' governments. It predominantly helps people in poorer countries and trains people to become nurses and healthcare workers in their own country. It also helps to try to eliminate diseases such as malaria by teaching people about how to avoid getting infected.

The UN and EU are overseeing bodies.

Ethical issues facing different communities

P4 ▶ Corporate social responsibility

Many companies now operate all around the world and their presence can have a massive impact on the communities in which they operate. These companies are known as multinational corporations. There is increasing pressure for businesses to be ethical and for this reason they create corporate social responsibility (CSR) programmes in order to help the local and national communities in which they operate. For example, the Ben and Jerry's Foundation is a charity that has employee-led action teams that distribute grants to surrounding communities. The company also: buys its brownies from the Greyston Bakery, a bakery committed to providing jobs for those who may otherwise be unemployed; is Fair Trade Certified; buys all of its milk from farmers who do not use growth hormones for their cattle; uses its funds to promote world peace, fight global warming and involve itself in local communities.

Globalisation

The process of **globalisation** means that we can phone a British company and be put through to a call centre in India or we can buy clothes from a high street store and find they have been made in China. The world is becoming more interconnected. Some people are opposed to globalisation as they argue that where production facilities have been **outsourced** (goods are produced in another country), those jobs are lost in the domestic country and fund the other country's economy. It also means that the multinational corporation that has outsourced the production gains power in the country where they employ people. These are often poorer countries where the labour is cheap (the reason for outsourcing the production). Globalisation has meant some low-paid workers in poor countries work in sweatshops. Opponents of globalisation have also argued that it has forced some farmers in developing countries to use genetically modified seeds as their only income is from the multinational corporations (usually European or American owned), which the farmers have no power to oppose. It is also argued that globalisation has forced some countries to sell off state-owned industries to get funding from the World Bank. On the other hand, globalisation means that we trade freely with each other, giving us the luxury of buying products from all over the world, and providing work for people in developing countries who may not otherwise be employed.

Many years ago, Britain had an overseas empire – it was an imperialist nation and dominated other countries for its own gain. Some people

Your assessment criteria:

P4 Examine the ethical concerns of the communities in which a selected business operates

 Key terms

Globalisation: *the process of the development of a more interconnected world*

Outsourcing: *the buying of goods and services from an outside supplier, sometimes in a different country*

 Design

Design a presentation about the Ben and Jerry's Foundation. Present it to the rest of the class.

argue that because of Britain's power, it influenced and therefore changed the cultures of other countries. Culture can be seen as the way we dress, the art and architecture we produce, our education, our etiquette and our opinions. Opponents of cultural imperialism criticise the advertising of large multinational companies. Around 75 per cent of TV adverts worldwide are in English, which makes the world increasingly Anglicised or Americanised.

Just as there are concerns that businesses are imposing western ideals on other cultures, so there are concerns that large multinationals contribute to wiping out wildlife. When multinational corporations move into a community, the land they build on is often home to both plants and animals. By using this land, the companies often destroy the ecological system – the relationship between plants and animals and the place where they live – which can result in the loss of species.

Key terms

Cultural imperialism: the dominance of one culture over another

Ecological system: a stable inter-relationship between plants, animals and the land in a particular local environment

Ben and Jerry's has a high-profile corporate social responsibility programme.

 Case study

In the late 1980s PepsiCo, the soft drinks and snack foods manufacturer, entered the Indian market. India was a highly regulated economy and PepsiCo had to work hard to sell its products there. The company made a number of promises, including one to work towards decreasing the terrorism that was affecting the Punjab by promoting agricultural activities. It was an offer the Indian government could not refuse.

However, PepsiCo has attracted criticism because of its alleged failure to honour many of its promises after it started operations in the country and after the liberalisation of the Indian economy.

1. What is meant by the term globalisation?

2. What benefits do the Indian people gain from PepsiCo's investment in the country?

3. What are the drawbacks of PepsiCo's investment in the country?

 Discuss

Set up two teams, one that opposes globalisation and one that supports it. Debate the pros and cons of globalisation using real examples to back up your points.

 Did you know?

The term 'cultural imperialism' appears to have emerged in the 1960s.

Further ethical issues facing communities

P4 Fair Trade

Fair Trade is about ensuring producers get paid fairly for their products; and the social, environmental and economic development of an area. Buying Fair Trade products means producers get a fair price for their goods, so they can continue producing and receive a social premium to invest in the development of their area. There are more than 90 coffees, teas, bananas, chocolate bars, juices, sugars and honeys that carry the Fair Trade logo. Fair Trade producers have to abide by certain conditions, including:

- fair working conditions

- business activities that ensure environmental stability

- development of the organisation

- looking after the welfare of producers.

Child labour

In poorer countries, children are often forced to work to bring in extra income for their families. Some unethical companies employ children as they are cheaper than adults. There are 218 million child labourers in the world, 14 per cent of whom are aged 5–17, so around 1 in 7 children in the world are child labourers (www.stopchildlabour.eu). This is unethical and corrupt and often leads organisations to try to cover up the use of child labour to reduce the possibility of negative publicity. Goods that have been made by child labour are often cheaper than ethically produced goods and therefore consumers are torn between ethics and money. This is similarly the case with Fair Trade goods, which are often more expensive than their non-Fair Trade counterparts.

Corruption and whistle-blowing

A further ethical issue facing communities is corruption. If someone who works for an organisation reports a concern that someone is doing wrong, this is known as whistle-blowing. Opinions about whistle-blowers vary. Some think they have the organisation's (and often the public's) interest at heart, whereas others think they are tell tales or grasses. A shocking example of a whistle-blower in the UK was Dr Bolsin, a consultant anaesthetist at the Bristol Royal Infirmary. He reported to the authorities that too many babies were dying during heart surgery. As

Your assessment criteria:

P4 Examine the ethical concerns of the communities in which a selected business operates

M3 Explain the ethical concerns of the communities in which a selected business operates and suggest measures that could be taken to improve corporate responsibility

Key terms

Child labour: the use of employees who are children

Whistle-blowing: reporting alleged wrong doing in an organisation

Research

Research other cases of whistle-blowing that have occurred in the UK in the last 10 years.

a result, a higher ethical standard in healthcare was developed in the UK and, after this, performance was measured and monitored in the NHS. Due to Dr Bolsin's whistle-blowing, the survival rate in children's heart surgery at Bristol Royal Infirmary increased from 70 to 95 per cent.

Look out for the Fair Trade logo next time you are in a supermarket.

M3 Improving corporate responsibility

In order to achieve M3, you need to explain the ethical concerns facing the communities in which a business of your choice operates. This means explaining the local, regional, national and global communities that are affected by its activities. You may identify that the business is not taking into consideration a certain aspect of an issue and therefore there is scope for them to improve. You will need to make valid recommendations for these improvements. A good place to start is to look at a company's corporate social responsibility programme and explain what else the company could do to help its local, regional, national or global community. You will need to explain why the activities of the business are an ethical concern for the communities.

Discuss

In groups, discuss the pros and cons of whistle-blowing. Consider the implication if the whistle-blower is wrong.

Research

Research the CSR programmes for each of the large companies in your local high street. Suggest ways in which these could be improved locally, nationally and globally.

Many companies have corporate social responsibility programmes to help their local communities.

Assessment checklist

To achieve a pass grade, my portfolio of evidence must show that I can:

Assessment criteria	Description	✓
P1	Explain the ethical issues a business needs to consider in its operational activities	☐
P2	Explain the implications for the business and stakeholders of a business operating ethically	☐
P3	Describe the social implications of business ethics facing a selected business in its different areas of activity	☐
P4	Examine the ethical concerns of the communities in which a selected business operates.	☐

To achieve a merit grade, my portfolio of evidence must show that I can:

Assessment criteria	Description	✓
M1	Assess how a selected business could improve the ethics of their operations	☐
M2	Assess the social implications of business ethics facing a selected business in its different areas of activity	☐
M3	Explain the ethical concerns of the communities in which a selected business operates and suggest measures that could be taken to improve corporate responsibility	☐

To achieve a distinction grade, my portfolio of evidence must show that I can:

Assessment criteria	Description	✓
D1	Evaluate the impact of a selected business's ethical behaviour on stakeholders and the business	☐

Index